CRYSTAL HEALING

A Vibrational Journey Through the Chakras

CRYSTAL HEALING

A Vibrational Journey Through the Chakras

by Hazel Raven

Raven & Co. Publishing

Disclaimer:

The information in this book is not intended to be a substitute for medical advise, diagnosis or treatment. If you have any concerns about your health consult a qualified medical practitioner. Neither the publisher nor the author accept any liability for readers who choose to self-prescribe.

Crystal energy is subtle, but powerful. If you are in any doubt about their use, consult a qualified crystal therapist. The Affiliation of Crystal Healing Organisation has a list of qualified therapists and approved crystal schools. All approved courses should be at least two years in duration.

ISBN 0-9538890-1-7

First Published in 2000 by
Raven & Co. Publishing
http://www.raven.org.uk
Printed by T. Snape & Co. Ltd., Boltons Court Preston Lancs.

Cover design by Martyne Raven
Chakra illustrations by Hazel Raven
All other illustrations by Graham and Hazel Raven
Photographs by Graham Raven

For information on bulk purchases or group discounts for this and other titles by Hazel Raven or details of vibrational medicine or crystal therapy courses - please contact:

Hazel Raven at **http://www.raven.org.uk**

For information on Martyne Raven's art work and jewellery designs go to:

http://www.raven.org.uk and go to the links page.

Dedicated to Avalokitesvara

I also wish to dedicate this book to all who strive for perfection this lifetime.

Other books by Hazel Raven
Crystal Healing - The Complete Practitioner's Guide
Angel Therapy - The Complete Practitioner's Guide
Heal Yourself with Crystals
Secrets of Angel Healing
co-author of
Book of Stones - Gemstone Encyclopaedia

Acknowledgements

I would like to thank my daughter, Martyne Raven, for choosing me to be her mother and for being the gifted artist who has allowed me to use 'the Angel of Ascension' Archangel Metatron, as the cover of this book. I also wish to thank my husband, Graham Raven, for his patience during the book's birth process. Thank you, Graham, for walking the path with me.

'Crystal Healing - A Vibrational Journey Through the Chakras' was the first book I intended to write - it has been with me for so long - but book one, 'Crystal Healing - A Complete Practitioner's Guide', had to come first...this was due to several factors, the most pressing of which was the need for a practical, safe, comprehensive practitioner's guide to crystal therapy.

Hazel Raven

December 1999

Spain

Foreword

Hazel Raven... I still remember vividly the vital surge of energy that poured through me when I first read her name in 1988. I recognised her as a major connection in my life: how major would not reveal itself until three years later. Wow, I thought, this lady is named after a tree and a bird - how Shamanic she must be.

And then I met her...

Incredibly energy-aware, Hazel has the ability to empower all who come into contact with her. She carries a delicious blend of courage, humility and vulnerability. She has so much to teach and does so from a space of clarity, consideration and communication. Her own Angelic aspect is clearly visible as she works and her love of the Crystal Kingdom is a delight to behold.

I am very proud of her for choosing to put aside the time to prepare this book. In this way she will touch more hearts than she could possibly meet personally. It feels very important to me that her unique way of viewing life, the universe and everything is made available to as wide an audience as possible. As she spreads her healing light, so she helps to raise the vibrational rate of the Earth's energy matrix.

I am personally honoured to regard Hazel as my teacher, spiritual sister, friend and constant source of love, inspiration and understanding.

I am sure that all who are attracted towards this book and dive into her pools of wisdom will emerge enriched by the treasures they find therein.

Zaria Et An Cullen TM. IACHT

Scotland

September, 1998

About the Author

Hazel Raven is a respected writer, teacher and holistic therapist - specialising in subtle-energy medicine - with over thirty years experience in this field. She is the founder member and course director of the Hazel Raven College of Bio-Dynamics.

Hazel Raven has been instrumental in gathering information and in practical research; she has also been involved with setting the United Kingdom standards for crystal therapy. She has been teaching crystal therapy since 1988 and has trained a dedicated team of professional crystal therapists and qualified tutors who are able to offer these training courses world-wide.

Hazel is clairvoyant, clairaudient and clairsentient and uses these gifts to enhance her healing work. Her style of teaching is inspirational and empowering.

Hazel is a qualified educationalist, who is a former vice-chair of the Affiliation of Crystal Healing Organisations and was previously treasurer for four years, is well respected by her colleagues in the field of complementary therapies and has served on the Inner Council of the British Complementary Medicine Association for many years as its crystal therapy representative for education.

Initiated as a Reiki Master in 1994, Hazel served on The Reiki Federations's Steering Committee as representative for obtaining validation for courses.

In May 1999, Hazel was asked to attend the Foundation for Integrated Medicine conference at the Commonwealth Institute in London, which was also attended by HRH The Prince of Wales, the Foundation's patron.

Hazel has always been aware of subtle-energies and the spiritual powers of flowers, trees, crystals, herbs, colour and sound to expand human consciousness. She has had a series of articles published and has appeared on television and radio, in the press and national women's magazines, including the Christmas 1997 edition of Cosmopolitan magazine, which featured her Angelic experiences.

For more details of the Hazel Raven College of Bio-Dynamic training courses, Angelic or Master essences please contact:

e.mail - info@raven.org.uk

http://www.raven.org.uk

Contents

Part 1:
Introduction **17**

Part 2:
The Chakras **23**

Master Chakras 23

Endocrine System 23

Root Chakra - Adrenals - Nerve Plexus
    Coccygeal 24

Sacral Chakra - Ovaries/Testes -
    Nerve Plexus Sacral 25

Solar Chakra - Pancreas -
    Nerve Plexus Solar 25

Heart Chakra - Thymus -
    Nerve Plexus Heart 25

Throat Chakra - Thyroid/Parathyroid -
    Nerve Plexus Cervical Ganglia Medulla 25

Third Eye Chakra - Pituitary - Nerve Plexus
    Hypothalamus Pituitary 25

Crown Chakra - Pineal - Nerve Plexus
    Cerebral Cortex Pineal 26

Life-Lessons 26

Chakra Correspondences 29

Root Chakra .29

Sacral Chakra 30

Solar Plexus Chakra 31

Heart Chakra 31

Throat Chakra 32

Third Eye Chakra 33

The Fourth Eye Chakra 34

The Fifth Eye Chakra 34

Crown Chakra 34

Part 3:
The Aura **37**

Seeing Auras 41

The Seven Kosas 42

Sheath One 42

Sheath Two .42

Sheath Three 43

Sheath Four .43

Sheath Five .43

Sheath Six 44

Sheath Seven 44

Part 4:
The Meridians **45**

Yin and Yang 46

Central Meridian 46

Governing Meridian 47

Connecting the Governing and
    Conceptual Vessels 47

Gall-bladder Meridian 47

Liver Meridian 48

Bladder Meridian 48

Kidney Meridian 48

Large Intestine Meridian 48

Lung Meridian 48

Stomach Meridian 48

Spleen Meridian 49

Heart Meridian 49

Small Intestine Meridian 49

Circulation-Sex Meridian 49

Triple Warmer Meridian 49

Vibrational Therapy for the Meridians 49

Vibrational Therapy for the
    Acupuncture Points 50

Acupuncture Points 50

Meridian List 51

Part 5:
Kundalini **53**
Yoga 53
Meditation Posture 56
Whole Body Experience 57

Part 6:
Karma **59**
Miasms 59
Samsara 59
Cause of Disease 59
Reality Perception 60
Tribal National and Global Karm 60
Alignment with the Higher Self 61

Part 7:
Crystals **63**
Selecting a Crystal 64
Sensations Experienced 65
How to Choose a Crystal 65
Method One - Vibration 66
Method Two - Intuition 66
Method Three - Scanning 66
Method Four - Kinesiology 67
Method Five - Resonance 67
Method Six - Pranayama 68
Method Seven - Hand Activation 69
Method Eight - Dowsing 69
Cleansing Your Crystal 70
Care and Storage of Your Crystal 73
Control or Master Crystal 73
Attuning to Crystals by Activating Them . . .73
Dedicating Your Crystal 73
Programming .73
Tuning 74
Energising Crystals 74

Charging Crystals 74
Reiki Web of Light 77

Part 8:
Crystal Webs of Light **79**
Crystal Systems 80
Hardness 81
Working With Crystal Energy
    Webs of Light 81
Quartz Crystal Webs 82
Quartz Crystal Webs for Meditation 83
Twelve Crystal Web 83
Merkaba Web .83
Pleiadean Star 84
Practical Geometric Exercises 84

Part 9:
Meditation **87**
Actual Meditation Practice 88

Part 10:
Color **91**
Make a Color Essence 94
Method 94
Mother Bottle 94
Stock Bottle .94
Dosage Bottle 95
Using the Color Remedies 95
Color Essence 95
Color Essence Body Cream 96
Color Essence Aura Spray 96
Solarized water 97
Gemstone or Crystal Solarized Water 97
The Vibrational Properties of
    Color Essences 98
Red 98

Rose Pink 98

Magenta 98

Pale Pink 99

Orange 99

Peach 99

Yellow 99

Emerald Green .100

Turquoise 100

Blue 100

Indigo 101

Purple 101

Violet 102

Amethyst 102

Lavender 102

Sun Gold 102

Silver 103

Iridescent Rainbow Light 103

White 103

Black 103

Grey 104

Brown 104

Color Meditation - The Rainbow Bridge . . .104

Part 11:
Sound 107

Sounds' Healing Powers 109

The Science of Sound 110

Using Sound in Therapy 113

Nature-Music Exercise 114

Toning 114

Vocal Sound Production 115

Mantra Meditation 115

Japa Meditation 116

Chants and Chanting 116

Humming 117

'Own' Name Exercise 117

Singing Bowl 118

Tibetan Singing Bowls 118

Part 12:
The Root Chakra 119

**Crystal Web of Light -
Grounding Into the Earth** **121**

Garnet 122

Clear Quartz 123

Ruby 123

Tourmaline 124

Black Tourmaline 124

Healing Meditation - Root Chakra 124

Kundalini Root Chakra Meditation 126

Hui Yin 127

Part 13:
The Sacral Chakra 129

Crystal Web of Light - Creative Fire **131**

Carnelian 132

Citrine 133

Clear Quartz 133

Garnet 133

Sunstone 133

Zincite 134

Healing Meditation - Sacral Chakra 135

Kundalini Rising Sacral Chakra
Meditation 136

Part 14:
The Solar Plexus Chakra 139

Crystal Web of Light - Lustrous Gem . . .**140**

Calcite 141

Citrine 142

Clear Quartz 142

Rhodochrosite .142

Topaz 143

Turquoise 144

Healing Meditation - Solar Plexus Chakra .145

Kundalini Solar Plexus Chakra Meditation .146

Breath of Fire 146

Part 15:
The Heart Chakra 149

Crystal Web of Light - Tranquil Heart . .152

Clear Quartz 154

Kunzite 154

Morganite 154

Rhodochrosite 155

Rhodonite 155

Rose quartz 156

Crystal Web of Light - Healing Calm . . .157

Clear Quartz 158

Larimar 158

Lepidolite 159

Moonstone 160

Rose Quartz 160

Sugilite 160

Crystal Healing Meditation -
Heart Chakra 161

Kundalini Heart Chakra Meditation 163

Alternate-Nostril Breathing 163

Technique 1 - Down-Flow 163

Technique 2 - Heart Consciousness Rising .163

Part 16:
The Throat Chakra 165

Crystal Web of Light - Sacred Sounds . .168

Apatite 170

Aquamarine 170

Clear Quartz 172

Iolite 172

Lapis Lazuli 173

Healing Meditation - Throat Chakra 174

Kundalini Throat Chakra Meditation 175

Resonance 175

Part 17:
The Third Eye Chakra 177

Crystal Web of Light - Inner Vision 179

Amethyst 181

Charoite 183

Clear Quartz 184

Iolite 184

Lepidolite 184

Sugilite 184

Tanzanite 184

Healing Meditation - Third Eye Chakra . . .185

Kundalini Third Eye Chakra Meditation . . .185

Kumbhaka Breath -
Super-Charge Upwards 186

Kumbhaka Breath - Balanced Breath 186

Kumbhaka Breath -
Calming and Grounding 186

Part 18:
The Crown Chakra 189

Crystal Web of Light - Pleiadean Star . . .191

Clear Quartz 192

Moldavite 192

Amorphous Nature - Inner Structure 193

Cosmic Birth - Growth Conditions 193

Verdant Green Hue - Color Vibration 193

Intense Resonance - Vibration 194

'Spirit' or Angel Guide - Inspiration 194

Healing Meditation - Crown Chakra 194

Kundalini Crown Chakra Meditation 195

The Bliss Breath 195

Part 19:
The Earth Star 197

Crystal Web of Light -
Earth Star Connector 199

Aragonite 201

Clear Quartz 201

Dioptase 201

Hematite 202

Labradorite 203

Obsidian 203

Smoky Quartz .205

Healing Meditation - Earth Star Chakra . . .206

Kundalini Meditation - Chanting Session . .207

Part 20:
The Soul Star 209

Channelling Meditation 210

Crystal Web of Light -
Ascension into Cosmic Consciousness . .211

Amblygonite 213

Angelite 213

Clear Quartz 214

Danburite 214

Moldavite 215

Petalite 215

Phenacite 215

Kundalini Seven Chakra Meditation 216

Glossary 221

Explanation of Back Cover 227

List of Illustrations

Root Chakra

Sacral Chakra

Solar Plexus Chakra

Heart Chakra

Throat Chakra

Third Eye Chakra

Crown Chakra

Earth Star Chakra

Soul Star Chakra

Chakra Placement

The Aura

Axes of Crystal Systems

Reiki Web of Light

Pleiadean Star Web of Light

Merkaba Web of Light

Twelve Crystal Web of Light

Crystal Web for Meditation

Part 1

Introduction

A Journey - in this book I wish to take you on a journey of self-discovery and personal empowerment. In my long teaching career of vibrational therapies I have seen the New Age holistic movement grow from what was considered alternative, weird and downright strange to being accepted by the general population as a natural and safe alternative to allopathic medicine. I am also aware that it is important to weave 'vibrational medicine' into a coherent understandable user-friendly format. May I even say I wish to bring clarity and understanding to our minds and world. As Byron said, 'a drop of ink may make a million think'.

As a child, before I had 'learnt' the word for a chakra, I was aware of spinning vortexes of light emanating from the human body....I saw them as not only wheels of energy but so very much more... I knew they were gateways to other worlds and dimensions....the higher chakras were gateways into realms of unimaginable beauty, peace and enlightenment. I was also aware of the luminous egg that surrounded all humans or, as I later learned to call it, the 'aura'. This luminous egg fascinated me; I was enthralled at the colors, shapes and energy movements it contained. I saw each person was very different and each individual had so much 'information' stored within this luminous egg. I could also see the damage people did, not only to themselves but to others, through their thoughtless self-centred words and actions.

I must admit, though, to my naivety as a child; I believed all human beings could see what I saw and experience what I experienced. I also thought everyone had contact with vast luminous beings of light, love and compassion or, as I later 'learnt' to call them, Angels. I now know all babies and young children can see these phenomena, but as they become 'earthed' into the current 'headset' or 'accepted tribal reality' they allow these divine 'gifts' to recede further and further until they rely solely on the five acceptable senses of sight, touch, taste, smell and hearing. Although I am aware that the sixth sense is still very active in all individuals - we all know that when we like or dislike a person instantly, usually on first sight, this is the powerful sixth sense in action - I truly believe that we should access the sixth sense far more than we do. We only have to 'download' the 'forgotten' information from the Akashic records, which in reality is the mind of God/Goddess, to fully utilize our divine birthright.

As I grew older I learned to keep silent about my gifts (the ones others let go of), the reason for my silence being my mother's total hostility caused by her dysfunctional fear. I learned never to say when someone was lying, or going to become ill or even to die. I knew, but I also knew I could not voice my inner knowledge. The one saving grace in my childhood was my maternal Grandmother, an enlightened soul who, for many years, had been a Spiritualist; she knew about my gifts because she possessed them too. Although she died when I was twelve years old, her wisdom and love have stayed with me for the last thirty-six years since her death. She had been light years ahead of her time and had even been a suffragette. Her personal charisma and powerful presence were awe-inspiring.

Chakras - I have already referred to the chakras as spinning energy vortexes of light and in this book I want to take you step by step through the chakra maze, as you will soon discover they are vitally important to your health and well-being. Each chakra is in reality closely associated with specific organs and endocrine glands. These spinning vortexes of energy are part of the subtle energy system, which forms the basis of the ancient Indian approach to healing our physical, emotional, mental and spiritual selves. The word chakra comes from the Sanskrit, meaning wheel or disk. The chakras can also be viewed as a step-down transformer for higher frequency subtle energies. The chakras process this subtle energy and convert it into chemical, hormonal and cellular changes in the body. Each chakra vibrates at a different frequency and on a different note. They also contain nadis, which are thread-like subtle paths of energy which flow from the chakras to various regions of the body and aura. The nadis represent an extensive network of fluid-like energies which parallel the body nerves in their abundance. In Eastern yogic literature the chakras have been metaphorically visualised as flowers. The nadis are symbolic of the petals and fine roots of the flower-like chakras that distribute the life-force (prana) into the physical body.

Aura - the 'luminous egg' or aura; incidentally, the word aura comes from the Greek word meaning breeze; in Sanskrit it is called Kosas or body sheaths. This energy envelope that surrounds and interpenetrates the physical body is made up of all the different energy shells that compose the physical, etheric, mental, astral and higher spiritual aspects of the multidimensional human form. As you develop your spiritual or inner vision through meditation, auras will become visible to you. This ability to see auras is your gift from God/Goddess; you just 'forgot' you had been given it.

Meridians - we will also work with the meridians. The ancient Chinese meridian theory is based on acupuncture meridians and was first discovered many thousands of years ago. It is a system of energy that flows throughout the body, providing protection to its inner mechanisms. The word meridian, as used in Chinese medicine, came into the English language through a French translation of the Chinese term jing-luo. Jing means 'to go through', or 'a thread in a fabric'; luo means 'something that connects or attaches' or 'a net'. In traditional Eastern medical systems - notably the Chinese healing system and the Indian Ayurvedic system - it has long been accepted that health is based on the continuous harmonious flow of energies. These systems believe that an intricate realm of subtle energy flows permeates the universe and that the physical, material world is but a gross manifestation of these energies.

Kundalini - one of the simple realities of life is that there are only a few spiritual Masters in Western society to whom we can turn for inspiration and enlightened instruction, especially into kundalini meditation. All too often the Gurus and Masters we do find are teaching an intense path that is beyond our everyday practical ability to participate in. I had myself read in an esoteric book that without a Master no one can progress on the spiritual path and that to awaken the kundalini energy unsupervised by a 'Master' was dangerous, leading to madness, ill-health or sudden death. You can imagine my deep confusion and despondency as I read this very difficult vague esoteric book and knew, without a doubt, not only had I activated my kundalini energy, but I was experiencing advanced stages of energy movement. During my following confusion, a dawning realisation happened - seeing that it had always been this 'way' for me, and my inner 'Divine essence' had never failed to guide me, I might just be all right. I was later to realise we are all our own Masters. You are your own Master too. We all possess a higher self, deep within, that's infinite, that is one with the 'All' or 'One-Thread-Soul'. The secret is learning to trust this Divine aspect and allowing it to gently guide you through meditation and self-realisation to enlightenment. I believe also it is no coincidence that you hold this book right now. I believe that your 'Divine essence' has drawn this book to you, at this very special time in your life, because you're ready to learn potent ways to advance into deeper communication with your own infinite self. Kundalini meditation is such a remarkable process for spiritual awakening; it is not based on complex theological arguments or culturally defined religious concepts, it is instead immediate, and the ultimate experience of the Divine essence within all of us. This creative energy of spiritual illumination, when properly released, can cause activation and alignment of all the major chakras.

Karma - is the reincarnational principle, sometimes stated as 'as ye sow, so shall ye reap'. It is viewed, therefore, as an energetic system of credits and debits, which allows the soul to experience the full range of perspectives on life. It is central to all Eastern religions and in the West we are told in Christianity 'do unto others as you would have others do unto you'. There are various schools of thought on Karmic patterning - that is, we come into this life with a certain set of life challenges factored into our energy systems. This 'prior programming' or predisposition determines our subsequent attitudes and behaviours. It also works with the law of cause and effect. This should make us look very seriously at our behaviour - knowing that what we give out we will have returned to us like a boomerang. The boomerang effect may be felt very quickly, even in this lifetime, or it may take many lifetimes to catch up with you. As we evolve spiritually we can release and heal a lot of negative Karmic patterns.

Crystal webs - quartz crystals, precious and semi-precious gemstones represent the lowest state of entropy possible because they have the most orderly structure in the natural world. All crystalline structures are formed of mathematical, precise and orderly lattice arrays of atoms. This stability has been utilised by scientists in many electronic situations. It has also been used by healers for centuries, too. By applying this coherent, stable, focused energy to dysfunctional energy systems within the human multi-directional energy circuits, they can quickly restore stability and optimum balance. This results in healing on every level. Quartz crystals, when used by a trained therapist, will always go to the areas which are most in need of restructuring; this energy seems to be self-regulating and results in optimum release of negative patterns which may have lodged in any level of the human system. Quartz crystals also resonate with the liquid crystals in your physical body and transfer to your bloodstream and to your circulatory system vital elements, in the form of intelligent energy fields which are essential for your health and for the rejuvenation of your body, while transmuting unwanted information that may be locked in your bones, tissues and unconscious mind. When crystals are used in geometric arrays they have an amplified effect and by combining the different gemstones and crystals to create a synergistic effect, you can amplify the overall potency of a crystal therapy session considerably.

Meditation - there is a power, an energy, which is available to each of us. We can begin to work with this energy and allow it to guide, inspire, strengthen and encourage us. It is available to all who seek to grow in a positive direction. This Divine source of wisdom is the Self. Once we become aware of our own inner light, our Divinity, our 'Divine Essence', our own source of unlimited goodness, we are never disempowered again. It will guide and nurture us if we let it, by sincerely seeking our own truth. Whether a person lives a spiritual life on his/her own, or is part of an organized tradition, the goal is the same: the attainment of peace of mind, purity and perfection or, as some call it, self-realization and enlightenment. Meditation practice will unleash your immense potential by stimulating harmonious, focused brain activity. This will improve your health and rejuvenate your body. It will also clear your mind of stress and improve your powers of concentration, bringing inner peace. This, in turn, will prevent or minimize the problems of senility.

Color - is an intimate part of our being. The human body and aura act as a prism in the sunlight. There is no doubt that our bodies are aroused and energized by some colors, or calmed and relaxed by others. Colors can restore peace, balance and harmony to our lives and make us healthy and well. Unfortunately the opposite is also true: drab, dull or negative colors also have the ability to adversely affect us and bring our already stressed-out vibratory rates to new levels of distress, imbalance, disease and disharmony. The health of all our internal organs, the circulation of the blood, the nervous, lymphatic and endocrine systems - in truth, all the workings of the body - are constantly altered by the colors to which we expose ourselves. Mentally and emotionally, color vibrations work on a deep level, changing our mood and our sense of well-being. Each major visible color has particular qualities that are linked to the chakras with which it resonates.

Sound - is created as the vibratory motion of particles and objects. Sound is among the most instant transformative and healing vibrational energies on the planet. It can relax us and make us calm, or move us to great heights of emotion and spiritual upliftment. Sound can restore peace, balance and harmony to our lives and make us healthy and well. Unfortunately the opposite is also true: sound also has the ability to adversely affect us and bring our already stressed-out vibratory rates to new levels of distress, imbalance, disease and disharmony. What is the difference in the sounds that make us healthy and those that distress us? Sound can affect us on all levels - physical, emotional, mental and spiritual. Beneficial sounds for us are often sounds that we consider 'sacred' or at the very least 'special' by evoking pleasant memories. These sounds seem to have the ability to charge and harmonize us. There are reasons for this. Knowledge of sound as a therapeutic and transformative force is ancient. The Mystery Schools of Greece, Rome, Egypt, Tibet and India had immense knowledge of sound as being the primary creative force in the universe. The ancients understood what the modern physicists now know: that all is in a state of vibration. 'The World is Sound', the ancient ones proclaimed, and indeed it is so.

If we examine the very basic tenets of many of the spiritual paths and world religions, we find a common thread in all of them. They all share the 'One' belief that the world was created through sound. Here are but a few examples. In Genesis, from the Old Testament, one of the first statements is, "And the Lord said 'Let there be light'." In St. John's Gospel, from the New Testament, it is written, "In the beginning was the Word, the Word was with God, and the Word was God". From the Vedas of the Hindu tradition comes the writing that, "In the beginning was Brahman with whom was the Word. And the Word is Brahman". The Ancient Egyptians believed that the God Thoth created the world by his voice alone. In the Popul Vuh, from the Mayan tradition, the first real men are given life by the sole power of the word. The Hopi Indians' story of creation tells of the animation of all forms on earth by having the Spider Woman sing 'The Song of Creation' over them. Many of us know of Pythagoras as the father of geometry. However, how many are aware that in the 6th century BC in Greece he had a mystery school that taught not only the 'magic' of numbers, but the healing powers of music. Pythagoras taught that the Music of the Spheres and the movement of the heavenly bodies could be perceived and reflected in the intervals of plucked strings. In the West, much of this ancient knowledge has all but vanished. Modern physics has verified that we are all vibrating atomic and sub-atomic particles. Everything has a resonant frequency - the frequency at which it most naturally vibrates - from the chair you may be sitting on to this book. Every part - cell, molecule, gene and organ - of your body also has a resonant frequency, as do all diseases, viruses and bacteria.

Personal and planetary evolution - sound, color and crystals are effective forms of vibrational therapy because of their unique ability to impact and influence not just the gross physical body, but all the subtle unseen hierarchical levels of human physiology, which include the etheric bodies, the acupuncture meridians, the chakras and nadis, and the mental, astral and higher spiritual bodies. In this book we will explore the function and integration of these many levels of energetic and spiritual physiology. We must ask ourselves just how all this information fits in with our divine purpose upon the planet Earth. Our comprehension of these higher levels of subtle anatomy and their influence upon our daily lives and health will help us to perceive how we are all intimately linked with the continually evolving divine energies of the soul. We will explore how our physical and higher bodies are specialized 'vehicles' which allow the full manifestation and expression of the soul's consciousness upon what we perceive as the dense Earth plane, which is in reality only an illusion of the incarnating ego.

The consciousness of each soul is actually a particularization of the greater spiritual consciousness which we refer to as God/Goddess. Various spiritual philosophies look to the time of our universe's creation period, when God/Goddess created all souls concurrently. It is said that God/Goddess created human beings in the divine image. This does not mean that God/Goddess has eyes, nose, ears, hair, pain, death, suffering and ignorance. This is man's image, not God/Goddess's. God/Goddess is what remains after all such qualifications have been negated. As each soul was created in that second, God/Goddess separated into smaller beings of light, which are energetic representations of the 'one' original vast being. Through the conscious evolution of these lesser 'gods' and the holographic connectivity of the universe, God/Goddess would enrich and develop tremendous potential for diversity and self-knowledge inherent in supreme consciousness. These first ethereal primal beings of light, or souls, developed ways of manifesting celestial energies of their consciousness through denser forms of expression.

The earthly personalities or incarnate egos 'forget' that they are manifestations of the one supreme intelligence, as the perceptual mechanisms of their brains and bodies create a physical sense of separation from each other, as well as from their Creator. Because of these feelings of separation from

Introduction

God/Goddess, human beings have created religion and rituals in an attempt to reunite themselves with the creative forces of nature and the physical universe which appeared outside themselves. Meditation is the vehicle we will employ to remove this illusion of separation. Despite the fact that the incarnating personality or ego loses (one of the by-products of meditation is remembering) the memory of its past lives at the moment of birth, the personality remains attached to the spiritual energies of the higher self through the connection of its higher vibrational bodies. Through many means, the soul tries to bring greater self-awareness to the incarnating personality via symbolic dreams, the manifestation of certain illnesses or bodily dysfunctions and occasionally through direct inner communication during the meditative state or prayer.

So through the 'self development' and meditation exercises in this book we can begin to strengthen our connectedness to our higher self and use the wisdom, understanding and the knowledge gained to heal ourselves into wholeness. The higher self contains all the memories and knowledge of the soul through its sojourns in many past-life incarnations. Within that pool of knowledge exists the transformational wisdom which will elevate the consciousness of the individual to understanding of its true divine spiritual origins, the transitory nature of life, death and rebirth and the cosmic significance of its existence and its connection to the Creator.

The journey to wholeness begins with a single step, a first dawning of realisation; by allowing the magic to happen, you open yourself to your true eternal perfect nature.

By following this thread of light you will find yourself once more 'consciously' woven into the crystalline-web of the 'One'. The Divine-One-Thread-Soul of the universe.

Part 2

The Chakras

Chakra is a Sanskrit word. It literally means wheel, disk, ring or circle. *Prana* (energy) is said to flow through the human body along the three main *nadis* (channels), namely, *susumna* (fire), *pingala* (male) and *ida* (female). Susumna is situated inside the physical spinal column. Pingala and ida start respectively from the right and left nostrils, move up to the crown of the head and course downwards to the base of the spine. These two major nadis intersect with each other and also with the susumna. These junctions of the nadis are known as chakras or wheels, which regulate the mechanism of the bodies. Even to think of a chakra as a wheel is merely not enough. It is, in metaphysical terminology, a vortex. Chakras pick up cosmic vibrations, or Universal Life Force, and distribute them throughout the body and aura via the *nadis*, *dhamanis* and *siras*.

The body is a replica of the universe, a microcosm of the macrocosm on the physical and spiritual levels. As you develop your inner knowledge, you will become aware of your own chakras and you will observe many changes in them as you advance spiritually. Although there are literally hundreds within the human body, we are most familiar with the seven main ones, which are aligned or 'embedded' within the spinal column. These moderators of subtle energy are envisioned in classic lore as a 'lotus' flower. Each chakra's lotus has a different number of petals. The number of petals is related both to Sanskrit symbolism concerning the configuration of subtle nerves, called nadis (think of these as the roots of the lotus flowers) that emanate from the particular region of the spinal column where the chakra is located, and also to the meaning of particular vowels and consonants in the Sanskrit alphabet. When these vowels are sounded correctly it causes awakening and spiritual growth in the particular chakra being 'sounded'.

Master Chakras

These seven main chakras are called 'master' chakras. They are also gateways between various dimensions, physical, emotional, spiritual, etc. On a physical level, chakras correspond to nerve ganglia, where there is a high degree of nervous activity, and to the glands in the endocrine system. Each person's chakras are unique, yet there are basic similarities among us all. When they are clear and free-flowing, vital optimum health results. When the energy centres (chakras) are blocked, split, damaged, distorted or inactive, we find ill health or dis-ease occurs. The aim of all of us is to maintain the free-flowing energy within the body, keeping it as clear as possible to maintain a happier healthier life. In the ancient yoga tradition it was important to conserve the energies generated within the body and prevent their dissipation, therefore *asanas* (postures) and *mudras* (hand positions), *pranayamas* (life-force-breath) and *bandhas* (seals or locks) were used. The heat so generated causes the *Kundalini Shakti* (Divine cosmic energy) to uncoil. The serpent lifts her head, enters the susumna and is forced up through the system of chakras one by one to the *sahasrara* (chakra at the top of the head). This journey upwards through the chakras is spoken of as 'Kundalini rising'. The Kundalini Goddess is represented as a coiled snake wrapped around a phallus, or *Lingam*, which represents male sexuality. Female sexuality is located primarily in the sacral (second) chakra.

Endocrine System

While anatomically unrecognized by current medical science, the seven major chakras are never-the-less metaphysically connected with all the different systems within the physical body. In this chapter on the chakras we will begin to explore how the chakras bridge the visible, physical body - in the form of the spinal cord, the autonomic nervous system and the endocrine system - with our 'subtle' body, that envelope of vibrational energy known as the aura. While orthodox medicine describes our physical system in terms of chemistry, what is now understood is that for any chemical action to happen a change in the electromagnetic energy of the body must occur first. This energy emanates from the mind and explains the importance of the mind-body link to our physical, emotional, mental and spiritual health. The endocrine system is central in controlling chemical messages, which include adrenalin, insulin, dehydroepiandrosterone (DHEA), progesterone, testosterone, oestrogen, serotonin etc. - these are secreted into the bloodstream from specific organs in the body to stimulate or inhibit certain essential physical processes.

A common question I am asked is what is a hormone?

In simple terms, hormones are chemical messengers that course through your bloodstream and enter tissues where they turn on switches to the genetic machinery that regulates everything from reproduction to emotions, general health and well-being. Hormones can be thought of as the life-giving force that animates you physically, mentally and emotionally.

Another question frequently asked is, where are hormones made?

Different glands and organs throughout the body produce hormones. For example, the pancreas produces the hormone insulin, whereas the ovaries produce oestrogens and progesterone. Other glands such as the pituitary and hypothalamus in the brain secrete hormones such as FSH (follicle stimulating hormone) and LH (luteining hormone) that control how much oestrogen and progesterone are produced by the ovaries.

Some hormones are composed of large proteins and others of small fatty substances derived from cholesterol. One class derived from cholesterol belongs to a family of hormones termed steroids. The steroid family is broken down into five major categories including the oestrogens (estradiol, oestriol, oestrone), progesterone, androgens (DHEA), testosterone, androstenedione, glucocorticoids (cortisol, cortisone), and mineral corticoids (aldosterone). Cholesterol is converted to the mother steroid hormone, pregnenolone, which is then further converted in the ovaries, testes and the adrenal glands to other hormones, as directed by protein hormone signals from the brain.

How much, and what type of steroid hormone is produced, is controlled by specific chemical messages from the brain. Each of the different steroid hormones is responsible for regulating thousands of unique and different cellular products needed for general cell maintenance and repair, as well as reproduction, immune modulation and brain function. In short, steroid hormones are powerful molecules essential for maintaining physical and mental health. So it is not difficult to see why an imbalance of any one hormone can throw your physical, mental and emotional health out of balance, causing aggravating and even serious health problems.

The endocrine system, along with the autonomic nervous system, helps maintain the parameters needed for optimum health by adjusting levels of hormone secretion to suit special demands. In the same way that an imbalance in one chakra affects the others, the nervous and endocrine systems are functionally interconnected and any disturbance in one part can lead to a malfunction elsewhere. In order to enlighten ourselves and gain a greater understanding of how the endocrine system links with the Master chakras we shall look at each pair in turn.

Root Chakra - Adrenals - Nerve Plexus Coccygeal

The adrenal glands cap the kidneys; they are triangular in shape. They are responsible for secreting a variety of hormones including those that regulate the body's metabolism of fats, proteins and carbohydrates and the ones that control the balance of salt in our body fluids. The adrenals also produce adrenalin, the hormone responsible for our basic primitive issues of survival, the fight or flight hormone.

Sacral Chakra - Ovaries/Testes - Nerve Plexus Sacral

The gonads, or male and female reproductive organs, are responsible for the secondary sexual characteristics, such as body hair and the depth of the voice. The testes in males control men's sexual development as well as their sperm production. In females, the ovaries produce the eggs. Oestrogens (estradiol, oestrone, oestriol) are predominantly female hormones, and in adults they are important for maintaining the health of the reproductive tissues, breasts, skin and brain. Excessive oestrogens can cause fluid retention, weight gain, migraines and over-stimulation of the breasts, ovaries and uterus, leading to cancer. Insufficient oestrogen levels can lead to hot flushes, vaginal dryness, rapid skin ageing, urinary problems, excessive bone loss and possible acceleration of dementia. An excess of oestrogen, relative to testosterone, is thought to play a role in the development of prostate problems in men. Most scientists now agree that by-products of oestrogen metabolism are the cause of both breast and prostate cancers. Emotional balance, sexuality and relationships are also the sacral chakra's domain.

Solar Chakra - Pancreas - Nerve Plexus Solar

As I have previously stated, the pancreas produces insulin, which regulates the blood sugar levels. It also is responsible for producing other essential substances which work on the effective digestion of food. The pancreas (pan = all and creas = creation) is situated just behind the stomach. The solar plexus chakra also has a direct influence on the adrenal glands, which are also responsible for producing glucocorticoids, primarily cortisol; these are produced in response to stressors such as emotional upheaval, exercise, surgery, illness or starvation. Cortisol plays an essential role in immune function, mobilising the body's defence against viral or bacterial infection, and fighting inflammation; however, chronic elevated cortisol levels suppress the action of the immune system and predispose to frequent infections. The solar plexus chakra also rules the digestive system.

Heart Chakra - Thymus - Nerve Plexus Heart

Located just above the heart, the thymus produces hormones that stimulate growth in early life. It also has a purifying role in the body by stimulating the production of lymphocytes, which form part of the blood's white cells' defence system, attacking invading organisms and providing immunity. Recently science has recognised that the auto-immune diseases, whereby the immune system attacks its own proteins, mistaking them for a substance that is foreign, have an emotional link and are not simply due to environmental or physical causes.

Throat Chakra - Thyroid/Parathyroid - Nerve Plexus Cervical Ganglia Medulla

Situated on either side of the larynx and trachea in the neck, the thyroid gland manufactures thyroxine, which regulates the metabolic rate of the body. This controls the body's efficiency in converting food into energy. The parathyroid gland, which lies just behind the thyroid gland, controls the calcium levels in the bloodstream. In addition to physical growth, these glands are also believed to affect mental development. The throat chakra is the link between the body and the head: it corresponds with balance and communication.

Third Eye Chakra - Pituitary - Nerve Plexus Hypothalamus Pituitary

The pituitary gland is located within a structure at the base of the skull, close to the eyebrows. Once called 'the master gland' of the endocrine system, it has since been found to be only a 'puppet' controlled by hormonal substances released by the hypothalamus, part of the brain. This gland influences growth, metabolism and general body chemistry, which includes the hormone producing contractions during labour.

Crown Chakra - Pineal - Nerve Plexus Cerebral Cortex Pineal

Once, not so long ago, scientists and doctors thought the pineal gland served no useful purpose. The pineal gland is tiny, about the size of a pea; it lies deep within the brain. The pineal gland produces melatonin (first discovered in 1958), which affects the pituitary, thyroid, adrenals, ovaries and testes. It is a master gland and is the subject of a lot of scientific research, especially in America, where supplements of melatonin are freely on sale to the general public, through chemists and health food shops. In Great Britain these supplements were banned in 1996. Melatonin is perhaps the most famous natural hormone supplement sold worldwide (except in Great Britain). Research scientist Professor Russell Reeiter's clinical studies in the early 1970's proved that melatonin is one of the most effective anti-oxidants ever discovered and is the only known compound which can diffuse into the body cells and savage free-radicals - a factor which may offer real benefits to those seeking long-term health and well-being. Melatonin is produced in the pineal gland and released in the body at night time. Its primary function is to regulate the body's sleep and wake cycle and control our 24-hour clock. Clinical studies have shown it has a direct affect in Alzheimer's patients and may play a protective role in heart disease and the maintenance of correct cholesterol levels. As we age, the body produces less of this hormone. The pineal gland and crown chakra are the control centre of the whole body.

Life-Lessons

Each of the seven master chakras has its particular emotional and spiritual lesson to be learned and applied. The chakras connect the organs, glands and nervous centres of the body with the vital forces which activate the physical body. The degree to which an individual is successful in understanding the particular life-lesson inherent in each chakra will determine the amount of subtle-energy flow which can move into the body to maintain correct physical health, emotional well-being, mental stability and spiritual growth. When a chakra is functioning abnormally because of improper attitudes, old self-deprecating message tapes, sentimental tribal conditioning, fear, guilt, hatred etc., the organs which receive vital flow from that chakra become affected.

Total avoidance of a particular life-lesson can result in blockage of the chakra and inadequate vital flow to the associated organs. When the subtle-energy flow due to chakra underactivity becomes evident, it will manifest in the related organs associated with that particular chakra. Underactivity causes degenerative, destructive or cancerous lesions, while conversely, over-exaggeration and over-focusing on a particular emotional issue cause the chakra to become overloaded with energy. This over-activity will cause over-stimulation of the associated glands, overproduction of cells in the form of tumour growth, and inflammation. We will look at the chakras and life-lessons - each chakra's lesson builds on the previous one, much as one would build any enduring structure. Unless the life-lessons are learned and the chakras are balanced one by one, it is useless to aim for spiritual growth. Not only is it useless, but it is also dangerous; without a strong foundation, the tower of your spirituality will come toppling down. For this reason, those who wish to grow to great spiritual heights must learn the life-lessons and balance the chakras one by one.

The developmental age and life-lesson of the root chakra is 1-8 years of age. It is associated with standing up for oneself. This means being 'earthed' and having a grounded reality, feeling good and taking care of the physical body. It also relates to letting go of fear and the past in order to move forward. It is the start of your journey on the earth plane. If you have not learned this life-lesson, you will react in a childish manner to threatening situations, usually by blaming others instead of taking direct personal responsibility. You will be the perpetual victim of your circumstances. You may have feelings of separation from God/Goddess, mental lethargy, spaciness, an unfocused mind, be incapable of stillness and have difficulty achieving your goals.

The developmental age and life-lesson of the sacral chakra is 8-14 years, its association challenging motivations based on sentimental tribal or social conditioning, as well as absorption, assimilation and reproduction. This means being able to take care of yourself emotionally, not just physically. Although prana flows throughout the entire body, the sacral chakra is considered to be the central distributor of pranic intake. When the life-lesson related to this chakra is fully understood it becomes evident that we take responsibility for our emotions and are able to take the rough with the smooth. We realise that both are just illusion and in truth we are responsible for our own emotional happiness, regardless of outside influences or circumstances. We no longer blame others for our own emotional problems. Our lives are filled with originality, creativity, gratitude and joy. We realise every second is precious and life is to be enjoyed. We are born anew moment by moment.

The developmental age and life-lesson of the solar plexus chakra is 14-21 years. It is associated with self-esteem and self-confidence, in other words learning to honour and love ourselves. We must establish a sense of personal power in relationship to self and our external relationships. This chakra teaches very firmly the lesson of being true to one's own beliefs, however unpopular or different from the 'current' acceptable tribal truth. Once you have learned to stand in your truth and accept personal responsibility, you will be able to overcome all obstacles in your spiritual path. You will also learn to be immaculate energy-wise and always behave in a pristine, impeccable manner to all you meet on your life journey.

The developmental age of the heart chakra is 21-28 years. Its life-lesson is forgiveness and compassion. On our journey through the life-lessons our focus has been with the lower chakras and building a strong balance of self-acceptance, self-love, self-honouring; this in turn has allowed us to love others and honour them too, for each one's uniqueness of being, allowing ourselves and others to follow our own unique path on our journey through life. This is unity within diversity, for if we cannot accept others exactly as they are, in this present moment, we will not be able to accept ourselves exactly as we are, right now, in this present moment. This is our test, our life-lesson of the heart chakra: unconditional love, compassion and forgiveness. We are challenged on this on a daily basis, but in order to move to the higher centres we must have this balance, otherwise we cannot successfully make this movement upwards, and when we begin to focus on the higher chakras, all our hatred, anger, resentment, bitterness and fear issues will come back to haunt us, only this time it will bring the full force of our focused mind with it. So before you move on, make sure you truly unconditionally love and have compassion for yourself and for all life, because when the mind looks at itself in the mirror of the soul, if you are not full of love, you will be full of hatred. This hatred will manifest as your own demons of darkness and if you are not fully balanced you will try to project them outwards and project them onto others, so seeking an escape route and someone else to blame. You and you alone are your only judge and jury; all illness and feelings of separation start with a lack of love. You need no one else to validate you, you know who you are: as the song goes "show your true colors, you are beautiful - like a rainbow".

The developmental age and life-lesson of the throat chakra is 28-35 years. Personal expression is the test and the goal is how to express yourself. "Walk your talk" as the saying goes! This means being aware of your communication on all levels, not just in the spoken or written word, but being aware of your unspoken communication too, your body language and your communication with God/Goddess and your higher self. Your body language speaks volumes, not just to others but to yourself. If you constantly affirm that you are depressed, sad or angry, be aware your body is listening to you with 100% concentration and will act on your communication. It will subconsciously give you exactly what you ask for. What you dwell on day after day attracts even more of the same; this is the universal law of resonance, like attracts like. Soon you will have lots of negativity to deal with. The universal law of resonance always gives you exactly what you ask for (even subconsciously) in ever greater abundance!

Your personal communication with others should be clear and precise too. You should integrate your mind with your heart before you speak; in this way you will have a balanced throat chakra.

The developmental age and life-lesson of the third eye chakra: well, there is no development age - some people never learn the lesson of emotional intelligence. Perhaps I should list how you can tell if you have learned this life-lesson. You will have access to all knowledge; when I say access, I mean you know through prayer and meditation how to access your own source of wisdom and divine personal communication direct from the Akashic records, the mind of God/Goddess. You receive inner guidance on a daily basis and can experience cosmic consciousness. You are not attached to material possessions, you know the transitory impermanence of these things; you know you are an eternal being of light, love, wisdom, truth and you are limitless, so why do you need to hold on to possessions, which are just illusions anyway? You have no fear of death or dying, you are not preoccupied with fame or fortune; you show the pathway to liberation to others by example. You experience astral travel, telepathy and all your past lives. At this level of development you perceive yourself as androgenous and you no longer require another person to complement you; you are complete in yourself. You can choose what, who or where you want to be; your life flows effortlessly. You can manifest your reality daily, as miracles occur naturally to you. Life is one 'big' miracle filled with joy, love and spiritual enchantment.

The developmental age and life-lesson of the crown chakra: well, there is no development age - some people never learn the lesson of selflessness. This lesson is a natural progression of the last one; by the time you reach this level of development you are one with the Divine, you can work miracles and are ready to merge your consciousness at the time of death with God/Goddess, or maybe you will choose to be immortal, as transcending the laws of 'nature' are no mystery to you. You will probably be able to live without food or water because you know that it is the pranic life force that supports and nurtures you, not the physical food and water.

So far we have explored the subtle-energy pathways which unite the major chakras to the normal functioning of the human body. Each master chakra furnishes subtle nutritive energy for the health and homeostatic maintenance of the body's combined physiological systems. An individual's stage of emotional growth, mental stability and spiritual evolution is directly related to the functioning, openness and activation of each master chakra. The amount and quality of chakric energy flow in turn affects the physiology of the physical organs of the body. If a chakra is blocked, or malfunctioning in some way, then there will be an associated difficulty in the organ or organs which receive energy from that major chakra centre. A thorough understanding of how emotional, mental and spiritual difficulties can create disease in the body is established on a broad working knowledge of how the chakras affect physical and mental illness. Perhaps one of the most effective and productive methods of opening, activating and cleansing blockages in the chakras is through the techniques of meditation. Although meditation initially is sought by many as a source of relaxation, it is so much more than that. In addition to providing relaxation to the body, meditation opens the mind to the energies of the higher self. It helps to clear the mind of day-to-day concerns of the earthly personality and allows higher information to be processed through the individual's consciousness. Most forms of meditation do this to some degree or another. However, certain meditative techniques are more potent and certainly far more powerful than others in accelerating this process of divine communication. In the chapter on meditation and especially the chapter on Kundalini we will begin to explore the different techniques in our personal vibrational journey through the chakra maze.

In actuality no unified world tradition regarding the nature and overall functioning of the seven master chakras exists. The Hindu and Buddhist traditions of India, for instance, differ significantly from the Tantric and Taoist traditions found in Tibet, China and adjoining Buddhist regions. Significantly there are many diverse traditions regarding the human energy centres - descriptions of which can be found in every deep spiritual tradition of all tribes and civilizations throughout the world.

In Western antiquity quite a number of esoteric groups, such as the Knights Templar, the Freemasons and the Gnostic Christian cults, dealt at very high levels not only with chakra systems but with Christ consciousness for attaining Kundalini awakening and advanced stages of ecstatic meditation. In the Qabalistic tradition a system of spheres or levels of consciousness was related directly to the physical body.

We have so far been reading about the chakras, a conceptual idea - now let's meet them one by one. It is relatively easy to turn your experiential consciousness towards your chakras. Let me guide you through a preliminary experiential exploration of your seven master chakras, so you can see how well your mind focuses your power of attention in each of the seven directions.

Chakra One: First, relax, be aware of your breathing, your heartbeat, your body balanced in the present moment........and in this expanded state of awareness, turn your power of attention to the bottom of your spine, where your body meets the earth in the sitting position........

Chakra Two: Now, while you remain aware of your breathing and whole-body presence, move your awareness up to your sexual centre, to your genital region........

Chakra Three: Now gently move your awareness up to your belly, to your third chakra's power centre......

Chakra Four: Now move your awareness gently up to the centre of your chest, your heart chakra......

Chakra Five: Now shift your awareness upwards to your throat, into your communication chakra.......

Chakra Six: Now effortlessly move your awareness to the point between your eyes and deep inside your brain: this is your intuitive sixth brow chakra......

Chakra Seven: Gently shift your awareness to the top of your head, to the crown chakra.....

Chakra Correspondences

1.   Root Chakra

Sanskrit name *muladhara* (*mula* = root, source; *adhara* = support, vital part). Also known as the base or earth chakra. Located in the perineum, the base of the spine, between anus and genitals. Associated with red, physical energy, physical health and fitness, gravity, self-preservation, survival, being grounded, adrenal glands, spinal column. All the solid elements of the body. Energy location: feet, ankles, legs, knees, thighs and large intestine. Energetic gateway between us and the earth, also energies of childhood and the past. When this chakra is developed, we are more grounded, solid and powerful at physical levels of survival. Knowledge of the past, present and future are bestowed when this chakra is fully activated.

Malfunction: osteoarthritis, obesity, haemorrhoids, constipation and problems associated with the feet, legs, bones and teeth. Mental lethargy, 'spaciness', incapable of inner stillness.

The first chakra (Earth) is masculine; solid; earthly; yang.

Element and ruling planet: Earth, Saturn - Astrological association: Capricorn.

Intake: protein.

Symbol: 4 crimson-red petal lotus flower, around a yellow square containing a downward-pointing triangle containing the *Bija* Lam. Here also is the *Brahma granthi*, or knot of *Brahma*, which must be forced open through rigorous *sadhana* and intense purification for the *kundalini* to rise. It is also the location of the resting *Kundalini* Goddess: she is said to lie coiled three-and-a-half times around this chakra. The three coils represent the three stages of *avastha* (mind), namely *jagrt* (awake), *svapna* (dreaming) and *susuptiin* (deep sleep). There is a fourth level, *turiya*, combining and transcending the others, which represents the last half coil. It is attained in *samadhi* (enlightenment).

Names of petals: vam, sam, sham, sam.

Sensory channel: smell.

Sound *Bija* Mantra: Lam (female) or Lang (male).

Musical note C

Associated creature: elephant.

Developmental age and life-lesson: 1-8 years. Standing up for oneself.

Sephira: Malkuth - Archangel: Sandalphon.

Gemstones: Ruby, Garnet, Zircon, Ruby Aura Quartz, Hematite.

Incense/Oils: Cedarwood, Patchouli, Myrrh, Musk, Lavender.

2.   Sacral Chakra

Sanskrit name *svadhisthana* (*sva* = vital force, soul; *adhisthana* = seat or abode). Also known as the water chakra or sweetness. Located in the sexual organs and upwards towards the navel. Associated with vitality, attraction, magnetism, desire, emotion, creativity, sexuality, water. Bodily parts: all fluid functions of the body, ovaries, testes, womb. There is great cleansing potential in this chakra associated with personality disorders related to the emotions: unbalanced sex drive, emotional instability, feelings of isolation. Social awareness and partnerships. The color orange is for creativity, wisdom and benevolence.

Malfunction: frigidity, impotence, bladder, kidney and uterine disorders, prostate problems, lower back pain. Fertility, impotency. Also fear, shock and guilt.

The second chakra (Sex) is feminine; liquid; flowing; yin.

Element and ruling planet: Water, Pluto - Astrological association: Cancer, Scorpio.

Intake: fluids.

Symbol: 6-petal orange-red lotus flower, containing a second lotus flower and an upward-pointing crescent moon. Within the moon lies the 'Makara', a fish-tailed alligator with a coiled tail. When this chakra is balanced you will 'flow'. Use this chakra as a primal spiritual centre. When this chakra is activated fully you become healthy and full of vitality. Meditation on the crescent moon gives control over the water element and confers psychic powers, intuitional knowledge and knowledge of astral entities. Many impure qualities are annihilated.

Names of petals: bam, bham, mam, yam, ram, lam.

Sensory channel: taste.

Sound *Bija* Mantra: Vam or Vang.

Musical note D

Associated creature: water dragon or a fish-tailed alligator with a coiled tail (*Makara*) or crocodile.

Developmental age and life-lesson: 8-14 years. Challenging motivations based on social conditioning.

Sephira: Yesod - Archangel: Gabriel.

Gemstones: Carnelian, Red Jasper, Orange Sunstone, Aragonite, Hessonite, Amber, Tangerine Quartz.

Incense/Oils: Jasmine, Rose, Sandalwood.

3.   Solar Plexus Chakra

Sanskrit name *manipuraka* (*manipura* = navel) situated in the navel; *manas* (mind) and *surya* (the sun). Also known as the power chakra or lustrous gem. Located between the navel and the solar plexus centre. Associated with fire, personal power, ambition, intellectual activity, combustion, anger, joy, laughter. Astral force, mental power, pancreas and adrenals. Also central nervous system.

Malfunction: stomach ulcers and other digestive disorders, also diabetes, low vitality, chronic fatigue and allergies. Over-sensitive to criticism, need to be in control, low self-esteem. Addictive personality, aggression.

The third chakra (Power or *agni*) is masculine; wilful; yang.

Element and ruling planets: Fire, Mars and the Sun - Astrological association: Aries, Leo.

Intake: starch, complex carbohydrates.

Symbol: 10-petal lotus flower. The petals are yellow, the centre contains a deep red downward-pointing triangle surrounded by three 'svastikas', symbolic of fire. The color yellow is for meditative analytical thought, intellectual activity, abundance, manifestation of your dreams. If you meditate on this chakra you will become dis-ease free and have no fear of fire, being able to control this element.

There is another important chakra (manas) which lies between the manipuraka and anahata chakras. It is the seat of the emotions, igniting imagination and creativity. When the manas and anahata chakras are activated together, they strengthen the heart and help you develop devotion to your spiritual path or goal.

Names of petals: dam, dham, nam, tam, tham, dam, dham, nam, pam, pham.

Sensory channel: sight.

Sound Bija Mantra: Ram or Rang.

Musical note E

Associated creature: ram.

Developmental age and life-lesson: 14-21 years. Self-esteem/self-confidence.

Sephiroth: Hod and Netzach - Archangels: Michael and Haniel.

Gemstones: Yellow Sapphire, Citrine, Golden Sunstone, Sunshine Aura Quartz, Amber, Amblygonite, Tiger Eye, Yellow Jasper.

Incense/Oils: Vetivert, Rose, Bergamot, Ylang Ylang, Cinnamon, Carnation.

4.   Heart Chakra

Sanskrit name *anahata* (= unbeaten or unstruck. A sound that is made without any two things striking). Located in the cardiac area, in the region of the physical and spiritual heart. Associated with compassion, love. Beliefs about love and relationships. One-ness, heart, thymus and the immune system.

Malfunction: lung disease, asthma, heart disease. Shallow breathing, high blood pressure, cancer. Problems with arms, hands and fingers. Fears about betrayal, co-dependent, melancholic.

31

The fourth chakra (Heart) is feminine; loving; integrating; yin.

Element and ruling planet: Air, Venus - Astrological association: Libra, Taurus.

Intake: vegetables.

Symbol: 12 deep rose-pink petal green lotus flower. The inner centre contains a green circle, two intersecting triangles make up a perfect six-pointed star, demonstrating the balance between the downward-pointing spirit descending towards matter and the upward-pointing matter ascending towards spirit. Meditation on the heart chakra gives the primal sound of *anahata* sound, the primal sound of *Sabdabrahman*. It also bestows pure qualities, cosmic love and various psychic powers.

Names of petals: kam, kham, gam, gham, nam, cam, cham, jam, jham, nam, tam, tham.

Sensory channel: touch.

Sound *Bija* Mantra: Yam or Yang.

Musical note F

Associated creature: black antelope.

Developmental age and life-lesson: 21-28 years. Forgiveness and compassion.

Sephira: Tiphareth - Archangel: Raphael.

Gemstones: (Green) Emerald, Green Jade, Green Tourmaline, Green Aventurine, Moldavite, Peridot, Malachite, Chrysoprase

(Pink) Rose Quartz, Morganite, Pink Tourmaline, Watermelon Tourmaline, Rhodochrosite, Kunzite, Smithsonite.

Incense/Oils: Rose, Bergamot, Melissa.

5.   Throat Chakra

Sanskrit name *visuddha* (= pure), which means purification. It is also known as the 'communication' chakra. Located in the throat region at the base of the neck. Associated with communication, self-expression, sound, voice, speech, writing. Active listening, thyroid gland, parathyroid, lungs, vocal cords, jaw, breath. Dreaming, imagination and out of body experiences. The power of choice, harmony with others.

Malfunction: stiff necks, colds, sore throats, thyroid and hearing problems, tinnitus, asthma. Masks of the self. Perfectionism, inability to express emotions, blocked creativity.

The fifth chakra (Throat) is masculine; manifesting; logical; yang.

Element and ruling planets: Ether (*akasha* in Sanskrit), Moon and Mercury.

Astrological association: Gemini, Virgo.

Intake: fruit.

Symbol: 16-petal blue lotus flower. Contained within the flower is a downward-pointing triangle, within which is a circle representing the full silvery-blue Moon. The color blue gives communication with divine guidance. When this chakra is fully activated you have a beautiful voice, your speech is clear and fluent. Your intellect increases, as does your understanding of the divine scriptures. You have complete knowledge of the past, present and future.

Names of petals (am, am, im, im, um, um, rm, rm, im, im, em, aim, om, aum, am, ahm).

Sensory channel: sound.

Sound *Bija* Mantra: Ham or Hang.

Musical note G

Associated creatures: white lion, *Airavata* the many-tusked elephant.

Developmental age and life-lesson: 28-35 years. Personal expression.

Sephiroth: Geburah and Chesed - Archangels: Khamael and Tzadkiel.

Gemstones: Lapis Lazuli, Blue Sapphire, Chrysocolla, Blue Calcite, Azurite, Blue Lace Agate, Larimar, Aquamarine, Turquoise, Aqua Aura Quartz.

Incense/Oils: Chamomile, Myrrh.

6a.   Third Eye Chakra

Sanskrit name *ajna* (= command), which means to know. Also known as the brow chakra or intuitive chakra. Located right between and just above the physical eyes, it corresponds to the space between the eyebrows, the *Trikuta*. Associated with intuition, pituitary gland, left eye, the base of the skull. The mind is looking directly at itself. The combined interaction of the pineal with the pituitary gland activates this chakra. The element is *Avyakta*, the primordial cloud of undifferentiated energy and matter.

Malfunction: headaches, nightmares, eye problems, poor vision, neurological disturbances, glaucoma. Learning difficulties, hallucinations.

The sixth chakra (Brow) is feminine; intuitive; mysterious; yin.

Elements and ruling planets: Mind and light - telepathic energy, Neptune and Jupiter -

Astrological association: Sagittarius, Pisces.

Intake: air.

Symbol: 2 large pure white lotus petals on each side of a pure white circle, within which is a downward-pointing triangle containing the *bija* seed letter Om. The color indigo (dark blue and dark violet) represents devotion to the truth - idealism, obedience, intuition and perception. The ability to look to the future. Indigo transmutes and purifies, it is the transformer. Indigo is the color of the priest or priestess. When you meditate on the third eye chakra and it becomes fully activated you can successfully destroy the karma of all past lives and become a liberated soul. Intuitional knowledge is obtained through this chakra; it is the seat of primordial power and soul. It is here that yogis consciously place their prana at the time of death. The color violet represents those who search for the spiritual truth in all life. This is the seat of true wisdom, through deep meditation. When this chakra is fully activated you are filled with joy and develop a spiritual aura. This is where the unmanifested and manifested meet. This is where yin and yang merge. This is where we move beyond dualism.

Names of petals: ksham, ham.

Sensory channel: light, sixth sense.

Sound *Bija* Mantra: Om

Musical note A

Associated creature: white owl.

Developmental age and life-lesson: (N/A) Emotional intelligence.

Sephiroth: Binah and Chokmah - Archangels: Tzaphkiel and Ratziel.

Gemstones: Iolite, Amethyst, Tanzanite, Sugilite, Charoite, Lepidolite, Fluorite.

Incense/Oils: Hyacinth, Violet, Rose geranium.

6b.   The Fourth Eye Chakra

Sanskrit name *soma* (= water).

Located just above the third eye chakra in the centre of the brain.

This chakra controls the body temperature and balances the power chakra in the solar plexus, bringing the male/female balance to the whole body system. The balance is maintained via the breath. Erratic breathing causes imbalances in the body and upsets this polarity.

Sensory channel: light.

Sound *Bija* Mantra: Om

Musical note A

Associated creature: eagle.

Developmental age and life-lesson: (N/A) Emotional intelligence.

Sephiroth: Binah and Chokmah - Archangels: Tzaphkiel and Ratziel.

Gemstones: Amethyst, Tanzanite, Charoite, Lepidolite.

Incense/Oils: Hyacinth, Violet.

6c.   The Fifth Eye Chakra

Sanskrit name *lalata* (= forehead).

Located at the top of the forehead. Its full activation brings man to be master of his own destiny.

Sensory channel: light.

Sound *Bija* Mantra: Om

Musical note A

Associated creature: white dove.

Developmental age and life-lesson: (N/A) Emotional intelligence.

Sephiroth: Binah and Chokmah - Archangels: Tzaphkiel and Ratziel.

Gemstones: Tanzanite, Diamond, Clear Quartz, Danburite, Phenacite, Azeztulite, Petalite, Clear Calcite, Selenite, Herkimer Diamond.

Incense/Oils: Violet.

7.   Crown Chakra

Sanskrit name *sahasrara* (= thousand), which means 'to multiply by a thousandfold'. Located at the crown of the head, known as the anterior fontanelle in a new-born child; is called Brahmarandhra, the "hole of Brahma". At the time of death the advanced meditator separates him/herself from the physical body, it bursts open and the prana escapes through it. Associated with enlightenment, cosmic consciousness, right eye, cerebral cortex, pineal gland, upper skull, skin.

Malfunction: confusion, lack of clarity, depression, obsessional thinking, sensitivity to pollutants, chronic exhaustion, epilepsy, Alzheimer's.

The seventh chakra (Crown) is masculine; pure bright light; yang - violet, gold, white.

Elements and ruling planet: Thought and cosmic energy, Uranus - Astrological association: Aquarius.

Symbol: The thousand-petal white lotus flower, on which are repeated the fifty letters of the *Sanskrit* alphabet. It is the abode of *Shiva*. Brilliance, bringing enlightenment, cosmic awareness, blissful reunion with source. Allowing the 'Holy Spirit' to flow downwards into our lives for the ultimate healing and inspirational power of the universe.

Enlightenment is to be filled with light, to comprehend the light, to function in the light, to radiate the light and merge with the light. When *Kundalini Shakti* is united with *Shiva* at the *sahasrara*, the *yogi/yogini* experiences extreme bliss. He/she attains the superconscious state and the highest knowledge.

Intake: fasting (Prana).

Sensory channel: experience - beyond self.

Sound *Bija* Mantra: of silence or silent OM.

Musical note B

Developmental age and life-lesson: (N/A) Selflessness.

Sephira: Kether - Archangel: Metatron.

Gemstones: Diamond, Clear Quartz, Danburite, Phenacite, Azeztulite, Petalite, Clear Calcite,

Selenite, Herkimer Diamond.

Incense/Oils: Lavender, Frankincense, Rosewood.

Part 3

The Aura

The peoples of ancient cultures knew and understood that beyond its physical material form the human body is a pulsing, moving, dynamic field of energy. They developed a deep understanding of these basic fundamental energies, called Universal Life Force, prana, chi or Qi. This pool of energy is drawn into and surrounds and permeates the human body and surrounding energy field known as the aura. (*Aura* is a Greek word meaning breeze). The aura consists of seven levels, subtle bodies or *kosas* (body sheaths). The seven levels correlate to the seven master chakras. The aura begins with the seen (physical body) and progresses to subtle and more refined vibrations as we go further away from the physical. Awareness of the levels of the aura is gained through meditation, contemplation and realisation. Very often, as we open spiritually, we begin to perceive a glow around the physical body. This is the first level and the most easy to view. The seven levels are enmeshed and interwoven in web-like energy-threads within each other, although each has a particular function, energy, awareness and realisation, which is reflected in the consciousness and is observable in all individuals. Even 'inanimate' objects have an aura or field of energy around them, especially crystals, trees, plants and flowers. Nothing in reality is 'inanimate', all is moving, vibrating, pulsing with life force and energy signatures.

In Yoga, the aura is known as the sevenfold knowledge and is to be integrated between the seen (*prakrti*) and the seer (*purusa*). They are, starting with level one, being the closest to the physical body:

> Integration of the body, *sarira samyama* - emerging consciousness (*vyutthana citta*)
> Integration of the senses, *indriya samyama* - restraining consciousness (*nirodha citta*)
> Integration of energy, *prana samyama* - individualized consciousness (*nirmana citta*)
> Integration of the mind, *mano samyama* - tranquil consciousness (*prasanta citta*)
> Integration of the intellect, *buddhi samyama* - attentive consciousness (*ekagrata citta*)
> Integration of the consciousness, *citta samyama* - fissured or rent consciousness (*chidra citta*)
> Integration of the soul, *atma samyama* - pure consciousness (*paripakva citta or divya citta*)

The Yoga Sutras of Patanjali (written 2,500 years ago) were the earliest - and are still the most profound and enlightening - study of the human psyche. In 11.27 he wrote "*tasya saptadha prantabhumih prajna*". This roughly translates as "its sevenfold province holds supreme knowledge of consciousness". He was referring to the seven sheaths, *kosas* or levels of the aura.

Yet even by saying there are seven layers or levels does not convey the energy correctly. How do you describe the indescribable, but we must begin somewhere. When someone asks me, as they frequently do, "what color is my aura?" or "what is in my aura?" I always feel like replying "which level?" When I view auras I can see many levels and by adjusting my 'focus' can 'tune' in to any particular layer. The other problem I have is I can see beyond the seven levels, into infinity, but to describe this is beyond the scope of this chapter. The other question I am asked is "how do you personally see auras?" This is a very difficult question to answer, because I was born with this ability. In reality it is a skill that everyone has access to. I only use my 'gift' as a diagnostic tool, as it is 'not appropriate' to be 'open' all the time, viewing each soul's confusion, pain, suffering and ignorance. Imagine being in a room full of color television sets, all tuned to different stations around the world, on full volume - you are getting the idea. I had to refine my awareness and now only choose to 'see' as a diagnostic tool, or when danger is evident - as in the case of a drowning child, my attention is drawn in that direction immediately. My gift also needs great discretion: I learned, very early in my life, to be silent at the appropriate time.

Unfortunately most people do not realise that they are so transparent and you do not have to be clairvoyant to know when someone is lying, cheating, stealing or committing any number of other 'deadly sins'.

The aura of an unevolved person will be very different to the aura of someone who is self-realised. All the stages inbetween these two vast polarities give myriad kinds and types of auras. When we progress spiritually we begin to find vast differences in the color, quality, texture, resonance and vibration or signature of each person on the planet. We have at the moment no totally accurate devices for measuring the aura, but in the meantime we have our own awareness which is automatic. I am sure we all know when we like someone or when someone is angry or sad: this we sense by direct contact of our aura with theirs. Every person projects some kind of vibration. Some people are a pleasure to be with and are an inspirational force. They have a certain prana, or energy, that they share with others. Then there are those who are negative and depressed; they seem to actually draw prana out of others. The reason for this is that there is a power contained in thought. It is subtle, yet it does exist and it is extremely potent. Whether a person is aware of it or not, they are constantly receiving and transmitting thoughts. The ability to communicate and perceive thought is developed to a higher degree in those who are said to be psychic. All thoughts have size, shape, weight, color and power. Those who are experienced in meditating can see this directly; it is a by-product, but not the goal of meditating.

As I have previously stated, there are no accurate devices for measuring the aura, but I have seen kirlian photography, aura photographs and aura video cameras; they are very limited in their application at the moment, but are interesting and quite revealing. I used an aura video camera last time I was in America, but I gave it problems. I was outside its scope, they could not capture a clear picture, due to my oscillation or resonance. Evidently, as I was told by the operator, "only crystals oscillate like this, I've never seen anything like it before". Research by Dr Hiroshi Motoyama, of Japan, and Dr Valerie Hunt, at UCLA, has measured the aura. Data from these experiments seemed to confirm the subtle energy field surrounding the human body.

All auras are different and change constantly as our thoughts, moods, environment and state of health change. A person with a spiritual aura is an inspirational joy to be with. It is very uplifting; they are full of light, usually white-gold, and they have a glow all of their own, just like the halos you see in old paintings of saints. As people develop spiritually they do have an amazing glow around their head, crown chakra and the higher chakras above the head. I always see 'Angels' around babies, children and those who are opening spiritually, especially the ones who work with the Angelic realm. We can all have Angelic help if we ask. But you do have to ask. Those souls who work with fairies have this energy visible in their aura, as do those who work 'shamanically', only their 'spirit guides' and 'helpers' are clearly visible. I will love to see the scientific equipment that can view these 'vibrations' in the aura.

When I talk of seven layers or levels each has a distinct function; they also alternate fixed, then moving. The fixed or structured layers appear to be every other chakra/aura layer. The root, solar, throat and crown are structured. These structures are web-like, with tiny lights that move along them at great speed, scintillating, fast, pulsing. The layers inbetween are fluid, moving, changing color and form, especially the emotional layer; they are only restrained by the structured layers. But in reality a person who is highly trained in meditation or very spiritually advanced can take these structured layers down and put them back up, if they wish to, at will.

The aura may become damaged by ill health, negative thought patterns, environmental pollutants, stress or poor breathing techniques. This can be 'viewed' and the damage may be repaired with the correct use and placement of crystals, gemstones or other vibrational medicine. Sometimes we find debris in the aura when someone repeatedly holds a negative thought pattern or addiction for a long time. Some of these thought patterns and addictions take on a life of their own and act as a possession, negative entity thought form or negative entity thought form shape; in time these can influence not only the person they are attached to but control other people's behaviour too. Colors and shapes are clearly visible within the aura, the colors reflecting which chakras are the most active or underactive, also where the person needs to pay special attention to restore pure color or vibrancy. Any imbalances will cause trouble in the overall vitality of the energy field. If a person regularly has spiritual thoughts the aura can be a very clear yellow or even gold, while a thought charged with anger and hatred is dark red, splattered with black. When you see grey in the aura it is always a bad sign too, usually very ill health has already manifested on the physical body. The exception to this rule is if someone has had a terrifying experience, a brush with death, like being blown up by a bomb, or a major car crash, or anything that has almost scared them to death; then the aura can be grey, but it should quickly recover once the person is safe and secure. The shapes and patterns in the aura represent energies which will block the spiritual, mental, emotional and physical health of a person. These can be removed with crystal energies.

I have even seen people with crystals in their aura, as well as flowers; some people I have observed have wings - very Angelic. A good way to observe auras is at the beach. Here people feel relaxed and happy; watch as they go in the sea, their aura (emotional level) turns the most beautiful shade of turquoise blue. Those who lie on the beach soaking up the sun's rays go golden-orange - yes, the sun is really energising. Or go for a walk in nature, where you will observe a person's aura going the most beautiful shade of emerald green as they relax and absorb the essence and energy of the trees and grass.

Karmic burdens and karmic predispositions or miasms (crystallized patterns of karma) are also viewed within the aura. This debris is a past-life carry-over and will cause problems, misery and mental or emotional instability. Very often we find damage in the aura caused by attachments, cords or ties. These are usually from outside causes, where one individual has damaged another. This can be very nasty to deal with, as it causes energy leakage or vampirism. These cords and energy drains need to be very carefully removed and the spaces where they have been need to be filled with positive, vital, loving, healing energy. I have also observed entities attached to people; they are very often sub-human and appear to be using their host in a parasitic manner.

On an even more interesting note, I am very surprised that 'the powers that be' have not investigated aura recording equipment, as wherever you go you leave your aura essence, or an energy signature, just as you leave your fingerprints over everything you touch. Just imagine, in the future the police will have energy recording devices at the scenes of crimes and will be able to match the signature to the perpetrator, just as they are developing at the moment with DNA testing. I can remember these machines being used in the legendary continent of Atlantis - where not only were they used to control crime, they were used to control and manipulate the population.

I personally can read energy signatures after a person has visited a particular place; each time I have verified it for its accuracy. I can also 'read' in a person's aura who has taught them particular healing techniques, especially those who have been attuned to the energy known as Reiki. This caused some people consternation when I said "did X attune you to Reiki?" and the Reiki person said "yes, how did you know?" "Well it was simply recorded in your energy field," was my reply. Of course your past lives are recorded in your aura too, as well as every thought, word or action. Your aura records 100% faithfully all this information, all the time.

When you evolve spiritually, you can cleanse your aura completely and become free of this information or, as it is sometimes known, karma, or miasms. We will deal with karma and karmic patterning, and miasms, in a later chapter.

We are surrounded by energy and energy patterns. Depending on our awareness, culture, expectations, intellect and perceptive abilities, this gives us our personal reality profile. Any time that changes occur, we become aware of the many billions of different energy currents and energy flows that live alongside us and the different sorts of beings that also inhabit our universe. All energy is omnipresent and all-pervasive; it only requires the correct energy shift or awareness to find it. You are most familiar with those we call sound, light, touch, taste and smell (third dimension). If you were able to alter at will your own bioelectromagnetic signature (vibration) in some way, it would be possible to connect your individual pattern to a slightly different pervading omnipresent model or pattern, thus altering your experiences, signature and comprehension and ultimately realisation. In ancient yogic philosophy, thought, form and sound are all the same, just as ice, water and steam are all the same substance.

We use the same process when we lie within a crystal web. This also happens when we hold a crystal in our hand and attune to its refined frequency or vibration. Each crystal modifies the physical and subtle bodies' energy relationship to its environment and allows access to other tiers (levels, worlds or, as the Qabalists would say, spheres) of information and, most of all, awareness perception. I became conscious of this process many years ago when I discovered that by placing certain crystals on or around the body we could expect and even predict a certain change in comprehension or perception. I have seen thousands of people 'feel' this 'shift' in consciousness or change of perception when using crystals. It usually takes years of meditation practice before this shift in consciousness occurs! So you can imagine my excitement as I watched the speed of awareness development within individuals who were not regular meditators. Some were even downright sceptics. The sceptics very often resorted to denial, although they initially felt the shift, but through fear of change or leaving themselves open to ridicule decided to block their spiritual growth. We all know the fear vibration and have felt it used against us many times by those who wish for their own selfish reasons to control or manipulate us.

As a child I was aware of the myriad different energies and energy systems; in fact I could not understand why others were not aware of these energies. I did not realise that they were not 'tuned' in to the frequencies that were my reality, my birthright. From the age of twenty I have studied these energies and energy realities. The native traditions of many peoples are very unlike those of the average westerner: their belief systems are very different. The more I studied, the more I became aware of the limitations we place upon ourselves. I also realised not only that 'healing' used different energy frequencies within the human body and aura (chakras, meridians, sheaths etc.), but that different frequencies and energy patterns are present and exist within the universal energy frequencies.

All energy begins with a central point which is the source of 'all'. In the Tantric view, sound, as a vibration of undifferentiated Intelligence, is the catalyst that sets into motion the unfolding of the manifest cosmos. This nothingness is comprised of all the energies and forces of the Divine Universe, existing in harmony beyond our understanding at a time before our existence. It has neither mass nor form, but it has the potential to become everything and anything. It is that first point from which we came and to which we will some day return.

View, if you will, the first primal movement that awakens the sleeping equilibrium of the Divine Intelligence and arouses the two active principles to carry out creation. This great cosmic vibration splits the Divine Intelligence into two streams of magnetic force, as two aspects are projected outward, male and female. The centrifugal positive male force is the ground from which the centripetal, negative feminine energy springs. It is the female that unfolds the universe into manifestation. They are the Father (*Bindu*) and Mother (*Nada*) aspects of the Supreme Power. God/Goddess in that one moment created all the lesser gods too, as all souls became manifest.

The act of creation, the act of Divine Intelligence manifesting from a place beyond physical reality and thus beyond our comprehension, as seen within the Qabala, gives a way of perceiving how we can each evolve and attain higher and greater knowledge or gifts. The Divine Intelligence began to manifest through stages its energies, acquiring greater density, much as steam condenses into water and then can change into ice: it is still the same, but different. Everything at some level or another is energy in motion; the electrons and protons that make up every atom of every substance and form have motion. According to quantum theory, matter is never quiescent but always in a state of motion. Macroscopically the materials around us may seem dead and inert, but modern physics pictures matter not as passive and inert, but as continuously dancing and vibrating. This vibrational movement continues as the energy moves further and further away from its source. It becomes heavier and denser and vibrates more and more slowly: but it does have the potential and the content of all the higher and finer vibrations within it.

We, as human beings, contain this energy of the all within our energy field. Through meditation and conscious attunement, we can cause our reality to shift into any desired frequency or vibration. Thus our aura can be used and manipulated by our awareness. This ability will become much more prevalent as we move further into the millennium and the frequencies become available to all within the earth vibration. This has been prophesied by many peoples in many countries. We, who choose to work with multiple frequencies or select the frequency reality of our choice, are the forerunners of the full millennium shift. It is no longer appropriate to just go along with the reality map we have been 'tuned' in to through our conditioning. We can in truth change our aura and energy signature at will.

Our thoughts and expectations create our reality, whether we are aware of this or not: what we think about or our mind dwells on day after day is brought into existence, along with its opposite quality. The real challenge is to gain control of the internal world we call the mind. This will facilitate our human evolution on a return journey home from the gross physical plane back to our source. In one case the force is centrifugal, in the other centripetal. As the thoughts or emotions you experience daily surround you, they can make you happy or sad, healthy or sick, tense or relaxed. Please remember - positive emotions strengthen your energy field or aura, bringing health, balance and vitality, whilst negative emotions or stress bring sickness, instability, mood swings, low energy and damage your aura. This is called the body-mind connection.

It works with the Universal Law of resonance; basically what we dwell on day after day becomes embedded in our aura. The negative or positive thoughts work with the karmic law of return: what you send out is returned amplified like a boomerang. The reason the energy is magnified is very simple: like attracts like! This makes some people very wary of negative thoughts and rightly so - for if you are not sending out positive loving energy and are instead deeply focused on negativity, the last thing you need is even more negativity! What you focus on attracts even more of the same energy; this law makes you very aware of your every thought, word and deed. What you give out will always be yours, you just attract even more of the same! This law can cause havoc when you consider all the negative emotional states people experience on a daily basis. I know from my own experience that we can change our field of reality. It is as simple as owning your thoughts, feelings, emotions - your vibratory pattern; pure mind power. When you are ready to accept responsibility for owning your own emotional energies and vibratory pattern, you will own and be Master of your aura, health and enlightenment.

In the chapters on each chakra we will work with the aura; they are linked, so we will keep this knowledge as a cohesive whole, too.

Seeing Auras

There are people who are born with the gift of seeing auras. Other people find that they can feel the aura surrounding a person: some people do it with their eyes closed, others with their eyes open. I use my gift as a diagnostic tool, as do others who share this gift. Basically, by using aura viewing or sensing, we can tell what kind of aura a person has and how to apply vibrational medicine to alleviate disease or re-balance the aura; this returns a person to optimum health and emotional well-being.

In my teaching of the crystal and vibrational courses I have discovered that almost everyone can develop this gift to some extent by allowing themselves to sense or feel the energy of the aura. Others have developed their inner vision and still others have completely developed aura vision.

I have developed a very simple technique for experiencing the aura of another person. First wash your hands and dry them thoroughly:

1.   Stand facing your partner, about three feet away from each other.

2.   Begin to sensitise and attune your hands by shaking them vigorously; this releases blocked or stagnant energy.

3. Briskly rub your hands together; this begins to concentrate the chi or prana into your hands and sensitises them.

4. Hold your hands with your palms facing each other, about nine inches apart. Feel the energy radiating and vibrating between your hands; play with this energy for several minutes.

5. Begin to form this energy into a ball and visualise it as bright yellow in color. When it feels right, place this yellow ball into the solar plexus area. This energises and focuses your mental body, allowing you to perceive auras more easily.

6. Now your partner drops their hands and you take your hands to the top of your partner's head and begin to feel and see their energy. Gradually and very slowly work down along both sides of the head and neck, shoulders, arms, pelvis, legs and feet, observing the energy in any way you can, via heat, cold, tingling, sensations, thoughts, emotions, feelings and color.

7. Your partner repeats the same process over your aura.

8. Ground, centre and focus yourself and share with your partner what you perceived in each other's aura.

The Seven Kosas (Body Sheaths or Aura) and Corresponding States of Consciousness:

Sheath One

Element of earth

Sheath - physical body (annamaya kosa)

Related chakra - Root

State of consciousness - emerging consciousness (vyutthana citta)

Knowledge of body - integration of body (sarira samyama)

Appearance - Pale blue or light silvery-grey-blue with tiny sparks of light moving very fast

State - Fixed

Close to the physical body

Level - One - Etheric (lower aspect)

Sheath Two

Element of water

Sheath - physiological body (pranamaya kosa)

Related chakra - Sacral

State of consciousness - restraining consciousness (nirodha citta)

Knowledge of energy - vitality, integration of senses (indriya samyama)

Appearance - Vibrant colors (when healthy and emotionally balanced)

State - Moving

1-3 inches around the physical body

Level - Two - Emotional/vitality body (lower base emotions aspect)

Sheath Three

Element of fire

Sheath - psychological body (manomaya kosa)

Related chakra - Solar Plexus

State of consciousness - individualized consciousness (nirmana citta)

Knowledge of energy - integration of energy (prana samyama)

Appearance - Yellow to gold depending on spiritual development

State - Fixed

3-8 inches around the physical body

Level - Three - Mental body

Sheath Four

Element of air

Sheath - intellectual body (vijnanamaya kosa)

Related chakra - Heart

State of consciousness - tranquil consciousness (prasanta citta)

Knowledge of energy - integration of mind (mano samyama)

Appearance - Pastel colors: when fully developed, a pastel rainbow infused with rose pink

State - Moving

6-12 inches around the physical body

Level - Four - Astral

Sheath Five

Element of ether

Sheath - the body of joy (anandamaya kosa)

Related chakra - Throat

State of consciousness - attentive consciousness (ekagrata citta)

Knowledge of energy - integration of intellect (buddhi samyama)

Appearance - Vivid bright blue

State - Fixed

12-24 inches around the physical body

Level - Five - Etheric blueprint

Sheath Six

Element of spirit

Sheath - the body of consciousness (cittamaya kosa)

Related chakra - Third eye (Brow)

State of consciousness - fissured or rent consciousness (chidra citta)

Knowledge of energy - integration of consciousness (citta samyama)

Appearance - Bright gold light flowing down from the higher self, when fully developed

State - Moving

24-30 inches around the physical body

Level - Six - Celestial

Sheath Seven

Element of thought

Sheath - the body of the self (atmamaya kosa)

Related chakra - Crown

State of consciousness - pure consciousness (paripakva citta or divya citta)

Knowledge of energy - integration of soul (atma samyama)

Appearance - Silvery-blue to shimmering-gold (the original blueprint)

State - Fixed

30-44 inches around the physical body (until self-realisation)

Level - Seven - Luminous egg

Part 4

The Meridians

The ancient Chinese meridian theory, based on acupuncture meridians, was first discovered many thousands of years ago. It is a system of subtle energies that flow throughout the body, providing protection to its inner mechanisms and dispensing life-giving nourishment. The word meridian, as used in Chinese medicine, came into the English language through a French translation of the Chinese term *jing-luo*. Jing means 'to go through', or 'a thread in a fabric'; luo means 'something that connects or attaches' or 'a net'.

In traditional Eastern medical systems - notably the Chinese healing system and the Indian Ayurvedic system - it has long been accepted that mental, emotional and physical health is based on the continuous harmonious flow of energies. These systems believe that an intricate realm of subtle energy flows permeates the universe and that the physical, material world is but a gross manifestation of these energies. In Chinese and Ayurvedic medicine, health is seen as the fluent and harmonious movement of energies at subtle levels. In the East, energies have various names. The Indian yogis call it prana; to the Tibetan lamas it is lung-gom. It is known as sakia-tundra or ki to the Japanese Shinto and the Chinese call it chi. In the West it is loosely translated as 'vital energy', 'vital force' or 'life force'. This energy is considered as having clearly distinct and established pathways, definite direction of flow and characteristic behaviour as well defined as any other circulation, such as blood, nervous, lymphatic and vascular systems.

The meridians, when viewed psychically, resemble a holographic energy template that connects the physical body with the first layer of the aura. The physical body cannot exist without an aura, and the first layer of the aura, the etheric, is the blueprint by which the physical body was manifested. Damage to the 'blueprint' will result in trauma and disease on the physical body, usually very quickly. The etheric layer of the aura, which interfaces with the physical body, has its main connection area at the witness point. The witness point is on your breastbone between your heart and your throat, just at the thymus.

The tubular meridian system appears to be divided into superficial and deep systems; these flow around and through the body on all levels. The body has twelve pairs of main meridians that flow each side of the body, as well as two specific meridians known as vessels. These twelve regular meridians correspond to each of the five yin and six yang organs. Together these constitute the body's energy system, which works to maintain the health of the whole organism. There are also many finer smaller net-like meridians called luo meridians. These meridians are pathways through which the energy of the universe circulates throughout the body organs and keeps the body and the universe in harmony. Illness or pain occurs when the pathway becomes blocked or weakened, disrupting the energy flow and breaking the body's overall harmony and balance.

Although it is one integrated system, each meridian has a starting point and an end point, which indicate direction of flow and function. Each meridian is named after an organ or function, such as lung or kidney, but these 'names' can be very misleading to the student, as the physical organ is only one tiny aspect of the type of energy over which a meridian has influence. The functions ascribed to physical organs by the Chinese rarely have any recognisable correlations to Western medicine and it is difficult not to get completely confused by trying to tie in the two very distinct systems. Meridians are not straight lines, their pathways have curves; they curl and sometimes zig-zag across the body. The

Chinese, in acupuncture, developed the use of needles to unblock these pathways. In shiatsu, the Japanese use direct thumb and finger pressure on acupuncture meridian points to achieve similar results. Reflexologists also work on acupuncture and acupressure points, but only those found in the feet. Through increased awareness of meridians one can practise crystal therapy more effectively, as meridians provide profound insight into the disease pathway and are therefore a most useful diagnostic tool.

Crystal therapy encourages positive changes throughout the body by stimulating the body's own healing potential, which is believed to be the result of stimulating and revitalizing this energy flow. Once you have identified which meridian(s) are dysfunctional it is relatively easy to bring them back into balance. However, always remember to think of the meridian system in its entirety and how each one works in harmony with the others to bring a complete sense of well-being. Each meridian operates at a unique, optimum frequency or resonance, which determines its vibrancy and flow. However, this frequency can be detrimentally affected through receiving too much or too little from the Universal Life Force. There are various schools of thought as to why such dysfunctions or miasms occur. Some say they stem from karmic patterning - that is, we come into this life with a certain set of life challenges factored into our energy systems. This 'prior programming' or predisposition determines our subsequent attitudes and behaviours. Similarly, many therapists believe that the deficient or excessive energy patterning of our energy systems, chakras, aura and meridians stems from our childhood and cultural experiences. They say that one way in which we cope with certain repeating situations is to try and protect ourselves by closing down the relevant chakra; this then would affect the meridian system. Another school of thought relates to miasms. Planetary miasms are stored in the collective consciousness of the planet and in the ethers. They may penetrate the physical body but are not permanently stored there. Acquired miasms are acute or infectious diseases or petrochemical toxicity acquired during a lifetime. After the acute phase of an illness, these acquired miasmatic traits settle into the subtle bodies and the molecular and cellular levels, where they ultimately may cause other problems. Whichever explanation resonates with you, never forget we always have a personal choice. We have a choice as to whether we accept or attempt to change the challenging situations which our predisposition causes us to attract. Knowledge is power, wisdom is applying that knowledge and love is transcending these predispositions.

Yin and Yang

Yin is seen as negative, passive, female, moon, interior, dark and reflective.

Yang is positive, active, male, sun, exterior, light and dynamic.

They are a pair of complementary qualities, constantly interacting and changing, and neither can exist in isolation from the other. Their affinity to each other has a direct effect on health, harmony and well-being. The meridians connect the interior of the body with the exterior and aura. Positive thoughts, feelings and emotions strengthen the meridians, whilst negative thoughts and emotions weaken the meridians. The two most important channels are the Governing and Conceptual Vessels, so we shall look at these two first.

Central Meridian (Conceptual vessel)

The Yin channel (the Conceptual Vessel) begins at the perineum, flows up the front centre of the body and ends at the tip of the tongue. This is a yin vessel which has a governing effect on all the other yin meridians. It has a major effect on conception. The yin meridians and organ functions - PERICARDIUM, large intestine, spleen, lungs, kidneys and liver - are related to storing vital essence. They are associated with generation, regulation, transformation and storage of energy, blood, fluids and spirit (shen). The specific connecting point for all yin meridians is the base of the sternum, where according to the Nei Ching all the energies are collected. This area of the solar plexus is very important for the overall well-being of the body.

Governing Meridian

The Yang channel (the Governing vessel) begins at the perineum and flows up the back centre of the body, over the top of the head and back down to the roof of the mouth. This is the main yang meridian and as such has a governing effect on all the other yang meridians and organs - small intestine, bladder, triple warmer, stomach, heart and gall bladder. The yang organ functions are primarily active and relate to breaking down food and fluids and the absorption of nutrients from them, the circulation of the derived 'nourishing energies' around the body and the secretion of unused materials. Located right at the crown of the head, known as the anterior fontanelle in a new-born child, is a unique connecting point for all yang meridians. The name of the point is 'Baihui' which means 'meeting point for 100 points'. This point governs all other points and all meridians in the body; according to Chinese philosophy it is a point of contact of the heavenly yang.

Connecting the Governing and Conceptual Vessels

To connect the heavenly yang energy and the earthly yin energy is very beneficial for the whole system on all levels, physical, etheric, emotional, mental etc. It is effortless to do and it is an ideal way to check your own energies are functioning and flowing smoothly, before you attempt any crystal or vibrational therapy work on others.

1.   Place the hands in the lap, with the right hand resting on the left, and pull the shoulders back ever so slightly and the chin in a little so that there is a small pull on the back of the neck; this will ease the blood-flow to the brain.

2.   Close your eyes and, with the mouth ever so slightly open, rest the tip of the tongue on the roof of the mouth touched to the highest point in the roof of the mouth behind the teeth. This placement of the tongue is vital because it naturally maintains the flow of energy to the head whilst keeping the jaw relaxed.

3.   The tongue connects these two important currents when touched to the highest point in the roof of the mouth. Allow your energy to complete the loop by letting your mind flow along with it. Start in the mouth and mentally circulate your attention with the energy. Eventually the current will begin to feel warm in some places as it loops around. Relax, try to bring your mind directly into the part of the loop being focused on.

4.   Experience the actual feeling of the flow of chi in that part of your body. Once the circuit is going smoothly, inhale as you go up the spine and over to the third eye, and exhale as you go down from the third eye to the perineum.

5.   You can complete as many circuits as you wish, finishing when you are ready or going on to meditate, with whatever meditation you choose. All through this book will be meditations which will focus on different aspects of personal healing and spiritual development.

Gall-bladder Meridian

Begins at the outer edge of the eye and finishes at the outer end of the fourth toe. It has a descending pathway (yang). As it circulates around the ear, it therefore directly relates to the ear. The gall-bladder meridian penetrates the lungs, liver, gall-bladder, spleen, large intestine and hip area. Meridian disorders include problems with the lungs, liver, gall-bladder, spleen, large intestine and hip area.

Liver Meridian

Starts at the outside of the big toe and ends just above the bottom of the ribcage either side of the sternum. It has an ascending pathway (yin). It has an internal branch which runs through the throat and affects the thyroid. Meridian disorders include liver problems; eye pain; obstructions in the throat; chest tightness; lung conditions; tightness in the solar plexus area.

Bladder Meridian

Begins at the inner canthus of the eye and ends on the outer edge of the little toe. It has a descending pathway (yang). It is the longest meridian line in the body. Meridian disorders are eye weakness, for example, red, itchy, weak or squint eyes; headaches in the crown of the head, in the forehead crossing over the head, and headaches caused by neck tension; forehead sinus; hair loss; pain and stiffness along the spine; haemorrhoids; bladder and kidney problems.

Kidney Meridian

Begins at the ball of the foot and ends where the collarbone and breastbone meet. The kidney meridian also penetrates the uterus/prostate in the body and according to Chinese medicine the kidneys store the Jing, a vital essence involved in reproduction. It has an ascending pathway (yin). Meridian disorders include uterus/prostate disorders; bladder weakness; digestive problems in the small intestine or colon; solar plexus and diaphragm problems; breast problems; lumps in the breast on the inner side; asthma; lung conditions and kidney pain.

Large Intestine Meridian

Begins on the face by the outer edge of the nostril and ends on the inner edge of the index finger. It has an ascending pathway (yin). Problems associated with this meridian are herpes; cold sores; colic; toxins; constipation or diarrhoea.

Lung Meridian

Begins just below the coracoid process on the shoulder and ends on the inner end of the thumb. It has an ascending pathway (yin). The lungs regulate respiration and are therefore responsible for the chi of the entire body. Imbalance in this meridian will result in all kinds of chest and skin problems; also asthma.

Stomach Meridian

Begins below the eye at the inner edge of the orbit and finishes at the outer end of the second toe. It has a descending pathway (yang). It affects the sinuses, throat, lungs, diaphragm, spleen, liver, gall-bladder, stomach, pancreas, duodenum, adrenal glands, kidneys, large intestine, small intestine and pelvic region;

also the appetite and digestion. If the stomach is out of balance, whatever is taken in, be it physical or psychic food, will not be utilized correctly; energy depletion, lethargy, weakness and debilitation are the results.

Spleen Meridian

Begins at the inner edge of the big toe and ends at the side of the chest just below nipple level. It has an ascending pathway (yin) and affects the spleen and pancreas. It is the crucial link in the process by which food is transformed into chi and blood. Emotional problems are also related to this meridian, for example, depression, PMT, irritability and concentration problems.

Heart Meridian

Begins at the forward edge of the armpit and ends on the inner edge of the little finger. It has a descending pathway (yang). The heart and small intestine meridians are coupled. The heart meridian gets its chi from the spleen meridian and in turn passes it to the small intestine meridian. If the heart meridian is strong and healthy, the emotions will be balanced. Imbalances in this meridian will affect the skin and cause weak wrists, angina and palpitations.

Small Intestine Meridian

Begins at the outer end of the little fingertip and ends at the start of the upper edge of the ear in a small hollow of the cheek. It has a descending pathway (yang). Meridian disorders are any heart condition; abdominal distension; headaches; poor circulation in the legs; indigestion; constipation; feeling cold and weakness in the legs.

Circulation-Sex Meridian (Pericardium, heart protector)

Begins at the outer edge of the nipple and finishes at the inside of the middle finger. It has an ascending pathway (yin). Meridian disorders include hot flushes and rapid heartbeat; heart pain; endocrine-related problems.

Triple Warmer Meridian (Triple heater)

Begins at the outside end of the ring finger (third) and ends at the outer edge of the eyebrow. It has a descending pathway (yang). Meridian disorders include ear problems - loss of hearing and earache; spontaneous perspiration for no reason; mental confusion; weakness; lack of energy.

Vibrational Therapy for the Meridians

As with *all* other subtle systems, and even the gross physical system, a tiny change in one area will create a larger overall effect. This puts responsibility on the vibrational therapist to be aware of the equilibrium of the overall energy systems of the client. To keep the meridian system in balance it is important to make sure there is not an excess of energy or a lack of energy in the system. Individual meridians or even sections of a meridian may be performing outside their standard ranges, but in a balanced system general equilibrium is kept by an overabundance in one area being balanced by a shortage in another.

What follows is a safe procedure for working on the meridian system with either color essences, crystals or flower essences, but you would be wise to become totally familiar with the meridian system before attempting the technique on others:

1. Use a list of the meridians to dowse or muscle test which meridian is out of balance. Remember that, apart from the Central and Governing meridians, all meridians are in pairs. So you will need to decide which side of the meridian pair needs balancing, or if both sides require balancing.

2. A practical illustration of an unbalanced meridian can be to gently touch one end-point with the first two fingers of your right hand. If that half of the meridian is out of balance a previously strong muscle test will go weak. Muscle testing all meridians in this way will quickly show where vibrational therapy is needed. By testing again, using the same vibration, you will be able to check on the effectiveness of the re-balancing.

3. It is unimportant which end-point is touched, so select the most convenient point for you or your client. You may even allow your client to touch the end-point if that is more convenient.

4. All twelve yin and yang meridians should be tested thoroughly using a systematic approach, as well as the Governing and Central vessels.

5. Find which color/crystal/flower will be effective in re-balancing a meridian. If you are dowsing, use a suitable list of colors, crystals or flower essences.

6. Once you have established which vibrational essence or crystal will be the most effective, place a drop(s) of the vibrational essence or crystal on the end-point of the meridian, either at the beginning or end, whichever is indicated by the dowsing or muscle testing. You may even need to place a different vibrational essence or crystal on each end of the meridian.

7. Once the re-balancing is complete, recheck all the meridians by either dowsing or muscle testing. Ground, centre and earth your client after all the treatment is finished.

The length of time it takes to rebalance a meridian will differ for each person. Some people integrate healing energy very quickly, others may take longer to fully consolidate the process. It is quite normal for this process to take several months for total integration. It is also vitally important to allow a rest period of several months which are free from any other form of healing. This ensures the correction has not only been fully integrated into the meridian system, but the body has stabilized to a balanced sustainable level.

Vibrational Therapy for the Acupuncture Points

Placing crystals on acupuncture points is another way of balancing meridians. This process is very powerful and great care should be taken not to over or under-stimulate any meridian. Once again, the length of time the crystal is on the acupuncture point will vary from person to person, as we are each unique in the way we handle and assimilate energy. It is advisable to take a break from other forms of healing whilst undergoing crystal healing using the acupuncture points. Always allow plenty of time for the body to integrate the crystal energy and advise your client to drink plenty of pure fresh water.

Acupuncture Points

1. Find out using dowsing or muscle testing which meridian is involved.

2. Find out whether the right or left channels need working on.

3.   Find the exact point on the meridian by tracing the path with your fingertips until the arm or pendulum indicate the exact right point. You must follow the natural flow of the meridian by tracing the normal direction (going in the wrong direction will weaken the meridian). It is quite common for the meridian to deviate from what is considered normal.

       You may wish to work with diagrams of the meridians.

4.   After you have marked the point, gently hold or place the crystal on the exact spot (take care to be aware of the energy assimilation by dowsing or using your fingertips to feel the energy flow). Sometimes the energy flow will be very subtle and at a deep level, which means you may have to rely on feedback from your client. It is important to ask your client to be aware of thoughts, feelings or emotions.

5.   When the assimilation is accomplished, re-test to check that all your work is complete.

6.   Ground, centre and earth your client after all the treatment is finished.

Meridian List

Conceptual - Yin   Governing - Yang
Bladder - Yang   Gall-bladder - Yang
Heart - Yang   Large intestine - Yin
Liver - Yin   Lung - Yin
Kidney - Yin   Pericardium - Yin
Small intestine - Yang   Spleen - Yin
Stomach - Yang   Triple warmer - Yang

Part 5

Kundalini

Kundalini is the cosmic power in individual human bodies. The Goddess is said to lie dormant coiled three and a half times around a lingam in the base chakra. The three coils represent the three stages of *avastha* (mind), namely *jagrt* (awake), *svapna* (dreaming) and *susuptiin* (deep sleep). There is a fourth level, *turiya*, combining and transcending the others, which represents the last half coil. It is attained in *samadhi* (enlightenment). Before the word 'kundalini' became fashionable, another term used to represent this divine power was *agni* (fire), that purifies and rises upwards like fire. This creative energy of spiritual illumination, when properly released, can cause activation, purification and alignment of all the major chakras. When the kundalini Goddess is awakened she makes a hissing sound like a serpent, hence it is also called serpent power. In kundalini meditation, the divine power that lies dormant in every human being is aroused and pulled upward through the chakras, one by one. At the top of the head the crown chakra is the seat of the highest consciousness, the place where the union of the individual and Absolute Consciousness takes place. This is expressed symbolically as the union of *Shakti*, or kundalini, with Lord Shiva.

The overall balance and harmony of the universe is maintained by a polarity of positive and negative, male and female, yin and yang, the static and the dynamic. Whatever exists in the universe, the macrocosm, exists likewise in human beings, the microcosm. The masculine principal passive ground force, Shiva, resides in the sahasrara, the seventh or crown chakra, bringing down the white light of cosmic energy. The Shakti, the feminine power, lies coiled at the base of the spine. She is the manifestation of cosmic power in the body and is in a dormant state of potential. Not a material force, she is a pristine psychic and spiritual power that underlies all matter, organic and inorganic. Due to the spiral-like upward action when aroused, it is referred to as serpent power, often depicted iconographically as a sleeping serpent, with the head pointing downwards, coiled at the base of the physical spine. The activation of kundalini leads to union with Lord Shiva - the state of spiritual enlightenment or supreme consciousness - or, as can be expressed, you are unifying heaven and earth - the ultimate spiritual marriage.

Yoga

In yoga - it is Hatha yoga that awakens the kundalini by disciplining the body, by purification of the subtle energy channels known as the nadis - this purification is very important; without the nadis being suitably purified, the pranic force is not at its full pristine potential. Through the physical asanas or body-postures the nervous system is toned and purified, enabling it to withstand the full experience of the powerful rising energy. Hatha yoga also teaches you to regulate the flow of prana by means of special body locks and energy seals, known as mudras and bandhas. Kriyas, special cleansing techniques, purify the inner organs of the physical body, and breath control, or pranayama, steadies, calms and focuses the mind. Vigorous pranayama, asanas, and meditation are insufficient, however, without the required mental purification. Until you can let go of the illusion of separation and see the divine aspect of the Supreme Being in others, as well as the self, the ego will remain impure and kundalini activation is not recommended.

The kundalini and her channel are not actually to be found in the gross physical body, although her effects can certainly be felt there. The channel is to be found in the astral counterpart, which is superimposed on the physical body. The seven master chakras and the sushumna nadi, the passage through which the kundalini rises, are also in the astral body, but they are interlinked to the physical body through the nerve plexuses and the spinal cord.

The most important of the 72,000 nadis, or astral subtle-energy tubes, is the sushumna, the physical representation of which is the spinal cord. On either side of the sushumna are the two important nadis known as ida and pingala, which correspond to the left and right sympathetic cords or nerves in the physical body. Prana, the vital life-force, flows through them. As long as it does this, a human being is bound by time, space, karma and the illusion of separation. However, once the kundalini has risen and activated the chakras in sequential order and the crown chakra has been fully activated and the light of the soul has flooded the head, the person now moves beyond the mundane ordinary physical limitations.

While Western medical science anatomically only recognises the gross form and functions, Kundalini yoga acts on a subtle but profound level. In order to activate the kundalini to rise, you must have a thorough working knowledge and deep understanding of not only the chakra system, but the three major nadis as well.

The sushumna nadi extends from the root or muladhara chakra, the second vertebra of the coccygeal region, to the sahasrara or crown chakra at the top of the head. The physical spinal column has inside it a central canal, in anatomy called the canalis centralis. The sushumna, located within the canal, has several sub-divisions inside it. Within the fiery red sushumna is the *vajra nadi*, or lustrous sun, which in turn contains another, the *chitra*, which is pale in color. Inside the chitra is a very fine, minute canal known as the *Brahma nadi* or, as it is sometimes called, the heavenly way. When the kundalini is activated it must first pass upwards through the *Brahma Granthi* or 'knot of Brahma'. The ida nadi is said to flow through the human body along the spinal column. The ida starts at the perineum, or root chakra, and moves energy upwards to the left nostril via the third eye chakra. The pingala nadi starts at the right nostril, over the third eye, moving energy from the crown of the head coursing downwards to the base of the spine. This major nadi intersects with the ida and also with the sushumna. These junctions of the three main nadis are known as the master chakras, which regulate the overall mechanism of the physical and subtle bodies.

There are various methods for locating the chakras and we have covered a lot of information in the chapter on chakras, but we need to study them further. When the kundalini force is initially awakened, it does not proceed directly to the sahasrara, or crown chakra, unless one is an exceptionally advanced meditator. It normally moves upwards sequentially, chakra by chakra. This involves great skill, concentration, purification and most of all patience to pull the kundalini energy upwards. It can be likened to giving birth; you may prepare yourself, and go through the labour pains, but it is impossible to tell the exact moment the kundalini will fully rise. There are many signs along the way, though, and by careful and thorough preparation it is just as joyous as giving birth to a new life. Unfortunately, just as in giving birth, no one can do it for you; in this process you are on your own. If you decide to train with a master and feel more confident with a 'midwife', I am sure you will attract to you the right person.

That is one of the most beautiful things with kundalini meditation. The simple act of deciding you wish to merge consciously with the divine literally moves heaven and earth to facilitate this process within you. Guidance in many forms is made available to you, as you open yourself to the cosmic currents of universal consciousness. I remember 29 years ago, when I started practising Hatha yoga, asking the universe to 'become more than human'. Since that day, every step of the way the universe has guided me, on my journey home to my cosmic source. Even if you feel isolated, believe me, a 'Master' will literally knock on your door. Your vibration will become magnetic, if your sincerity is constant. You will attract an enlightened soul to aid you. All you have to do is recognise the 'Master' when they arrive, as you will be tested. This is to see if, not only are you ready, but have the right motives. You must also make sure the Master is right for you. It is necessary to find a Master you are comfortable with. Very often the true Masters are hidden or not well known; they choose their students, not the other way round.

The speed at which the kundalini power is aroused depends on the person's purity, clarity, stage of evolution, nature and overall purification of the nerves, chakras, meridians, aura, karmic debris and spiritual evolution. This is nevertheless combined with the person's yearning and dedication for liberation and cosmic union with their divine aspect. Even when the kundalini is raised to the ajna chakra, it is difficult to keep it there. Only great yogis are able to keep it there for any length of time. When the kundalini finally rises from the ajna to the sahasrara, union takes place. But even here it does not remain long. Only after lengthy and continual dedicated practice does the evolved adept experience permanent union and final liberation.

Nature awakens the power and gives the student knowledge as they are ready. Until they are able to absorb it totally, nothing of deep importance is revealed to them. Even if it is, the information will not be fully understood and acted upon. There are numerous other exercises, both physical and breathing, to facilitate chakra meditation and here we will begin the awakening process.

Before commencing any of the following gentle kundalini exercises, you need to ask yourself the following questions:

> Are you fearful of the kundalini process? If so, please deal with your root chakra fear and survival issues by learning self-discipline.
>
> Are you cleansed of emotional debris? If not, please release negative feelings and cleanse your sacral chakra.
>
> Are you on a personal power trip, or do you see the kundalini process as a way of being superior to others? If so, please cleanse your solar plexus chakra.
>
> Are you possessive? If so, please cleanse your heart chakra.
>
> Are you truly open to your full spirituality? If not, please cleanse your throat chakra.
>
> Are your five lower master chakras balanced? If they are not, please work through some of the basic chakra balancing exercises in the meditation section of this book. Do you feel good about the kundalini process? If so, feel free to try some of the breathing exercises and meditations.

The techniques I am teaching in this book are often drawn from ancient teachings by such Yogic Masters as Patanjali, who, in his Yoga Sutras, systemised the ancient Yogic practices of his spiritual culture some several thousand years ago. I also recommend taking a course in Hatha yoga, because working directly with the physical postures or asanas will steady your body and mind; this will definitely assist your kundalini-awakening process. I personally practise my favourite Hatha yoga postures every day. I also have to say that it is a mistake to think that the Yogic tradition is the only path to spiritual awakening. Many other ancient and modern techniques are equally effective, as your 'Divine Essence' will always guide you.

Another basic fundamental misconception of kundalini energy awakening and movement is the premise that kundalini rises - just rises. The simple experiential truth is that the life-force energy flows both up from the earth through our bodies and also down through the seventh (crown) chakra into our bodies from above. It is fundamental to understand and experience that our human bodies are receptors both from above and below. When our chakra system is functioning correctly, a mystic balancing takes place within the unified heart chakra, the balance of love in action, the meeting place of heaven and earth. As I have already stated, the sushumna has several sub-divisions inside it. The kundalini channel has inner movement.

The sushumna is a fiery red subtle energy, with an upwards momentum.

The vajra, lustrous sun, is golden in color and flows downwards.

The chitra, pale in color, is a cosmic light which finally ignites the final stage.

The Brahma nadi, the heavenly way, is an upwards movement that floods the body with light.

If you open your kundalini channel in a balanced fashion, there are four distinct phases; as each phase is completed you will experience the next level. First your sushumna must become clear; many people experience this clearing, which can appear to be fiery, and think their kundalini has risen. It has not, just the channel has been cleared. This experience can be distressing. There are many possible symptoms of the kundalini rising. Some are very pleasant, others are uncomfortable in the extreme. All the latter are caused by resistance or lack of preparation. Symptoms include waves of heat or cold; hot needle-like shooting pains along the acupuncture meridians, especially in the left foot and left side of the body; tension, pressure or pain at the third eye and crown chakras. Pain in the spine, muscle spasms, unconscious muscle movements in the head and body, orgasmic energy in the spine and various parts of the body, spontaneous unsolicited past-life recall, the instant ability to do pranayama and Hatha yoga, hearing voices, high-pitched sounds, the unsolicited ability to do unusual things (powers or siddhis). A number of individuals also report roaring sounds and high-pitched whistles in the head, followed by a brilliant sensation of light flooding the entire being and then a feeling of total bliss.

There may be emotional turmoil and damage to the nervous system by overloading the energy body before it is ready. Erotic dreams may haunt you (sacral chakra imbalance). If you are not well grounded (first chakra), you may feel as if you are going crazy. In truth, kundalini rising may appear to the unenlightened very much like psychosis or paranoia. Frequently, illness may also be associated with abnormal function in more than one chakra, because an individual may have multiple emotional blockages. These symptoms have also been called physio-kundalini syndrome or complex. During the process of kundalini activation, all impurities and blockages in the chakras are released and burned away. There is a complete additional change in the nervous system and brain, as the refined energy begins to flow. The negative painful side-effects of kundalini activation are not experienced by everyone. In truth, it is not necessary for any painful experiences. It can be total pleasure.

The key, as I have already stated, is meditation practice. The more stored pain and tension in the body, the more discomfort will be experienced. The good news is, kundalini, as a developmental process of daily meditation, is a natural means by which human beings may release the stresses that have accumulated within the physical and subtle bodies over a lifetime, and by which they may open their channels to creative expression and divine attunement with higher levels of subtle vibrational input or resonance. Not only are stresses released, but once the activation is complete, the body and brain become not only more efficient at handling stress, but eventually immune to all stress and stress-related disorders. Through its transformational effects on the nervous system, kundalini eliminates stresses from the physical and subtle bodies as rapidly as they occur, thus preventing the accumulation of new stresses. This process is constant as long as kundalini meditation is practised on a daily basis.

The truth is, once kundalini practice is established, it is so blissful that the thought of missing a day would be unthinkable, not to mention foolish, for who would want to truly miss a blissful life experience? The other fact is that once kundalini meditation is established as a regular routine, it can be accomplished in minutes, or even less, and the kundalini Goddess reminds you when it is time to meditate and will spontaneously rise.

Meditation Posture

The traditional kundalini posture is to sit in a comfortable steady posture with the spine and neck held erect but not tense. This helps steady the mind and aids concentration. The psychic current must be able to travel freely from the base of the spine to the top of the head. Any comfortable cross-legged posture provides a firm base for the body. It makes a triangular pathway for the energy flow, which must be contained rather than dissipated in all directions and keeps the lungs free to move naturally with as little effort as possible. If you sit on the floor in the traditional cross-legged Hindu and Buddhist position, I recommend a pillow or folded blanket under your bottom, with your knees and feet on the floor, so your spine is raised just a bit off the floor. Place your hands on your thighs, palms upward, and join your thumbs to your index fingers. Now pull the shoulders back ever so slightly and the chin in a little so that there is a small pull on the back of the neck; this will ease the blood-flow to the brain. Close your eyes.

If you can't sit cross-legged, sit on a straight-backed chair with your feet flat on the floor, your knees level with your hips, and your spine upright. Many people prefer this chair meditation posture at least some of the time. You can also lie on your back, on the floor sometimes, and it will give you a different meditation experience - usually sensory ventures into other states is heightened when lying down in a sleep posture. These trance-like dream-meditations can be very intense. I would suggest you try both methods, which will lead to balance in your kundalini meditation practice. Many people prefer to sit upright to begin the day in meditation and to lie down to finish the day with a more dream-like meditation. It is possible to do short chakra meditations whilst standing up, walking or dancing - meditation in action - until your whole experience of life is in an expanded state of consciousness.

Whole Body Experience

This primary expansion meditation will always be used to begin each kundalini session. You must learn this process of consciousness expansion and commit it to memory. This is the bed-rock that underpins the process. If you can't experience yourself as a whole unified entity, you will have missed the starting point of the kundalini energy.

1. Begin with the awareness of the physical sensation of the air rushing in and out of your nostrils with every new breath; feel the pranic life energy filling your lungs.

2. Expand your awareness to include the movement of your chest and stomach as you breathe.

3. Expand your awareness to include your heartbeat and allow your attention to come alive in the present moment.

4. Experience your muscular sense of balance in the present moment; feel the energy of Mother Earth's gravity, her divine force field.

5. Expand your awareness to include your whole body at once; effortlessly experience yourself in the present moment.

6. Now, while maintaining awareness of your whole-body presence, expand your awareness to focus on each of the master chakras in turn, allowing seven breaths for each chakra.

7. Now let go of individual chakra-focusing and be aware of all the chakras together as one energy system. Feel your entire energy system at once, including your aura. Open yourself to experience whatever energy is flowing around you......allow yourself to make contact with the actual energy of yourself, your personal kundalini presence.

8. Allow yourself plenty of time to come back to everyday normal waking reality and write down your experience, or draw a picture of the experience if you are more visually orientated.

We can employ our awareness of our breathing experience, heartbeat and balance to lead us into whole-body awareness. Whole body consciousness prepares us for the fundamental act of focusing our power of undivided attention on our master chakras, our energy centres along our spinal column.

These two important kundalini meditation vehicles or processes, breath awareness and chakra focusing, form the very first part of the kundalini activation. Our awakening programme will deepen as we begin to explore other kundalini meditation vehicles: chanting and visual meditation. Chanting will be covered in the section on sound healing and visual meditation will be explored in the meditation section.

Each chakra will have a chapter dedicated to it, which will also include a kundalini meditation, as well as a healing meditation and crystal web of light to bring about profound but gentle deep personal healing and spiritual insight and development. If you are not yet ready for kundalini meditation - focus completely on the chakra healing crystal webs of light and healing meditations. You are being given the choice. Once you are healed and whole, try the kundalini meditations.

Part 6

Karma

Karma is a Sanskrit word - meaning the sum total of a person's actions in this and previous lives. The past actions, good or bad, are carried as traits or miasms over to each new life. This brings continuing opportunities for growth and spiritual development. This is the reincarnational belief. The principle is sometimes stated as 'as ye sow, so shall ye reap'. It is viewed, therefore, as the soul's energetic system of credits and debits, which allows the incarnate being to experience the full range or scope of all attitudes and perspectives on life. It is central to all Eastern religions and in the West we are told in Christianity 'do unto others as you would have others do unto you'.

Miasms

There are various schools of thought on Karmic patterning - that is, we come into this life with a certain set of life challenges factored into our energy systems. This 'prior programming' or predisposition determines our subsequent attitudes and behaviours. It also works with the law of cause and effect. This should make us look very seriously at our behaviour - knowing that what we give out we will have returned to us like a boomerang. The boomerang effect may be felt very quickly, even in this lifetime, or it may take many lifetimes to catch up with us. As we evolve spiritually we can release, cleanse and heal a lot of negative Karmic patterns. That is the true goal of human life.

Samsara

Each lifetime we can evolve to higher states of conscious awareness, until all pain and suffering are released. Suffering begins and ends with illusion. The first illusion is desire; this is created by the feelings of separation, driven by the ego, which bind us in chains of ignorance, causing suffering. It is the ego that feeds attachments, in the form of ignorance, or materialistic pursuits. Until all desire for material attachments is released, we are bound on the wheel of illusion or, as the Buddhists say, *Samsara*: life after life, endlessly, until we release all desires. We are then empty, no longer bound by these incessant desires. Each soul fragment has to find its own way back to its source, the mind of God/Goddess, for in reality there is only the One mind, the One God/Goddess. The fragments or little egos are only a splintered holographic reflection of the whole. It is like looking at one of the cells in your body through a mirror and saying "that is you" - it is but only a tiny reflected piece of you.

In the Buddhist tradition the wheel of life is depicted graphically as a whole process which craving, hatred, envy and ignorance cause living beings to circle in states of unsatisfactoriness. It includes depictions of the six realms of *devas, asuras*, humans, animals, hungry-ghosts and hell-beings, which combined represent all the mental states unenlightened living beings can experience. So an enlightened person acts, but without any egotistical volition. Thus their actions are described in Sanskrit as *akarya* - creating no new karma.

Cause of Disease

We need to explore the cause of disease, in order to understand the process. Some therapists believe illness is caused by karmic patterns or miasms, as they are sometimes called. There are various schools of thought as to why such dysfunctions or miasms occur. Some say they stem from karmic patterning - that is, we come into this life with a certain set of life challenges factored into our energy systems. This 'prior programming' or predisposition determines our subsequent attitudes and behaviours. Similarly, some therapists believe that the deficient or excessive energy patterning of our energy systems, chakras, aura and meridians stems from our childhood and cultural experiences. They say that one way in which we cope with certain repeating situations is to try and protect ourselves by closing down the relevant chakra; this then would affect the meridian system. Another school of thought relates to miasms. Planetary miasms are stored in the collective consciousness of the planet and in the ethers. They may penetrate the physical body but are not permanently stored there. Acquired miasms are acute or infectious diseases or petrochemical toxicity acquired during a lifetime. After the acute phase of an illness, these acquired miasmatic traits settle into the subtle bodies and the molecular and cellular levels, where they ultimately may cause other problems. Whichever explanation resonates with you (you can accept all three), never forget we always have a personal choice. We have a choice as to whether we accept or attempt to change the challenging situations which our predisposition causes us to attract. Knowledge is power, wisdom is applying that knowledge and love is transcending these predispositions by dispelling illusion with truth - thereby gaining enlightenment.

Reality Perception

All illness and disease occur due to our faulty perception of reality. These errors in our perception keep us from existing harmoniously with our fellow beings and ourselves. These faults in perception then manifest as illnesses. Our perception can also be faulty due to karmic patterning, where we repeatedly hold misconceptions as to the true nature of reality. These errors in our perception often manifest as illness within the physical body. Depending on our reality impediment, the disease will manifest in the organs that most closely resonate with the chakra ruling the particular life-lesson. As an example, the difficult life-lesson of loving unconditionally, not only others, but ourselves, causes blockages of energy flow through the heart chakra. These eventually manifest as physical afflictions of the heart, thymus gland, lungs and shoulders.

Interestingly, illness may not be related at all to this lifetime, but be a carry-over from previous lives, or even a national miasm or karmic patterning that has been absorbed into the individual energy-body, which has then manifested on the physical body as an illness. Negative patterning can be absorbed from the environment or even the media. This is tribal, national or even global karma and is caused when you allow others, however well-meaning, to influence your way of life and thinking. By doing so you give your spiritual power, your enlightenment process, away.

Tribal National and Global Karma

In order to find our own healing, our own enlightenment, it is necessary to understand tribal, national and global karma. We must let go of our self-imposed limitations, restrictions and personal fears. We must learn to flow and expand our consciousness, learn how to bring more light into our darkness or shadow side. On the path to our own personal wholeness, healing and health, we must confront our deepest fears, phobias, pains, hurts and shame.

Very often we desperately try to ignore our shadow side; these are the parts of us that we have judged, rightly or wrongly, to be bad, ugly or shameful. We have been conditioned since our births to conform to other people's ideas of good and bad, right or wrong. This is our personal 'conditioning', our 'robotic programming'. This programming *does* serve a vital function: it makes us easier to control and manipulate. These rules of good or bad constantly change, depending on our personal circumstances and present life situation; they are influenced by our religious beliefs, teachers, parents, relatives, politicians, scientists, the media and our peers. These rules do not represent Eternal Divine Truth, only the current civilisation's accepted truth. As we, as individualised perfect expressions of the sacred life force, claim our Divine birthright, personal power and enlightenment, we will have to confront all our demons of darkness and shine the light of truth into these murky recesses. These demons of darkness or karmic patterning will otherwise manifest as illness, pain and feelings of separation from our source of love, inspiration and wisdom. We must draw the quality of our Divine essence into our physical body; this purges the negativity and fully activates 'the Divine essence within'. We must also learn to shield ourselves from all unkind energies which seek to use our energy and manipulate our energy field for their own benefit. We must also learn to dissolve all negative energy within our environment; this we can do in service to others. As each soul becomes enlightened and releases all negative karma, we can raise the energy level of every being on the planet.

Alignment with the Higher Self

When we are truly aligned with our higher selves we dissolve all negative karma, regardless of its cause. The best way of totally healing ourselves into enlightened awareness is to learn to meditate and become aware of the vibrations that affect our spiritual growth, both positively and negatively. Vibrational medicine will, in the future, render all diseases and illnesses null and void. In the intervening time, we can enlighten ourselves by learning to use vibrational medicine on our own energy field, and then on others. This process of vibrational medicine is simple, safe and effective, especially if we work with the loving creative forces of the universe. In each chapter on the master chakras we will use specific crystal webs of light that will cause old diseases and negative patterning to simply fall away. These will be augmented with sound, color, meditations, gem essences and affirmations.

Part 7

Crystals

Hold a clear quartz crystal, examine it carefully, admire its beauty, see its radiance and perfection. As you hold it gently in your hand it is possible to begin to feel the very subtle vibrations, resonance or oscillations, not only in the hand but also at various points in the body as the vibrations move to the parts which perhaps need alignment, strengthening or re-structuring. As you become more aware of its energy, feel the synchronised vibration it programmes into your energy field. Quartz crystals, these miraculous forms of nature, are an outward expression of the atomic orderliness that exists in their inner structure. Quartz crystals or silicon dioxide (SiO_2) occur in profusion throughout the earth's surface. They are a white, transparent substance when found in their pure state (no impurities - inclusions, crevices, fractures and different mineral particles). They have a hexagonal form and broadcast the complete spectrum of wavelengths - the visible colors and the low and high frequencies not perceived by us, such as radio waves, infra-red radiation and ultraviolet light etc.

Crystals have a spontaneous natural allure to almost everyone, especially children. This is understandable when you comprehend the influence of light and subtle magnetic fields on the human energy structure and on the cellular level of the physical body. (Even if you are not consciously aware, your subconscious and superconscious are). As crystals can go into a state of resonance with you, you will feel their spontaneous attraction and they will respond positively to you. They are marvellous life-forms of mother-nature in the process of divine evolution, just like you, just like me, just like the cosmos. Crystals resonate with the liquid crystals in your body and transfer to your bloodstream and to your circulatory system vital elements, in the form of intelligent energy fields which are essential for your health and for the rejuvenation of your body, while transmuting unwanted information that may be locked in your bones, tissues, subtle-bodies and unconscious mind. You can also programme clear quartz with a thought of love, a thought of prosperity, healing, compassion, joy or protection.

Crystals:

*   Cohere, focus and amplify energy or prana
*   Relieve and release stress
*   Increase your personal healing power and healing potential
*   Stop burn-out and energy depletion or energy drain
*   Stimulate harmonious focused brain activity
*   Restore the energy structure of your body and aura
*   Stimulate healing, personal growth and spiritual development
*   Re-connect you with inner levels of your Divine essence
*   Create carrier waves of pure positive vibrant energy
*   Improve your health, rejuvenate your body and calm your mind
*   Transfer intelligent encoded healing information to the bloodstream
*   Transmute unwanted information that may be locked in your bones, tissues, subtle-bodies and your unconscious mind

Acquiring your crystals and gemstones will be an enjoyable magical adventure. It is a journey of discovery and self-discovery that can last a lifetime. Once you have been initiated into the crystal world and have made your very first contact with the devic stone consciousness you will never view the world the same. Crystals and gemstones cost very little in their tumbled form, but you can pay much more for an exquisite or rare specimen such as phenacite. Some of the sources for stones are rock shops, mineral shows, the Internet and metaphysical fairs: New Age stores are springing up everywhere as the consciousness of the planet shifts into a higher vibration. Try to find a place that has a wide variety and choice of beautiful crystals and gemstones and whose owners know the correct names, mineral content and vibrational properties. Perhaps you may be lucky enough to find beautiful stones while walking on the beach, or along the side of a river or even up in the mountains. Remember, the earth is full of crystals and gemstones.

Most crystal therapists are aware how important it is to know not only the source but where crystals and gemstones come from and by what means they were mined: for example, strip mining is the cheapest, but also causes the most destruction to our planet. It goes against the harmony of the devic kingdom. When you are selecting stones for personal healing, ask the salesperson questions such as: Where were the stones mined? What are the therapeutic properties? Buying crystals and gemstones must be a beautiful empowering experience, one that is not only enjoyable, but educational. Don't be rushed or intimidated into buying a crystal just because you feel browbeaten by the salesperson. I would suggest looking at the list below, which gives you tips on buying:

1. Damage - the more blemishes a crystal has, the less effective it will be, especially in the case of quartz crystals. If they are chipped, cracked or broken, primarily on the tips of the terminations, then they are useless for directing energy and may well even damage your energy field.

2. Clarity - for certain types of vibrational healing a crystal or gemstone must be as pure and clear as possible. This rule holds for all semi-precious gemstones and especially quartz points.

3. Shape and size - does the shape attract you? If you are buying stones for body layouts, flat shapes or cabochons are best. The size of your clear quartz crystal is also important; you should find one that fits your hand. If you are practising chakra cleansing techniques, it is no use having a crystal that makes your arm ache because it is too heavy.

4. Rarity - rare stones are more costly, especially if they are currently mined out, so be aware of this fact and be prepared to pay more for these special purchases.

5. Inclusions - sometimes inclusions are very attractive. If the stone is full of rainbows it brings light and joy to the owner; often you will find 'pictures' of animals, landscapes or Angels inside a stone which make it more attractive for you personally. The great exception to this rule is if you follow Vedic astrology: then the clearer and purer the gemstone the better and it is best to buy these from specialised dealers only.

6. Vibration - does the crystal resonate with your energy field, harmonics and frequency? If it does, you will experience sensations of harmony, balance, clarity and positiveness. Also with clear quartz the type can make a lot of difference; the list of different types is in part one of my first book, 'Crystal Therapy'.

Selecting a Crystal

All crystals and gemstones are naturally tuned to particular vibrations, frequencies and energy harmonics. See which crystal captivates your eye or attracts your attention. It is usually the first one that we feel drawn to that will be 'our' crystal. When you are in attunement with a crystal, you will experience sensations of resonance, balance, harmony, joy, compassion, wisdom or love. It will give you a feeling of wholeness and completion.

Sensations Experienced

*   Energetic charge or tingling on your skin or in your hands
*   Humming sensations
*   Electric charge
*   Dampness or sweating, a moistness in your hand on rubbing the stone
*   Breeze or cool wind-like energy across your skin
*   Flow of energy from the termination of the crystal
*   Cold
*   Heat
*   Pulsing or vibration
*   Heat from the termination of the crystal
*   Twitching in your fingers or hand
*   Immediate sense of being centred and balanced
*   Sound or audible humming in your ears
*   Glowing light or a visible energy field
*   Odour or scent
*   Flush or wave of heat through your body
*   Feelings of being enclosed by the crystal energy field

How to Choose a Crystal

Choosing crystals and gemstones is an intuitive act of love. So take a very deep breath and release all negative thoughts and emotions, still your mind and focus completely on the crystals as you hold them one by one. Your intention will be known. If you only wish to use the crystals, rather than becoming their partners, the crystals probably will stay 'dead' or their energy may withdraw. Part of the spiritual work of the crystal devas is to work with the human spirits. If your intention is to become a partner, much more of their 'magic' manifests in your life. Allow yourself to notice which stones feel good to you. If a stone feels good to you it probably will be the right one for you. You may like to use a pendulum, or ask a friend to help with muscle-testing techniques. Also allow your inner 'guru', the 'Divine Essence Within' and the crystal devas to be the teachers. Do not listen to or be too prejudiced by other people's thinking and advice, however well meant. Ask for guidance from the point of love and wisdom within yourself. If you are working from the point of love and humility you will always be helped by the crystal devas. In the West we have a very superior attitude and, in our ignorance, we tend to believe we are the highest evolved energy in the universe; if we are, it does not look good for the future, when we view all the wars, famine, disease, suspicion, prejudice and hatred humankind has visited on one another.

A cautionary word - it is wisest not to tune in to unclean stones. The implications of tuning in to uncleaned crystals and gemstones are immense. You will run the risk of absorbing any residual negative vibrations which have been left on the stones from whoever has handled them prior to you, be it the miner, wholesaler, retailer, jeweller or any previous customer. It is very important that all crystals are cleansed before you attune to them. Cleansing is important and will ensure that any residual disharmonies are removed from the stones. There are many New Age shops and suppliers who understand how important it is metaphysically for their crystals and gemstones to be cleansed before they sell them. If the shop you buy your crystals from is not energetically aware, only choose by sight and leave the 'tuning' in till later, after you have had time to cleanse them completely. The other places to avoid attuning to crystals and gemstones are museums, where they have never had any cleansing.

Method One - Vibration

Because all crystals and gemstones are naturally tuned to a particular frequency, vibration, resonance or energy harmonics, when you attune to a stone you will experience a sensation that is appropriate to that stone's harmonic range or resonance: this very often is a feeling of harmony, peace, compassion, balance or wholeness.

Selecting a crystal or gemstone by its vibration:

1.   Raise the sensitivity in your hands by washing them in warm water, then dry them thoroughly.

2.   Begin to sensitise your hands by shaking them; this releases blocked energy.

3.   Briskly rub your hands together; this begins to concentrate the chi or prana into your hands and begins to sensitise them.

4.   Hold your hands with your palms facing each other, about nine inches apart. Feel the energy radiating and vibrating between your hands; play with this energy.

5.   Begin to form this energy into a sphere and visualise it yellow in color. When it feels right, place this yellow sphere into the solar plexus area. This energises your mental body, allowing you to perceive the energy of the crystals more easily.

6.   Take a deep breath and relax. Release all negative thoughts and emotions, still your mind and focus completely on the crystals as you hold them one by one. Your intention will be known.

7.   Hold several different crystals, allow plenty of time with each stone. Normally you will find your receptive left hand (if you are right-handed) finds this process easier than your right hand. The reverse may be true if you are left-handed.

8.   Make a mental note of which stone feels good to you personally. If it intuitively feels 'right' to you it is definitely the 'right' one for you at this time.

9.   When you have finished, ground, centre and focus yourself.

10.   Write down the experience, for future reference.

Method Two - Intuition

1.   Take a very deep breath and release all negative thoughts and emotions.

2.   Still your mind and focus completely on the crystals as you look at them one by one. Your intention will be known to the crystals.

3.   Hold each crystal or gemstone in your mind and feel the energy or vibration; if it intuitively feels good to you, it has a natural affinity with you.

4.   When you have finished, ground, centre and focus yourself, then write down the experience, for future reference.

Method Three - Scanning

This method of scanning involves passing your hand slowly over several crystals until you can detect a crystal that feels hotter/cooler/stronger vibration/pulse etc.

1.   Raise the sensitivity in your hands by washing them in warm water, then dry them thoroughly.

2.   Begin to sensitise your hands by shaking them; this releases blocked energy.

3.   Briskly rub your hands together; this begins to concentrate the chi or prana into your hands and begins to sensitise them.

4. Hold your hands with your palms facing each other, about nine inches apart. Feel the energy radiating and vibrating between your hands; play with this energy.

5. Begin to form this energy into a ball and visualise it yellow in color. When it feels right, place this yellow ball into the solar plexus area. This energises your mental body, allowing you to perceive the energy of the crystal more easily.

6. Now take a very deep breath and release all negative thoughts and emotions, still your mind and focus completely on the crystals. Your intention will be known to the crystals.

7. Pass your left hand slowly over several crystals and begin to feel and see their energy. Gradually work along each crystal, observing the energy in any way you can, via heat, cold, tingling, vibration, pulse, etc. If you are left-handed, work with your right hand.

8. When you have finished, ground, centre and focus yourself.

9. Write down the experience, for future reference.

Method Four - Kinesiology

Kinesiology or muscle testing is one very effective means of selecting personal stones. This very simplified version really is extremely useful.

1. You need to find another person to work with.

2. Extend your right arm at shoulder height.

3. First test your normal muscle strength by having the other person rest two fingers on your extended arm and press down gently but firmly while you resist.

4. Then, with your left hand, hold the crystal or stone on your witness area, which is at the thymus, the area where your physical and etheric bodies meet.

5. Ask the question "Is this the right crystal for me to wear or carry?" or "Is this a good gemstone for me to use for self-healing? Is this good for meditation?" "Is it good for channelling?"

6. After each question, have the other person do the same finger test on your extended arm, while you resist.

7. If your arm remains strong, you have made the right choice. If your arm becomes weak, try again with another stone.

8. When you have finished, ground, centre and focus yourself. Write down the experience.

Method Five - Resonance

There are many other methods of choosing your crystal or gemstone. My favourite is to use resonance, which is connected breathing technique. I 'discovered' this technique as a child, using rhythmical, connected, fine breaths which are long, slow and deep, allowing us to connect to, and experience, the vibrational aspect of the energy that drives the breath. This energy is our divine essence. When using this technique you will reach a point where you feel as though you are 'being breathed'. As you continue with this breathing practice you will experience it aiding you in maintaining and restoring health and vitality and increasing longevity. This is due to its pure and perfect nature.

Step one: Hold a clear quartz single terminated crystal in your right hand with the termination pointing away from you.

Step two: Take a long deep breath in and breathe out very slowly as though a candle flame is in front of you and your breath must be so gentle as not to blow it out.

Step three: Begin to breathe in a connected way, where each inhale flows naturally into each exhale with no pause. The Buddhists call this 'chasing the breath'. The re-birthers call it rhythmical breathing.

Step four: Breathe finely and slowly, through the nostrils, until you feel the resonance or oscillation.

Step five: Slowly bring your right hand and crystal to the witness area at the thymus - this area is where your physical and etheric bodies meet - and continue to breathe slowly and calmly.

Step six: Allow the crystal consciousness to merge with your energy field. As you do so you will become aware of the crystal's consciousness; this will indicate, by its resonance with your energy field, if this is an appropriate crystal for you.

Step seven: When you have finished, ground, centre and focus yourself.

Step eight: Write down the experience, for future reference.

The Buddhists say that correct breathing keeps the body calm - calm breath, calm body, calm mind.

The crystal consciousness is much slower and calmer than our normal everyday vibration. This is one of the reasons why we, as humans, find it so very therapeutic and beneficial to our health, vitality and well-being to work with the crystal consciousness. The crystal energy is also much more focused than most human minds; crystals do not scatter their energy as humans do. Using connected breathing resonance allows us to access the crystal vibration with greater ease.

Resonance is a phenomenon that occurs throughout nature. At the level of the atom, it has been found that electrons whirl about the nucleus in certain defined energetic orbits. In order to move an electron from a lower to a higher orbit, a quantum of energy with a special frequency characteristic is needed. This is because the electron will only accept energy of the appropriate frequency to move from one energy level to the next level. If the electron falls from the higher frequency to the lower frequency orbit, it naturally will radiate energy of that same frequency. The required atomic frequency is referred to as the 'resonant frequency'. Molecules and atoms have special resonant frequencies that will only be excited (caused to move) by energies of very precise vibratory characteristics. A perfect example of this is the singer who is able to shatter a wine glass by singing a precise high amplitude note and does so by delivering it in the precise resonant frequency of the glass. Another example of resonance is demonstrated by the phenomenon of energy exchange between tuned oscillators. As an example we will use two perfectly tuned Stradivarius violins placed at opposite ends of a small room. If we pluck the E string of one violin, the observer will view the sister violin's E string also begin to vibrate and 'sing' in harmony. This happens because the E strings of the violins are carefully tuned and responsive to a particular frequency. The E strings can accept energy in the E frequency because that is their resonant frequency. The E strings of the violins are like the electrons of the atoms. They will vibrate at a new energy level only if they are exposed to energy of their resonant frequency.

Method Six - Pranayama

Breath-work - this is a very important tool as you develop spiritually.

Step one: Another way to find a crystal you feel empathy with is to hold your crystal in your right hand and take a deep breath.

Step two: Hold your breath until you feel your body begin to vibrate or oscillate.

Step three: As you exhale and relax, point the termination of the crystal towards the palm of your left hand, at a distance of two to six inches.

Step four: Begin slowly to move the crystal in a clockwise circular motion. You will begin to feel a sensation in your left hand reflecting the movements of the crystal.

Step five: Begin to move your right hand further and further away from your left hand, keeping the circular motion intact. Move your hand as far away as you can, until you no longer feel the crystal sensation in your left hand, then begin slowly spiralling the crystal back in, then out, then in.

Step six: Continue in this manner until your left hand feels a sensation of lightness, tingling or heat. This will indicate the suitability of the crystal for your energy-field or purpose.

Step seven: When you have finished, ground, centre and focus yourself.

Step eight: Write down the experience, for future reference.

Method Seven - Hand Activation

This technique of hand activation and attunement will remove all the energy blocks within your hands and will aid you in your crystal healing practice. It is also good for those who work as Reiki or spiritual healers. Regular use of this technique will enhance your health and well-being also. The hand represents the whole of the body, so in fact you are carrying out a crystal healing session on yourself each time you use this simple technique.

1. Hold your breath until you feel your body vibrate or oscillate.

2. As you exhale and relax, point the termination of the crystal towards the palm of your left hand, at a distance of two to six inches, and slowly move the crystal in a clockwise circular motion. You will begin to feel a sensation in your left hand reflecting the movements of the crystal. Begin to move your right hand further and further away from your left hand, keeping the circular motion intact.

3. Move your hand as far away as you can, until you no longer feel the crystal sensation in your left hand, then slowly spiral the crystal back in, then out, then in.

4. Continue in this manner until your hand feels very light and full of energy.

5. Repeat the process on the back of your left hand.

6. Then trace round the outline of your hand three times with the termination of the crystal.

7. Put your crystal down, close your eyes and feel the difference between your left and right hands. Often the 'crystallized' one will feel very large and full of energy, while the un-crystallized one will feel heavy and small.

8. Repeat the whole process, this time on your right hand, holding your crystal in your left hand.

9. Throughout this process be aware of the crystal's energy field interacting with yours; ask yourself if this crystal is appropriate and suitable for your purpose. This method is a very effective means of selecting personal stones.

10. When you have finished, ground, centre and focus yourself.

11. Write down the experience, for future reference.

Method Eight - Dowsing

Dowsing with a clear quartz pendulum has many diagnostic and healing applications, but in the context of choosing an appropriate healing gemstone or crystal for a particular therapeutic application it is one method that many people feel attracted to and indeed prefer. It also is a very ancient method of divination, perhaps the oldest energetic 'technology'. The pendulum is operated as a 'device' suspended on a silver chain from the hand of preference, which is held above the crystal or gemstone in question, while mentally or physically asking 'yes' or 'no' questions. The pendulum interacts with your energy field via your intent. Your pranic energy flows into the clear quartz pendulum and into its energy field; this energises it. This combined field of the quartz pendulum and your energy then interacts with the field of the crystal or gemstone in question, causing the clear quartz pendulum to move. The mechanical output (movement) of the pendulum is dependant upon unconscious nervous output induced by psychic perceptual functioning; this is dependant on the medium of expression being the tiny unconscious skeletal muscle movements. These are triggered by the electrical changes in the nervous system of the physical body as a means of translating unconscious psychic data into conscious diagnostic energetic information.

1.   Make sure your own personal energy system is flowing smoothly and you are grounded, centred and in balance. Make sure your clear quartz crystal pendulum is suitably cleansed, dedicated and programmed.

2.   Once your energy is interacting with the pendulum, you will need to establish your 'yes' movement and your 'no' movement. These can be clockwise for yes and anti-clockwise for no. If you establish a different movement for yes and no, that is fine too; as long as you know which is your yes, and which is your no, it matters not at all.

      This method of dowsing involves holding your pendulum over each crystal or gemstone in turn, whilst asking yes/no questions as to their suitability for the therapeutic use in question.

3.   When you have finished, ground, centre and focus yourself.

      You could also use a list of gemstones and hold your pendulum over each gemstone on the list until you find the correct gemstone for your therapeutic application.

Cleansing Your Crystal

This is the next stage. No matter who may have given it to you, always cleanse your crystal to remove any negative vibrations or physical dirt. It is very important that all crystals are cleansed before and after use. This will ensure that any residual disharmonies are removed from the stones. This you can do with water, sound, smudging etc. Again, be guided by your own inner knowledge. Only use a technique that truly 'resonates' with your energy field.

Natural water cleansing - this is particularly suited to those born astrologically under a water sign. First find a source of pure, clean, fresh water. This may be a stream, waterfall, river or spring. Hold your crystal under the flowing water until you feel all the dirt or stored negative vibrations have left it. When this process is complete you will feel your crystal is pure and vibrant. It is now ready to be used or, if it is a clear quartz crystal, programmed, charged or dedicated. Please check that your crystal is safe in water. Some crystals, such as talc, halite or selenite, are water soluble.

Saltwater cleansing - purely from a scientific angle, I would never use saltwater on a crystal, as this process will, in a short time, damage the crystalline structure and split the crystal or make it appear cloudy, dull, or darker. Remember, salt is also a crystal. Salt will get into any other crystalline structure, causing irreparable structural damage; also, direct contact with salt may produce chemical reactions with some crystals, making the stone lose its shine or change its color. Laying an opal in salt is sudden death for the crystal, due to the salting process of water extraction. If you want to try cleansing with the salt vibration, I recommend you place the crystal in a large bowl of sea salt, allowing enough salt to completely cover the crystal. Leave it buried for as long as your intuition tells you. You could also dowse for the correct amount of time. Wash your crystal with plenty of fresh, clear, clean pure water after its salt immersion. Laying an opal in salt will damage it by extracting the water. You can lay the opal - or any crystal that might react negatively to salt - in a small glass dish that is embedded in a larger glass dish full of salt.

Smudge cleansing - this technique is particularly suited to those born astrologically under an air sign. The burning of herbs or incense is a sacred practice held in common by many traditions. In American Indian tradition the practice is called 'smudging' or sometimes 'smoking', even though the herbs may not be inhaled. Smudging, practised traditionally, takes many forms. Sometimes the herbs are tied in a bundle and called a 'smudge stick'. There are certain herbs that lend themselves to braiding, such as sweet-grass. To smudge cleanse a crystal or gemstone you need a safe container that is heat-proof. Ceramic and glass bowls or abalone shells work well. There are also special chalices designed for smudging. Unless you use a chalice, place a layer of soil, sand or salt in the bottom for insulation, before adding your charcoal and herbs. Some people place the herbs on quick-lighting charcoal, which is available from many New Age shops, health food stores and Bible and Christian supply shops. (Smudging is similar to Catholic and Orthodox incense burning, for which Bible and Christian supply shops carry prepared charcoal blocks). Place either sage, cedar, copal, lavender, fennel or sweet-grass into the container and light the herbs using a candle or lighter. Matches are not very efficient because it takes a while to get the herbs smoking.

If you prefer to light your whole bundle or braid, hold it in a candle flame until the smudge glows red hot. Blow out the flame; it will smoulder for at least a few minutes. You will need a bowl or shell to catch the hot ashes. The bundle or braid of herbs will eventually go out by itself. Should you need to put it out before it does, you can tap it out as you would a cigarette or cigar. Putting water on it to put it out is messier and considered disrespectful to the fire spirits. The idea of burning herbs is to release their fragrance and energy, not to fill your room or lungs with smoke. Burning excessive amounts of smudge can lead to respiratory distress and other respiratory problems. Show consideration for other people when burning smudge. Avoid burning smudge in the same room as infants and anyone who is pregnant and those who suffer from respiratory problems, or those who have asthma or respiratory allergies. Avoid fire hazards; never smudge around flammable substances and never leave burning smudge, charcoal, candles or fires unattended. Smudging is also used during healing work and prayer. The Native Americans believe it helps them to connect to their spirit helpers. The smoke carries their intention to the sky world. Allow the smoke to pass around the crystal, gently carrying away any harmful, stagnant vibrations to the elements of air to be dispersed and transmuted. If you are using this technique indoors, be sure to keep a window open to allow the stagnant vibrations a place by which to exit. Burning incense and herbs can also be used to cleanse your aura, before meditation and healing sessions. It can also be used to cleanse rooms, before or after healing sessions.

Bay leaf - used in the autumn to protect from colds and flu.

Cedar, Cypress, Juniper - to consecrate and make sacred.

Fennel - repels evil energies.

Lavender - protection and cleansing.

Mint - cleansing and uplifting.

Mugwort - healing, divination and dream work. Unsafe for pregnancy.

Pine - purifying.

Resin, Copal, Balsam, Gum, Sap - embodying the four elements.

Sage - clears negative energy, foreign energy and entities from oneself.

Sweet-grass - grounding, protection and making sacred.

Wild tobacco - traditionally used to connect with sacred beings and wisdom.

Earth cleansing - this technique is particularly attractive to the earth signs amongst us. This method is extremely useful when you feel your crystal is particularly negative. By placing it in the earth you are returning it to its 'Great Mother' for realigning, nurturing and cleansing. Crystals love this experience; they simply enjoy the whole process of earth placement. After you have buried your crystal in the earth, please mark the place with a twig or other marker if you want to find it again. Also be aware that if your pet has watched you enact this ceremony it may try to dig up your crystal to help you! This cleansing process can take some time. Once again, allow your inner guru to let you know how long to leave your crystal in the earth. Please note, however, that you may have a soil that will damage your gemstone. Some soils are very acid, so please check before you bury it, otherwise you may find your crystal has been damaged.

Fire cleansing - fire signs love this one and it's quick, which also appeals to fire signs. Simply pass your crystal very quickly above a small candle flame, taking care not to burn yourself or the crystal. I always use a white candle for this 'Grandfather' fire ceremony. This is a quick dynamic process, which is instant and very effective. Please note, however, that you must never put an opal near fire, as fire will damage it.

Another technique with fire is to surround your crystal or crystals that need cleansing with small tea lights, normally four, one for each direction. You can leave them in place until the candles burn out, which is normally four hours or for as long as you feel is the right length of time. This process also works very well to burn off negativity from the human aura. In the case of humans you may need up to 12 small candles. Begin by lighting one, then two, three, etc. until you can feel the effect of the flames in your auric shell. You may even hear hissing sounds from the candles as negative energy is burned away. I like to use this technique often.

Flowers or petals for cleansing - gather petals or flowers of any kind you feel attracted to. Very often you may feel a particular vibration is needed for each crystal or gemstone. Obvious flower choices would be lavender for cleansing, roses for love, chamomile for soothing: the list is endless. Place your flowers or petals in a clear glass container and leave the crystals completely covered by the flowers for at least twenty-four hours. This process is gentle and nurturing.

Rice cleansing - fill a clear glass bowl with plain brown rice (uncooked) and place your crystal or gemstone in the rice. Make sure your crystal is completely covered. Leave it for twenty-four hours and safely discard the rice afterwards (do not eat it). The rice will have absorbed the negative vibration from the crystal, leaving it clean and ready for re-use in whatever way you choose.

Sound cleansing - for this process you will need a crystal singing bowl, bells, a gong, ting-shaws, rattle or drum. Simply allow your chosen sound to 'wash' over the crystal, purifying, cleansing and freeing it of any stuck or negative vibrations. This process can take a little time, but it is very effective for large quantities of crystals which may all need cleansing at the same time.

Toning - you may use a mantra such as Om to cleanse a crystal or gemstone. This is quick and efficient, bringing a powerful cosmic vibrational energy to aid you in this way, which is very empowering to both you and your crystal. You may also charge or energise your crystal with your favourite mantra. For Reiki or Karuna Masters and practitioners you can use the name of the Reiki or Karuna symbol that is used for clearing negative energy.

Breath cleansing - this technique was given to me by a Native American elder. Simply breathe into your crystal three times with the view of clearing any unwanted vibration from your crystal or pendant with your breath. I would never use this technique on a crystal I was using in healing others, but I feel it is fine for my own personal crystals; it imbues them with my energy and my pure vibration and stops other vibrations from intruding into the crystals' energy fields.

Crystal cleansing - you may decide to cleanse your crystal by placing it on an amethyst bed or cluster. This is a very powerful and effective method, but please be aware that if your crystal is softer than amethyst (7) it may become scratched and dull. The other problem with this technique is that the amethyst cluster is so powerful it will remove other vibrations completely. In other words, if you leave the crystal on it too long it will have lost its original vibration and have absorbed the amethyst signature, which may take some time to dissipate from your crystal.

Care and Storage of Your Crystal

When you purchase or are given a crystal or gemstone, you have to 'care' for it. Remember it is a sacred unique piece of Mother Earth that you will be able to cherish for ever. This means finding a position for it where it is safe, secure and is in harmonious surroundings. This facilitates its vibration to work with you and for you. Please make sure your crystal is content and honoured. Do not put it in your pocket, to be scratched, chipped and knocked by your keys and loose change, but maybe in a small pouch or on a special healing shelf or altar. If it is a pendant, please take very special care of it. Do not allow others, however well meaning, to touch your pendant or personal crystals. Please do not wear a pendant in the shower or bath. Wearing pendants in the sea or swimming baths is not a good idea, as your pendant chain may break. Also, take your pendant off at night and place it on your bedside table or altar.

Control

Or master crystal - crystal vibrational therapists normally work with a 'control' or 'master crystal'. This is your own personal resonance crystal. You may use this for all your crystal healing work. It is your main crystal. It is your best friend or ally and your guide into the crystal kingdom. It usually is a clear quartz single terminated point, between 3" and 10" long, 1" to 3" thick. It may be a powerful masculine focused water-clear laser quartz or the type of milky quartz crystal from Madagascar which has a soft feminine energy. Perhaps you will be attracted to a clear quartz point from Arkansas, USA, with a balanced male/female energy.

You will try not to let anyone touch your control crystal, because it will be tuned into your energy vibration or resonance. You may have more than one control crystal in your life. As you grow in knowledge and understanding, another control crystal may be attracted to you. When this happens, release the original control crystal with love and pass it on to do other work. If you do not have a control crystal as yet, be assured that one will be attracted to you in the course of your crystal healing work, if you so desire.

Attuning to Crystals by Activating Them

Crystals oscillate to a natural healing frequency that is activated by your intent (your focused mental energy). This is achieved by techniques such as meditation and visualization. Crystals are therefore compatible tools with which to harmonise and balance the chakras. All you need to do to unlock this vibrational healing potential is to focus your mental energy on the crystals when using them.

Dedicating Your Crystal

Simply dedicate your crystal to your highest good and the good of all, then fill it with the appropriate image, finally filling the crystal with love and compassion. These are the vibrations you are best to work with and the only vibrations to use when healing others. You may prefer to enact a simple ritual and dedicate the crystal, asking that "it is my pure intent that from this moment on this crystal may only be used in the name of love and compassion and always for the universal highest good of all".

Programming

Please note that only clear quartz crystals can actually be 'programmed'. All other crystals, minerals and gemstones automatically contain their own specific programme, via their mineral and vibrational make-up. That is why you must choose your crystal with great care for the specific purpose you have in mind. It is always wisest to consult a qualified crystal therapist who has completed a full professional crystal course, before committing yourself to an expensive purchase. You can also take a course yourself. There are excellent courses run by many organisations worldwide. Allow yourself to be guided to the course that resonates with you. In other words, follow your heart: if you feel joy and excitement, this will be the right course for you. When you enquire about courses, always ask how long the facilitators have been working with crystals, how long they have been running crystal courses, are they qualified tutors and, most of all, how their course will develop your inner knowing, wisdom and compassion.

To programme your clear quartz crystal, simply hold your cleansed quartz crystal between your hands in a prayer position at your heart chakra, concentrate on the energy of your choice and fill your crystal with this energy. Say "I intend this crystal to be an effective tool for healing/meditation/absent healing/scrying/dream interpretation, etc". You may enact a simple ceremony. Or you may like to programme your crystal during a meditation. Please remember, positive emotions strengthen your energy field, bringing health, balance and vitality, whilst negative emotions bring sickness, instability, mood swings and low energy. So always remain positive emotionally when programming your clear quartz crystal.

Tuning

When you have cleansed your crystals you 'activate them', like turning on a radio, but to receive a 'broadcast' you must tune the dial to the correct station. Also the 'frequency' you choose when tuning depends on your purpose. Say "I intend this crystal to be an effective tool for healing/meditation/absent healing/scrying/dream interpretation, etc".

Energising Crystals

This is like 'programming' and it is useful when you feel your crystal needs a positive charge of energy, filling the clear quartz crystal with sunlight, moonlight, sound or storm energy, Reiki, Angel energy, Karuna or Pranic healing.

Charging Crystals

Charging is like 'programming', filling the clear quartz crystal with sunlight, moonlight, storm energy, Prana, Karuna or planetary energy. You may even feel that you associate your particular stone or crystal with a totem or power animal. Many people also fill their crystals with Angelic healing energy, which instantly lifts the vibration of any stone. It is also possible to fill your crystal with a specific sound or color vibration for more individual healing energies. Clear quartz will also hold the charge of air, earth, fire and water or any combination of the four.

Moonlight - is feminine, liquid, yin, calm, intuitive, still, mysterious, hidden. To energise your clear quartz crystal with moonlight, simply place your cleansed crystal outside during the three days of the full moon. If you wish to have a banishing energy within your crystal to help you let go of negative thoughts, habits, people or situations, simply place your quartz crystal out of doors in the three days of the dark moon. You may enact a simple ceremony of dedication and thanks to the moon during this process for more immediate results. The moon influences certain crystals naturally: these are moonstone, labradorite, pearl, snow quartz and mother-of-pearl.

Sunlight - is associated with fire, personal power, agni (Lord of fire), ambition, intellectual activity, combustion, anger, joy, laughter, expansion, movement, yang. To energise your clear quartz crystal with sunlight, simply place your cleansed crystal outside on a sunny day. You may enact a simple ceremony of dedication and thanks to the sun during this process for more immediate and powerful results. The sun influences certain crystals naturally: these are ruby, garnet, citrine, gold, golden labradorite and sunstone.

Starlight - is associated with cosmic awareness, universal energies, brightness, expansiveness, wishing and wish fulfilment. To energise your clear quartz crystal with starlight, simply place your cleansed crystal outside on a clear night, or you may wish to fill it with a particular star energy. Maybe you already have a guiding star or star-being contact. You may enact a simple ceremony of dedication and thanks to the stars and the star-beings during this process for more immediate and powerful results. It is also possible to use your clear quartz crystal for wish fulfilment. Simply go outside on a clear starry night, look up to the stars and think about the wish you want fulfilling. If it is in the name of love and light and the highest universal good of all beings, your wish will be fulfilled. The stars influence certain crystals naturally: these are iolite, moldavite, star sapphire and asterised quartz.

Angel energy - is associated with hope, protection, warmth, love, compassion, universal energies and guidance. To energise your clear quartz crystal with Angelic energy, simply hold your cleansed crystal in your left hand; left is for receiving. You may enact a simple ceremony, asking the Angels of light, love and protection to place their pristine energies within the crystal. Alternatively you may already work with a particular Angel, such as Archangel Michael for protection, or Archangel Raphael for healing. Simply ask your Angel to place their energy within the crystal. Please give thanks after the dedication ceremony. This process is immediate and powerful. The results are always swift and pristine. The Angels influence certain crystals naturally: these are angelite, seraphinite, selenite and danburite.

Karuna - is the energy of compassionate action. To energise your clear quartz crystal with Karuna, simply hold your cleansed crystal between your hands in a prayer position at your heart chakra and meditate on the energy of compassion and compassion for all beings. Remember the most compassionate thing you can do for all beings is to become enlightened. This then raises not only your vibratory rate, but the vibration of all who come into contact with you. You may enact a simple ceremony of dedication and thanks to all enlightened beings, both in the physical realm and those from other realms during this process for more immediate and powerful results. The influences of the Karuna energies are contained in certain crystals naturally: these are morganite, rhodocrosite and aquamarine.

Storm - the element of storm is the most transformational of all the elements. It is a combination of air, earth, fire and water. This synergy of energies is very powerful and not to be worked with lightly. It is sudden and powerful and embodies the creative and destructive forces of nature. It also combines the yin/yang vibration and, as such, has a point of perfect balance. The earth is renewed by the storm vibration as it quickly cleanses and purifies the environment. If you wish to work with this powerful rebirth energy, place your crystals outside before a thunderstorm reaches you, allow them plenty of time to absorb the energies and wait for the storm to finish before you go outside again to retrieve your crystals. Some 'stones' are already working with this vibration, such as herderite, fulgurite, moldavite, Tibetan tektite and phenacite.

Earth - this energy is associated with physical energy, gravity, self-preservation, being grounded and deep healing. To energise your clear quartz crystal with the earth element when you wish to work with the energy of abundance, strength and deep healing to reconnect you to your roots, or when you feel spacey or detached from reality, simply place your crystal back into the earth. By placing it in the earth you are returning it to its 'Great Mother' for realigning, nurturing and the magic of abundance. Crystals love this experience; they simply enjoy the whole process of earth placement. After you have buried your crystal in the earth, please mark the place with a twig or other marker if you want to find it again. Also be aware that if your pet has watched you enact this ceremony it may try to dig up your crystal to help you! This cleansing process can take some time. Please note, however, that you may have a soil that will damage your gemstone. Some soils are very acid, so please check before you bury it, otherwise you may find your crystal has been damaged. You may enact a simple earth healing ceremony of dedication and thanks to the Earth Mother for deep healing and connection; if you do this during the process you will find a more immediate and powerful result. The earth influences all the crystals she has given birth to.

Water - this primal element is associated with emotions, cleansing, tears and all fluid functions of the body. To energise your clear quartz crystal with the water element, simply find a source of pure, clean, fresh water. This may be a stream, waterfall, river or spring. Hold your crystal or place your crystal under the flowing water. You may enact a simple ceremony of dedication and thanks to the element of water during this process for more immediate and powerful results. The water element influences certain crystals naturally: these are enhydros, water sapphire, river-tumbled pebbles, aquamarine and aqua aura quartz.

Fire - this regenerative element is associated with heat, personal power, agni (Lord of fire), ambition, intellectual activity, combustion, anger, joy, laughter, expansion, movement and yang. To energise your clear quartz crystal with the fire element, simply light a white candle and place your crystal in front of it. Ask the crystal to absorb the energy of fire or you may use any source of the fire element that will not damage you or the crystal and is appropriate to the fire element. You may enact a simple ceremony of dedication and thanks to the fire during this process for more immediate and powerful results. Fire influences certain crystals naturally: these are fire agate, fire opal, pumice, Mexican fire opal and sunstone.

Air - this element is associated with movement, breath, lightness, freedom and spirit. To energise your clear quartz crystal with the element of air, simply place your cleansed crystal outside on a windy or breezy day. You may enact a simple ceremony of dedication and thanks to the element of air during this process for more immediate and powerful results. The element of air influences certain crystals naturally: these are amethyst, selenite (with air bubbles in) or any crystal that contains air bubbles. Moldavite and other tektites very often contain air bubbles; this is ancient air, which is full of prehistoric memories.

Color - to energise your clear quartz crystal with a particular color vibration, simply hold your cleansed crystal between your hands in a prayer position at your heart chakra and meditate on the energy of the color you wish to work with. Feel the crystal begin to radiate the color vibration of your choice. Alternatively you can wrap your clear quartz crystal in a cloth of the color you wish it to absorb, or place it on a colored gel. You may enact a simple ceremony of dedication and thanks to the elements of color during this process for more immediate and powerful results. The influences of color are contained in all colored crystals and gemstones naturally.

Tree - to energise your clear quartz crystal with a particular tree vibration, simply hold your cleansed crystal between your hands in a prayer position at your heart chakra and meditate on the energy of the tree you wish to work with. Feel the crystal begin to radiate the tree vibration of your choice. Alternatively you can place your clear quartz crystal in or near the tree you wish it to absorb, or place it on a leaf, blossom, fruit or photograph of the type of tree. You may enact a simple ceremony of dedication and thanks to the elemental/deva of the tree during this process for more immediate and powerful results. The elementals of certain trees naturally influence fossilized wood and amber; this is ancient energy, which is full of prehistoric memories.

Flower - to energise your clear quartz crystal with a particular flower or plant vibration, simply hold your cleansed crystal between your hands in a prayer position at your heart chakra and meditate on the energy of the flower or plant you wish to work with. Feel the crystal begin to radiate the flower or plant vibration of your choice. Alternatively you can place your clear quartz crystal in or near the flower or plant you wish it to absorb, or place it on a leaf, blossom, fruit or photograph of the type of flower or plant. You may enact a simple ceremony of dedication and thanks to the elemental/deva of the flower during this process for more immediate and powerful results. The elementals of certain flowers and plants influence amber, which may contain pollen or pieces of flower or plant material; this is ancient energy, which is full of prehistoric memories.

Prana or Reiki - to energise your clear quartz crystal with Prana or Reiki, simply hold your cleansed quartz crystal between your hands in a prayer position at your heart chakra, meditate on the energy of Prana or Reiki and fill your crystal with this energy. You may enact a simple ceremony of dedication and thanks to all enlightened beings, both in the physical and those from other realms, during this process, for more immediate and powerful results. You can then carry your crystal around with you, or give it to someone else who needs healing. Another traditional way crystals are used with Reiki is to write down on a piece of paper any problem you are experiencing and place it under the Reiki crystal, intending that the Reiki energy flows constantly into the problem to create a solution or healing that is to the highest possible good of all. You must charge the crystal once a week to maintain the strength and integrity of the energetic link. Another way to use crystals and Reiki is the Reiki web of light.

Reiki Web of Light

Reiki is a powerful, mysterious healing energy and by combining crystals with the Reiki we have seen amazing, tremendous positive results from this technique. The Japanese word REIKI means power and a Reiki attunement can only be facilitated by a Master who has personally been attuned to the Reiki energy. For those crystal therapists who are not attuned to Reiki, the following crystal web of light will still be effective, especially if you use Prana or chi for activation.

A crystal web of light can be established and charged with Reiki to heal, protect or manifest a goal for 48 hours or longer after it has been charged. In addition, the Reiki web can be used by your guides and higher self as a connection to transmit healing and help your clients. Don't rush choosing your crystals for the web of light; we often find that it is better to allow the 'right' crystals to come into your life. You may already possess some clear quartz crystals. If so, these should be considered as possible candidates for your Reiki web. One more question you should ask yourself before you begin is: do the crystals you have chosen wish to participate in the web of light? Do they feel right for this device?

When you are ready to create your web of Reiki light you will need 8 clear quartz crystals:

> 6 small (2")
> 1 medium (4")
> 1 double terminated (2-3")

Your clear quartz crystals should be totally cleansed before using them by placing them under running water for one hour. Say a prayer over them during this process of purification, asking the crystal Angels or devas to help guide you as you set up this web of light. Also ask the spirit of the water to cleanse your crystals. Then ask the crystals to help you manifest your highest spiritual purpose this lifetime. You may also attune your quartz crystals to the energies of the sun, moon and earth by placing them in the earth with the terminations pointing out for the three days of the full moon. Do this in a safe place where they will be bathed in the appropriate energies. Say a prayer over them each evening, asking for the creative powers of the universe to help you.

Next, you must prepare a special place for your Reiki web of light. It should be a place that only you have access to, or at least a safe place. It could be your Reiki altar or shelf, a desk top or window-sill.

From your 8 crystals, the medium-sized one is your control or master charging quartz crystal.

Place the 6 small quartz crystals at equal points around a circle of about 12" in diameter pointing inwards. This will create a hexagon or six-sided figure. This is the optimum web for working with quartz crystals. Clear quartz crystals contain the full spectrum of white light energy (white light contains all colors and all energies, so this enables you to help yourself and your clients on every level of their bodies and minds). Clear quartz crystals are master healers and are the only programmable crystals on the planet at this time. Lastly, place the double terminated crystal in the centre. This completes the web of light. The next steps are:

1. Choose a photograph of yourself and sign your name on the back.

2. Draw the four Usui Reiki symbols on the back, along with their names.

3. Include a powerful affirmation such as: "I am perfectly protected with divine love, compassion and wisdom; I now allow myself to heal on every level of my being, as I fulfill my highest spiritual goals this lifetime" or "Reiki guides and Angels, heal and guide me in all I do" or "I am a channel for Reiki healing, love and compassion; the more I use my Reiki the stronger it becomes until I am of great service to all I meet" or " I now connect with the divine essence which dwells within me, as I allow the Reiki energy to flow into my life". Use any of these or a combination of them or be creative and make up your own affirmation to suit you personally.

After your crystals have been purified and blessed and you know how you will arrange them and your photograph is ready, your next step is to charge your crystals with Reiki. Take each quartz crystal individually and hold it in your hands; allow Reiki to flow into the crystal, filling it with Reiki energy for at least 10 minutes. As you do this, say a prayer asking your Reiki guides and Angels, Archangels and all beings of love and light to assist you in the process of charging your quartz crystals with Reiki energy. You can also do a Reiki attunement on each crystal if you are a Reiki Master. This gives them an even greater charge of higher frequency energy.

As you charge each crystal, place it in its correct position on the Reiki web of light. After the crystals are in position, do not move them, as this will weaken their energy connection. Then charge your master crystal in the same way.

Your master crystal will be used to keep your Reiki web charged with positive healing energies. Charge it with Reiki the same way as the others. Then, while holding it in your right hand, begin drawing out pie-shaped sections above the web, imagining the energy coming out of your master crystal and charging the web of light. Start with the central double terminated crystal and move to an outer crystal, then move counter clockwise to the next outer crystal and back to the centre, then back out to the same outer crystal you just came in from, and so on, making pie-shaped movements and moving around the web in a counter-clockwise direction.

As you do this, repeat an affirmation/mantra/prayer such as: "I empower this web with love, with light, with compassion, with healing, with wisdom; I empower this web with love, with compassion, with light, with healing, with wisdom, to heal, to heal, to heal; I empower this web with joy to heal, to heal, to heal; I call on my Reiki guides and Angels to empower this web with love, with love, with love, to heal, to heal, I am filled with compassion for all beings". Again feel free to create your own positive affirmation/mantra/prayer that feels perfect for you.

Meditate with your master crystal each day or night and use it to charge your Reiki web of light each and every day. If you miss the odd day, do not worry, but you must keep your web charged for it to remain activated. You must work with it regularly to obtain the best positive results. For greater empowerment you may draw the four Usui Reiki symbols over the web with your master crystal and charge the web regularly with your master crystal. If you have a person to whom you would like to send Reiki or a project or goal you would like to empower with Reiki, write it out on a piece of paper and draw out the four Reiki symbols. Then Reiki it between your hands and place it within your web of light. Your crystal Reiki web will continue to send Reiki to the person or to manifest your goal or project. You may also place other crystals in the centre of the Reiki web of light and I would suggest looking up the properties of the different crystals and gemstones in the relevant sections of this book to find which crystal would help you.

Part 8

Crystal Webs of Light

Quartz crystals, precious and semi-precious gemstones represent the lowest state of entropy possible because they have the most orderly structure in the natural world. All crystalline structures are formed of mathematically, precise and orderly lattice arrays of molecules. This stability of quartz crystals has been utilised by scientists in many electronic situations. The crystalline structure will respond in characteristic, predictable and precise ways to a broad spectrum of energies including pressure, sound, electricity (electron flow), light, heat, microwaves, gamma rays, radiation, physical stress, bioelectricity and consciousness (thoughts and emotions). The response of quartz crystal has also been employed by healers for centuries. (Healers use the focused power of their intent). By applying this coherent, stable, focused energy to dysfunctional energy systems within the human multi-directional energy circuits, they can quickly restore stability and optimum balance. This results in multi-directional healing or energy restructuring on every level. Quartz crystals focus coherent energy, when used by a trained therapist, and will always go to the areas which are most in need of restructuring; this energy seems to be self-regulating, due to its orderly structure, and results in optimum release of negative crystalline patterns which may have lodged in any layer of the human energy system.

Quartz crystals also resonate with the liquid crystals in your physical body and transfer to your bloodstream and to your circulatory system vital elements, in the form of intelligent energy fields which are essential for your health and for the rejuvenation of your body, while transmuting unwanted information that may be locked in your bones, tissues and unconscious mind. This effect can be felt very strongly with the pineal gland, which has an overall controlling effect on the whole system. The pineal gland has long held great mystical knowledge; this secret, but sacred gland, known to the advanced meditator, has properties which appear to have caught the attention of some of the scientific community in the form of research into the hormone it produces (melatonin). When crystals are used in geometric arrays they have an amplified effect and by combining the different gemstones and crystals to create a synergistic effect, you can amplify the overall potency of a crystal therapy session considerably.

The internal structure of minerals has been resolved only this century, by the use of X-rays, although for about 200 years it has been acknowledged that crystals are almost incredibly regular. This is not at once instantly apparent, for crystals of the same substance, such as quartz, have faces that seem almost infinitely variable in their size and shape: it is only when the angles between corresponding pairs of faces are measured that the regularity becomes apparent. The angle between the same two faces in all crystals of the same mineral species is constant. It is now known that this is because the constituent atoms pack together in a definite and orderly way. Crystals were studied long before this was appreciated, however, and from a study of external shape alone it was supposed that crystals were symmetrical and could be grouped according to their symmetry.

To fully understand the structure of crystals it is useful to know something of the atom itself. An atom is said to be the smallest part of an element, giving the term element the meaning more commonly assigned to it in practical chemistry. However, each atom is now known to be a complex system consisting of planetary particles each with a unit of negative electrical charge, which are called electrons, surrounding a heavy nucleus containing a number of positively charged particles called protons. There are a similar number of protons to electrons, so producing, by balancing the positive and negative charges, an electrically neutral atom. Except for the hydrogen atom, all the nuclei of atoms also contain a number of uncharged particles called neutrons, whose possible function is to act as a cement against the repulsive action of the positively charged protons to each other. An atom contains three elementary particles, two of which, the proton and the neutron, have approximately equal weight or mass, and the electron has a mass much smaller. An atom may be considered as consisting of a core - small and compact - surrounded by a 'cloud' of electrons describing orbits which may be circular or of varying ellipticity. The electrons, the protons and the neutrons spin on their own axes, so that the atom is a highly dynamic system. Each of the chemical elements is made of like atoms, atoms which have the same nuclear charge or, as it is better known, atomic number; that is, they have the same number of protons. While the number of protons determines the nature of an atom, not all the atoms of a given element possess the same number of neutrons, therefore such atoms will vary in their weight. The configuration of the planetary electrons around the nucleus is important, for the chemical properties of an element, chemical compounds, and the formation of crystals depend a great deal upon the disposition of the electrons. The electrons circle the nucleus in all directions as a 'cloud' in given orbits which may be described as the average of their movements, the radius of which defines a 'shell' or energy level. If the atom gains or loses one or more electrons it ceases to be electrically neutral and becomes what is known as an ion, the gain of electrons producing negatively charged ions called anions and the loss producing positive ions called cations.

This is the simple basis, as all substances are built upon this foundation. In nature we find no more than 83 different, stable atoms; they are distinguished from each other only by the number of their elementary particles. Not all of the elements in a chemistry book can be found in minerals. Some are absent because they do not form bonds (noble gases) and some because they were created by humans in laboratories and atomic reactors (plutonium etc). From the compounds of these few elements, the majority (over 95%) of the 4,000 known minerals are formed. These elements in fact make up over 99.9% of the earth's crust. Each of them has its own unique properties and the compounds of these elements formulate the characteristic features of minerals.

Atoms and molecules are not themselves geometric shapes. However, they are organised spatially in exact geometric patterns, known as 'crystal lattices'. This perfect order is explained by the fact that individual atoms and molecules of the mineral are packed together as tightly as possible during their growth, which is partly due to the strong electromagnetic forces exerted on them at this time, and partly due to the pressure around them as they form. The internal structure of any crystalline substance is constant and the outward shape of a crystal must have a definite relationship to this structure. Therefore, ideally, a crystal shows a symmetrical arrangement of the various surfaces, which are usually flat but in diamond and a few others may be curved. These plane surfaces are called faces: they may be of two kinds, like and unlike. Crystals made up of similar faces are termed simple forms. A cube or octahedron is an example of a simple form. The characteristic shape of a crystal is known as its habit. While the interfacial angles are always the same for crystals of the same mineral, the form of crystals can differ greatly, and for reasons which are not clearly understood. In gem minerals it has been noticed that a different habit can occur in crystals of the same mineral which come from different localities or are of a different color. For example, aquamarine (which is a beryl) is usually found as long prismatic crystals, while pink beryl (morganite) usually forms crystals which are short and tabular.

When a mineral has a chemical composition the same as another mineral, but crystallises in a different system, the effect is termed dimorphism, or collectively polymorphism. For instance, diamond and graphite are both carbon, but crystallise in the cubic and hexagonal system respectively, and the rhombohedral calcite has the same chemical make-up as the orthorhombic aragonite.

Crystal Systems

On the basis of their symmetry, crystals can be grouped into seven crystal systems. One other 'crystal' system, amorphous, is not technically crystal: this is because it is without structure, due to the formation, which is so rapid that no crystal structure has had a chance to form. The systems are:

Cubic
Tetragonal

Orthorhombic
Monoclinic
Triclinic
Hexagonal
Trigonal
Amorphous

Hardness

Bound up with the atomic bonding of a substance is the property of hardness. A high degree of hardness in a precious stone is necessary, for only hard substances can take and retain a good polish. A practical means of assessing hardness was proposed by the German mineralogist Friedrich Mohs (1773-1839), who in 1822, after extensive experiments, chose 10 well-known and easily obtainable minerals and arranged them in order of their 'scratch hardness' to serve as standards of comparison. Albeit the numbers of Mohs' list have no quantitative meaning, it is commonly called the Mohs' scale and still forms a universally accepted standard of hardness amongst mineralogists, gemmologists and crystal healers. The Mohs' scale is as follows:

10.	Diamond
9.	Sapphire
8.	Topaz
7.	Quartz
6.	Orthoclase
5.	Apatite
4.	Fluorite
3.	Calcite
2.	Gypsum
1.	Talc

The numbers on Mohs' list are not quantities, they represent an order only. Diamond is enormously harder than any other mineral and the gap between 10 and 9 on the list is far greater than that between any other of the numbers. The number 7 on the Mohs' scale is an important one, as any gemstone must be at least as hard as this if it is to withstand being regularly worn in jewellery. Stones such as peridot or green demantoid garnet are only suitable for occasional wear. Opal, pearl, amber and coral are also very soft and great care should be taken if they are worn as pendants.

Working With Crystal Energy Webs of Light

The atmosphere or energy field in which we live, work and sleep will have a lasting effect on our health. Our personal environment is very important, not only to our physical body, but to all levels of our being, from the gross physical body to the most subtle levels. Over time, the effects of televisions, computers, sockets and electrical cables can influence our bio-magnetic energy field and damage our aura, which in turn has a direct result on the physical body. This has been substantiated by those people who live near electricity pylons. Depression, suicide and multiple illnesses have been the result of prolonged exposure. This means that we can use healing crystals in our daily environment to obtain fast positive results. The important point to remember is that the crystals are effective across a suitable radius. Whenever you are in the radius of influence of a crystal or cluster you always feel mentally, emotionally and physically better.

Various geometric arrangements using clear quartz crystals will be employed in each chapter on the chakras; we will utilize them on and around the physical body and aura. Their unified field of energy and influence will work on all levels of the subtle bodies. The use of energy webs in this fashion not only builds a wall of healing energy, but utilises the sacred geometry of the creative forces of the universe. All manifestation starts from geometric patterns, the 'word' of God/Goddess made manifest.

Crystallography is the study of the divine symmetries of these atomic structures, the outer expression of their inner divine orderly structure. In the section of this book on sound healing, we will explore the use of sound, but it is of interest in this section too. In ancient Egypt, the hieroglyph for music was also that for joy and well-being. The Vedic-Sanskrit scholars of ancient India, and the philosophers of the school of Pythagoras, in Classical Greece, regarded all physical forms as manifestations of music; as we shall discover, the relative proportions of musical sounds parallel the physical proportions of natural and architectural shapes. These ancient doctrines held that life and health depended upon a continuum of ratios, geometric patterns and harmonic relationships, from within the mind and through the body, out to society and the natural world. Many of us know of Pythagoras as the father of geometry. However, how many are aware that in the 6th century BC in Greece he had a school that taught not only the magic of numbers, but the healing powers of music.

Perhaps the most profound scientific work showing the power of sound to affect shape and form was researched by Dr Hans Jenny, a Swiss medical doctor and scientist who spent ten years of his life examining the effects that sound had on shape and formation. Jenny photographed plastics, pastes, liquids, powders, mercury, glycerine gel and other substances as they were being vibrated by sound. The results of these experiments are truly awe-inspiring, for they show extremely organic shapes being created from inorganic substances merely by exposing them to different sound frequencies. The different substances, which were once blobs of inorganic matter, take on varying geometric forms and begin to look like living creatures: starfish, human cells, microscopic life.

In his book, "Cymatics", Dr Jenny wrote: "Now it is beyond doubt that where organization is concerned, the harmonic figures of physics are, in fact, essentially similar to the harmonic patterns of organic nature...we have the certain experience that harmonic systems such as we have visualized in our experiments arise from oscillations in the form of intervals and harmonic frequencies. That is indisputable." According to Dr Jenny, harmonious shapes and harmonic frequencies are inter-related. Through Jenny's experiments and research we have proof - that different sounds create different forms. Modern physics has verified that we are all vibrating atomic and sub-atomic particles. Everything has a resonant frequency, the frequency at which it most naturally vibrates, from the chair you may be sitting on to this book. Every part of your body also has a resonant frequency and ideal shape. This pattern is your original blueprint, which may become damaged by internal or external influences.

There is another concept which the ancients understood and which will eventually be recognized by modern scientists. This is the concept of "intention," the understanding that thought, vibration, resonance or sound has the ability to transmit the intention of the one creating the thought, vibration, resonance or sound to the one receiving the thought, vibration, resonance or sound.

Quartz Crystal Webs (Triangulation - See the Crystal Energy Web of Light - Inner Vision).

These are very effective healing energy webs. They are a fundamental geometric energy of initial creation; as such you should become proficient at placing them correctly around yourself and your clients.

Place three quartz crystals around yourself or, if working with another, the client, who can be either lying or sitting. If this is used for healing, the one above the head - or, if sitting, behind the back - should point away from you or your client.

The other two quartz crystals should be placed in such a position as to form a triangulation, pointing in towards yourself or the patient.

Pass your control crystal around yourself or the patient three times to join up the quartz crystals.

Allow 20 minutes for integration of the energies.

On no account must you leave your client unattended. Be ready to remove the crystals sooner, if your client has integrated the crystal energy very quickly.

Quartz Crystal Webs for Meditation (Triangulation - See the Crystal Energy Web of Light - Inner Vision).

The same quartz triangulation may be used for meditation, the difference being that the quartz crystal above the head (if in supine position) or behind the back (if in the Yoga position) should point towards the body. This allows for a considerable build-up of unified positive energy. If sitting in the Yoga position, a clear quartz crystal may be held in either hand, with the terminations either facing in or out. Experiment with holding them in different ways to find the optimum energy flow for yourself. Generally it has been observed that energy enters from the left-hand side and exists through the right-hand side.

Proceed as before. If used on yourself, do not stay in this longer than 20 minutes, until you are more experienced with the crystal vibrations.

For a client, allow 20 minutes for integration of the energies.

On no account must you leave your client unattended. Be ready to remove the crystals sooner, if your client has integrated the crystal energy very quickly.

Various quartz crystal configurations, or quartz triangulations, create certain energy patterns which will help the body to re-balance its vibrations and heal itself.

Twelve Crystal Web (Configuration - See the Crystal Energy Web of Light - Creative Fire).

The energy produced in this web is very powerful; the influence of the pattern is much greater than the sum of its parts. It is used for intense healing situations, or advanced meditation sessions.

1.   The most common system is to have the patient lying in a supine position, encircled by twelve clear quartz crystals:

> one by the head,
> one by the feet,
> five evenly spaced on each side of the body.

2.   Take a thirteenth, or your control crystal, in your hand and by passing it over the twelve crystals surrounding the patient's body you will create a unified vibrational healing field of energy around the patient.

3.   Have the patient lie in this position, allowing 20 minutes for integration of the energies.

4.   On no account must you leave your client unattended. Be ready to remove the crystals sooner, if your client has integrated the crystal energy very quickly.

5.   This type of crystal formation is used for full body, full energy system healing.

Merkaba Web (Star of David - See the Crystal Energy Web of Light - Sacred Sounds).

Another energy system is to have the patient sit on the floor in a Yoga fashion, holding a quartz crystal in the palm of each hand with the points facing in or out depending on the energy flow of the patient. (If the person is right-handed, the left hand should have the point facing towards the body and the right hand would hold a quartz crystal with the point facing away from the body. If the person was left-handed the reverse would be true. If the patient was ambidextrous you would have to check on the energy flow most suitable for them.)

Place six quartz crystals around them in the formation of a six-pointed star, with one point directly behind them and one point directly in front of them. Merkaba, the star of David, is also known as the seal of Solomon or the symbol for your holy Guardian Angel within your heart chakra. It also equates with yin/yang, agni/soma and the infinity symbol.

This type of healing is specifically used to enhance spiritual vibrations and awareness or for healing of karmic issues. Use your control crystal by standing over them and passing your control crystal in a circular motion (clockwise), connecting the six quartz crystals surrounding the client.

Do this twelve times, then allow them to rest in this position.

Allow 20 minutes for integration of the energies.

On no account must you leave your client unattended. Be ready to remove the crystals sooner, if your client has integrated the crystal energy very quickly.

You could also experiment with a rose quartz, citrine, or amethyst triangulation: each would give a different experience and outcome.

Pleiadean Star (Configuration - See the Crystal Energy Web of Light - Pleiadean Star).

This crystal web uses 7 clear quartz points, placed to form a Pleiadean star. The terminations should point towards the body.

Practical Geometric Exercises

The following exercises are designed specifically to help you develop a deeper understanding of geometric shapes and their effect on the energy system of the human body and aura. You will employ concentration, followed by contemplation and then finally move into meditation. It's good to learn concentration, then graduate to contemplation, and then finally move into deep meditation.

The fundamental difference between concentration and contemplation is that in concentration you imagine an object very concretely in front of you. You are different than the object that you project or imagine in front of you. In real contemplation, you experience yourself as the object, so you are there; you are experiencing from the inside. In meditation you merge your consciousness with the geometric shape and become the shape; this changes your perception of reality. By experiencing alternate realities we begin to understand how limited our everyday waking reality is; this frees up a lot of psychic energy and aids our spiritual growth.

You can also cut out the following geometric shapes in paper and sit down or lie on them; each will modify your energy field and give you a different perspective on reality. You could also draw out the following shapes on the floor. Square, triangle, circle, hexagon, octagon.

Some concentration, contemplation, meditation practices:

*   Practise your choice of these exercises for at least one minute several times a day.
*   As you get better at them, increase the time you spend on the exercise.
*   Begin by practising them with your eyes closed.
*   After you become proficient with them that way, practise with your eyes open.
*   Start with the ones that appeal to you the most.
*   Move into meditation space when you are proficient at contemplation.

1.   Imagine the outline of an equilateral triangle made out of pure light hanging perfectly still in the air in front of you.

   Hold that image as long as you can.

   This practice will give you a sense of balance, composure and confidence.

2.   Imagine the outline of a square made out of light hanging perfectly still in the air in front of you.

   Hold that image as long as you can.

   This practice will give you a sense of strength, security, stability and foundation.

84

3. Imagine the outline of a circle made out of light hanging perfectly still in the air in front of you.

   Hold that image as long as you can.

   This practice will give a blocked person a sense of flowing and moving of energy and grace.

4. Imagine a cube drawn out of light hanging perfectly still in the air in front of you.

   Keep one side of the cube facing you.

   With your imagination, as you inhale push that face backwards so that another face comes forward.

   As you exhale bring that face forward so that the other face goes backwards.

   This practice will give you control over your visualization and will develop your will power, increasing your sense of personal ability and self-worth. You will also find stability and inner strength in the cube. This exercise also gets you to work with the power of the breath.

5. Imagine a tetrahedron - a pyramid which has four faces that are all equilateral triangles - made of pure pristine clear quartz crystal hanging in the air in front of you.

   Keeping the crystal tetrahedron perfectly still, imagine that you are able to move around it, so you see from one angle, then another, then the top, then the bottom.

   This practice will give you control over your visualization and will develop your personal will power, increasing your sense of personal ability and self-worth. You will gain a deep understanding of the quartz crystal's sacred energy and manifestation.

6. Imagine yourself sitting inside a crystal tetrahedron, an angle to your back and facing a face.

   This gives you a sense of poise, composure, peace, harmony, tranquillity, self-control and security.

Part 9

Meditation

Many distinctive meditative traditions have come into being throughout the world during the last seven thousand years; each has generated specific theologies, ceremonies, visualisations and rituals through endless generations of deep profound spiritual exploration. Despite the apparent differences, all meditation and prayer of all traditions is one-goal orientated; the common theme is bringing human beings into direct experiential contact with the spiritual authenticity of the universe. By definition, there can be only one Infinite Presence, one Universal Creative Source, One Thread Soul. So, even though various human civilizations have generated quite interesting and diverse ways for accessing spiritual reality, the Divine Presence we seek communication with is always the same. Once we evolve and learn to look beyond concepts, we become emancipated - free to encounter - through personal, direct spiritual illumination - the divine radiant core of love and life that is our centre, our own personal consciousness. We can begin to work with this energy and allow it to guide, inspire, strengthen and encourage us. It is accessible to all who seek to grow in a positive direction. Once we become conscious of our own inner light, our Divinity, our 'Divine Aspect', our own source of unlimited goodness, we are never disempowered again. It will guide and nurture us if we let it, by sincerely seeking our own truth. Whether a person lives a spiritual life on his/her own, or is part of an organized tradition, the goal is the same: the attainment of peace of mind, purity and perfection or, as some call it, self-realization and enlightenment.

Let me list what meditation practice will do for you:

* Liberate your immense potential
* Enhance your health and emotional well-being
* Rejuvenate your body and improve your sense of self-worth
* Clear your mind and improve your concentration
* Amplify your personal healing power
* Stimulate harmonious, focused brain activity
* Restore the energy structure of your body and aura
* Awaken healing and personal growth
* Free subconscious hidden knowledge
* Release intuitive forces that genuinely evoke transformation
* Bring inner peace and tranquillity
* Improve your creativity by releasing past-life talents and divine gifts
* Prevent or minimize the problems of senility
* Give your life a sense of purpose, direction and joy

On a day-to-day basis, meditation is sought by many for relaxation and this is fine, for meditation will relax you - by clearing yourself of your daily concerns of your earthly personality, this allows access to higher information. The whole process of meditation is to bring about transformation. Normally this can be gradual, usually interspaced with periods of intense illumination. The one thing you can be sure of is that meditation will cause changes to happen in your subtle-energy anatomy. Specifically, your chakras will become activated and cleared of emotional debris and your divine presence or kundalini energies within the root chakra eventually will make their climb up the subtle pathways within the spinal cord to reach and activate the crown chakra. This evolutionary process will be facilitated at the meditator's own pace.

Meditation practised daily, over a period of many years, results in the gradual upliftment of the kundalini energies, which in turn opens and evolves each of the chakras from the root up to the crown in sequential order. As each chakra opens, subtle stresses that have developed throughout your life are slowly dissipated. This releasing of the blockages to life energy flowing through the chakras is greatly due to the kundalini force, but in reality it is also the gradual realizations of emotional and spiritual life lessons which must be learned before proper functioning of the chakras can be experienced. The process of meditation actually assists in understanding why you had blockages in your energy system; this is augmented by direct personal experiential contact by your higher self.

There is a vast difference in the chakras of an advanced meditator and someone who has not fully activated their chakras. As you evolve spiritually, the quality, vibrancy and resonance of the chakras is enhanced. In traditional lore the most important point to remember about the chakras is that, in a relatively unawakened person, the chakra lotus flower is envisioned as hanging downward from above the chakra. Thus the energies are being directed downwards, to sustain basic survival activities and materialistic pursuits. As you meditate on the chakras for a time, sending conscious attention and energy to each centre in sequential order, the lotus flower begins to turn upwards, so that kundalinin energy is directed upwards instead of only being spent on outward survival, materialistic pursuits and routine mental functioning. Of course this is a symbolic image, but it visually carries a very real relevance to what happens energetically during meditation and spiritual evolvement.

Actual Meditation Practice

The two senses that are the strongest are sight and sound; they are able to hold the ego's attention the longest, so in the relevant chapters on the chakras they will be worked with most, although there are other methods which we will employ. If you find it difficult to meditate, you may need to find out what kind of person you are, as with anything 'new' we all have different ways of learning or viewing the world: head, heart, or hand, otherwise known as cognitive, affective or psychomotor domain, also known as intellectual, emotional or practical in nature.

You need to find out what kind of personality you have (what is your incarnating personality's ego trap). Are you an intellectual giant, who likes to conceptualise ideas and ask millions of questions to hopefully to gain a deep thorough understanding before you can 'accept' knowledge? Or are you emotionally led and have great heart intuition and get an emotional feeling for the truth, the true nature of reality? Or do you like to physically feel the effects of wisdom, as they directly affect your physical and subtle body? Or are you a mixture of all three, as most people are?

In order to gain spiritual wisdom and attain personal growth towards empowered enlightenment, you will have to let go of your old outdated concepts, thoughts, feelings and emotions. You will have to become empty, before you can be filled, for as the old Buddhist saying goes, "you can't fill a pot that is already full" - you will have to make room inside yourself for your new self to grow, mature and fully take root, otherwise your meditation practice may be erratic. Remember, no one can do it for you. There are no quick fixes and it may take years to learn to 'meditate' correctly, but it is well worth the effort involved. In learning to meditate you have to 'wake' yourself up and become aware of the current 'drama' you are involved in. We will use in each chapter on the chakras two kinds of meditation, kundalini and healing, crystals, sound in the form of mantras, color, gem essence - and, above all, your divine essence will be employed in 'awakening' you.

Many people begin meditation in a goal-oriented state of mind, aiming towards their conceptualised ideal imaginary state of mystical bliss and total enlightenment. As you will discover quite quickly, these concepts are counter-productive; it is not a competition. There is in fact nowhere to go, nothing to do, no future, no past - you are already there, all that you are really seeking is right inside you, we just need to wake you up - to the immense power and beauty that is you. There is in reality only the eternal present moment. Its rediscovery is the theme of all meditation.

Meditation

The great cosmic joke of all time is - we are already enlightened. In the Christian terminology we are already living in the Christ Spirit, we are the Second Coming, that was the message brought to us all two thousand years ago. We are the Buddha, as they say in India. As the Zen tradition points out so clearly, there is "nowhere to go and nothing to do" to gain enlightenment. For those who work with Angels, we are the Angels. For those who work with the Ascended Masters, we are the Masters. For those who work with Spirit guides, we are our own guides. We are everyone and everything; in truth there is nothing outside us. This is all we have to remember, as we begin to gently awaken ourselves from our deep slumber.

Meditation can be seen as the process through which we rediscover our true identity beyond the confines of three-dimensional chronological time. The correct way to meditate is with calm eagerness to 'view' what is happening in your meditative expanding consciousness right now. Use your breath and heartbeat, they are the keys. You are breathing right now, in this present moment. Your heart is beating right now, in this present moment. You have energy flows in your body - tune into them; you are surrounded by a sea of cosmic energy - experience it. Your divine inner Master at the 'centre' of your being is waiting for you to tune into its illuminatory presence.

True meditation is simple, easy, safe and effective. The following are practical points regarding the basic techniques and stages of meditation.

They are basically intended for the beginner, although even the most accomplished meditator will find a review of them useful.

1. Have a regular time, place and practice.

2. The most effective times are dawn and dusk.

3. Try to have a separate room for meditation.

4. Keep it free from other vibrations and influences.

5. Purify it with incense and have a large amethyst crystal (an amethyst cluster will also work) to focus on.

6. When sitting, face north or east to take advantage of favourable magnetic vibrations.

7. Sit in a comfortable steady posture with the spine and neck held erect but not tense. This means that the base of the spine needs to be higher than the knees, thus tilting the pelvis forwards to a position where the spine naturally remains upright when relaxed. The easiest way of doing this is to put a small, firm cushion beneath the base of the spine. The psychic current must be able to flow unimpeded from the base of the spine to the top of the head.

8. Sit cross-legged; this forms a triangular path for the energy field and stops it dissipating in all directions.

9. Command the mind to be still for a specific length of time. (This states your focused intent).

10. Forget about the past, present and future, focus on the eternal 'now'.

11. Consciously tune in to your normal breathing pattern.

12. Allow your awareness of your breathing to expand effortlessly.

13. In the middle of your breathing experience your heartbeat.

14. Experience your sense of balance as gravity pulls on your body and your muscles respond with perfect precision to keep upright.

15. Allow your awareness to expand to encompass the whole of your body and aura.

16. Allow your eyes to gaze on the amethyst crystal.

17. Focus on the amethyst crystal, then slowly allow your eyes to close, being aware of any after-image or impression.

18. Become aware of the amethyst crystal begging to relax your whole energy field.

19. Let the chant Om rise up and manifest inside you, perhaps vocally as well.

20. Repetition of the Om mantra will free your mind; allow the Om to vibrate throughout your whole body and aura, until there is nothing else but pure vibration.

21. Experience this pure vibration; it will lead to pure thought, in which sound vibration merges with thought vibration.

22. With your eyes closed, concentrate on the space between the eyebrows; it is here that the Ida and Pingala, sacred conduits of energy, merge. It is here that the Ida and Pingala, the pair of opposites, generate what is called the third eye, that lies within the brain. This activates the pituitary and pineal gland into cosmic consciousness. It is here that the earthly opposites unite, where yin and yang become one

23. With practice, concentration develops, then contemplation, then meditation - duality disappears and meditation begins; over time, samadhi, the superconscious state, is reached.

24. Begin the practice of meditation with twenty-minute periods and increase to one hour. If the body is overcome by jerking or tremors, control them and keep the energy internalised.

25. Allow yourself plenty of time to come round to 'normal' everyday waking reality after meditation practice, at least in the beginning.

   If you don't have an amethyst crystal, you could use rose quartz or clear quartz. If you don't have a crystal, just follow the meditation steps but omit the crystal gazing; you will still experience deep states of meditation. The amethyst crystal merely aids your spiritual progress and awakening.

Part 10

Color

Color is an ancient method of natural healing. There were schools of color healing in ancient Egypt. In his book, *"The Seven Keys To Color Healing"*, the famous color researcher, Roland Hunt, writes: "In the ancient temples of Heliopolis, Egypt, the force of color was used, not only to aid worship, but also as a healing agent. These temples were oriented so that the sun shone through in such a way that its light was broken up into seven prismatic colors and suffering ones were bathed in that special color which they needed to restore health". Color surrounds and affects everyone, but few people realise how color can be used in a therapeutic form. Color plays a large part in our lives and whether we are aware of the effects or not it is a very powerful force. The colors that surround you can make you happy or sad, healthy or sick, tense or relaxed. There is no doubt that our bodies are aroused and energized by some colors, or calmed and relaxed by others. Colors can be restorative - and they can make you agitated, lethargic or ill. The health of all our internal organs, the circulation of the blood, the nervous, lymphatic and endocrine systems, in truth all the workings of the body are constantly altered by the colors to which we expose ourselves. Mentally and emotionally, color works on a deep level, changing our mood and our sense of well-being, as well as others' perception of us. Leonardo da Vinci as quoted in *"The Seven Keys To Color Healing"* maintained "that the power of meditation could be enhanced tenfold if carried out under the influence of violet rays passing through the stained glass window of a quiet church."

Humans are not the only creatures on our planet who are affected by color. In the animal, insect and plant worlds color can mean survival or extinction. Color is used to attract, repel, camouflage, ward off danger and send sexual signals. Color is intrinsic to life and it is as significant to our species as it is to the plant and animal kingdoms. We must become consciously aware of the language of color for our own physical well-being, emotional happiness and spiritual upliftment.

Nature has furnished us with color to support not only the body, mind and emotions, but also the spirit. It nourishes our whole system, supplying a vital energy that is an essential part of life. We respond to color actively or passively in all that we do. Light waves affect us every minute of our lives and penetrate our energetic system, whether we are awake or asleep, sighted or blind. Our growth, blood pressure, body temperature, muscular activity, sleep patterns and immune system are all affected by light rays. The colored rays affect not only our physical bodies, but our emotions, moods, mental faculties and our spiritual nature. We all have an intimate relationship with color. We often give ourselves an intuitive color treatment by choosing jewellery or clothes of a certain color, or by surrounding ourselves with specific colors in our homes, offices and gardens. Most of our reactions are, however, unconscious and it is only when we start to use the qualities of color in an informed way that we harness this wonderful vital force to improve the quality of our lives and our overall sense of total well-being.

The universe is a magnetic field of positive and negative charges, vibrating constantly to produce electromagnetic waves. Each of these has a different wavelength and speed of vibration: this forms the electromagnetic spectrum. We can see about 40 per cent of the colors contained in sunlight. So although white light looks colorless it is made up of assorted definite color vibrations, which have not only wavelengths but also a "corpuscular structure". The radiant energy of pure sunlight is a vital component in nourishing our bodies, minds and spirits. Each color vibration has its own quality. Sight is your dominant sense, occupying some three-fifths of your conscious attention.

91

As shown by Newton, white light is composed of all the colors of the rainbow intermingled. By passing a narrow beam of white light through a glass prism it can be spread out into a whole series of spectrum colors according to their wavelength. There are only six main color names (or seven if one includes indigo). Red is the longest wavelength we can see and has the slowest frequency and vibration. Its energy is passionate, warm and stimulating. Violet has the shortest wavelength and the quickest vibration. It is calm, cool and purifying.

At either end of the visible spectrum of light are very many wavelengths we, as humans, cannot see. Ultraviolet light is just beyond violet and further beyond this are electromagnetic rays with increasing frequencies as the wavelengths get progressively shorter: these include X-rays and gamma rays. At the other end, infrared light is found just beyond red light. Just as red has warming qualities, although it gives off more concentrated heat (these qualities are utilized in infrared lamps), beyond this are electromagnetic rays with increasing wavelengths and decreasing frequencies: these include radio waves. The ancient Yogic mystics have long been able to see colors outside the 'normal' range during meditation.

The human eye consists essentially of a flexible lens of changeable focal length, limited by a diaphragm (the iris), through which light is focused to form an inverted image as the retina, which lines the back wall of the eye. The retina is connected with the brain (where all messages of light and color are translated into sensations) by the optic nerve. Impulses from the right eye travel to the left side of the brain, while those from the left side travel to the right half of the brain. This action of the nerve fibres means that they actually cross over, in part of the brain called the optic chiasma. The sensory layer of the retina consists of small rod-like structures interspersed with shorter conical bodies, which are known respectively as rods and cones. Only the cones are thought to be sensitive to colors and only the cones are capable of acute vision. A small central area known as the yellow spot near the emergence of the optic nerve contains cones only, and it is here that the image of an object is focused for the clearest possible vision. The cones that are sensitive to green light are situated directly in the middle of the retina, allowing light to fall in the centre of the eye. This will make the green color the most relaxing on the eyes and, in turn, the mind.

The rods, on the other hand, are the structures which enable us to see to some extent in a dim light: for this reason they are the chief feature in the retina of a nocturnal animal. The rods contain a reddish substance (rhodopsin), commonly called the visual purple, which is rapidly bleached on exposure to light. The visual purple can thus only begin to form in the dark, and its presence can make the sensitivity of the eye several thousand times greater than it is in bright light - hence the power of the dark-adapted eye to see objects which would be quite invisible before this transformation has had time to take place. Rods therefore are more light sensitive, allowing us to see in dim light, but do not record color, only shades of gray.

There have been many theories of color vision and a final answer to all problems connected with this intricate subject is still to be found. For most practical purposes, however, the 'three color' theories, particularly the Young-Helmholtz theory, serves very well. According to the simplest form of this theory, the human retina contains three varieties of cone, which are sensitive to the red-yellow, green, and blue-violet parts of the spectrum respectively. It is assumed that three light-sensitive chemical compounds are present in these different groups of cones, each of which undergoes a breakdown when exposed to light of the correct wavelengths, transmitting messages to the brain. The spectral regions where these receptors are active overlap considerably. Thus in the central part of the spectrum all three will be functioning, though the green receptors will be much more active than the other two, which will function alone at the extreme ends of the spectrum. The action of these three receptors in varying strengths permits all familiar sensations of color by persons of normal vision.

More recent work seems to indicate the presence of not merely three but as many as seven different types of receptors. About 10 per cent of men and less than 1 per cent of women are in some measure color-defective, or are color-blind. In such persons it is supposed that one or more of the red, green or violet-sensitive color receptors is not functioning, thus limiting and distorting to a lesser or greater degree the perception of hue.

However, not all the light impulses received through our physical eyes are used solely for the purpose of sight. Nervous impulses from the eyes travel not only to the visual cortex of the brain but also via the hypothalamus to the pituitary and pineal glands. We find, therefore, that many body functions are stimulated or retarded by light, and different colors of light have specific effects on the brain and central nervous system. The pituitary gland, known as the 'master gland' of the endocrine system, is first affected by colored light. It produces substances that regulate the hormones produced by the endocrine glands. These hormones regulate our body functions, which include growth patterns, sleep, our temperature control, our sex drive, our energy levels, our metabolic rate, and appetite. It has been discovered that our pineal gland, located deep within our brain, is also sensitive to light. This gland is our internal body clock, producing a substance known as melatonin, which controls our sleep cycles and also inhibits sexual maturation. Daylight suppresses the production of melatonin and at night the lack of sunlight increases its production. The quality and amount of the light reaching the pineal gland will also alter with the changing seasons.

Therefore the proportions of the colors within sunlight, according to the season, cause our body functions, like those of plants and animals, to mimic the energy of the seasons. In summer we are full of vitality and life and very active, whilst in the winter months we feel sluggish, depressed and inactive. Color affects us even when our eyes are closed. Light is required for our cells to function normally and individual colors affect them by causing changes in growth and behaviour patterns. There is a lot of research in progress at the moment into S.A.D. or Seasonal Affective Disorder. You can even purchase SAD lamps that mimic the effects of sunlight on the human body. SAD is typically identified in certain individuals by their symptoms: feelings of deep depression (even feeling suicidal), but only in the autumn and winter months. This is due to the shorter daylight hours and lack of bright light. These individuals may also put on extra weight in winter and lose it in the summer months. Many SAD lamp users have found that they no longer feel depressed in winter or put on excess weight. I have tested several of these SAD lamps for myself and clients, therefore I can personally attest to their effectiveness.

As we become more aware of the influence of color in our lives, the next step is to use it for its therapeutic properties. One very effective way is to make color essences or color tinctures. Distilled water may be placed in direct sunlight in either a bottle of colored glass or one that has been wrapped in a suitable colored see-through material. During the exposure to the pranic forces of sunlight, the distilled water becomes activated with a positive charge with the energetic frequency of the particular color filter used. The essence prepared can be given orally to treat the appropriate disorder. Color therapy, or chromotherapy, has many forms and applications.

The use of color tinctures or hydrochromatic therapy uses the principle by which pure distilled water may be imprinted with vibrational color characteristics for the purposes of healing. Each major visible color has particular qualities or resonance linked to the chakra with which it vibrates. An understanding of the nature of the chakras and their energetic links to the body's physiology is all that is needed for using a particular color essence to ameliorate specific dis-ease, emotional states or even for spiritual development. You can use any of the following methods to help you choose which color essence would be appropriate for you:

*   Use a pendulum and dowse over a list of colors to find one that will help you.
*   Get a friend or relative to help you with kinesiology.
*   Intuitively choose one.
*   Use the color essence appropriate to the dis-eased part of your body.

However you decide, it is relatively easy to make an essence for yourself.

To make a color essence you will need:

1. A colored gel or colored glass or piece of colored material.

2. A small bottle of purified water or distilled water (from the chemist or pharmacy). Distilled water is the best as it contains no impurities or energetic signature. This facilitates, when energized by the pranic forces of sunlight, the optimum energetic interaction, which allows the color essence to fully interact not only with the physical body but all the subtle bodies as well. Water is a universal storage medium of vibrational energy; when activated by the solar energies it allows a therapeutic essence to be made.

3. A clear glass container or you could use a colored container, but you must make this part of your color essence.

4. Brandy or other preservative.

5. Glass dropper bottle (not clear).

6. Three pure quartz crystals with terminations. (These are to be placed around your color essence during preparation, to keep out unwanted outside energies.)

Method:

Add purified water from the chemist to the clear glass container, place your chosen gel/cloth/glass over the clear glass container.

Surround the container with three clear quartz crystal points in triangulation, pointing inwards, to keep away unwanted outside energies.

Leave your container in a place where it is unlikely to be disturbed by negative energies and away from pets, pests, etc.

Charge it in sunlight as required.

Dowse, meditate, etc. to find out how long to leave it. Normally three hours is sufficient, but if using the full sun method and the temperature is over 80 degrees, the water will start evaporating, so you will need less exposure time. The normal procedure is to leave it in direct sunlight for several hours during the early morning sun. The solar pranic energies are most potent in the early hours of the day. As with flowers and gemstones, certain etheric properties from the color become transferred to the water, which becomes charged with their particular vibration.

The original mixture is used to make a mother bottle.

A stock bottle is then made from the mother bottle.

The dosage bottles are made as required from the stock bottle.

Mother Bottle

Contains one-third of your original mixture and two-thirds brandy or other spirit.

You must fill the mother bottle with brandy before placing the water from the bowl into the mother bottle, otherwise the vibration of the color essence could permeate the brandy bottle where it could enter other storage bottles being prepared then or in the future.

This mother bottle will keep for ever if stored correctly.

Stock Bottle

Dowse to find out how many drops of the mother bottle should be placed in the stock bottle.

It is wise to add seven drops, whether the size of the stock bottle is several drams or several ounces, because color essences work with the influence of the seven dimensions. If you use less than seven drops to the stock bottle, it will still work, but the effects may not permeate all levels and dimensions. If your color essence is from a very high vibrational color you may need to place up to twelve drops to maintain access to the higher chakras above the head and the corresponding dimensions. Then fill the bottle with one half brandy, one half purified water.

Dosage Bottle

Dowse to find out how many drops of the stock bottle should be placed in the dosage bottle (dark glass, with dropper). This may vary, but as with the stock bottle the number of drops will correspond to the dimensional access. Then fill with one-third brandy, two-thirds purified water (or alternatively all water, in which case the dosage bottle must be kept in the fridge and will only last two weeks).

*   Label all bottles with the color and state whether mother, stock or dosage bottle.

*   Give the date made and, on dosage bottles, the expiry date and the number and frequency of drops required.

*   Your name and telephone number should also be added.

*   Store with a clear quartz crystal, suitably programmed.

*   The area you store them should be a 'clean space' and it is wise to take special precautions. Before storing the essences, first wash the area with distilled water using an organic cloth, such as linen or cotton. After cleaning the area leave it empty for several days prior to use.

*   You could also store them under a pyramid. If you have a lot of bottles to store you may need four clear quartz crystals, one for each corner of the space.

*   Never leave the bottles in sunlight, because extreme heat can damage the color essences; cold temperatures are all right, however.

*   Also remember to keep them away from harmful energies and environmental pollutants.

*   Do not keep different varieties too close together or, in time, there will be a transference of energy from one to another.

*   Remember - the more you dilute the original mixture, the stronger the vibration.

*   You can make crystal, gemstone, flower, tree or other energy essences in a similar way.

Using the color remedies:

Color Essence

Taking color remedies is a very personal process; how often and for how long you take a essence will depend on how quickly your body integrates the color vibration. This will also depend on the circumstances surrounding the emotions or dis-ease you are treating. If your mood is merely transitory or you're in a small crisis situation such as a job interview or driving test, you may require only one dose, but if you've been feeling the same for a longer period there is no set time limit as to how long you can take your chosen essence or remedies. The same goes for illness: long-standing problems may take longer to respond. They can be taken by anyone of any age. They work in harmony with your body and are 100% natural and can be used with any conventional or complementary medicines and treatments. If you are using the color essence for treating a long-standing or chronic condition, I have found it is best to review the essence and its actions at least once a fortnight. This is the time when you will decide whether to change the essence for yourself or your client or to continue for another two weeks.

If you are taking a color essence for spiritual development, you may need to review it more often, as they can be integrated very quickly by those who are energy aware (we are talking about minutes and seconds, rather than days). Also, if you are taking the color essence in a group situation, especially for group meditation or spiritual attunement or alignment, the integration period is very fast, almost instant. This is due to the amplification of the overall group energetic dynamics. If you are taking the color essence in an Earth 'power' area, such as Stonehenge, Glastonbury, Sedona or the Pyramids in Egypt, the essences will be amplified and the integration period substantially reduced.

These are some of the different methods of taking a color essence:

1. Place 1 to 7 drops directly under the tongue. For spiritual development you can take up to 12 drops.

2. Dilute 1 to 7 drops in a small glass of mineral water and sip slowly throughout the day until relief is obtained. Up to 7 essences may be taken together if required.

3. Rub a few drops on your palms, then pass your hands through the aura using a sweeping motion.

4. Rub a few drops on your palms, then inhale deeply from your cupped hands.

5. Put a few drops in the bath. For spiritual development you can use up to 12 drops.

6. Put a few drops in your washing, with the washing powder.

7. Add 1 to 7 drops directly to massage oil.

8. Apply to the temples before meditation.

9. Use on the meridian system instead of a crystal. It will be just as effective as placing a crystal or gemstone on the meridian point(s).

Color Essence Body Cream

This is made by placing seven drops of the color essence or essences (you may use up to seven different essences together) into an aqueous cream. (You will need to keep this refrigerated or use a preservative in the cream).

Do not ingest this color cream, it is for topical use only. Its effectiveness will be felt in the aura and directly within the body because it is absorbed trans-dermally.

1. Apply to the area of the body that is manifesting a painful vibration or feels sore, tense or congested.

2. Apply to the palms of both hands before giving a therapy session.

3. Apply to the temples before meditation.

4. Apply to the temples before sleep.

5. Apply in a circle around the waist for complete auric integration or protection.

Color Essence Aura Spray

This is made by placing seven drops of the color essence or essences (you may use up to seven different essences together) into a spray bottle filled with purified water. (You will need to keep this refrigerated or use a preservative in the water).

1. Rub a drop or two on the palms of both hands.

2. Rub a drop on the pulse points: wrist, throat, forehead, back of neck, soles of both feet.

3.   Rub a few drops on your palms, then pass your hands through the aura using a sweeping motion. (Aura cleansing).

4.   Rub a few drops on your palms, then inhale deeply from your cupped hands.

5.   Spray directly into the aura, especially any areas that may feel stuck or congested.

6.   Spray around your room.

7.   Put a few drops in the bath.

8.   Put a few drops in your washing, with the washing powder.

9.   Add to massage oil.

10.   Spray directly on the body.

Solarized water

This is a simple way of drinking sunlight-charged water. You can literally bottle the sun's force by placing a bottle of clear mineral water in the sun for one day. Sip slowly. It is wonderful and natural. It rejuvenates and revitalizes you. The subtle effects of sunlight are critical in charging water: it relates to the prana that is contained in sunlight. The Hindus have known for millennia about the pranic beneficial power of sunlight. So have the Chinese; they call it Chi. Prana or Chi permeates everything; it gives life to every cell in the body and a balanced supply is necessary for maintaining optimum physical health, emotional well-being and mental agility and optimism.

Gemstone or Crystal Solarized Water

You can add gemstones and crystals to solarized water too; this is a wonderful way of using the crystal vibration - by drinking it, allowing the body to gently absorb the crystal energy. The effects may be a little slower than taking a gem essence, though.

It is a good way to boost other therapy treatments.

Red, orange and yellow (magnetic) gemstones are good 'drinks' in the morning; if you take them later in the day the effects may keep you awake all night.

Green (balance) gemstones are perfect at lunch time - but you can 'drink' them at any time.

Pink (integration) gemstones are used for attuning to relationship energies at any time of the day or night.

Blue, indigo, purple and violet (calming) gemstones are only 'taken' in the afternoon or at night. They are good for meditation or relaxation.

1.   Fill a clear glass tumbler, glass jug or bottle with pure spring or filtered water.

2.   Place the suitably cleansed, dedicated, programmed etc. crystal or gemstone very carefully into the water.

3.   Leave the glass/jug/bottle in a position that allows the sunlight to fall upon it. Even thirty minutes will make a difference to the water. I would suggest seven hours is best. The longer the exposure time, the stronger the effect.

Red, orange or yellow gemstone water must be sipped very slowly. (Yellow gemstone water must not be taken after 6 pm because of its elimination effect).

Green, blue, indigo and violet gemstone water can be taken a little faster.

Experiment with your level of sensitivity.

Shut your eyes and take a sip of solarized water.

Then take a sip of water from the same source without solarization.

See if you are able to notice a difference. (If you don't detect a difference, do not worry: you will still get the benefit from solarized water.)

Some sensitive people can detect a difference after the water has been instilled with crystals for only five minutes. Try it yourself. Then try it after twenty minutes' exposure and so on up to twelve hours. Some gemstones are easier to detect than others. Do not solarize gemstone water for longer than twelve hours, otherwise the water becomes too intense.

The Vibrational Properties of Color Essences

Red - Ray of Passion: Slowest vibration of the spectrum: Infra-red

Parts of the body: genitals and reproductive organs; gonads, ovaries; regulates adrenalin release into the bloodstream; blood; circulation; eases stiff muscles; feet; legs, knees, hips. Avoid red for all angry conditions, agitation, hyperactivity, fever, ulcers, high blood pressure, swellings, inflammation and nervous disorders. Also never place red or a red crystal anywhere near the third eye, or shine a red light anywhere near the eyes or top of the head.

Uses:

* Survival issues
* Dynamic, removes fear
* Action, life-force, courage, stamina
* Detoxification by removing inertia
* Warms the body, stops chills
* Restores the will to live
* Increases physical energy and can be used if you are feeling tired.
* Signifies and arouses lust, desire, armour, intensity

Stones Red jasper, ruby, garnet.

Rose Pink - Ray of Love: White and red in perfect balance

Parts of the body: aids digestion; any part of the body that you dislike or feel is un-lovely.

Uses:

* Spiritual love, universal love, compassion
* Forgiveness
* Affection, romance
* Comforting and nurturing
* Use after an operation or dentistry
* This is the color of love
* Ideal for developing a loving attitude, for yourself and others
* Gives emotional balance

Stones Rose quartz, rhodochrosite, rhodonite, pink tourmaline, morganite.

Magenta - Ray of Spiritual Upliftment: Red and violet in perfect balance

Parts of the body: the entire endocrine system; clears fungus conditions and warts

Uses:

* Releases sorrow
* Infra-red and ultraviolet in perfect balance for divine creativity

Stones Magenta-colored tourmaline, almandine garnet.

98

Pale Pink - Ray of Affection: The whiter shade of red

Parts of the body: all.

Uses:

*   For the newborn
*   For birth and re-birth
*   For new beginnings
*   For mid-life crisis
*   For bereavement and loss (very gentle action)

Stones Rose quartz, rhodonite, pink tourmaline, morganite, kunzite.

Orange - Ray of Creativity: Red and yellow in perfect balance

Parts of the body: lower back, lower intestines; abdomen and kidneys; governs the adrenal function; aids digestion. Never place orange or an orange-colored crystal (carnelian) anywhere near the third eye, or shine an orange light into the eyes.

Uses:

*   Ameliorates grief, bereavement and loss (trauma)
*   Enhanced creativity
*   Optimism and positive view of life
*   Ameliorates bronchitis and asthma
*   Useful during the menopause
*   Balances hormones and aids fertility
*   Helps ease fears and phobias
*   Very motivating, balances body energy levels, increases vitality
*   Eases constipation

Stones Carnelian, amber, orange calcite, sunstone (orange).

Peach - Ray of Compassion: Red, yellow and white in perfect balance

Parts of the body: emotions; lungs; digestive system; skin.

Uses:

*   Eases breathing problems
*   Eases painful and difficult memories
*   Relaxation and rejuvenation
*   As orange, only much more gentle

Stones Peach-colored carnelian, peach calcite, peach moonstone.

Yellow - Ray of Wisdom: Brightest color of the spectrum

Parts of the body: pancreas; solar plexus; liver; gall-bladder; spleen; middle stomach; nervous system; digestive system; skin.

Uses:

*   Mental agility and learning enhancement
*   Sunshine
*   Wisdom and intellect stimulation
*   Concentration aid
*   Upliftment, freedom, laughter and joy
*   Weight loss for body and mind, increases self-control

* Breaks down cellulite
* Cleanses the body of toxins
* Raises self-esteem and brings feelings of total well-being
* A very good communication color
* Helps to stimulate conversation, prevents shyness and gives courage
* Prevents mental confusion

Stones Citrine, topaz, golden calcite (especially stellar beams), sunstone (golden).

Emerald Green - Ray of Balance: Yellow and blue in perfect harmony

Parts of the body: thymus; heart; lungs; shoulders and chest.

Uses:

* Personal growth
* Brings harmony and balance in all areas
* Attunement to nature and the devic kingdoms
* Eases claustrophobia
* Helps to balance hyperactivity in children
* Balances and stabilizes the nervous system
* The ray of great healers and healing
* Soothes emotions
* Reduces mental confusion

Stones Emerald, malachite, green calcite, chrysoprase, green aventurine, moldavite, green tourmaline.

Turquoise - Ray of Truth: Blue, green and yellow in perfect harmony

Parts of the body: throat; chest; thymus gland; arms and hands.

Uses:

* Natural tranquilliser
* Calms the nerves
* Ameliorates emotional turmoil
* Heartfelt communication
* Good for 'healing' relationships
* Used for overcoming self-sabotage
* Used for centering
* Balances the emotions during a coping crisis and nervous stress
* Ameliorates panic attacks

Stone Turquoise.

Blue - Ray of Communication

Parts of the body: thyroid and parathyroid; upper lungs; jaw; arms; base of the skull; and body weight.

Uses:

* Seeker of truth and knowledge
* Combats fear of speaking the truth
* Reduces fevers and calms hot conditions where there is too much heat in the body
* Eases stiff necks and stiff-necked attitudes
* Heals ear and throat infections
* Natural pain reliever
* Aids weight loss by encouraging communication, thereby releasing stored words

Color

*   Blue can help bring down high blood pressure
*   Good for the sickroom and for those terminally ill
*   Eases menstrual cramps and haemorrhoids
*   Royal color of integrity
*   Calms the mind
*   Helps you to think more clearly
*   The intellectual and mind color
*   Will soothe your soul

Stones Blue sapphire, azurite, lapis lazuli, blue topaz, blue lace agate, Siberian blue quartz, blue tourmaline.

Indigo - Ray of Devotion: Balance of dark blue and dark violet

Parts of the body: the pituitary gland; the skeleton; lower brain; eyes and sinuses.

Uses:

*   Aids intuition and spiritual knowledge
*   Strongest painkiller of the rainbow spectrum
*   Releases negativity from the skeletal structure
*   Astral antiseptic and astral toxin release (clears negative thought forms)
*   Kills bacteria in food, water or air
*   Clears pollution on all levels
*   Ameliorates chronic sinus complaints (unshed tears)
*   Eases insomnia
*   Releases migraine headaches and pain
*   Ameliorates overactive thyroid conditions
*   Breaks up tumours and growths
*   Helps ease kidney complaints
*   Indigo helps to control diarrhoea
*   Eases bronchitis, asthma, lung conditions
*   Lowers high blood pressure
*   Ameliorates back problems, especially sciatica, lumbago, any spinal complaint
*   Transmutes and purifies negativity
*   Good for spiritual teachers and writers
*   Indigo can be addictive
*   Indigo is the domain of mystery and psychic understanding
*   The ray of artists and the acting profession

Stones Iolite, blue tourmaline.

Purple - Ray of Spirituality: Balance of blue and red: Highest and fastest vibration in the rainbow

Parts of the body: the pineal gland; top of the head; the crown; brain; scalp.

Uses:

*   Ameliorates internal inflammation
*   Eases heart palpitations
*   Aids the correct function of the immune system
*   Ameliorates bruises, swellings and black eyes
*   Very intense energy, so a little goes a long way (never shine the purple vibration into the client's eyes. Only use with closed eyes or on the back of the client's head).

Stones Amethyst, purple fluorite, sugilite, charoite.

101

Violet - Ray of Spiritual Service: Paler than purple, not as intense

Parts of the body: the pineal gland; top of the head; the crown; brain; scalp.

Uses:

*   Spiritual dedication
*   Calms emotional turbulence
*   Eases eye problems and eye strain
*   Used for past life regression
*   Aids intuition
*   Aids psychic abilities
*   Allows for full soul development
*   Clears karmic debris

Stones Amethyst, purple fluorite, sugilite, charoite.

Amethyst - Ray of Protection: Paler than purple, much more blue than red

Parts of the body: the pineal gland; top of the head; the crown; brain; scalp.

Uses:
*   Gateway to the soul
*   Enables you to 'see' visions
*   Stops addiction and addictive traits within the personality
*   Allows psychic protection
*   Draws out pain
*   Aids the balancing of the immune system when citrine yellow is used as the stabilizing color
*   Cleanses and purifies anywhere it touches

Stones Amethyst, purple fluorite, sugilite, charoite.

Lavender - Ray of Sensitivity: Pale purple

Parts of the body: any area that has body armour, or holding on to tension.

Uses:
*   Lavender will gently allow you to let go of pain
*   Lavender clears anaesthetics from the body
*   Lavender will allow you to be more open, fragile and sensitive in a positive feminine way
*   Will ameliorate drug addiction
*   Will ameliorate pain

Stones Lavender-colored amethyst, lavender fluorite, charoite.

Sun Gold - Ray of Knowledge and Understanding (The end of the rainbow is the pot of Gold)

Parts of the body: thyroid (underactive); pancreas; solar plexus; liver; gall-bladder; spleen; middle stomach; nervous system; digestive system; skin.

Uses:
*   Aids assimilation of knowledge
*   Aids assimilation of vitamins
*   Vitality and spiritual abundance
*   Eases irritable bowel syndrome
*   Ameliorates underactive thyroid problems
*   Ameliorates scars and scar tissue
*   Helps ease the male menopause
*   Rids the body of parasites and parasitic energies on all levels
*   Attunement to the Sun and Solar Lords of Light

Stone Gold.

Silver - Ray of Reflection

Parts of the body: kidneys; all fluid functions; menstruation; the mind.

Uses:

*   Shielding and reflective
*   Flowing, graceful fluidity brings freedom from emotional hang-ups
*   Attunement to the moon, stars and cosmos
*   Allows intuition and inner guidance of the divine feminine within
*   Good for dissolving negative relationships
*   Can help those troubled with schizophrenia symptoms

Stone Silver.

Iridescent Rainbow Light - Supreme Ray: Cosmic Light: Brilliance

Parts of the body: affects all areas of the body and aura; multidimensional.

Uses:

*   Restores a person's vibrancy
*   Used for positive change
*   Used as a 'cure all' by color therapists
*   Clears rooms of negativity
*   Clears the aura of negativity
*   New beginnings

Stones Very clear quartz, phenacite, danburite, diamond, Herkimer diamond, petalite, clear calcite.

White - Ray of Peace: Contains all other colors

Parts of the body: collective functioning of the whole endocrine system; white of the eye; teeth.

Uses:

*   For peace and tranquillity
*   Begins the process of initiating well-being
*   Exposes the hidden, lost or forgotten
*   Pristine, lightness, openness
*   A fresh start, just like a blank page
*   Purity, calming and soothing

Stones Clear quartz, snow quartz, white moonstone.

Black - Ray of Mystery: Holds all the other colors captive by absorbing them

Parts of the body: when seen in the aura it means dis-ease: not normally used in color therapy.

Uses:

*   Contains, holds and hides
*   Deep, dark and secret seeds can be unearthed with black
*   It can be protective, womb-like
*   It can be used for protection and authority, even intimidation
*   Winter personalities love this color

Stones Black tourmaline, obsidian, deep-colored smoky quartz, snowflake obsidian.

Grey - Ray of Restriction: Used by those who conform or want to hide

Parts of the body: never use in healing; when seen in the aura, dis-ease is evident.

Uses:

* Used as armouring
* Puritanical

Stones Hematite, grey agate.

Brown - Ray of the Earth Mother: Deep inside the earth the seed lies waiting for spring

Parts of the body: not normally used in healing except for russet red browns, which are warming, comforting and can attune you to the Earth and the animal kingdoms.

Uses:

* Stability, earthing, solid and caring
* Basic security
* Tunes you in to nature

Stones Brown agates, smoky quartz, mahogany obsidian.

Color Meditation - The Rainbow Bridge

This next meditation is very powerful: it will change your life if you let it. So let us take a look at the rainbow. We have no need to search in the sky, or look very far, we are the rainbow, it lies within each and every one of us, within our integrated chakra system and aura. So we will work our color healing meditation through the chakra system in sequential order. We use the seven master chakras, as each master chakra gives off its own unique color signature. When a person is healthy, strong and vibrant, so is the chakra color and we find the human body and human aura is a resplendent vibrant rainbow. When there is a serious physical, emotional, mental or spiritual imbalance or illness, certain colors will look impure, dirty, dim or drab; sometimes a color can even be absent altogether.

1. Sit in a comfortable steady posture with the spine and neck held erect but not tense. This means that the base of the spine needs to be higher than the knees, so tilting the pelvis forwards to a position where the spine naturally remains upright when relaxed. The easiest way of doing this is to put a small, firm cushion beneath the base of the spine. The psychic current must be able to flow unimpeded from the base of the spine to the top of the head.

2. Sit cross-legged; this forms a triangular path for the energy field and stops it dissipating in all directions.

3. Command the mind to be still for a specific length of time.

4. Consciously regulate the breath; begin with five minutes of deep breathing.

5. Focus on the base chakra and visualise or feel a vibrant red light bringing activation, healing, balance, strength and integration. When all energy movement/sensation is completed, allow the red light to change to a beautiful violet color and gently feel/visualise it moving up to the next chakra.

6. Focus on the sacral chakra and visualise or feel a glowing vibrant orange light bringing activation, healing, balance, creativity and integration. When all energy movement/sensation is completed, allow the orange light to change to a beautiful violet color and gently feel/visualise it moving up to the next chakra.

7. Focus on the solar plexus chakra and visualise or feel a glowing yellow light bringing activation, healing, warmth, balance and integration. When all energy movement/sensation is

completed, allow the yellow light to change to a beautiful violet color and gently feel/visualise it moving up to the next chakra.

8. Focus on the heart chakra and visualise or feel a comforting green light bringing activation, healing, balance, integration and acceptance. When all energy movement/sensation is completed, allow the green light to change to a beautiful violet color and gently feel/visualise it moving up to the next chakra.

9. Focus on the throat chakra and visualise or feel a soothing blue light bringing activation, healing, balance, integration and peaceful flowing communication. When all energy movement/sensation is completed, allow the blue light to change to a beautiful violet color and gently feel/visualise it moving up to the next chakra.

10. Focus on the third eye chakra and visualise or feel a soothing indigo blue light bringing activation, healing, balance, insight and integration. When all energy movement/sensation is completed, allow the indigo light to change to a beautiful violet color and gently feel/visualise it moving up to the next chakra.

11. Focus on the crown chakra and visualise or feel the calming violet light bringing activation, healing, balance, purification, integration and wisdom. When all energy movement/sensation is completed, allow the violet light to cascade out of the crown chakra and into the aura. Visualise or feel it like a fountain, as it cleanses, activates, heals and purifies the whole of the auric shell.

12. Allow yourself plenty of time to come back to everyday reality

Part 11

Sound

Sound is generated as the vibratory motion of particles and objects. The vibrations that manifest as sound portray an energy, a sonic vibrational pattern, that is found throughout nature - not only within ourselves and our world, but far beyond, into the realms of moon, stars and the cosmos. The vibrational patterns of sound possess the key to understanding the patterns of manifestation and organisation of matter in the physical universe. As scientists and healers begin to understand the relationship between the vibrational patterns of sound and the inner structure of matter, they will harness them by tapping into a whole new universe of ideas and applications of energy for healing and technology. Due to the limitations of human physiology, our own ears can only detect an infinitesimal fraction of the vast vibratory spectrum. On the cosmic scale, sound is a universal, unseen power, able to bring about profound changes on many levels: physical, emotional and spiritual. This chapter looks at how you can harness and direct the power of sound - as the vibratory energies of your own voice, and as sounds from the world around - making them resonate through your body and mind, to bring physical and emotional well-being, and in the context of this book awaken spiritually.

Sound is among the most transformative and recuperative emotional healing energies on the planet. It can relax us and make us tranquil, or move us to great heights of passion. Sound can restore balance and harmony to our lives. Conversely, sound also has the ability to adversely affect us and bring our already stressed-out vibratory rates to new levels of imbalance, disease and disharmony. What is the difference in the sounds that make us feel balanced, centred and at peace and those that distress us?

Sound can affect us on all levels - physical, emotional, mental and spiritual. Beneficial sounds for us are often sounds that we consider 'sacred'. These sounds seem to have the ability to energize, renew, centre and harmonize us. There are reasons for this. Knowledge of sound as a therapeutic and transformative power is very old. The Ancient Mystery Schools of Greece, Rome, Egypt, Tibet, China and India had great knowledge of sound as being the primary creative force in the universe. The ancients knew what the modern physicists now understand, that all is in a state of constant vibration. "The World is Sound," these ancient mystics proclaimed and indeed it would appear to be so. Let us examine the basic tenets of many of the spiritual paths of the world: we will find a commonality in them. They all share the belief that the world was created through sound. Here are but a few examples. In Genesis, from the Old Testament, one of the first statements is, "And the Lord said 'Let there be light!' " In St John, from the New Testament, it is written, "In the beginning was the Word, the Word was with God, and the Word was God." From the Vedas of the Hindu tradition come the writing that, "In the beginning was Brahman with whom was the Word. And the Word is Brahman." The Ancient Egyptians believed that the God 'Thot' created the world by his voice alone. In the Popul Vuh, from the Mayan tradition, the first real men are given life by the sole power of the word. The Hopi Indians' story of creation tells of the animation of all forms on earth by having the 'Spider Woman' sing the "Song of Creation" over them. Ancient Celtic tradition describes the revelation of the "Word" to the 'Son of the Three Shouts' (a Seer) as forming all life. Many of us know of Pythagoras as the father of geometry. However, how many are aware that in the 6th century BC in Greece he had a school that taught not only the magic of numbers, but the healing powers of music? Pythagoras taught of the Music of the Spheres and the movement of the heavenly bodies could be perceived and reflected in the intervals of plucked strings. Another ancient system associating musical notes with subtle-energy systems of the body is the Five Element Theory of acupuncture and Chinese medicine. The Chinese model views Earth and the human body in terms of the five elements of creation, which are earth, water, fire, wood and metal - each has a corresponding sound.

Today, in the West, much of this ancient knowledge has all but vanished. However, we are now in the process of rediscovering that lost wisdom and adding to it through information and understanding obtained from modern science. Perhaps the most profound scientific work showing the power of sound to affect shape and form was researched by Dr Hans Jenny, a Swiss medical doctor and scientist who spent ten years of his life examining the effects that sound had on shape and formation. Jenny photographed plastics, pastes, liquids, powders and other substances as they were being vibrated by sound. The results of these experiments are truly awe- inspiring, for they show extremely organic shapes being created from inorganic substances merely by exposing them to different sound frequencies. The different substances, which were once blobs of inorganic matter, take on varying geometric forms and begin to look like living creatures: starfish, leaves, human cells, microscopic life.

In his book, "Cymatics", Dr Jenny wrote: "Now it is beyond doubt that, where organization is concerned, the harmonic figures of physics are, in fact, essentially similar to the harmonic patterns of organic nature...we have the certain experience that harmonic systems such as we have visualized in our experiments arise from oscillations in the form of intervals and harmonic frequencies. That is indisputable." According to Dr Jenny, harmonious shapes and harmonic frequencies are interrelated. Through Jenny's experiments and research we have proof - that different sounds create different forms. This phenomenon is one of the basic principles of healing with sound, the principle of "resonance." Modern physics has verified that we are all vibrating atomic and sub-atomic particles. Everything has a resonant frequency, the frequency at which it most naturally vibrates, from the chair you may be sitting on to this book. Every part of your body also has a resonant frequency.

Music is a special type of sound. It not only pleases our ears. The patterns of its vibratory motions encapsulate a system of rhythms, relationships, proportions and harmonies that exist throughout the natural and the human-made world - from the movements of the planets around the Sun to the growth of cells and plants, to the sacred numbers and ratios of ancient beliefs and religions, to art, architecture and mathematics. Music is a universal human language: of initiation in rites of passage, as a guide through the labyrinths of expanding consciousness, and as a route to profound healing and spiritual fulfilment. People have used sounds, particularly musical sounds, naturally and therapeutically through the centuries. The origins of healing by sound and music can be traced into prehistory and beyond, into the realm of myth, religion and soul memory. In ancient Egypt, the hieroglyph for music was also that for joy and well-being. The Vedic-Sanskrit scholars of ancient India, and the Greeks, as well as other cultures, understood music to be mathematical and, as Pythagoras taught, they made the equally interesting connection between sound, music and the science of astronomy. In "Poetica" Aristotle stated that poetry was comprised of language, rhythm and sound. He also pointed towards the potency of sound vibrations to influence human thoughts and emotions. The philosophers of the school of Pythagoras regarded all physical forms as manifestations of music; the relative proportions of musical sounds parallel the physical proportions of natural and architectural shapes. These ancient doctrines held that life and health depended upon a continuum of ratios and harmonic relationships, from within the mind and through the body, out to society and the natural world. The same ratios and harmonics were manifested as sound and music.

Correctly applied sound could bring about cures by restoring the musical integrity of the body and soul. Ancient prescriptions often included rhythmic singing and chanting, from a traditional selection of sacred melodic sequences. The peoples of ancient cultures perceived earthly music as an echo or resonance of cosmic music; they obeyed the same divine laws. If these earthly sounds reflected the divine laws, they had the power to ease pain and suffering and promote health and healing. Cosmology and musical theory were therefore developed on parallel principles, which govern the design and making of musical instruments, composing and performing and the attitude of the listener. Humanity, correctly aligned in 'tune', could sing in vibratory consort with the stars in this quest for universal harmony. The sheer power of music to evoke emotional response has been a recurring theme of poetic and musical celebration. Music can bypass the mind's logical and analytical filters, to make direct contact with profound feelings and passions deep in the memory and imagination. This, in turn, produces physical, psychological and spiritual reactions.

Physical effects can be introduced in other ways. Energies, including sound energy, are morally neutral. That is, they can be used for good or ill. Sound is a potent force; when abused it can irritate, disorientate, injure, even kill. Reverence for all life, and a sense of moral responsibility, are imperative for the appropriate use of sonic energies. This sense of responsibility and burden of accountability was deemed a requirement of students of classical philosophy in ancient Greece and Rome, when healing music was carefully chosen to ensure health, purity and a stable character.

Sounds' Healing Powers

Healing mantras, chants and incantations have very ancient obscure origins. The knowledge of sounds, rhythms and words of power have survived centuries of materialism and they maintain a living heritage for the future. Egyptian medical papyri from 2,600 years ago refer to incantations as cures for infertility, rheumatic pain, and insect bites. In about 324 BC, the music of the lyre restored Alexander the Great to sanity. The Old Testament records that David played his harp and lifted King Saul's depression. The Essenes and Therapeutai used secret, sacred words for healing. And in Hellenistic culture, flute playing eased the pain of sciatica and gout. Knowledge of sounds, rhythms and chants was an essential ingredient in the healing power of the shaman, the medicine man or woman, and the Druidic priest-doctors of Celtic cultures.

The great scholars and teachers of medieval and Renaissance times recognised music's central importance in the understanding of the universe and humanity. The physician Thomas Campion, remembered for his exquisite lyrics and vocal compositions, practised psychological healing of depression and similar problems through his songs in the reign of Elizabeth I. In Jacobean England, Thomas Cogan and Richard Brown treated their patients with music. The nineteenth century saw scientific research into the psychological effects of music, by measuring its effects on respiration, heart rate, circulation and blood pressure. As a result of this research, selected musical sequences have successfully relieved specific kinds of pain. Gradually, the value of music and sound as therapeutic techniques won a measure of recognition, especially in areas of mental health, psychological rehabilitation and occupational therapy. The acoustic principles of resonance apply not only to musical instruments, but also to the human body. As the sound waves enter the aura and physical body, sympathetic vibrations occur in its living cells, which help to restore and reinforce healthy organisation. The high water content of the body's tissue helps to conduct sound and the overall effect is likened to a deep massage at the atomic and molecular level.

Vibrational healing is often described as healing through the use of sound - either the sound of the voice, animated instruments like the didgeridoo or drum, or inanimate instruments like a tuning fork or synthesizer. Voice, animated instruments and inanimate instruments are in decreasing order able to "reflect" the condition of the client. Besides their own characteristic qualities (determined by vocal cords or shape of instrument for instance), they can add a dimension that is helpful to improve the condition of the client. A healer has in general a recognizable voice, but the specific sounds or melodies that are used with a certain client depend on the condition of that client in that moment of time. The same principle applies, for instance, for a didgeridoo: it has a certain base-tone, but the specific overtones and effects that are created depend on the client. Partly it is the healer who generates these sounds, but partly it is the instrument itself that allows certain sounds to emerge. The more a healer is in harmony with the instrument, or the more animated an instrument is, the more the healer will be able to let the instrument play its own sounds in reflection of the client.

The sounds that are used in a therapy session induce a shift in consciousness that helps the clients to get unstuck from their belief in disease or misfortune. Actually, it is the sound working through the energy centres of the body that effects the healing, causing the rapid shift in consciousness by activating, cleansing, balancing and aligning the chakras.

The Science of Sound

Sound is motion. Specifically, sound is vibrational motion - produced as objects move to and fro, or oscillate, in the manner of a swinging pendulum. At a fundamental level, sound is the motion of atoms and molecules coming from objects - from a mosquito's tiny wings to a gale-thrashed tree - originating from the movement of the millions of atoms and molecules that make up such objects. In fact sounds come from objects as small as an atom or as large as a star.

To produce sound, an object must vibrate, or move to and fro. Each complete to-and-fro movement - of a guitar string or tuning fork, for example - is known as one cycle. The string or tuning fork vibrates at the rate of hundreds of cycles each second, the exact rate depending on the musical note of the fork. The number of to-and-fro cycles in one second is known as the frequency.

Frequencies of sounds are a major factor in determining their use in sound therapy. They are measured in units called Hertz, usually abbreviated to Hz. One Hz is one vibration or cycle per second. Tap your finger on a surface once each second and in effect you are making a sound with a frequency of one Hz. At such a low frequency, however, your ears detect the individual cycles as separate throbbing sounds. Only when cycles move above 20 Hz do your ears perceive them as moving. High-pitched sounds have more oscillations, or cycles, per second than low-pitched ones. A high-pitched sound is represented by waves that are pressed closer together than low-pitched sounds. This means the wavelengths of high-pitched sounds are shorter than the wavelengths of low-pitched sounds. We talk of "low-pitched" sounds such as the rumble of thunder and "high-pitched" sounds like a mouse's squeak. Low-pitched sounds have low frequencies and high-pitched sounds have high frequencies. To give an approximate idea of frequency ranges, a rumble of thunder is 20-40 Hz (cycles per second) and a squeaking mouse about 3,000 Hz. The note C, in the middle of a piano keyboard, is 256 Hz. Perhaps not by coincidence, this frequency is approximately in the centre of the frequency of human conversation, which is generally 200-400 Hz.

Sound waves travel from their source at a speed of about 339 metres per second (759 mph); this is the speed in air, at sea level, and at a temperature of 19C. Other substances conduct sound faster. In steel its speed is 5,000 metres per second (11,200 mph) and in glass 5,600 metres per second (12,500 mph). Although its speed is faster, the sound usually fades away faster in denser substances. The speed of sound in water is 1,500 metres per second (3,350 mph). The human body is two-thirds water. The speed at which sounds pass through tissues and organs depends largely on the water content, and this has important implications for sound's therapeutic effects.

The amount of movement in vibrating atoms and molecules facilitates the loudness, or volume, of a sound. In simple terms, if an air molecule vibrates to and fro only slightly, it represents a soft sound. If it vibrates more dynamically, travelling further in each oscillation, it facilitates a louder sound. A sound's volume is another factor that has important bearings on its value in sound therapy. Volume can be thought of as the height or amplitude of the sound wave, and expressed graphically. It is measured in units called decibels, dB. Most people cannot detect sounds much below 20 dB. Conversational speech is about 60 dB, a loud orchestra or rock concert around 80-90 dB, and the threshold of pain from sound 120 dB. Living things may die if exposed to sounds above 150 dB - an ultimate expression of the power of sound and vibration.

The human ear is a very complex structure of astonishing sensitivity. Not only is it the organ of hearing. It also enables you to be aware of the position and movements of your head, and the direction of gravity, so contributing to your sense of balance and motion, and your ability to make smooth co-ordinated movements. Your outer ear collects sound waves. These funnel along your outer ear canal, which is about 25 millimetres long and gently s-shaped. The sound waves impact on your eardrum, or tympanic membrane, at the end of the outer ear canal. The eardrum is like a tightly stretched membrane of skin, measuring only 10 millimetres by 8 millimetres. Vibrating air molecules transfer their kinetic energies to it, causing it to vibrate in sympathy with the frequencies (pitch) and amplitudes (volume) of the sound waves. The sound waves, converted into vibrations in solids, pass along three tiny bones, known as the hammer, anvil and stirrup. These in turn convey the vibrations to your cochlea, a fluid-filled, snail-shaped organ deep in your head, just behind your eye. The cochlea transforms the physical vibrations in its fluid into electrical nerve signals and routes the signals along auditory nerves to the brain. In your brain, the signals are sorted and analyzed, compared with a memory bank of sounds, recognized and identified. This happens subconsciously. Only patterns of sound which your subconscious deems important are brought to your attention and you hear.

As a baby develops within the womb, the rudimentary ears appear within a few weeks of conception. By four-and-a-half months, the ears are complete and functional. Therefore, for half of its time in the womb, the baby can hear and respond to sounds. Relaxation sessions to music for mother and unborn baby, and a peaceful musical background at the time of birth, should be calming and helpful.

When we talk of hearing 'sound' we refer to a limited frequency range. Most people cannot detect sounds with frequencies of much less than 20 Hz, or in some cases 17 Hz. Below this the vibrations can be felt in the body, but not heard. Sounds with frequencies too low for us to detect are called infrasonic. Similarly, most people cannot detect sounds above 20,000 Hz. In general children can hear up to this limit. Sounds with frequencies which are too high for us to hear are known as ultrasonic.

The theory of disease, observed by the ancients, and now speculated on by certain scientists such as Itzhak Bentov in his book "Stalking The Wild Pendulum" is that illness is an out-of-tune behaviour of the body. When something becomes diseased, its frequency changes and it begins to vibrate differently. Through sound, it may be possible to apply harmonizing vibrations which will cause the body to become in tune again. Here we need to look at crystals again. As I stated earlier, "quartz crystals, precious and semi-precious gemstones represent the lowest state of entropy possible because they have the most orderly structure in the natural world. All crystalline structures are formed of mathematical precise and orderly lattice arrays of atoms. This stability has been utilised by scientists in many electronic situations." Entropy is a term which describes the tendency towards disorder of a system. The greater the entropy, the greater the disorder. In general, most systems within the physical universe tend towards increasing positive entropy and more disorder over time, as basically things tend to fall apart. (When a body dies and the life force vacates the physical form, the remaining unoccupied shell returns, via micro-organisms, to its raw constituents). Illness and disease is the breaking down of harmony or resonance; by applying the solidified geometric crystalline patterns of sound to the physical body and aura, we stop the positive entropy and this brings healing.

In a strong healthy body, every organ, bone, tissue and other part is producing balanced frequencies that create a healthy harmonic of the entire body. Dr Peter Guy Manners, a British scientist who has created the Cymatic Instrument, which projects sounds into the body for healing, describes this phenomenon of resonant frequency healing this way: "A healthy organ will have its molecules working together in a harmonious relationship with each other and will all be of the same pattern. If different sound patterns enter into the organ, the harmonious relationship could be upset...they may establish their disharmonious pattern in the organ, bone tissue, etc., and this is what we call disease. If, therefore, a treatment contains a harmonic frequency pattern which will reinforce the organs, the vibrations of the intruders will be neutralized and the correct pattern for that organ re-established. This should constitute a curative reaction."

With healing sounds, the aim or intention of the individual creating the sound is to align with Divine Will and higher consciousness. If the world began with the creator God/Goddess making Sound, then the ultimate aspiration of healing sound is for the sounder to unite with this Sound. Healing sounds from many different traditions can vary in their use of frequencies. These traditions will often use very different tonal scales and rhythms than we are accustomed to hearing in the West and we may find these sounds initially extremely peculiar, or out of tune and quite disharmonious. However, once we get past this first response, we may find that these sacred sounds have extraordinarily transformational consequences.

Many of the sacred healing sounds on the planet are rich in high frequency sounds, called harmonics or overtones. These sounds are thought to energize the cortex of the brain and stimulate health and well-being. Harmonics, or overtones, are geometrically related sounds that occur whenever a natural sound is manifested. Harmonics are the sounds within all sounds, responsible for the tone color or "timbre" of an instrument and our voices. The mathematics of harmonics display universal and predictable principles corresponding to an underlying framework found in chemistry, physics, botany and the study of other sciences.

The use of harmonics as healing sounds may be found in many Shamanic and mystical traditions. Overtone chanting is a centuries-old technique, usually practised in a religious or ritual context, across the world: in Tibet, Siberia, Mongolia and Northern India; in Buddhist communities in China, India and Japan; in the Andes of South America; in Bulgaria and Romania and the rest of Europe; and in Central Africa. Traces of the technique remain in Spanish flamenco music, itself of Indian origin. It is even believed that overtones were known in medieval convents and monasteries. The clues suggest that highly decorative group singing may have combined with the architecture, producing astounding esoteric harmonics.

Overtones exist in every vocal sound, but here the sound practitioner developed the ability of creating multiple overtones or "vocal harmonics" and singing two or more notes simultaneously. These sounds were used by chanters as a means of invoking different deities and energy forces and for balancing the chakras. Listening to recordings of Tibetan Monks chanting in this "One Voice Chord" can be a transformational experience. The monks utilize a fundamental frequency that is deep, it seems to be almost inhuman, like the growl of some wild beast. Coupled with this tone is a much higher voice which sounds like the voice of an cherub singing in harmony. These two distinct sounds come from the same person, a Tibetan Monk, and they are the result of ritual sound practices. The creation of harmonics is based upon vowel sounds. The singing and elongation of these vowel sounds is found in most of the major chanting in the world, from Hindu and Tibetan mantras to Sufi and Qabalistic practices. For example, we have "Oooooooommm" and "Aaaaaameeen", "Aaaaallaaaah", "Ahaaooohhnn" and "Yaaaaah Waaaaay". Through this form of 'toning', resonance of the physical body and the brain occurs, when the reciter focuses, on becoming one with the sound.

In the Australian Aboriginal traditions, the sacred sounds are produced by an instrument called the didgeridoo, a hollowed-out tree limb. When it is blown, using a technique called "circular breathing" (which allows for the creation of a continuous stream of air and therefore a non-stop sound), the result is a single tone, very deep and extremely rich with harmonics. Those of you who have heard this sound may have found it comparable to the "Tibetan Deep Voice," which is also very deep with distinct overtones. These two extremely similar sounds were created by two very distinct civilizations. It could have been, as their ancient legends indicate, that the initial human creators of these sounds first heard these sounds in 'dream time' or meditation and then tried to create them in the physical body, one using the voice, the other using an instrument.

The chanting of a sacred sound coupled with the intention of invoking specific beings or energy forms may create what British scientist Rupert Sheldrake called "morphic" fields. These are energy fields that create shape and form. In many of the ancient sounding traditions, the recitation of the name of an entity will eventually bring forth that entity and allow one to unite with it. Many times these sacred names are called in the recitation of Sanskrit mantras. However, this ancient practice is found all around the world. It is based upon an ancient understanding of sacred sound. In many of the creation myths, the Creator God/Goddess would think of an object and then sound its name. The Being would first visualize the object to create, placing intention upon this. Then the Being would vocalize the sound of the object, creating its frequency and bringing it into being.

A typical example of this would be the Buddhist "Om Mani Padme Hum," an invocation to the Avalokitesvara, the Bodhisattva of Divine Compassion. When coupled with the intention and visualization of invoking this great beneficial being, the vocalization of this chant will have the result of producing a field of enormous compassion. The Tibetans have a highly developed and extremely powerful practice of this in which they utilize extraordinarily specific visualizations of "mandalas." Whether it is in the Sufi, Christian, Hebrew or any of the countless other traditions, including shamanism, this sounding of the sacred names of the Divine is utilized as a deeply spiritual practice to invoke the Divine.

It is customary for this sounding of these 'words of power' to be slow and repetitive, creating a phenomenon known as sonic "entrainment" in which the brainwaves of the listener lock in resonance with the brainwaves of the chanter. This is one way of creating altered states - by slowing down our brainwaves. Much sacred sound puts us in resonance with frequencies that are within the alpha or theta brainwave range, 7 to 12 Hz, and 4 to 7 Hz, respectively. Many of the environmental sounds seem to resonate to this spectrum of sound and particularly to a frequency called the Schumann resonance, 7.83 Hz, which may be the resonant frequency of planet earth.

Environmental sounds may be among the most healing on the planet, for they are the reverberation of the earth celebrating herself. Whether it is the sound of the sea, bird song, or whales calling, these sounds soothe us for two reasons: first, for the tranquillizing visualization they evoke for us; second, for the entrainment they create within.

We breathe with the sounds.

Our hearts beat with these sounds.

Our brains sing with these sounds.

Our spiritual nature is awakened with these sounds.

Many of the sacred rhythms particularly Native American, employ at their core a heartbeat which we entrain and match when listening to them. Our heartbeat, respiration and brainwaves slow down due to the repetitive rhythms created. Another method of creating altered, transformational states is to overdrive the brain and put us into a trance state. This is true of many of the polyrhythmic sounds of the sacred music of Africa and Bali. The over-driving of the psyche which follows can energize us to the point of what seems to be the loss of self-control. Something much deeper has taken over.

Using Sound in Therapy

We are all unique vibratory beings, in a constant state of fluidity and flow. On a basic cellular level, there may be generic tones for specific organs. However, we may be lacking certain information regarding the proper understanding of this. Along with a frequency for the structure of the organ, there may also be a modulated frequency which is the pulse of the organ (how the organ interacts with the various energies which pass through it, whether it is slow or fast etc.) The brain, for example, pulses at different frequencies (alpha, beta, delta, theta) but these are not the frequencies of the tissues of the brain. So there may be very different types of sonics which influence and affect any organ.

A system exists for working with sound and the chakras which uses the note "C" for the root chakra and goes up the chakras diatonically ("C", "D", "E", "F" etc.) so that the seventh or crown chakra vibrates to "B".

* One of the best ways of beginning to work with music for its therapeutic properties is to create a musical prescription for yourself.
* Find out what types of music you respond to best.
* What specific music makes you feel joyful, uplifted or energized?
* What music makes you feel sad or low in energy?
* Write down the music that elicits different responses and use this music when you want to create a feeling or a mood.

* No one piece of music will affect everyone the same - especially when it comes to our personal emotional responses. As a therapist you cannot expect someone else to have the identical experience that you do with any music. However, frequently with our own experiences, if we have had a specific emotional response to listening to particular music, we will usually have a similar response when listening to that music again. When working with others, we should find out what music works best for them in order to help create their musical prescription profile. It could be possible that a person is blocked from enjoying certain types of music because the sounds resonate imbalances within them. As I found out when running crystal courses, what appeared to most of the group to be heavenly music could elicit in some individuals a response close to being their personal idea of hell!

Nature-Music Exercise

As a useful awareness procedure, go out into the open air sometimes and focus your ears and mind on the natural sounds that surround you. Make a list of those you hear and your reactions to them. Appreciate singing birds, humming insects, rustling leaves, swishing grass, barking dogs and whinnying horses, the sound of the waves, etc.

Which are most obvious or hidden away?

Do you tend to notice sounds by volume, loudest first, or by frequency, low pitch first?

Toning

Refers to sounds which are a language for the multidimensional transmission of light, color, vibration and geometries. These tones break up dysfunctional energy patterns and energy blockages. In this section I have given you the seed sound or *bija* I have personally used for twenty-nine years. These are ancient Sanskrit syllables known as *varnas*. Varna means color and all sounds have a corresponding color in the invisible world. They are the ones I use in my teaching, group work and with my clients. I can personally vouch for their effectiveness in restoring the human chakras to perfect balance and alignment, but there are many other systems for toning. All ancient peoples used sound as a potent force in their spiritual and healing work.

Each chakra or energy centre has a corresponding tone which we use to vibrate that chakra:

    root - lam or lang
    sacral - vam or vang
    solar - ram or rang
    heart - yam or yang
    throat - ham or hang
    third eye - om
    crown - silent - om

By using the seed sounds or *mantras* we can change our frequency or vibratory rate to align with our perfect body and mind, bringing in the energy of our higher God/Goddess nature. These holy energy forms of meditation restore harmony and much more. Every time I have used them in group work all the participants have made huge shifts in their consciousness and healing awareness. It is said that if we have the name of God/Goddess on our lips in the last moment of life, our spirit will pass directly to that sacred space of being. That is how sacred and powerful these spiritual sounds are.

You will derive the most benefit if you tone for yourself, but it is possible to tone for others. Also, toning with others is very effective in group work; the energy produced is magnified and those who are new to toning quickly gain strength from those more experienced in the art.

Vocal Sound Production

Every musical instrument has three features which combined are responsible for sound production. These are an exterior, or source of energy; a vibrator, determining sound and pitch; and resonator, adding tonal qualities. Your own voice - regardless of any preconceptions you may hold - is a musical instrument of great power. Its exterior is the breath from your lungs; its vibrator is your vocal cords, in the voice-box or larynx; and its resonators are the air cavities and structures of your mouth, throat, sinuses and nose.

Similarly, vocalisation is divided into three main processes. These are phonation, or making the sound; resonance, or the harmonic enhancement of the sound; and articulation, the shaping and moulding and delivery of vocal sounds into linguistic forms we call words. As you carry out the vocal toning exercises, always work through the physical sensations of phonation, resonance and articulation. Allow yourself to feel them taking place within you. And above all listen to yourself. Aural feedback, listening to your utterances, is a vital part of the toning process.

The secret, as ever, lies in your creative imagination. Just as you have a mind's eye, you also have a mind's ear. Hear sounds mentally, before you release them. This should convey the right message to your vocal mechanism, so that you actually tone at your perfect level.

To enhance the vibratory effect it is good to hold a clear quartz crystal in your hand. This amplifies and focuses the sound into the chakra or chakras being worked with. You can also 'charge' a crystal with toning.

During a crystal therapy treatment you can increase the effect by placing a single terminated clear quartz crystal over the chakra being balanced, with the point towards the person's head, and begin to sound the tone for that chakra.

Repeat the tone several times until the quartz crystal and the corresponding chakra begin to resonate with the sound. Continue this process until the chakra is re-balanced or the blocked energy is released.

You can do a complete quartz crystal chakra vibratory balancing session in this way for your client, remembering to use only clear quartz crystals. You could even have a complete chakra balancing set that you keep only for this technique.

When toning for yourself, you can place the tips of your fingers very lightly on the chakra you are toning for until you feel the resonance (vibration) in that chakra - although after a while even that is unnecessary as the effects will be felt throughout the physical body and aura.

Other methods of toning are to allow any vibratory sound to come out spontaneously. This method is very good for releasing pain, anger, rage, anguish, hatred, sadness, hostility, grief, frustration or any emotion that needs clearing which is blocking that chakra.

Toning is used to intensify meditation, for clearing emotional debris, healing, alignment and just for the sheer love of it.

The Usui Reiki system of natural healing using the symbols' sounds has also proved very potent; you can even buy tapes of the chanting Reiki Masters. Another example of using sound in healing is drumming, which is useful for attaining altered states of consciousness and healing.

Mantra Meditation

Is often called "Mantra Yoga", considered to be a part of "Nada Yoga", which means the "yoga of sound". The word '*yoga*' means to "link with God" and this is the ultimate goal of all yoga. Although Hatha yoga is used by many as only a means to keep good physical condition, in reality this is but a by-product of yoga. The physical postures or "asanas" are to help bring the body and senses under control in order to prepare for meditation. Ultimately the mind will be also brought under control. These sacred sound vibrations are known to promote healing on all levels, whilst, at the same time, awakening the

115

chakras within our ethereal or subtle bodies. Mantras are always sung to a melody (raga), although it is generally monophonic, or individual sounds which may 'seem' to be without harmony.

Mantras, being sacred sound vibrations, are composed of sacred seed syllables representative of and containing within great spiritual power or cosmic energy. The *Bija* - within each mantra is its seed, which is its source of potency. These break up dysfunctional energy patterns and energy blockages. Utilising mantras allows us to concentrate and focus this spiritual energy. The mantras are believed to descend via the masters of wisdom, from the subtle realms of the *Anahata*, the primeval or cosmic ether. (Anahata is also known as the universal heart). They have been translated into very definite syllables with rhythm and melody.

The word "mantra" is composed, in Sanskrit, of two root words: "man" means "mind" or "thinking", and "tra" to "release" or "free" or "strengthen". Therefore the meaning is "to free the mind and thinking" from the material sphere of consciousness and to be able to transcend the wheel of "samsara" or "birth and death within this physical world". Chanting mantras promote oneness and harmony on all levels, as it awakens the spiritual self, the 'Divine Essence within'. Once awakened, ultimately the spiritual self turns within to the source of all power and can direct spiritual energy not only for personal benefit but for the good of all sentient life.

Rishis mantras have always come down from master to student, beginning with the ancient seers, mystics, visionaries or rishis. It is said that unless a mantra is received from an authorised source it will be ineffectual. Therefore this process has been kept intact since time immemorial. If no 'guru' can be found to initiate you into mantra, Swami Vishnu Devanada suggested "select any mantra that seems appropriate. It should be repeated mentally with faith and devotion every day. This in itself has a purificatory effect, and the realization of God-consciousness will eventually be attained." In a very real sense, mantras are eternal - their source of power and purpose belongs to God/Goddess. From traditional Buddhist chants to the waves of sincere devotion rising spontaneously from your own heart - these are all threads of tradition weaving the seamless robe of unity. Accumulated energy resides in the mantric sound, which through age and repetition gathers a "life of its own". The energy of your chosen or given mantra will help you; it will carry you as a novice through the early stages of mantric discipline. Gradually mantra becomes your respected friend, a tower or pillar of strength to support your sincere resolve. Mantra study and practice is a lifelong task - if you are drawn to using it in your meditation practice, remember to make haste slowly.

Japa Meditation

Sound the sonic seed of all matter - "In the beginning was the Word, the Word was with God, and the Word was God". The word of the Bible is the *Sabdabrahman* of Hindu *tantra*. Word, sound and mantra are integral parts of Indian cosmology and cannot be separated from it. Taking cosmological principles out of the realm of theory, japa or mantra repetition puts them to work in a basic, realistic way. It is the path 'home' from the microcosm to the macrocosm; it is the vehicle that carries the individual back to the Source. Its sole purpose or aim is to help you make the vital connections, so that you can experience the point at which you are one with the Universe. Japa meditation may also be silent - just sounded in the mind and heard by your inner ear. To sound the 'Om' mentally is very popular. The Om or AUM, is called the first mantra. The Sanskrit symbol for the Aum (Om) has great significance - the long lower curve represents the dream state, the upper left curve is the waking state, and the central curve projecting to the right is the deep, dreamless sleep between them. The crescent on the upper right symbolizes the veil of illusion, maya, and the dot beyond it is the transcendental state of illumination.

Chants and Chanting

Are rapidly growing in popularity as a tranquillising and rejuvenating activity; they provide the opportunity for spiritual experience and unity with the cosmos. Sacred songs, hymns, psalms and mantras have long been used as a source of solace, inspiration and group expression. Chants are very often related to Shamanic practice, or where we have a group of 'mixed' belief systems, or when we are participating in dances of 'Universal Peace'. One chant that I have used with many groups is:

"O Great Spirit, Earth, Sea, Air and Sky - you are inside and all around me".

Another popular one is: "Earth my body, water my blood, air my breath and fire my Spirit"

or perhaps one from the White Eagle Lodge:

"Let the Light Shine"

or a Celtic one:

"Awen" Ah.....ooh...nn.. A Celtic Aum.

or a Goddess one....

"We have come from the Goddess and to her we shall return, like a drop of rain"

Humming

Explore reverberations within your body's own air chambers by humming. We naturally hum when contented and happy and absorbed and at one with the situation. The position is simple, with your lips closed... "mmmmmmmmmmmm". Humming is a very quick way of activating and balancing the throat chakra. Prolonged focused humming can, with practice, completely clear the aura of any emotional debris. The humming sound.... induces resonance....

1.   Very gently, as softly as possible, begin to allow your vocal cords to vibrate as you exhale, generating a very quiet humming sound with your lips closed.....and your eyes closed as well....

2.   At the bottom of your exhale...fall naturally silent....and inhale silently....feel the vibrations continue throughout your body from your humming a moment before......this is resonance....

3.   Continue with this humming meditation for a number of breaths until you feel you are becoming pure sound yourself......pure resonance.....pure vibration.....

4.   Then allow yourself to be quiet, while you continue breathing....allow the vibrations in your body to remain in your consciousness.

'Own' Name Exercise

Or 'owning' your name. Many years ago, I was 'taught' to 'own' my own name. There is great importance and benefit in 'owning' your own name; you should feel comfortable with it - on all levels. Remember, words have power. By understanding your name, you can also 'feel' or ascertain a lot of past life and karmic energy around it. So I would like to pass this process on to you. I have also found many people on the 'spiritual' path change their name - either through initiation or choice. I can remember one of my students who had been to visit the Damanhur community in Italy saying how wonderful it was and how each group member as they joined this sacred group had to take a 'new' name, one of a plant and one of an animal, fish or bird. The community's theory was that this helped them to live in harmony with the Earth. I can still remember the look on her beautiful face as it dawned on her - yes - Hazel Raven. Your name is a flowing stream of connected sounds, but because it represents a person, a living breathing divine aspect of the God/Goddess force, these sounds are invested with great meanings, memories and assumptions.

Say your name - several times - very slowly and carefully. Be aware of the movements involved, your breath, and the shape and flexibility of your tongue and lips. How do you hold your body - is there any resistance to your name? Do you say your name with joy? Next - repeat your name in its natural rhythm. Notice how the stresses on certain letters form a rhythmic sequential pattern. Speak the rhythm, now sing it, form it into a musical phrase by singing it as a song. Experiment with different tunes. Does your name feel right to you? Sometimes you may feel you need to alter your name a little; perhaps you are happier with your middle name? Or, if a woman, your maiden name? Or abbreviate your name? Do you have a nickname? Is there some 'other' name you would rather be called by?

Finally - I want you to use your creative imagination to hear with your 'mind's ear' your name spoken very gently by the wisest, most compassionate voice you can imagine. This will be the sound of your 'Divine Essence' calling you home on 'wings of light'.

Singing Bowl

Fabricated quartz crystal bowls are claimed to be the sound of light. Those who work with them say they are a deeply transformative vibrational experience. (I am one of those who work with them and I have been using them since 1991). They bathe the listener in harmonic waves which deeply effect healing in every cell. Quartz crystal bowls re-balance and cleanse abnormal functioning or 'blocked' chakras. Dysfunctional chakras affect the subtle energy bodies: the sounds of the crystal singing bowls release the 'blocked' energy, allowing healing to occur. Crystal singing bowls are also used to aid meditation and develop deeply spiritual experiences. They have been used for space clearing and 'Earth Healing' at the times of the full moon. They will also create structured water, which is beneficial to radiant good health. Care should be taken, however, never to place a quartz crystal singing bowl on the body of your client. If the quartz was to shatter it could very seriously damage your client, who would be showered in thousands of sharp pieces of glass-type quartz. (I have never see this happen for myself, but I have been told of this happening by a very reliable source). Two more cautionary notes are: quartz crystal singing bowls of the same size (dimensions) and same note (harmonically tuned) should never be played too close together, as the vibration from one could shatter the other. Finally, some very sensitive people find them too intense when played indiscriminately, especially at New Age fairs. Remember, the bowls will amplify the players' thoughts and energies and send them out to pollute the atmosphere; it is much better to only play them in a sacred way for healing and meditation.

Tibetan Singing Bowls

Are made from 'seven' holy metals and are extraordinarily vibrant, as are meditation gongs from Burma and Chinese temple bells: all these have similar effects to the quartz singing bowls.

Small personal symbols or 'ting-shaws' have been used over each chakra to cleanse it, before a healing session; they can also clear or activate a crystal.

You can use any instrument - ethnic, modern, exotic or familiar - as an aid to meditation, once the inner significance is recognised. If you feel an instrument calls your inner attention, be it a drum, flute, harp, piano or even a didgeridoo...all can be used.

Part 12

The Root Chakra

The first chakra is frequently referred to as the Root Chakra. It is our most powerful contact and reflects our personal relationship to this Earth, the beautiful planet we live on, whose energy field we interact constantly with from the moment of our conception via the force of gravity. In Sanskrit the word for this chakra is *muladhara*. The direct translation is *mula* - root, *adhara* - support. It is also known as the base or earth chakra. In fact, the physical nerve bundle at the base of the spine that is associated with the root chakra resembles a massive root system that leaves your spine and runs down both legs as the sciatic nerve. This is the largest peripheral nerve system in your body, about as thick as your thumb as it leaves the sacral plexus at the bottom of your spine and spreads just like a great root system down each leg, all the way to the very tips of your toes and the heel of each foot. The root chakra is physically located in the perineum, the base of the spine, halfway between anus and genitals. This chakra is associated with physical energy, physical health and fitness, gravity, self-preservation, survival and being grounded. It is the energetic gateway between us and the earth, also energies of childhood and the past. When this chakra is developed, we are more grounded, solid and powerful at physical levels of survival. Knowledge of the past, present and future are also bestowed when this chakra is fully activated.

The root chakra, even though some people think of it as lowly, is directly linked to the crown chakra. Without a strong foundation it will be impossible to fully activate the crown chakra. It would in fact be completely absurd, not to mention downright dangerous, to turn your full undivided focused attention to your crown chakra without a solid, grounded, balanced reality - although in some Hindu schools of Yoga, where the crown chakra is seen as the primary chakra, there is generated, instead of a male/female balanced awakening of the whole chakra system in sequential order, a very masculine blasting of energy up the spine and out of the crown chakra. I will never teach this kind of meditation practice, but it is taught to satisfy personalities who hunger for instant enlightenment. Unfortunately, I have personally seen the 'casualties' of the big blast theory and their shattered lives. *"Make haste slowly"* as the old saying goes.

Each chakra is envisioned in classic lore as a lotus flower. Every chakra has a different number of petals. The number of petals is related both to Sanskrit symbolism concerning the configuration of subtle nerves, called nadis, that emanate from that particular region of the spinal column where the chakra is located, and also to the meaning of particular vowels and consonants in the ancient Sanskrit alphabet. Thus, the symbol of the root chakra is a four-petal crimson-red lotus flower, around a yellow square containing a downward-pointing white triangle containing the *Bija* symbol Lam. The natural name of the root chakra, according to ancient Yogis who learned to listen directly to the sound emanating from their awakened chakras, is LAM in the Hindu tradition, and a slightly altered and even more powerful LANG in the Tantric Buddhist tradition of Nepal and Tibet. The LAM sound is of a feminine nature because of the sound finishing with closed lips, while the LANG is a masculine force, which finishes with open lips. It is up to you which sound you use to awaken and balance your root chakra, but it would be wise to use the female LAM when you are in a gentle mood and the masculine LANG when you need more energy. Here in the root chakra is also the *Brahma granthi*, or knot of *Brahma*, which must be forced open through precise *sadhana* and intensive purification before the *Kundalini* will rise.

The colors associated with this chakra are the bright shades of red, scarlet and crimson. As you begin to focus on this chakra, you will first envisage the lotus flower opening from a bud, with the 'warmth' of your focused attention. Over a period of time you will become aware of the flower beginning to focus

119

upwards; this is a good sign. It means you have stopped wasting your energy on basic survival mechanism and ordinary fear-based tribal mental pursuits. The root chakra, as its name suggests, connects you to your roots - your 'tribe', your birthplace, your culture, your foundation and your earliest relationships, which can influence you all your life. If these early relationships were unbalanced, due to a dysfunctional family life, it is very important to look at your roots, otherwise you may find problems with your physical health, overall vitality and enthusiasm to complete your goals. Strength, courage, endurance, perseverance and stamina are key words that relate to this primary energy centre.

The yellow square in the centre of the lotus flower represents the solid element of Earth. In the centre of the square is a white triangle: this represents the power and purity of the trinity. In the centre of the triangle is the lingam, a symbol for male sexuality. Around the lingam is the location of the resting place of the *Kundalini* Goddess. She is said to lie coiled three-and-a-half times around this chakra. The three coils represent the three stages of *avastha* (mind), namely *jagrt* (awake), *svapna* (dreaming) and *susuptiin* (deep sleep). There is a fourth level, *turiya*, combining and transcending the others, which represents the last half coil. It is attained in *samadhi* (enlightenment). Around the yellow square is a white circle, which in turn represents the ultimate circular unity of every dimension of the universe. There are four red lotus petals around the periphery of the circle, then there is a white space around the petals; this signifies the pure white light and void of the human consciousness.

The first chakra, with its Earth element, is masculine. All the chakras have a polarity and as you move upwards through the Master chakras, in sequential order, they alternate male, then female. It is vitally important to fully understand these dualistic polar opposites, as by their combined action we have the unifying manifesting power of the Universe, the One. All your chakras are interlinked, of course, but truly understanding your chakras is a prerequisite for any crystal therapist, whether an amateur (working on healing the self) or a qualified crystal therapist working on or advising others. You need to memorise all the information on the chakras. To return to yin and yang, masculine and feminine, neither is better than the other, regardless of any cultural bias you may have been indoctrinated into - only by truly understanding manifestation can you rise above duality and dualistic concepts - please remember unity in diversity.

The first chakra (Earth) - root - is masculine; solid; earthy; yang; male sexuality - balanced and paired to the crown chakra.

The second chakra (Water) is feminine; liquid; flowing; female sexuality; yin - balanced and paired with the third eye chakra.

The third chakra (Fire) is masculine; power; wilful; yang - balanced and paired with the throat chakra.

The fourth chakra (Air) is feminine; loving; integrating; yin - balanced in the centre.

The fifth chakra (Ether) is masculine; manifesting; logical; yang - balanced and paired with the solar plexus chakra.

The sixth chakra (Spirit) is feminine; intuitive; mysterious; yin - balanced and paired with the sacral chakra.

The seventh chakra (Cosmic) is masculine; pure bright light; yang - balanced and paired to the root chakra.

The root chakra should always spin clockwise in a male body and anti-clockwise in a female body. The master chakras in sequential order follow clockwise, then anti-clockwise. So in a male body it goes - clockwise, anti-clockwise, alternating through the chakras to finish at the crown chakra with clockwise. In a female body it goes - anti-clockwise, clockwise, alternating through the chakras to finish with anti-clockwise.

If you have any physical dis-ease or chronic ill-health you must give extra special attention to this primary chakra. In order to grow to great spiritual heights and consummate the marriage of Heaven and Earth (crown and root chakras), you must have a strong physical body. Your physical body is your only vehicle with which to make this transition into enlightenment.

The glands, organs and parts of the body directly influenced by the root chakra are the blood (by its color association in haemoglobin), adrenal glands (by the adrenaline release mechanism in fight or flight), spinal column, nose (the root chakra rules the sense of smell), all the solid elements of the body - bones and teeth, your sciatic nerve, lower back, prostate, feet, ankles, legs, knees, thighs and large intestine. Physical malfunctions include osteoarthritis, obesity, haemorrhoids, constipation and problems associated with the hips, feet and legs. Mental lethargy, 'spaciness', incapability of inner stillness are also malfunctions of this chakra's unbalanced energy.

The Archangel Sandalphon is your guide with this chakra. Sandalphon is the twin of Archangel Metatron, who rules the crown chakra. Other guides you may encounter in this primary root chakra are Lord Ganesha, the four-armed, elephant-headed Hindu god who teaches you to overcome all obstacles on your spiritual path, or the great brown bear of the Native American tradition, who teaches you the sacred lore of roots, herbs and how to go inside to find deep personal healing.

Crystal Web of Light - Grounding Into the Earth (Prana Activation)

Crystals: 2 garnets, tumbled, faceted or natural
               1 ruby, tumbled, faceted or natural
               4 black tourmaline wands
               2 clear quartz points

Uses: This is for when you feel disconnected from the earth, or if you have been travelling over a long distance and need to rebalance the energy field and clear it of unwanted outside energies and influences. It is also for anyone who has survival or fear issues: it will help them to take positive action in their life. It gives protection from nightmares, by bringing inner stability to a troubled mind. It will bring out the 'Spiritual warrior', increasing health and life force. The energy of strength, courage, endurance, perseverance, tenacity, durability, forbearance, vigour, fortitude, stamina and self-mastery - these are the signs of a balanced base or root chakra. It will keep you grounded, solidly anchored to the earth, bringing a feeling of vigorous good health and boundless vitality. It will help you to understand the energy of gravity, allowing you to connect to the vastness of the earth's energy grid. When you are fully 'earthed', nothing can shake you. Without a strong foundation and fortitude you will be blown about like a leaf in the wind. In order to develop metaphysically you must have a sturdy foundation, otherwise you will not be able to grow to great spiritual heights.

It helps release the symptoms of an unbalanced base chakra, which are: when it is too closed, deformed or blocked - emotionally needy, low self-esteem, self-destructive behaviour, fearful. The symptoms of an overactive base chakra are: bullying, over-materialistic, self-centred, engaging in physical foolhardiness. In our present materialistic society we plunder the earth, giving no thought to our children and their future. This crystal web teaches you to care for the planet and accept your Divine birthright as a custodian of the earth and guardian of peace. This crystal web of light also holds a magical key to the Spirit Kingdom of the animals. Meditating or focusing with the powerful earthy energies whilst in this web will activate your passage of power into the 'totem' animal energy or consciousness, where you will find your own animal 'Guardian Angel'; this will be an energy that is trustworthy, sincere and reliable. It will work with you in all realms and dimensions as your teacher, mentor, guide and friend.

It is also helpful for those who have insufficient red energy in their auric shell and as such suffer from fear and survival issues, as well as being good for rheumatism and arthritis. It releases feelings of guilt and shame. It stops you being manipulated by others, especially sexually. It is used for male impotence and prostate problems, as well as lower back pain. It also has the potential to connect your base chakra with your crown chakra, bringing a flow of positive life force to the whole chakra system. It is good for the 'Kundalini Shakti' yoga activation of the base or root chakra and can be used for all problems of the feet, legs and hips. This crystal web of light has proved useful for those who are frigid emotionally, sexually or spiritually.

1 ruby placed on the base chakra (for Kundalini activation).

1 garnet at the top of each leg (where the limb joins the trunk).

1 black tourmaline beneath the feet in the earth star chakra, 1 black tourmaline above the head in the soul star chakra and the remaining two tourmalines placed at elbow level, so that the tourmalines form a cross.

1 clear quartz point in the left hand pointing inwards, 1 clear quartz point pointing outwards.

Process:

1.   Cleanse all the crystals and programme the clear quartz for healing.

2.   Choose a warm comfortable place where you can lie down undisturbed for at least an hour. Never rush a crystal web of light process. View it as a sacred healing space, so you need to make sure it is energetically clean. Make sure you are wearing warm, loose, comfortable clothes.

3.   Relax by consciously becoming aware of your breathing and heartbeat; you can play soothing music, light candles and burn incense.

4.   Lay the stones around and on the body, then hold the quartz in your hands.

5.   Allow 20 minutes to facilitate the integration of the crystal vibration.

6.   Feel free to remove the crystals sooner, if you have integrated the crystal energy very quickly - remove the crystals in reverse order of placement.

7.   Make sure you are fully grounded, centred and balanced.

8.   Cleanse your crystals (using your chosen method).

9.   Finish by giving thanks and asking mentally that all the healing work you have just accomplished is closed, sealed and protected with Divine love and wisdom. Give yourself sufficient time to integrate the crystal therapy session. As a guideline it is suggested a period of twice the length of time you were actually lying in the crystal therapy web.

Garnet

Garnets have long been carried by travellers to protect against accidents far from home. In legend, garnets light up the night and protect their owners from nightmares. In mythology, Noah used a garnet lantern to navigate the Ark at night. The ancient world is full of praise for the carbuncle, the glowing red coal of a gemstone we now know as garnet. The name garnet probably comes from pomegranate. Almandine red garnet is traditionally the birthstone for January. It has always been a warrior's stone - set into shields and sword hilts to give protection in battle. It is known as a stone of health and life force.

Almandine garnets certainly contain the energy of strength, courage, endurance, perseverance, tenacity, durability, forbearance, vigour, fortitude, stamina and self-mastery. These are the signs of a balanced base or root chakra. They keep you grounded, solidly anchored to the earth, bringing a feeling of vigorous good health and boundless vitality. They help you to understand the energy of gravity, allowing you to connect to the vastness of the earth's energy grid. When you are fully 'earthed', nothing can shake you. Without a strong foundation and fortitude you will be blown about like a leaf in the wind. In order to develop metaphysically you must have a sturdy foundation, otherwise you will not be able to grow to great spiritual heights. Garnet is also helpful for those who have insufficient red energy in their auric shell and as such suffer from fear and survival issues, as well as being good for rheumatism and arthritis.

Affirmation: My body is my spirit's home. I now activate my 'Divine Essence' to guide me on every level.

Clear Quartz

Quartz is the most common mineral on the face of the earth. It is found in nearly every geological environment and is at least a component of almost every rock type. It frequently is the primary mineral. It is also the most varied in terms of varieties, colors and forms. The water-clear colorless quartz is known as rock crystal and receives its name from the hardy mountain climbers of ancient Greece, who first came upon it gleaming in hidden caves near their sacred mountain, Mount Olympus. They called it *'krustallos'*, meaning ice, for they believed it to be water forever frozen by the Gods.

Many Native American healers, especially the tribal Shamans of cultures throughout the world, have quartz crystals among their collections of power objects. Clear quartz is the 'Master Healer' or 'cure all' because it contains the full spectrum of the visible 'white' light (iridescent rainbow cosmic light) and as such it will work on every level of our being, physical, emotional, mental, astral, spiritual, etheric etc. It is acknowledged as the only 'programmable' crystal. Clear quartz also contains the double helix spiral of Universal Life Energy. Working with, holding or meditating with this 'Master' energy of the supreme ray will unlock not only deep memories but facilitate healing by quickly removing the 'blocks' or stagnant energy which may cause or have caused illness or distress within any level of the body.

It is also used for amplifying one's concentrated attention and intent. When healing energy is directed through the clear quartz crystal, it is transmitted into the body of the patient and distributed to the areas most in need of energy balancing. There is an intelligence contained within this focused energy that always directs it to the areas displaying a lower vibration or 'block'. Quartz crystal allows for easy access to altered states of consciousness and it will assist the movement of energy flowing between the chakras. It can also be used to bring about 'Kundalini' activation. Use clear quartz crystal when you need to bring clarity and light to a situation, or when you need to bring about a change, major or minor. Clear quartz is considered a cure-all by many crystal therapists. There are many types and uses.

Affirmation: My consciousness transcends normal thoughts and the ordinary senses. I now move into a deeper state of awareness and personal mastery. I am open to coincidences that add magic to my life.

Ruby

Ruby is the fabulous gemstone for those born in the month of July. Ruby is the superb scarlet variety of corundum, the second hardest natural mineral known. The word red is derived from the Latin for ruby, *rubeus*, which is derived from similar words in Sanskrit, Hebrew and Persian. The intensity of color of a fine ruby is like a glowing coal, probably the most intensely colored substance our ancestors ever saw. Ruby has been the world's most valued gemstone for thousands of years. Ruby was said to be the most precious of the twelve stones God created when he created all things and this "lord of gems" was placed on Aaron's neck by God's command. The Bible says that wisdom is "more precious than rubies". In the ancient language of Sanskrit, ruby is called *ratnaraj* or "king of precious stones" and *ratnanayaka*, "leader of precious stones".

It is no wonder they ascribed magical powers to these fires that burned perpetually and never extinguished themselves. Ruby instills in the wearer a passion for life, truth, courage, wisdom and perseverance. It introduces dynamic leadership qualities. It emits the energy of cheerfulness and creativity. Ruby is for the pioneers, those who must go first, bravely into uncharted territory. Ruby is raw power, drive and will-power. Ruby works primarily on the genitals and reproductive organs. The glands of the body connected to ruby are the gonads and ovaries. Ruby also prompts the release of adrenaline into the bloodstream when there is danger, aggression or pain. The blood and the circulation are a focus of the ruby vibration. Muscles, which give the power to act, are also governed by ruby and of course the deep red ray is seen as raw life force, so ruby rules the blood and helps with anaemia; also it will warm the body when it is chilled and can be used to counteract hypothermia.

Rubies have been worn in the navels of belly dancers and have been used to stimulate sexual power and potency. The signature of ruby is growth at any cost and it can be too powerful for some sensitive souls.

You really have to understand the resonance of rubies to be completely comfortable in their vibrational field. If someone is stressed and irritated, avoid ruby completely, as it will inflame the condition. The bright red scarlet, crimson and flame are clean, pure, pristine forms of ruby; when used spiritually, it is devotion that transfigures Divine love into Divine will. Ruby will stimulate the heart chakra when consciously directed, raising, then transforming the raw power of the base chakra into devotion, piety, adoration, worship, reverence and enlightened religious zeal. Ruby works very well with those who have a strong 'spiritual devotional' energy to the 'ultimate liberation' of the human race from suffering and ignorance into enlightenment.

Affirmation: I now allow passion into my life to burn away all obstacles on my spiritual path.

Tourmaline

Tourmaline's name comes from the Sinhalese word *'turmali'*, which means 'mixed'. There are many unique properties of tourmaline. First, they are piezoelectric, which means that when a crystal is heated or compressed (or vibrated) a different electrical charge will form at opposite ends of the crystal (an electrical potential). Conversely, if an electrical potential is applied to the crystal, it will vibrate. It becomes a polarized crystalline magnet and can attract light objects. This property was noticed long ago, before science could explain it: in the Netherlands, tourmalines were called 'aschentrekkers' because they attracted ashes and could be used to clean pipes! Secondly they are pleochroic, which means that the crystal will look darker in color when viewed down the long axis of the crystal than when viewed from the side. This property goes beyond the idea that the crystal is just thicker in that direction. Even equally-dimensioned crystals will demonstrate this trait.

Tourmaline is a favourite among crystal therapists. The tourmaline family as a whole gives off a very focused directional energy; this can be very useful when one wishes to 'work' within a particular chakra that may be too open, blocked, distorted or split. They can still be used for body layouts to direct the energy flow; they are also good for moving energy between the chakras. For working on the meridian system you need to point the termination in the direction you wish the energy to flow. They also make exceptionally good meditation stones and are used to make a wonderful healing gemstone essence.

Black Tourmaline - Gives protection from negativity and heavy energies. It has been used to deflect the negative energy from all electrical equipment and especially computers. It also grounds heavy, stagnant or negative energy; as with all tourmalines it is very directional. It has been used as an energy deflector, as it is an excellent stone for those with potential for exposure to excessive amounts of radiation. It will protect against the negative thought forms and even the evil 'eye' of another. It has been used to help people after operations and chemotherapy. It is used for problems of the spine, feet, legs and for nervous disorders. It is also good for kidney and adrenal problems.

Affirmation: I now choose to heal myself on every level and become free of all dis-ease.

Healing Meditation - Root Chakra

1. Choose a warm comfortable place where you can lie down undisturbed for at least an hour. Never rush a meditation. View it as a sacred healing space, so you need to make sure it is energetically clean. Make sure you are wearing warm, loose, comfortable clothes.

2. Breathe slowly, encouraging energy to flow up and down your nervous system.....and begin to relax your body. Go through your whole body, starting at your feet, and consciously relax each part, moving up and finishing at your head. Allow yourself to really let go and relax, feel yourself sinking into the floor or bed....

3. Visualize yourself on a warm tropical sandy beach.....it is just before sunrise, the start of a new day......you feel the energy of daybreak....as the earth begins to stir at the dawn's approach.......an air of expectancy and excitement floods through your body as you listen to the gentle lapping waves................

4.   Sit down on the sandy beach and place your hands on the warm clean soft sand; really feel the sand between your fingers........

5.   Become aware of the weight of your body as the gentle pull of gravity holds you in its tender embrace......turn your full attention to your root chakra, as it makes contact with the warm soft sand.......you are now going to let go of all thoughts and outside stimulations and experience an overwhelming vibrant red color that will come flooding up into your root chakra from the ground below.....

6.   As the flush of red comes upon you, a strange spinning feeling will come right at the base of your spine, where you sit on the warm sand.......you will suddenly feel your body extending down to the centre of the earth.....as this happens you will feel what it's like to be perfectly balanced atop a spinning planet.

7.   Allow this energy and feeling to stay with you as long as is comfortable....gradually building up in future sessions to longer....and longer.....

8.   When you are ready, allow the vibrant red energy to flood your lower body.........allowing it to move to your heart...........here it activates your seed atom....this is the same permanent atom that dwells in all people from the soul's original creation through all incarnations.......this divine spark looks like a star.......it expands your philosophical skills to gradually understand concepts of God....

9.   Now focus your attention on your crown chakra; imagine a cap of a thousand pristine white petals hugging your head........through the centre, where the petals meet, is an opening through which pours white cosmic brilliant light.......this is your link with the Divine source, your connection to everything that was, is, or will be......

10.   Allow this light to pour into your head, your throat, your chest and into your heart......here it merges with the red and transforms, using divine alchemy, into pink........healthy pink......allow the pink energy to move around your body.....flowing and moving to wherever it is needed, bringing warmth, love, healing........really let go.....allow any thoughts, feelings or emotions this energy unearths to be released; use your breath and breathe out any negative thoughts, feelings or emotions as they arise.....really breathe them away....

11.   Stay with this energy as long as you like; it can heal a lot of stored pain and anger. By mixing the brilliance of the white cosmic light of divine guidance in with the red you can transmute and release all disease; pink relaxes the body ready to receive healing.....it makes you more receptive.....to spiritual beauty, universal love and compassion.......pink expands...it shows you a beauty that extends beyond the physical plane......it teaches you how to fulfill your potential.

12.   When you are ready and all energy movements have ceased, begin to become aware of your energy field, your aura; by now it should be a healthy shade of pink and glowing nicely with warmth and relaxation.....you should stay where you are for five more minutes......keep breathing out any pain or negativity.......this can continue for some time......so.....let it go...

13.   Come out of meditation very slowly, like a cat having an after-nap stretch.

As well as tuning you in to the Earth and your root chakra, this meditation tunes you into your crown chakra for divine guidance, especially for healing. Once you fully activate your higher self you will find healing follows very quickly. It also opens your heart chakra with the red, then cosmic brilliant white, which merges into the pink. The pink makes your body really relax, which makes you open and receptive to healing on all levels. Use pink after a person has been assaulted in any way. Use this meditation as often as you need it. For those who wish to go further, please read the Kundalini meditation following.

Kundalini Root Chakra Meditation

1.   It is necessary to be seated comfortably, so sit in a relaxed steady posture with the spine and neck held erect but not tense. This means that the base of the spine needs to be higher than the knees, so tilting the pelvis forwards alters your posture into a position where the spine will remain upright but relaxed. The easiest way of doing this is to put a small, firm cushion or rolled up towel beneath the base of the spine, whether you are sitting cross-legged on the floor or on a chair. If in a chair, another small firm cushion in the small of the back prevents lolling into the chair and keeps the lungs free to move naturally. The spiritual current must be able to flow unimpeded from the base of the spine to the top of the head.

2.   It is best if you can sit cross-legged; this forms a triangular path for the energy field and stops it dissipating in all directions. Place your hands on your lap, palms upwards, left hand on top of right. Then place your right thumb on top of your left thumb. This is your primary hand 'Mudra'. You need to employ this hand position throughout all your kundalini meditations.

3.   Without making any effort to alter your breathing, simply tune in to the actual physical sensations you feel in your nose as air rushes in and out of your nasal passage......with every new breath.......be sure to relax your jaw and tongue........at the same time tune in to the sounds created as the air rushes in and out of your nose.....feel the sensations in your chest as you breathe..........

4.   Allow your awareness to expand to include the tip of your nose......your hands and fingers.....your feet and toes....your whole body, here in the present moment....relax and enjoy the pure experience of effortless breathing and deep meditative calm......tune in to your heart beating.

5.   As you inhale slowly, consciously focus upon the sensation of energy flowing up from the earth into your root chakra and then on upwards in sequential order through each chakra......now as you exhale slowly, open up to receive a spontaneous flow of energy from above......experience a downflow of light, insight and power into your body....moving through each chakra in turn until all seven chakras have been illuminated from above.....and you are empty of air...........then again, without effort, let your breath spontaneously come rushing into you; allow energy to flow up from the earth into your chakras all the way to the crown........rather than just visualising this, see if you can actually feel this experience happening inside you.....

6.   Again, after the full inhale, reverse the experience...opening to the downflow of universal energy into your personal energy system....continue with this pattern for a number of breaths....

7.   We need to apply our primary energy seal or 'Bhanda' at this point. So contract the Hui Yin point (Moola Bhanda) - the sphincter contraction - and just allow your breathing to come and go effortlessly......and without any hesitation, allow the sound for the root chakra to come into your mind...LAM.....let the word begin to vibrate in your mind before you begin to vocalize it......simply hear the sound in your inner realms of consciousness.......now again, without effort, allow the sound to come alive within your vocal cords, with your lips closed.....this subtle chanting is so powerful.....it needs to be employed for a number of breaths before opening the lips.

8.   Now, in your own time, spontaneously let your lips open and form the L sound as you exhale...make this consonant sound with your tongue touching the roof of your mouth.....feel the vibration reaching all the way down to your root chakra.....now let your tongue fall away from the roof of your mouth and allow the soft A sound, followed by the M sound, to be made all in the same exhale.......continue to focus on the root chakra........and continue with this chanting as long as you like...............

9.   Now visualise or look directly at the root chakra mandala....use the one in this book......become aware of the chakra mandala.... as you focus on the energy movements, colors and shapes it contains.......

10.   Continue to visualise or gaze at the mandala as long as you desire....only when you feel completely ready, visualise or feel your root chakra begin to turn upwards.....towards your crown chakra....this brings spiritual energy into your root chakra and allows for your full attention to be focused upwards towards your spiritual development and enlightenment.......

11.   At some point begin to sound the LAM again......bringing auditory vibration into harmony with visual vibration......do the Hui Yin (Moola Bhanda) contraction again and the breath energy movement up and down the spine.....feel yourself going even deeper into the root chakra experience.........then just relax, breathe without effort and be open to feeling a new experience throughout your chakra system....very gently open your eyes and feel the new energy flow of your body......don't forget to reverse the root chakra to point downwards as you once more anchor yourself on the earth plane of ego existence......

Hui Yin or Moola Bandha: A muscular contraction of the Hui Yin point is a necessary part of first chakra awakening; it is exceedingly important to devote a great deal of time and patience to it in meditation sessions. If you don't become deeply immersed in this special kundalini awakening, you can forget the rest of the kundalini awakening programme - this is crucial. The Hui Yin point is between the anus and the genitals. It relates to the sphincter muscles of the anus - while using the breathing as a pump to raise kundalini up the spine, high frequency Chi enters your system. This point must be held for the entire time you are practising a kundalini meditation. Contraction is to prevent Chi from escaping from this point. Therefore, it is important to practise holding this point to build up your co-ordination and muscular strength in this area. Practise contracting the muscles in this area 20 times in a row and then holding them as long as you can. Also practise contracting these muscles continuously while you go about your daily activities. As you continue it will become easier and easier and you will be able to contract them for longer periods of time. Your muscular co-ordination will develop so that you will be able to isolate the different muscle groups into back, middle, and front. It is the middle area that it is important to hold. This is similar to the kagel birth exercise for women.

Illustrations

Axes of crystal systems with examples of crystal formations of each group

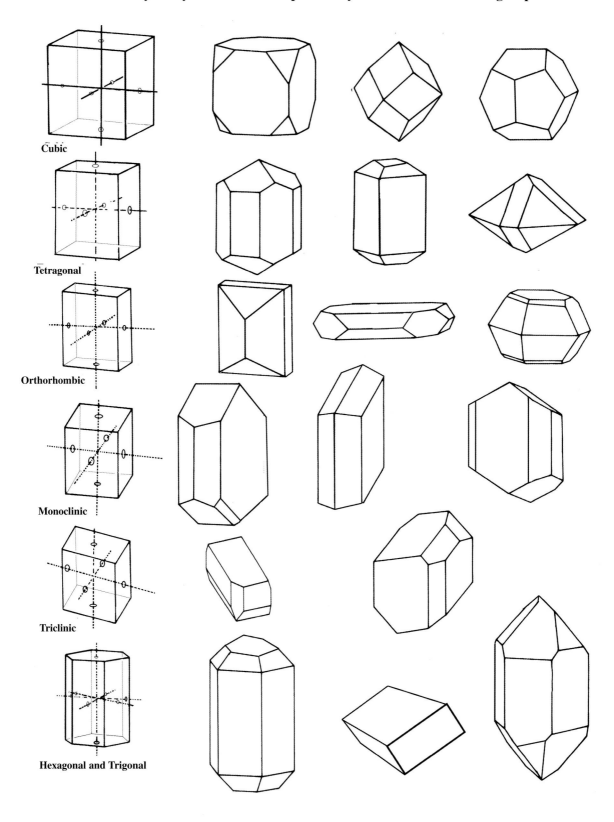

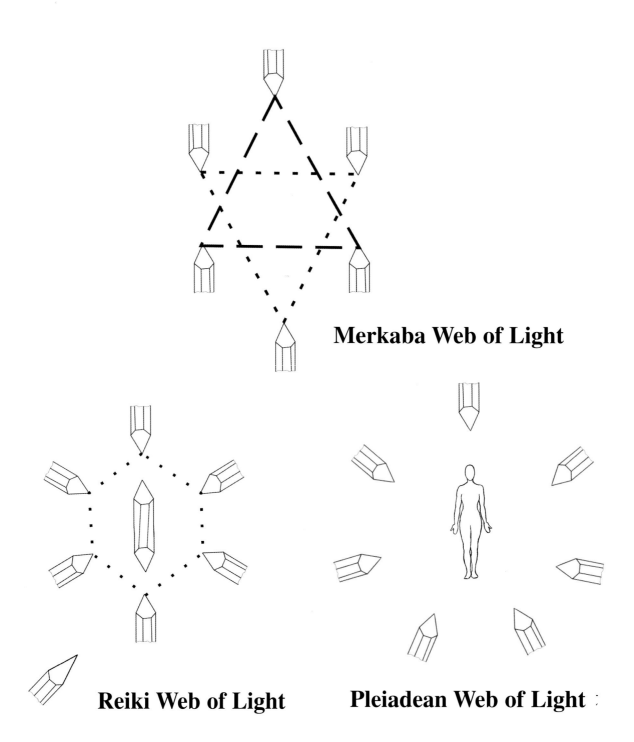

Merkaba Web of Light

Reiki Web of Light   **Pleiadean Web of Light**

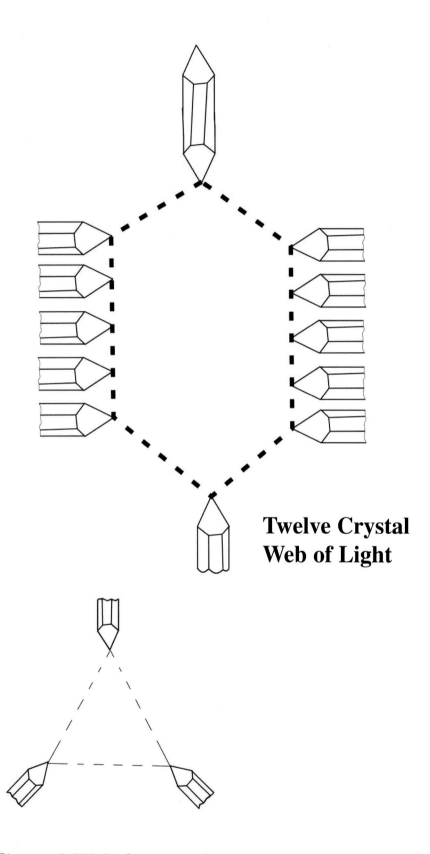

**Twelve Crystal
Web of Light**

Crystal Web for Meditation

The Aura

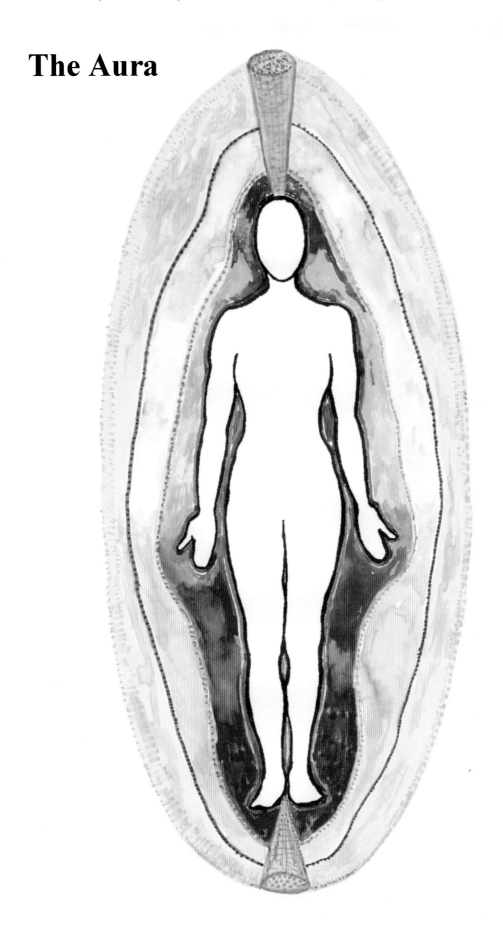

Chakra Placement

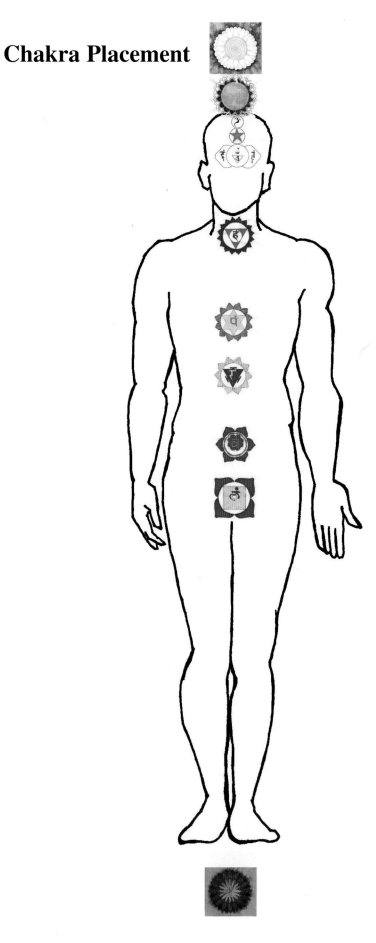

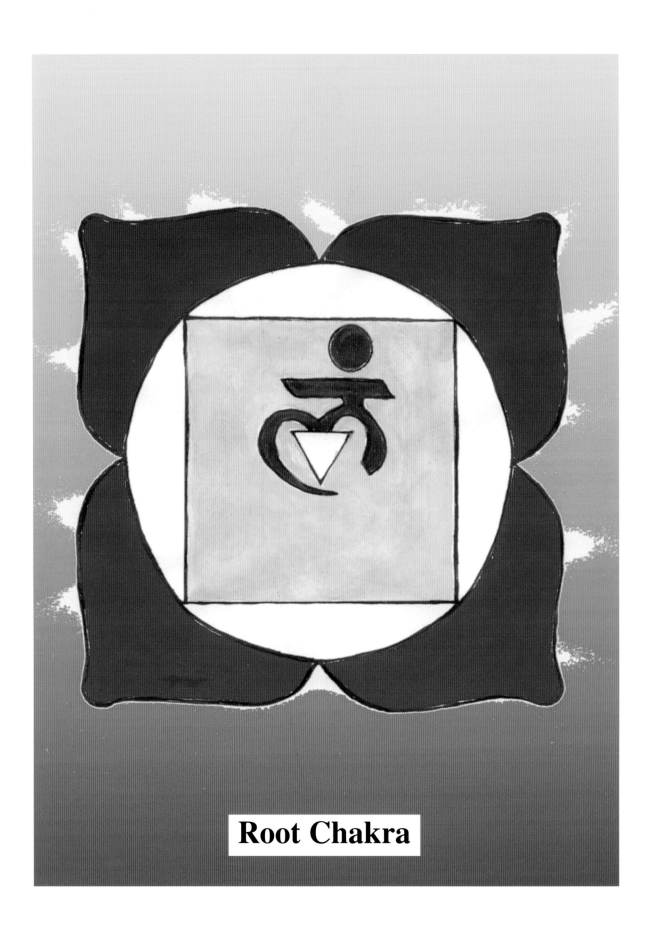

Root Chakra

Sacral Chakra

Solar Plexus Chakra

Heart Chakra

Throat Chakra

Third Eye Chakra

Crown Chakra

Earth Star Chakra

Soul Star Chakra

Part 13

The Sacral Chakra

The principal function of the second chakra is to manifest primal creative energy in the form of functional 'sexual' resonance - which the nervous system then transmutes by divine alchemy into the higher spiritual force that powers enlightenment. The second chakra is thus an essential ingredient in the opening of the higher chakras; without the 'pressure' of this chakra's raw sexual power transmuted into spiritual energy, all hope of perfectly balanced higher chakra functioning is futile. The Sanskrit name of this chakra is *svadhisthana*; the direct translation is *sva* - vital force, soul; *adhisthana* - seat or abode. It is commonly known in the West as the water or sexual chakra or sweetness. In Hindu scriptures the second chakra is located in the sexual organs and upwards towards the navel, although it is not easy to draw a line between where the root chakra finishes and the sacral chakra begins, due to the position of the genitals, which dwell in both chakras. The area on the spine where the sexual ganglia leave the spinal cord and move down and forward to the sexual organs is located very high and close to the navel.

In the last chapter we saw how the root chakra provides the basic energy for strong masculine actions related to survival; now, with the second chakra, we switch into its opposite polarity, as it brings us directly to the flowing, nurturing, emotional, feminine power needed to conceive and give birth to a new life. From the opposites we begin to explore manifestation. Chinese scriptures which examine yin and yang, male and female, black and white, night and day, teach us the constant of change, of the balance of opposites. Your breathing is a perfect example of yin and yang in perfect harmony, the in-breath and the out-breath. Through the movement of opposites manifestation takes place.

Without the in and out breath of life your physical body dies. This constant dance of energy, this interaction between the chakras, is vital for harmony. When we become overly fixated with any one of the chakras, we cause a disturbance in the integral essential balance of yin and yang in our bodies. We then end up either physically ill, emotionally distressed, mentally disturbed or spiritually unbalanced - or all of the above together. Your body has the innate ability to heal itself so, during the meditations and spiritual development I personally teach, you will always be guided to give conscious attention to all your chakras in any one session.

Looking deeply within the second chakra we find it associated with water, vitality, attraction, magnetism, desire, creativity, sexuality and emotion. The word emotion comes from the Latin movere, which means "to move" and e, which means "out". The second chakra, therefore, is wholly linked to our emotional movements and movement in all its forms. There is great cleansing potential in this chakra associated with personality disorders related to the emotions. The bodily parts it rules are all fluid functions of the body, kidneys and bladder, lymphatic system, reproductive system, breasts, tongue, fat deposits, skin. It links the physical and mental energies. An unbalanced sex drive, emotional instability, feelings of isolation can also be healed through balancing this chakra. This energy centre also gives you your social awareness and relates to your partnerships. Other malfunctions are: frigidity; impotence; bladder, kidney and uterine disorders; some prostate problems; middle back pain; fertility; asthma; bronchitis; gout; gallstones and obesity. This chakra also deals with purification and removal of poisons from the intestines. Physical lethargy and apathy, also the emotions of fear, shock and guilt, are under the domain of this feminine chakra.

The symbol for this chakra is the six-petal orange-red lotus flower, containing a second lotus flower: this represents the various intensities of the emotions. By meditating on this chakra you learn to turn the

129

tidal wave of your emotions upwards - to feel them flowing through your body, bringing spiritual surrender. An upward-pointing crescent moon in the centre is where the attention must be fixed when meditating on this chakra. This gives command over the water element and confers psychic powers, intuitional knowledge and knowledge of the astral plane. Because the moon is part hidden, portrayed as a crescent, it gives the feeling of the yin/yang balance needed to manifest cosmic awareness within the body. Within the moon lies the *'Makara'*, a fish-tailed alligator with a coiled tail. This water dragon of ancient Asian mythology is unable to live in captivity; it would rather die than lose its freedom of liquid movement. It is very important to remember, as you shift your attention from the first chakra to the second, to open yourself to a liquid, feminine, emotional surrender. In traditional Hindu folklore, the kundalini energy is always portrayed as a feminine goddess and to awaken this latent power of the kundalini is definitely to awaken a feminine force. If you find that you are afraid of the mysterious, feminine, yin dimension of your personal energy system, then you will need to spend a lot of time learning to 'surrender' to your higher spiritual nature. In the Christian terminology it can be thought of as "Thy will be done", not my will, or your entire spiritual development will be hindered, if not halted altogether. The best way of finding this 'surrender' energy is through breathing techniques. The ones taught in the kundalini meditations are perfect for developing the surrender needed - especially going deeper and deeper into your exhale, allowing your lungs to be 'empty' of air for longer periods of time, brings direct knowledge of the depths of your being and direct personal contact with your divine connection and personal crystalline resonance.

Although each of the master chakras is envisaged in sacred lore as a lotus flower, this is only a representation. The lotuses are not the map, merely the signposts, which initially begin to help you make sense of these vast mysterious energy centres. The study of the chakras is a lifetime pursuit, as each chakra is a complete universe within itself. Perhaps an understanding of this can be gained by studying the 'sounds' of the chakras. These mantras are what are called essence-sounds. They have been heard deep in meditation both by the great Masters of ancient times and by contemporary Masters as well. The master chakras are swirling vortexes of energy (they resemble, when viewed from a particular distance, spiralling galaxies that we see through our telescopes; likewise, atoms are miniature galaxies with their own spinning vortexes and central fixation points - this gives us our major clue to the nature of not only the universe but also ourselves. As above, so below; we are a directed replication of the universe, the microcosm of the macrocosm. The swirling, spiralling vortex of energy creates a particular tone, just as a spinning top will make a particular humming sound, which is audible to our physical ears. The chakras, though, have an infinitely more intricate vibrational quality; in fact each chakra is an immense symphony and each person's chakras make a symphonic sound distinctive to that person. So we are on the brink of an extraordinary vast sphere of reality when we begin to tune in to the subtle vibratory realm of reality generated by the energy centres in both our own bodies and those of people around us. The traditional sound for the sacral chakra is the *bija* mantra VAM in the Hindu tradition, and a slightly altered and even more powerful VANG in the Tantric Buddhist tradition of Nepal and Tibet.

The orange ray is primarily associated with this chakra, as is the color red. The first three chakras all are associated with red, but in the sacral chakra it is defined as the marriage of the physical red with the intellectual of the yellow. This gives the color orange, which is for creativity, activity, rejuvenation, wisdom and benevolence. When this chakra is balanced you will 'flow'. When this chakra is activated fully you become healthy, full of vitality and originality. Your originality originates from validity - you no longer need outside forces to validate your existence; once your kundalini has been awakened your freedom is never in doubt; indeed the color orange stands for freedom.

Your guide to this chakra is Archangel Gabriel. He is the divine messenger whose arrival in your life signals a time of unprecedented spiritual growth and change, as you release all your old fear-based concepts of who you think you are as defined by others and begin to experience yourself as you truly are, an unlimited being of love, wisdom and compassion. Your other guide is the kundalini goddess herself.

Crystal Web of Light - Creative Fire

Crystals:
          1 carnelian, tumbled or faceted
          2 citrine, tumbled, faceted or natural
          1 garnet, tumbled, faceted or natural
          1 sunstone/golden labradorite, tumbled, faceted or natural
          1 zincite natural point
          12 clear quartz points

Uses: This crystal web is aimed primarily at the sacral chakra. When the sacral chakra is out of balance, the next chakra above - the solar plexus - and the root chakra below will have a greatly impaired functioning too. A balanced sacral chakra is shown when you trust your own feelings, you are creative and feel good about expressing your creativity. If your sacral chakra is too open you will feel emotionally unbalanced and find yourself living in a fantasy world. The other signs of being too open in the sacral chakra are aggression, sexual manipulation of others or sexual fixation. If you are too closed you will be over-sensitive to others' energy, feel guilty for no reason or be frigid or impotent physically and spiritually.

The crystal web of creative fire has been used to aid fertility. Physically, it can help with problems of the lower back, lower intestines, the abdomen, the kidneys, all fluid functions of the body, ovaries, testes, womb and impotency. The sacral chakra is also associated with vitality, attraction, desire, emotion, creativity, sexuality and water, fear, shock and guilt. There is a great cleansing potential released when this crystal web of light is used for healing personality disorders related to the emotions. Creative fire can help to ground and focus thoughts and emotions. It has been utilised to protect the user from hatred, envy and rage. It also lifts the spirits, banishing negativity. For those who suffer from existential fears, past physical abuse, vitality-sapping illness or any long-standing mental anguish, it is a good on-going supplement to their life force and should be used on a regular basis.

This crystal web can also help with the life lessons of uncovering the motivations influencing your choices, which are based on past conditioning. It really helps you fully understand what motivates you; in other words, who or what in your past is pulling your strings now? Creative fire gently removes these emotional snares and transmutes them into positive loving energy. It really makes you look what sacrifice you make to suit others? Dysfunctional relationships are toxic to both people involved. Try saying 'no' next time - you don't even have to explain. It also makes you aware of how much you nurture yourself; it asks about taking responsibility for your own health and body, taking regular gentle exercise like walking or Yoga. It also asks 'is your life sweet?' - or has all the sweetness gone out of your life? If it has, creative fire can initiate positive change so you regain your sweetness. If you are not happy in what you do, how can you advance spiritually? Creative fire is also a forceful combination for clearing and activating the heart and lower three chakras, bringing in the ability to create your own reality; this is a powerful manifestation of the divine will in action. This will work in assisting you in clearly implanting your envisioned dream into the etheric pattern. The combined signature is strong, stimulating and creative when used correctly in crystal therapy.

1 carnelian placed at the sacral chakra.

2 citrine, one placed in the palm of each hand.

1 garnet placed on the heart chakra.

1 golden labradorite placed at the solar plexus chakra.

1 zincite placed at the navel, point upwards.

12 clear quartz single terminated crystals placed evenly around the body. The terminations should point towards the body.

Process:

1.   Cleanse all the crystals and programme the clear quartz for healing.

2. Choose a warm comfortable place where you can lie down undisturbed for at least an hour. Never rush a crystal web of light process. View it as a sacred healing space, so you need to make sure it is energetically clean. Make sure you are wearing warm, loose, comfortable clothes.

3. Relax by consciously becoming aware of your breathing and heartbeat. You can play soothing music, light candles and burn incense.

4. Lay the stones around and on the body and hold the citrine in your hands.

5. Allow 20 minutes to facilitate the integration of the crystal vibration.

6. Feel free to remove the crystals sooner, if you have integrated the crystal energy very quickly.

7. Remove the crystals in reverse order of placement.

8. Make sure you are fully grounded, centred and balanced.

9. Cleanse your crystals (using your chosen method).

10. Finish by giving thanks and asking mentally that all the healing work you have just accomplished is closed, sealed and protected with Divine love and wisdom.

11. Give yourself sufficient time to integrate the crystal therapy session.

12. As a general guideline it is suggested a period of twice the length of time you were actually lying in the crystal therapy web be allowed for integration.

Carnelian

Carnelian's signature is strong, stimulating and creative; when used in crystal therapy it has the full potential to balance the sacral chakra completely. The sacral chakra is located in the sexual organs and upwards towards the navel. When the sacral chakra is out of balance, the next chakra above - the solar plexus - and the root chakra below will have a greatly impaired functioning too.

A balanced sacral chakra is shown when you trust your own feelings, you are creative and feel good about expressing your creativity. If your sacral chakra is too open you will feel emotionally unbalanced and find yourself living in a fantasy world. The other signs of being too open in the sacral chakra are aggression, sexual manipulation of others or sexual fixation. If you are too closed you will be over-sensitive to others' energy, feel guilty for no reason or be frigid or impotent. Carnelian has been used to aid fertility. Physically, carnelian can help with problems of the lower back, lower intestines, the abdomen, the kidneys, all fluid functions of the body, ovaries, testes, womb and impotency. Carnelian is also associated with vitality, attraction, desire, emotion, creativity, sexuality and water, fear, shock and guilt. There is a great cleansing potential released when this crystal is used for healing personality disorders related to the emotions. Carnelian can help to ground and focus thoughts and emotions. It has been utilised to protect the user from hatred, envy and rage. It also lifts the spirits, banishing negativity. For those who suffer from existential fears, past physical abuse, vitality-sapping illness or any long-standing mental anguish, carnelian is a good on-going supplement to their life force and should be carried or worn on a regular basis.

Always check with kinesiology for the correct period of wearing duration; as with all crystals you must check on a regular basis the correct time period of use. Carnelian can also help with the life lessons of uncovering the motivations influencing your choices, which are based on past conditioning. It really helps you fully understand what motivates you. In other words, who or what in your past is pulling your strings now? Carnelian can also accelerate the healing process of broken bones, torn ligaments and strained muscles. You could apply it in a gemstone cream or as a gemstone aura spray, or even wrap a tumbled stone into the bandage.

Affirmation: I trust my own feelings, I am creative and I feel good about expressing my creativity.

Citrine

Natural citrine (yellow quartz) is not common and occurs only sparingly in many large quartz deposits. As such it is greatly prized by crystal therapists and healers. Most of the yellow and brownish-yellow quartz which in the past was often sold under the misnomer 'topaz' is heat-treated amethyst. Most material comes from Minas Gerais, Brazil, but almost all of the Brazilian material is heat-treated amethyst. Citrine gets its name from the French word for lemon, 'citron': many citrines have a pale lemon color. In ancient times, citrine was carried as a protection against snake venom and the evil thoughts of others. Although the darker orange colors of citrine, sometimes called Madeira citrine after the color of the wine, have generally been the most valued, in modern times many people prefer the bright lemony shades.

Citrine is a lustrous gem of a stone which holds the key to a balanced solar plexus chakra. A balanced solar plexus or power chakra, as it is sometimes known, is shown by the following characteristics: personal power; spontaneity; positive mental attitudes; joy, hope and freedom from emotional hang-ups and inhibitions; a keen thirst for knowledge, wisdom and spiritual understanding. So, if you choose to wear citrine, get ready for a life filled with wonder, delight, enthusiasm, expansion, originality, honesty, justice and self-confidence. People just feel great around citrine energy, of that there is no doubt; it banishes negativity and deep gloom. Yes, citrine certainly holds the answer to depression; it has a general 'feel good' factor. Citrine will also help you think through your difficulties and encourages you to explore all avenues, leaving no stone unturned until you find the best solution. It stimulates mental wisdom and is very penetrating; it will aid your total concentration. Citrine loves new ideas and looking at the world with fresh 'eyes', but it hates hesitation, procrastination and ignorance and can be impatient.

Citrine aids communication, so if you sometimes feel 'tongue tied', wear a citrine pendant and you will find you eloquently have no shortage of words. On a higher level, citrine will aid intuition and telepathy, bringing spiritual wisdom. If your solar plexus chakra is blocked, underactive or distorted, you will be overly concerned with what others think, be fearful of being alone, insecure and need constant reassurance. If your solar plexus chakra is too open or spinning too fast, you will be angry, controlling, workaholic, judgemental and superior. Citrine is one of the best stones of our time for M.E. and relieving energy drain. It brings abundance on all levels and has been called the 'merchant's stone', because carrying or wearing a citrine has a positive beneficial effect on cash flows, easing the burdens associated with too little money.

Citrine works first of all on the pancreas, then all the other organs associated with the solar plexus chakra: liver, gall-bladder, spleen and middle stomach. We store anger in the liver and the solar plexus is where our emotional upsets will register first. Citrine knows how to remove this stored pain; it also knows how to rid the body of toxins and cellulite. It is the great eliminator. It relieves constipation. Constipation is holding on to the past. Citrine tones and cleanses the system, the mind and the emotions. So if you want to let go and lose some mental, emotional or physical weight, join the enlightened crystal weight-watchers and wear a citrine. As a gem essence it is used for menopausal flushes, menstrual difficulties and hormone problems, stomach ulcers, fatigue, allergies and diabetes.

Affirmation: I deserve all the love, respect, joy and prosperity that flows into my life. I am open to receiving all that is good.

Garnet - See the Root Chakra for details of properties.

Clear Quartz - See the Root Chakra for details of properties.

Sunstone (Golden Labradorite)

Oligoclase is not a well-known mineral but has been used as a semi-precious stone under the names of sunstone and moonstone. Sunstone has flashes of reddish color caused by inclusions of hematite or goethite. The display is produced from lamellar intergrowths inside the crystal. These intergrowths result from compatible chemistries at high temperatures becoming incompatible at lower temperatures and thus a separating and layering of these two phases. The resulting shimmer effect is caused by a ray of light entering a layer and being refracted back and forth by deeper layers before it exits the crystal. This refracted ray has a different character than when it went in and it produces the moon-like glow. There are two types of 'sunstone' available at the present time. The orange one shows brilliant reflections due to inclusions (usually goethite or hematite); the other, from Oregon in the USA, is a lovely fresh transparent yellow.

The orange sunstone is used in bringing in vibrant solar energies in meditation and body layouts, for connecting with one's own source of light, transmuting dark or negative energies into positive healing energies. It is very yang in nature and emits a strong energy of leadership and positive personal empowerment. It works on the sacral chakra, lower back, lower intestines, abdomen, kidneys, bladder and ovaries. Orange sunstone is very magnetic and attracts the energy of making things happen now. It makes you take action in your life; the time for procrastination and hiding your light away is past; rather than just dreaming of the life you would like, live the life you want to live right now - no more postponement, deferral, delay or stalling. It is a strong stone, which links you in to your intuition. It removes inhibitions, sexual hang-ups, self-imposed constraints, repression and emotional hang-ups, even emotional hook-ups. The emotional hook-ups from others are energies other people have placed within your energy field to control or manipulate you in some way. They can be very debilitating and draining on your energy field. Sunstone gently removes these emotional snares and transmutes them into positive loving energy. Sunstone really makes you look what sacrifice you make to suit others. Dysfunctional relationships are toxic to both people involved. Try saying 'no' next time - you don't even have to explain. Sunstone also makes you aware of how much you nurture yourself; it asks about taking responsibility for your own health and body, taking regular gentle exercise like walking or Yoga. It also asks 'is your life sweet?' - or has all the sweetness gone out of your life? If it has, sunstone can initiate positive change so you regain your sweetness. If you are not happy in what you do, how can you advance spiritually?

The Oregon sunstone, sometimes known as golden labradorite, is believed to be among the most beneficial stones for the third chakra - the solar plexus - the stomach, spleen, liver, gall-bladder, adrenal glands, nervous and digestive systems. It has a warm sunny nature. It helps you to develop your own originality. It is expansive to the mental body, allowing for integration of knowledge, clarity and wisdom. It is ideal for developing originality and enlightened leadership. It makes you sociable, without being dependant. It gives you the power to be an individual, to be unique, while celebrating your continued connection to humanity. The spiritual warrior relies on inner strength, tempered by the belief that guidance comes from a Divine force. This strength becomes honed and refined through facing and overcoming external challenges. As you learn to honour and value yourself, the inner chant of "I am not worthy" finds less and less space within your energy field. Only by truly honouring and loving yourself can you hope to act out of love and compassion for others. Sunstone teaches you that when you suppress your psychic sensitivity it leads to blockages around the solar plexus chakra; these manifest as excess weight around the middle, digestive problems and stomach ulcers. Sunstone is excellent for weight loss and healing digestive problems.

Affirmation: I tune in to the energies of the Sun; my enlightened personal power is becoming stronger every day.

Zincite

Informed sources tell us that the Polish zincite is a curious occurrence that was formed as a consequence of zinc smelting, growing spontaneously in the air vents or chimneys of the smelters. They have a spectacular red/orange and gold color with eye-catching crystal formations. Metaphysically, the energies are well attuned to the lower three chakras, bringing an enhancement of overall life force, as well as confidence, strength, creativity and courage. Zincite provides for the synergy of personal power, freedom, strength and endurance in all endeavours. Zincite is the 'creative fire' of magnetic manifestation. It encourages activity, it has flamboyance and an air of expectation and excitement around it. It is not for the faint-hearted, if you decide to wear it. Its untiring energy is fearless, as it re-energizes depleted energy systems. If you are feeling pessimistic or dwelling on past events, depressed, or in shock, zincite is a very good crystal to work with. Zincite helps you let go of the past, of painful memories, shock, trauma, psychological paralysis and the fear of moving forward. Zincite is the crystal that pulls you through, breaks down barriers, shatters blocked energies.

Its energy is very easy to direct and extremely focused, almost as focused as laser quartz. It has been used extensively in body layouts as a creative fire to not only regenerate depleted energy systems but to energize creativity. Those who have worked with the layouts report that creative abundance has been achieved in all areas of their lives. It is good for menopausal symptoms and the 'empty nest' syndrome; it gives freedom to the spirit and aids intuition - the gut instinct. Zincite removes energy blocks throughout the system, restoring the natural flow of vitality in the meridian system. It can open the kundalini channel and is a great re-energizer. With conscious use it will anchor the light body into the physical body. Zincite treats hair, skin and prostate gland problems. It is good for M.E., candida and all immune system disorders, intestinal disorders, assimilation, bowel disturbances, kidney complaints, mucus, catarrh, asthma, bronchitis, epilepsy, mental disorders, rheumatism, torn ligaments, broken bones, infertility and phobias. It has been extensively used to treat AIDS patients and those with severe immune system disorders. Zincite's focused energy has been used to open gateways - portals into other realms of consciousness.

Affirmation: Life can be a succession of wonderful, beneficial experiences - if I choose it to be so.

Healing Meditation - Sacral Chakra

1. Choose a warm comfortable place where you can lie down undisturbed for at least an hour; never rush a meditation. Breathe slowly, encouraging energy to flow up and down your nervous system.....and begin to relax your body.....

2. Visualise yourself on a warm tropical sandy beach.....it is just before sunrise, the start of a new day......you feel the magnetic energy of daybreak, as the earth begins to stir at the dawn's approach.......an air of expectancy and excitement floods through your body as you listen to the gentle lapping waves.................

3. Sit or lie down on the sandy beach and place your hands on the warm clean soft golden sand.... really feel the sand between your fingers........as you do so you become even more aware of the sounds of the sea.....the gentle lapping of the waves has a hypnotic effect on your mind and it allows you to focus inwards to become aware of the tides of life within your own body.......

4. As you feel yourself relaxing more and more into your body, experience your heartbeat....blood flowing in your veins....revitalising you....energising you........your every breath celebrates life......the life force.....that is you.....

5. I want you to sense or visualise a beautiful orange light beginning to grow around your sacral chakra....feel its warm orange glow.........allow it to grow as large as possible.......when you can't contain it any longer, as you feel it is just growing too big to hold in that area.....allow it to flow through your whole body......like a great tidal wave of warmth........

6. Now focus your attention on your crown chakra....imagine a cap of a thousand pristine white petals gently hugging your head........through the centre, where the petals meet, is an opening through which pours a beautiful violet ray of liquid light.....

7. Allow this light to pour into your head, your throat, your chest and into your heart.....down through your stomach and into your sacral chakra.....the beautiful violet ray is the transmuting energy to raise the vibration and completely heal and balance the sacral chakra.......allow it to purge your sacral chakra of old pain, hurt, humiliation, rejection, loss, bereavement, shocks and fears.....allow it to heal all emotional trauma that you may have carried for years, even since before your birth.....

8.   The violet ray carries the ancient energy of the sacred violet flame of transmutation....this is not earthly fire.....but cosmic fire of total purification and deep soul protection.......it gently cleanses away all the stored putrefied negative emotional issues of low self-worth and fear-based realities.......allowing them to dissolve with dignity.........violet is a very dignified color.....

9.   Allow the violet flame to wash through your body and aura, bringing peace, purity, protection and transformation..........stay with this energy as long as you like....it can clear a lot of emotional trauma...............

10.   When you are ready and all energy movements have ceased, begin to become aware of your energy field, your aura.....by now it should be purified and protected....you should stay where you are for five more minutes......keep breathing out any emotional pain............this can continue for some time......so.....let it go...come out of meditation very slowly, like a cat having an after-nap stretch.

Kundalini Rising Sacral Chakra Meditation

1.   Sit in a comfortable steady posture with the spine and neck held erect but not tense. The psychic current must be able to flow unimpeded from the base of the spine to the top of the head.

2.   Sit cross-legged; this forms a triangular path for the energy field and stops it dispersing in all directions. Place your hands on your lap, palms upwards, left hand on top of right. Then place your right thumb on top of your left thumb. This is your primary hand 'Mudra'. You need to employ this hand position throughout all your kundalini meditations.

3.   Without making any effort to alter your breathing, simply tune in to the actual physical sensations you feel in your nose as air rushes in and out of your nasal passage......with every new breath......be sure to relax your jaw and tongue........at the same time tune in to the sounds created as the air rushes in and out of your nose.....feel the sensations in your chest as you breathe..........

4.   Allow your awareness to expand to include the tip of your nose......your hands and fingers.....your feet and toes....your whole body here in the present moment....relax and enjoy the pure experience of effortless breathing and deep meditative calm.......tune in to your heart beating.....

5.   As you inhale slowly, consciously focus upon the sensation of energy flowing up from the earth into your root chakra and then on upwards in sequential order through each chakra......now, as you exhale slowly, open up to receive a spontaneous flow of energy from above......experience a downflow of light, insight and power into your body....moving through each chakra in turn until all seven chakras have been illuminated from above.....and you are empty of air............then again, without effort, let your breath spontaneously come rushing into you......allow energy to flow up from the earth into your chakras all the way to the crown........rather than just visualising this, see if you can actually feel this experience happening inside you.....

6.   Again, after the full inhale, reverse the experience...opening to the downflow of universal energy into your personal energy system........continue with this pattern for a number of breaths....

7.   Then contract the Hui Yin/Moola Bhanda point - the sphincter contraction - and just allow your breathing to come and go effortlessly......and without any hesitation, allow the sound for the root chakra to come into your mind...LAM.....let the word begin to vibrate in your mind before you begin to vocalize it......simply hear the sound in your inner realms of consciousness.......now again, without effort, allow the sound to come alive within your vocal cords, with your lips closed.....this subtle chanting is so powerful.....it needs to be employed for a number of breaths before opening the lips.....

8. Now, in your own time, spontaneously let your lips open and form the L sound as you exhale...make this consonant sound with your tongue touching the roof of your mouth.....feel the vibration reaching all the way down to your root chakra.....now let your tongue fall away from the roof of your mouth and allow the soft A sound, followed by the M sound, to be made all in the same exhale.......... continue to focus on the root chakra and continue with this chanting as long as you like........

9. Now visualise or look directly at the root chakra mandala....use the one in this book......become aware of the chakra mandala......as you focus on the energy movements and shapes it contains.......when you are ready, visualise or feel your root chakra begin to turn upwards.....towards your crown chakra....this brings spiritual energy into your root chakra and allows for your full attention to be focused upwards towards your enlightenment.......

10. When you are ready, as you inhale imagine you are drawing up energy of a sexual nature and force from the root chakra.....from the very depths of your being...allow it to flow into your genitals....hold your breath for a moment on full, this allows the charge to be absorbed into your sacral chakra.....then simply let go of the air in your lungs as you breathe out.........just allow yourself to become empty in an effortless fashion........now consciously inhale and draw the energy upwards again......hold your breath for a moment on full....feel the charge of liquid excitement beginning to fill your sacral chakra.........then simply let go of the air in your lungs as you breathe out.........just allow yourself to become empty in an effortless fashion......

11. Continue in this breathing pattern until you feel a charge building up in your sacral chakra.... now you need to employ the next energy seal or bandha.....focus your awareness on your lower spine and push backwards very gently....if you get this movement right you will feel a very definite 'sensation' of gentle pressure on your spine and it will intensify the sacral chakra movement considerably.....

12. You can allow the energy to flow up your spine if it feels too much of a charge........if you can, though......really allow yourself to plunge into the liquid depths of your sacral chakra.......when you are ready, visualise or feel your sacral chakra begin to turn upwards.....towards your crown chakra....this brings spiritual energy into your sacral chakra and allows for your full attention to be focused upwards towards your enlightenment.......

13. Without any hesitation, allow the sound for the sacral chakra to come into your mind... VAM.....let the word begin to vibrate in your mind before you begin to vocalize it......simply hear the sound in your inner realms of consciousness.......now again, without effort, allow the sound to come alive within your vocal cords, with your lips closed.....this subtle chanting is so powerful.....it needs to be employed for a number of breaths before opening the lips.....

14. Now, in your own time, spontaneously let your lips open and form the V sound as you exhale...make this consonant sound .....feel the vibration reaching all the way down to your sacral chakra....allow the soft A sound, followed by the M sound, to be made all in the same exhale..continue to focus on the sacral chakra and continue with this chanting as long as you like.

15. Now visualise or look directly at the sacral chakra mandala......use the one in this book......become aware of the chakra mandala.... as you focus on the energy movements and shapes it contains.......continue to visualise or gaze at the mandala as long as you want....

16. When you are ready, allow the liquid energy you have created to flow up your spine through all your chakras in sequential order.........and pour out of the top of your head like a fountain of light............this sacred divine energy brings your whole energy field to life..........

17. Allow yourself plenty of time to integrate this new awareness. You need to practise this meditation on a daily basis; it is the culmination of the first and second chakra kundalini activation you have learned thus far........don't forget to reverse the root chakra to point downwards and the sacral chakra to point outwards.....as you once more anchor yourself on the earth plane of ego existence......

Part 14

The Solar Plexus Chakra

So far we have discovered that the root chakra is firmly fixed in the element of earth and the water chakra is concerned with the fluidity and movement of water; now we need to move upwards into the solar plexus chakra, which is aflame with the element of fire. If we move up the human torso a little further we discover the heart chakra, which is imbued with the magical quality of air. Thus, in the human body, within our own spinal column below the neck we have all the basic elements of earth, water, fire and air. They interact and complement each other beautifully when balanced. We are each unique as well and sometimes this balance is hard to achieve. So in this chapter we will explore the element of fire, but as we do so we must be aware that in order for fire to burn it must be fuelled from below and fanned by the air element of the heart chakra above, and this gives us a clue to major blockages in the solar plexus chakra. In order to balance the solar plexus chakra completely we need to engage the lightness and airiness of the heart whilst having a grounded reality. Remember, it is hard to think clearly when your stomach is too full or you are very hungry, although fasting is useful for calming the mind.

The traditional Sanskrit name for the solar plexus chakra is *manipuraka*; which means jewel of the navel. It is also known as the power chakra, navel chakra or lustrous gem. It is indeed located at the navel, but its effects are felt from just below the navel to just below the tip of the sternum. As with all the chakras we must always keep in mind that their locations are not static; they are located in slightly different places in different bodies. They also drift up and down the spine a little depending on one's spiritual and emotional condition. It is interesting to note that the medical profession recognises this area as being related to the sun - hence everyone is familiar with the term solar plexus. In China and other Eastern countries this chakra has been held in high regard due to the attention over millennia to the tradition of the male-dominated martial arts. In the martial arts tradition it is located just below the umbilicus and is a potent point for the gathering of chi. The best way to experience this chakra is through meditation - this will leave you in no doubt where your sun centre is located. This third chakra's polarity is masculine, explosive, flammable, wilful, powerful and yang.

Traditionally this third chakra is associated with the logical functioning of the mind. This means it also rules our intellectual prowess, thought processes, will power and energy manipulation on all levels, especially the astral and cold-hearted wilful aggression. It is also associated with the fire of anger and hatred, personal power, ambition, combustion, happiness, joy, laughter and fun. It rules and assimilates energy for the pancreas and adrenals, also the central nervous system, stomach, liver, gall-bladder, spleen and eyesight. Malfunctions include stomach ulcers and other digestive and eating disorders, also diabetes, low vitality, depression, phobias, chronic fatigue and allergies, constipation, flatulence, headaches and poor skin conditions due to faulty elimination. Negative emotions such as oversensitivity to criticism, a need to be in control, low self-esteem or the addictive personality, as well as sluggishness, negative thinking, boredom, cowardice, being judgemental, sarcastic, acidic and impatient. The yellow ray is associated with this chakra. The color yellow is for meditative analytical thought, intellectual activity, abundance and the manifestation of your dreams. The solar plexus is the junction that absorbs all the emotions. Emotional upset will register here first.

We are looking at the chakra that rules our present society in all its technological energy manipulating glory. We have all seen the explosive energy of the atom bomb, a triumph for the negative energy control of the solar plexus chakra. The world witnessed the dubious domination of others in Hitler, and most of the dictators of the last fifty years who have heartlessly damaged or destroyed the lives of countless millions. And the American-led business atmosphere of the eighties was a triumph of the solar plexus chakra power-play. Remember this chakra is raw power which can lead to enlightenment or annihilation.

Just as all life on this planet needs the energies of the sun to survive, we too need our sun centre. This chakra will assist us when perfectly balanced to move beyond the polarities of the two lower chakras' wilful desires, which are selfish and ego-led, into the manifestation of personal and planetary joy. As we evolve spiritually and take control of our personal power and personal responsibility we step outside the limiting rigid mental strait-jacket of late twentieth-century analytical thought patterns - moving into the abundance of personal responsibility and global abundance. It is also said "If you meditate on this chakra you will become dis-ease free and have no fear of fire, being able to control this element". A balanced solar plexus chakra is shown when we are optimistic, self-confident, original, tolerant, honest, just, flexible, adaptable and focused. The traditional sound for the solar plexus chakra is the *bija* mantra RAM in the Hindu tradition, and a slightly altered and even more powerful RANG in the Tantric Buddhist tradition of Nepal and Tibet.

The symbol for this chakra is the 10-petal lotus flower. The petals are yellow, representing wisdom, and the centre contains a deep red downward-pointing triangle surrounded by three *'svastikas'*, symbolic of fire. The three represents the combined energy of the three lower or physical realm chakras, because as we move into the higher chakras we shall move into the element of spirit. The creature associated with the solar plexus is the wild ram, which is an independent beast, not liking to be dominated or restrained, but it does have a remarkable sense of balance and poise and it is very powerful, much more so than in relation to its size.

There is another important chakra, *manas* - which means mind. This lies between the manipuraka and anahata chakras. It is the seat of the emotions, igniting imagination and creativity. When the manas and anahata chakras are activated together, they strengthen the heart and help you develop devotion to your spiritual path or goal. This helps you bring your dreams into reality. Your guides to this chakra are Archangels Michael and Haniel. Michael teaches you protection of the innocents. He carries the sword of truth; this helps you to cut away all illusion that may block your spiritual growth. Haniel teaches wisdom and mercy with divine use of will.

Crystal Web of Light - Lustrous Gem

Crystals:
        3 calcite, natural or tumbled, in red, orange and clear
        1 citrine, tumbled, faceted or natural
        1 rhodochrosite, tumbled, faceted or natural
        1 topaz, faceted or natural
        1 turquoise, tumbled, cabochon or natural
        5 clear quartz points

Uses: The crystal web - lustrous gem holds the key to a balanced solar plexus chakra. A balanced solar plexus is shown by the following characteristics: personal power; spontaneity; positive mental attitudes; joy, hope and freedom from emotional hang-ups and inhibitions; a keen thirst for knowledge, wisdom and spiritual understanding. So, if you choose to use the crystal web - lustrous gem, get ready for a life filled with wonder, delight, enthusiasm, expansion, originality, honesty, justice and self-confidence. It quickly banishes negativity and deep gloom. Yes, this web certainly holds the answer to depression; it has a general 'feel good' factor. It will also help you think through your difficulties and encourages you to explore all avenues, leaving no stone unturned until you find the best solution.

It stimulates mental wisdom and is very penetrating; it will aid your total concentration. It teaches you to explore new ideas and look at the world with fresh 'eyes'. It also stops hesitation, procrastination, ignorance and impatience. This crystal web aids communication. On a higher level, it will aid intuition and telepathy, bringing spiritual wisdom.

If your solar plexus chakra is blocked, underactive or distorted, you will be overly concerned with what others think, be fearful of being alone, insecure and need constant reassurance. If your solar plexus chakra is too open or spinning too fast, you will be angry, controlling, workaholic, judgemental and superior. This crystal web is helpful for M.E. and relieving energy drain. It brings abundance on all levels, easing the personal burdens associated with too little money. It works first of all on the pancreas, then all the other organs associated with the solar plexus chakra: liver, gall-bladder, spleen and middle stomach. We store anger in the liver and the solar plexus is where our emotional upsets will register first. It will remove stored pain; it also knows how to rid the body of toxins and cellulite. It is the great eliminator. It relieves constipation. Constipation is holding on to the past. This crystal web tones and cleanses the system, the mind and the emotions.

3 calcite - one red placed on the root chakra; one orange placed on the sacral chakra; one clear placed on the third eye chakra.

1 citrine placed just below the navel.

1 topaz placed on the solar plexus chakra.

1 rhodochrosite placed on the heart chakra.

1 turquoise placed on the throat chakra.

5 clear quartz single terminated crystals - one in each hand, pointed end towards the shoulders; one towards the sole of each foot; one pointing at the crown.

Process:

1. Cleanse all the crystals and programme the clear quartz for healing.

2. Choose a warm comfortable place where you can lie down undisturbed for at least an hour; never rush a crystal web of light process. View it as a sacred healing space, so you need to make sure it is energetically clean. Make sure you are wearing warm, loose, comfortable clothes.

3. Relax by consciously becoming aware of your breathing and heartbeat; you can play soothing music, light candles and burn incense.

4. Lay the stones around and on the body and hold a clear quartz in each hand.

5. Allow 20 minutes to facilitate the integration of the crystal vibration.

6. Feel free to remove the crystals sooner, if you have integrated the crystal energy very quickly.

7. Remove the crystals in reverse order of placement.

8. Make sure you are fully grounded, centred and balanced.

9. Cleanse your crystals (using your chosen method).

10. Finish by giving thanks and asking mentally that all the healing work you have just accomplished is closed, sealed and protected with Divine love and wisdom.

11. Give yourself sufficient time to integrate the crystal therapy session.

12. As a general guideline it is suggested a period of twice the length of time you were actually lying in the crystal therapy web be allowed for integration.

Calcite

Calcite is a common and widely distributed mineral. It is a rock-forming mineral that is a major constituent in calcareous sedimentary rocks (limestone) and metamorphic rocks (marble). It may be precipitated directly from sea water and it forms the shells of many living organisms which on death accumulate to form limestone. In areas of hot springs it is deposited as travertine or tufa, and stalactites and stalagmites of calcite are common in caves of limestone.

Calcite is the biggest cleanser of negative stored energies within the human system. Its vast array of colors works on all areas of the body and aura, from the gross physical to the finest layers of the etheric.

Clear/rainbow inclusions - these bring cleansing, clarity and brilliance to all the chakras. Use clear/rainbow calcite when you want to bring about change, major or minor, in your life. Its brilliance allows you to wipe the slate clean, to start again. This shaft of pure cosmic light gives you new beginnings, free of all the old pain and sorrows. Clear calcite gives you the opportunity of bringing the Divine essence of the soul into all the levels of your being to facilitate deep soul healing. Many crystal therapists make use of clear calcite in healing, as it supports clearer perception of the truth by gently cleansing the eyes - not just the physical eyes, but the third, fourth and fifth eye - so as to fully activate the crown chakra into perfect alignment with the higher self and the Merkaba vehicle for ascension. The first incarnational experiences in this world were ones that were not in bodies such as we now have, and indeed, when we were floating in the ethers and the mists above this world, before it became more solid, that was our true nature, our true geometry, our true bodies, what we would call the light vehicle or the Merkaba. Clear calcite clears and activates all chakras and heals all conditions: it is a 'cure-all'. Used for detoxification, it is a crystal antiseptic. It also clears a room of negativity; the power of brilliance, iridescent rainbow light, will clear away old blocks and stagnation. It also makes an excellent gem essence, which is used as a 'cure-all'.

Red- this 'gentle' red crystal will work primarily on the genitals and reproductive organs. The glands of the body connected to red calcite are the gonads and ovaries. Deep red calcite understands what prompts the release of adrenaline into the bloodstream when there is danger, aggression or pain - thus its connection to releasing fear. Red calcite will destroy that which is holding up your growth; it is an excellent detoxifier. It releases stagnant energy blocks from every level of your life, not just the physical body, via cleansing and releasing stagnation within the base or root chakra. It is especially useful for healing problems of the hips, legs and feet, bringing stability and strength of will. It also gives you the power to move forward and to take action and it can ease stiff muscles and joints.

Orange - for stimulation of second chakra sexual energies, clearing negative energies there; regeneration and creativity. Also heals the reproductive system. Orange calcite is useful for any intestinal disorder or irritable bowel syndrome and kidney complaints. It also clears away any mucus or catarrh that may be in the system. Orange calcite can bring relief from emotional fear and emotional paralysis and can be used in cases of mental breakdown, depression, accidents, rape, divorce or suicidal feelings. Orange calcite restores equilibrium by releasing known and unknown fears and phobias.

Affirmation: I am cleansed of all negative thought patterns; I now allow myself to learn through joy, happiness and success.

Citrine - (See the Sacral Chakra for details of properties.)

Clear Quartz - (See the Root Chakra for details of properties)

Rhodochrosite

Rhodochrosite received its name from the Greek for rose colored, but has been known also as 'Rosinca' or 'Inca rose'. In a massive form its pink and white bands are extremely attractive and are often used in semi-precious jewellery. Rhodochrosite is often carved into figurines and tubular stalactitic forms are sliced into circles with concentric bands that are truly unique in the mineral kingdom. The material may be likened in its banding, but not color, to malachite. Occasionally, very fine quality crystals are found that are transparent; these are usually cut into faceted stones and they have the strongest energy of the peach-rose-pink ray. It is often used with malachite in crystal therapy, where it produces positive results, not only in the right use of power, but in this combination it brings in the energy of compassion, so that a greater understanding of the energy of Divine will-power is fully manifested.

Rhodochrosite is not the gentle loving energy of the rose quartz pink ray, but is the active energy of Divine love in action of the peach-pink ray. It facilitates the energy of compassion, but not pity. It does not encourage the sympathetic use of the pink ray, but rather the dynamic use of the peach-pink ray, whereby a greater understanding of the need to learn through the emotions is fully comprehended. Mankind has a great capacity to learn through the emotions; this has been clearly demonstrated in the twentieth century, where the use of instant communication or global news has moved whole nations as a single soul to end war, famine or disease and brings in the energy whereby the aggressive and destructive behaviour of others can no longer be hidden or tolerated. It is the energy of the enlightened reformer, as has been witnessed so many times this century when we have seen Live Aid, the release of Nelson Mandela, the end of the Vietnam war and the demise of the Iron Curtain. Its message is: let's change the world with enlightened love, as we can no longer tolerate the massive abuse of the solar plexus chakra by the few who manipulate, control and exploit the masses.

Rhodochrosite helps ease trauma and clears traumatic events from the heart, solar plexus and sacral chakras. It clears old pains, hurts and memories and will purify the base chakra, sacral chakra, solar plexus chakra and heart chakra; it will restore Divine balance to these areas. Rhodochrosite balances the energies of the heart and reproduction system. It is good for stomach, lungs, heart, reproductive areas, liver, kidneys and the intestines. Rhodochrosite is very enlivening to the mental body; it brings creative self-expression. It really wakes you up and gives boundless energy and enthusiasm. For those of you who are not into compassion, but are turned on by passion or eroticism, rhodochrosite is good for that too; if you feel unloved or unlovely, try the energies of rhodochrosite to give a boost to your love-life.

Affirmation: I am compassion in action.

Topaz

Topaz is a wonderful gemstone that has been used for centuries in jewellery. Topaz is the hardest silicate mineral and one of the hardest minerals in nature. The crystals can reach the incredible size of several hundred pounds. The Ancient Egyptians said that topaz was colored with the golden glow of the mighty sun god Ra. This made topaz a very powerful amulet that protected the faithful against harm. The Romans associated topaz with Jupiter; so did the Indians in ancient Vedic astrology. Legend has it that topaz dispels all enchantment and helps to improve eyesight. The ancient Greeks believed that it had the power to increase strength and make its wearer invisible in times of emergency. Topaz was also said to change color in the presence of poisoned food or drink. Its mystical curative powers waxed and waned with the phases of the moon: it was said to cure insomnia, asthma and haemorrhages. The most colorful gem, yellow topaz, is the birthstone for those born in November.

Topaz facilitates the deep understanding and acceptance of Universal Laws. These are not man's laws, but cosmic laws. This crystalline energy works through the laws of attraction and manifestation: it's electric! It can 'plug' you in to the cosmic web of Divine light. It allows for these cosmic realisations to become manifest in your everyday waking reality. It gives a good perception of the underlying reality behind the truth of personal integrity, ritual, cause and effect and making sure at all times you are energetically pristine. It does not ask for blind devotion though, but it does ask you to open your eyes, to go beyond your self-limiting belief system into the full understanding of personal power, choices and freedom. It does improve your eyesight, inner and outer. A sanctuary of healing awaits you with the topaz vibration.

Yellow Topaz - is revitalizing; it has the energy of the ancient Egyptian Sun God Ra. It brings a feeling of energy, power and vitality to the user. It is used for liver, gall-bladder, spleen, pancreas, stomach disorders, anger, emotional upsets, the skin and nervous system; also any problem that is associated with the mental body, toxins and elimination, including negative mental attitudes that have stopped emotional or spiritual growth. It can help with eating disorders, both anorexia and overweight problems; the solar plexus chakra that it governs is responsible for both extremes. It is a powerful stone and, when worn, carried or used in meditation, will bring personal power and self-mastery.

Golden Yellow Topaz - can activate contact with the higher self, the Divine aspect, that dwells within each and every one of us. It brings immortality - you are already immortal, but you may have forgotten that you are! You are an eternal being of infinite light, love, compassion, wisdom, truth and joy. This crystal just reminds you of this fact; it then encourages you to behave in the enlightened way. It manifests healing on all levels. It makes a wonderful gemstone essence, as do all colors of topaz. This gemstone's energy is attraction; it can attract into your life favourable 'happy coincidences' that will advance healing and spiritual growth. It is very beneficial to the meridians and can clear blockages or underactivity very quickly.

Affirmation: I allow myself a sanctuary of peace - a special time every day for personal contemplation and meditation.

Turquoise

Some say that in the thirteenth century turquoise was named in the mistaken belief that it came from Turkey. That may be true or it may be that the name comes from the Persian word for turquoise, *firouze*, since Persia has been a major source of this gemstone for thousands of years. In any case, the blue of this gemstone is so vivid and distinct that it has given its name to the color. Turquoise is one of the oldest known gem materials. The Egyptians were mining turquoise in 3,200 BC in the Sinai. The blue of turquoise was thought to have powerful metaphysical properties by many ancient cultures. Montezuma's treasure, now displayed in the British Museum, includes a fantastic carved serpent covered by a mosaic of turquoise. In ancient Mexico, turquoise was reserved for the gods; it could not be worn by mere mortals. The Apache believed that turquoise helped warriors and hunters to aim accurately. The Zuni believed that it protected them from demons. In Asia it was considered protection against the evil eye. Tibetans carved turquoise into ritual objects, as well as wearing it in traditional jewellery. Ancient manuscripts from Persia, India, Afghanistan and Arabia report that the health of a person wearing turquoise can be assessed by variations in the color of the stone. Turquoise was also thought to promote prosperity. The color can change with exposure to skin oils.

Turquoise is a healer for the emotions of the heart. It teaches you to talk from the heart. It loves the sharing of emotional wisdom, heartfelt communication; it loves togetherness and family. It brings people together and gets them communicating. It is also a good crystal to wear if you have to speak in public. It calms the nerves and 'feeds' the central nervous system; thus it is helpful in healing situations of nervous stress or breakdown. It helps panic attacks and emotional shock. Turquoise subdues fevers and cools inflammation of the nerves; it is particularly good for the pain of neuralgia. Turquoise is a good crystal to wear when you have to make decisions, as it encourages self-questioning. It is also a good stone to wear when you wish to overcome self-sabotage; use it to centre yourself.

Turquoise helps you strengthen your voice: a person's voice is a good indication of overall health and vitality. It gently purifies the throat chakra; you can tell if someone's throat is blocked, they have to keep clearing it every few minutes. Turquoise teaches true communication - not idle chatter, but purposeful thought-out communication. It is about personal expression combined with personal responsibility. Above all, turquoise helps you find your true path in life, your path with heart, so you can walk your talk with truth and dignity. Turquoise is good for 'channelling' and communication with spirit guides and Angels. Its beautiful blue color is very expansive. It contains the essence of *shunyata*, the vast blue emptiness, stretching in all directions, absolutely clear, pristine and radiant. By this blue sky stretching into infinity we can gain an understanding, a feeling for the expansiveness and freedom which could be ours if we did not allow our horizons to become narrow, clouded and limited, if we did not permit our minds to become fixated and hypnotized by cravings and worries centred on what really are empty passing phenomena.

Turquoise is an excellent meditation stone. It has also been worn and carried as a talisman against demons and evil entities. Turquoise can be carried, worn, used in body layouts or made into a gemstone essence or aura spray. It aids focused meditation. Physically it has been used for stomach ulcers, fatigue, weight problems, allergies, diabetes, the digestive system, muscles and muscle cramps, heart disease, high blood pressure, cancer, shallow breathing problems, sore throats, neckache, thyroid problems, hearing problems, tinnitus, asthma, headaches, nervous complaints, nightmares, dizziness and panic attacks.

Affirmation: Great Spirit, teach me to speak from an enlightened heart.

Healing Meditation - Solar Plexus Chakra

1.   Choose a warm comfortable place where you can lie down undisturbed for at least an hour. Never rush a meditation. View it as your own sacred healing space. You need to make sure it is energetically clean. Make sure you are wearing warm, loose, comfortable clothes......

2.   Breathe slowly.....encouraging energy to flow up and down your nervous system.....and begin to relax your body......go through your whole body starting at your feet and consciously relax each part, moving up and finishing at your head.....allow yourself to really let go....and deeply relax....feel yourself sinking into the floor or bed........

3.   Visualise yourself on a warm tropical sandy beach.....it is just before sunrise, the start of a new day......you feel the magnetic energy of daybreak....as the earth begins to stir at the dawn's approach.......an air of expectancy and excitement floods through your body as you listen to the gentle lapping waves.................

4.   Sit down on the sandy beach and place your hands on the warm clean soft golden sand.....really feel the sand between your fingers........as you do so you become even more aware of the sounds of the sea.....the gentle lapping of the waves has a hypnotic effect on your mind and it allows you to focus inwards..... you feel yourself relaxing more and more into your body..... experience your heartbeat....blood flowing in your veins....revitalising you....energising you.........your every breath....celebrates life......the life force.....that is you.....

5.   Now I want you to gaze towards the horizon......you are going to watch the sun rising very slowly into the sky.....as you see the first rays of dawn you begin to become aware of a warmth in your solar plexus....as the sky grows bluer and bluer.... and the sun rises higher and higher into the cloudless turquoise blue sky, you are aware of the warmth in your solar plexus growing warmer and warmer.........feel the energy movement this warmth creates........

6.   As you gaze at the sun....you see a shaft of pure golden yellow coming out of the sun...the lance of the sun......bringing energy, healing, wisdom and personal power......allow your eyes to close and focus on the solar energy that is now inside you.....allow this golden sunlight to fully activate your solar plexus............

7.   Now focus your attention on your crown chakra; imagine a cap of a thousand pristine pure white petals gently hugging your head........through the centre, where the petals meet, is an opening.......you feel another shaft of pure liquid sunlight as it gently caresses the top of your head....it then flows into your crown chakra ......the quickest way to open the crown chakra is with sunlight.......allow the energy of the sun to be absorbed into your crown chakra....feel it flowing down into your head, throat, neck, chest and into your solar plexus chakra.....from there it flows downwards through your abdomen and out of your legs and feet........bringing energy and vitality to every cell, every fibre, every molecule of your being.......

8.   Now, just allow the red of the earth to be drawn up through your feet........allow it to flow into your solar plexus chakra.......allow the red and golden yellow energy to merge and flow together.......begin to expand....................activating your mental body.....this will bring clarity and focus...............allowing you to walk your true path..........back to radiant good health and personal power.......

Kundalini Solar Plexus Chakra Meditation

In the *Upanishads*, one of the main collection of Yogic instructions from ancient India, there is a very special kundalini breathing exercise called 'breath of fire'. This technique is a direct way of increasing the flow of kundalini energy in your third chakra. Use it at your own discretion, in great moderation.

Please keep in mind that in a complete kundalini meditation session the solar plexus pranayama 'breath of fire' you are about to learn is always done after you have completed the meditation on the first two chakras.

So I will outline the first two again briefly to start you off. It is also important to remember that when you come to the 'breath of fire' section it is performed with very little air actually in the lungs. It is the opposite of slow deep breathing. It is radically different. It will energize the solar plexus chakra. So in the beginning, when you are just learning the 'breath of fire', try not to overdo it......remember the solar plexus chakra is combustion.....an explosion of energy......

1.   First focus on your breathing, heartbeat, balance, then expand your awareness to encompass the whole of your body.

2.   Contract the Hui Yin point, then focus on the energy, breathing it up and down the spine.

3.   Next chant the root chakra mantra LAM...and visualise the root chakra turning upwards.....

4.   Now meditate on the root chakra mandala.

5.   Next draw the kundalini energy into the sacral chakra, with each new inhale.

6.   Without any hesitation, chant the mantra for the sacral chakra VAM.

7.   Now meditate on the sacral chakra mandala and put the sacral chakra bandha on and visualise the sacral chakra turning upwards.....

Breath of Fire

8.   Now rapidly contract your belly muscles, so that you force the air out of your lungs through the mouth almost instantaneously (this is similar to coughing, there is a sound....Huh....but it is made only softly in the throat. The breath of fire is different from the cough.....it is all one controlled movement. The exhale is also centred on the solar plexus energy centre, rather than in the throat. The most important thing to remember is that the exhale happens almost instantaneously, with a very aggressive power - total controlled force.)

9.   After the exhale, relax your breathing muscles completely for a short time, so that air flows very quickly into your lungs through your nose, replacing the forced discharge of air. (Again, the coughing inhale is similar to the 'breath of fire' inhale, except in this case it is smoother and under conscious control and through your nose. Also, you only make one exhale contraction per breath, where with a hacking cough you make several belly contractions with each breath.)

10.   Just as soon as the air has rushed into your lungs to replace what you had pushed out, again push the air out with a strong sudden exhale, contracting your diaphragm and abdominal muscles. Let the Huh....sound come out of your throat with each of these exhales, then instantly relax and let air rush in through your nose.......continue in this breathing pattern for as long as is comfortable and you feel deeply centred in your third 'fire' chakra...........then just relax and allow your breathing to slow...........

11.   Breathing easily......you are now ready to employ the solar plexus energy seal or bandha...this bandha is not subtle....you must pull your stomach muscles in....try to make your navel (umbilicus) touch your spine.....once again you will feel a very distinct change in your solar plexus chakra when you have employed this energy seal correctly........

12. You are now ready to focus on and vocalize the third chakra mantra...RAM....as before, allow the sound to manifest in your mind....feel it effortlessly rising from your inner being........as the Rrrrrrr sound generates tremendous power in your solar plexus region, feel it energising the solar plexus chakra.....opening yourself to the sound of the universe, as it joins you in sounding the RAM........continue for as long as you want..............when you are ready visualise or feel your solar plexus chakra begin to turn upwards.....towards your crown chakra....this brings spiritual energy into your solar plexus chakra and allows for your full attention to be focused upwards towards your enlightenment.......

13. Now visualise or look directly at the solar plexus chakra mandala....use the one in this book......become aware of the chakra mandala as you focus on the energy movements and shapes it contains.......

14. Continue to visualise or gaze at the mandala as long as you want.........

15. When you are ready, allow the fiery energy you have created to flow up your spine through all your chakras in sequential order.........and pour out of the top of your head like a fountain of light............this sacred divine energy brings your whole energy field to life...........

16. Allow yourself plenty of time to integrate this new awareness.......you need to practise this meditation on a daily basis; it is the culmination of the first, second and third chakra kundalini activation you have learned thus far.......don't forget to reverse the root chakra to point downwards and the sacral and solar plexus chakras to point outwards.....as you once more anchor yourself on the earth plane of ego existence......

There is no doubt the daily practice of asanas...the physical postures employed in Hatha Yoga... makes the use and implementation of the bandhas in the Kundalini Yoga meditation programme easier....if your spine is stiff and rigid, you need to practise Hatha Yoga to free your body enough to be able to hold the bandhas for prolonged periods of time during the kundalini meditation. It is the same as holding any trance posture. In many ancient cultures holding a 'pose' or 'sacred posture of power' brings about a change in the vibration in the energy field and a shift of consciousness. In kundalini meditation practice we 'hold' the body in certain postures; this has a profound effect on all levels of the body and aura. Over time you will notice a remarkable and sustained shift in not only your vibrational awareness, but a deepening knowledge in the quality of your spiritual power, insights and heartfelt personal happiness and compassion.

Part 15

The Heart Chakra

Before we move into the heart chakra, we need to just recap on the three lower chakras. They relate very much to matter and the physical world of day-to-day survival, procreation, of energy manipulation and personal mastery over the physical realm. We are now moving into the presence of a magical quality we call love. There is no doubt that humans are preoccupied with this energy centre - there must have been thousands of songs written containing the word love - yet if you analyse all of them, very often you will find it is not the principle of true love they contain, but conditional love - which is the reason why so many of these love songs have reference to broken hearts and unfulfilled longings within their lyrics. Can a heart be broken? It can certainly feel like it, if you have attachments in your personal loving energy. Remember, human love never stands on its own, free of attachments - it is empowered by the energetic interplay of the first three chakras. Within the seven-fold chakra system it is only when we have fully merged the energy from the top three chakras through the heart and combined them with the energy of the lower three chakras that we can actually love unconditionally. If you can't love yourself and others unconditionally, how can you hope to create a pure home for God/Goddess to dwell in?

When there is an ample balanced flow of energy from above and from below, the heart chakra is radiant with compassion or, as I like to express it, radiating compassion. At this point I would like to bring in Avalokiteshvara, who could be described as the quintessential Bodhisattva, for he is the Bodhisattva of Compassion, and compassion is the distinguishing mark of a Bodhisattva. It is the heartfelt longing to rescue all living beings from the burning house of samsara which makes a Bodhisattva a Bodhisattva. *Ishvara* means lord, and *Avalokita* is usually translated as 'the one who gazes down'. So Avalokiteshvara is the Lord of the *Dharma* who looks down with infinite compassion on any being in a state of suffering. His sphere of involvement is universal. He is the central figure in the *Prajnaparamita Hridaya* (Heart *Sutra*), where he expounds the Perfection of Wisdom. His mantra is *'Om mani padme hum'*. He appears in many diverse forms, any of which can be meditated upon; so far 108 have been identified in Buddhist literature. This diversity is hardly surprising when you take into account the preoccupation of Buddhist meditators with the exploration of compassionate states of mind. The one most used is the vision of Avalokiteshvara emerging from the blue sky of *shunyata*; he is brilliant white, standing erect on a white lotus and moon mat, and holding in his hand the wish-fulfilling gem of *Bodhichitta*. He is surrounded by what appears to be a vast aura of white light - but looking more closely it dawns on us that what we are really gazing at is a figure with a great many arms, which form a tremendous circle of white light that stretches out in all directions. Each arm is reaching out to help the suffering beings, as the beautiful blue eyes gaze downwards compassionately. Several of the hands hold sacred implements which symbolize Avalokiteshvara's measureless resourcefulness in helping beings move towards Enlightenment.

So in Avalokiteshvara we come to recognise our need to move the energy of the lower three chakras upwards towards enlightened love. Avalokiteshvara also teaches us another important lesson in dissolving the seeds of duality; enlightenment transcends all gender differences. As an illustration of this, Avalokiteshvara, who in India and Tibet is definitely a male figure, became transformed in Far Eastern Buddhism into a compassionate goddess. In China she is known as Quan Yin, and in Japan as Kannon or Kwannon. Like Avalokiteshvara, Quan Yin can take a number of forms, of which perhaps the best-known in the West is the White-Robed Quan Yin.

The Sanskrit name for the heart chakra is *anahata*, which translates as unbeaten, unstruck, unhurt, bright or clean. The deeper sacred meaning of this word is 'a sound that is made without any two things

149

striking'. We need to explore this a little further: in the intuitive understanding of Yogic tradition there exists at the very centre of each chakra a nucleus called the seed or *bija*. From this seed emanates a vibration: this is both a sound and an essential energy resonance pattern that governs that particular chakra. This seed sound governs the overall development of the particular energy centre. So when we meditate on the fourth chakra we must hold this concept uppermost in our minds. By sounding the mantra we can develop our heart chakra in accord with our divine cosmic blueprint. The sound, as the name *anahata* implies, is its creation come forth by no known means; it originates from the void and manifests in the heart chakra. As I mentioned before, in the sound chapter of this book, in many religions, sound vibration is considered to be the originating power of manifestation in the universe. Whenever you choose to chant the *bija*-mantra for each of the chakras, you are tuning your entire physical, emotional, mental and spiritual being to the exact sound of the chakra - and aligning yourself with the mysterious centre of your chakritic universe.

The heart chakra is located in the cardiac area, in the region of the physical and spiritual heart. It is associated with the element of air - or, as many people prefer to call it, prana. In ancient times the spiritual masters knew from direct inner revelation that each breath, and the air taken in with each breath, was magical, determining the quality of life and vitality in each individual. It was therefore decided that the air must hold a mystical, life-giving substance, which they termed prana. Prana has been described as the subtle all-pervading, divine energy of eternal life - invisible but vital. A hundred years or so ago, the scientists discovered a substance called oxygen, which they explained does fuel our every movement on this planet - so is oxygen prana? In one way, yes, but in another, no. No one fully understands what oxygen is. The scientists know some of its properties, but the deeper they look into its sub-atomic activities, the less they really understand the reality of the air we breathe. The mystery becomes bigger as the scientific knowledge grows more massive. The only real way to understand this mysterious substance called prana is through direct contact with it during meditation.

In Chinese philosophy underlying all aspects of Chinese medicine is an outgrowth of viewpoints on our relationship to the universe around us. The Chinese see human beings as a microcosm within the universal macrocosm. The principle demonstrated by the inner workings of humans is reflected in the universal relationships of energetic flow. They call this energy *Qi* or *ch'i*; they give its explanation as a unique substance that flows from the environment into the physical body. The Chinese feel that chi is an energy of both nutritive and cellular-organisational characteristics which supersedes the energetic contributions of ingested food and air. Therefore this chi is a type of subtle energy which permeates our environment. Since the heart chakra is closely tied to the expression of love and compassion, it is naturally considered to be an important centre of nurturing. Most of the organs associated with the heart chakra nurture and promote life and vitality throughout the rest of the body. The lungs take in air, oxygen or prana from the atmosphere. The heart pumps the blood to the lungs, where oxygen, prana or chi are taken in and distributed to the rest of the body's organs. In the digestive system, more nutrients are added to the bloodstream, where the circulation can distribute them to the rest of the physical body. The breasts are also located at the level of the heart chakra; they are dedicated in females to the nurture of another being. Therefore the ability to nurture oneself, as well as other people, is linked to the development of the love nature of the heart centre.

As the heart chakra becomes more open and free-flowing with cosmic pranic energy, the capability to unconditionally love oneself and others is substantially increased, along with a greater flow of life force or chi to all the organs it supplies. At a psychological level, the heart chakra deals with the emotions that bind individuals in various loving relationships. The act of nurturing is fed by the different emotional feelings generated by the heart chakra. Feelings of love, compassion, empathy, are a direct outpouring of spiritual growth. Therefore the heart chakra is important in developing higher levels of consciousness. When these elements are lacking in the personality, it indicates a severe dysfunction or energy block within the heart chakra. Interestingly, one of the most important links between the heart chakra and a physical organ is seen in the relationship between the heart chakra and the thymus gland. For years the medical profession thought it was 'normal' for the thymus gland to display atrophy in size and function as an individual grew older - this view is being revised, as physicians begin to delve into the energetic relationship between the heart chakra and the thymus gland. It is possible that the age-related involution of the thymus gland is not a universal phenomenon; in those who do have thymic-atrophy in later years it will be shown that there is a direct relationship between loneliness, depression, blockages of the heart chakra and glandular function. Researchers in the field of psychoneuroimmunology are examining the subtle-energetic links between emotions and immunological function. It has already been established that physiological links between human emotions and illness do exist - so it will not be long before full understanding of emotions and the thymus gland that plays an important role in the regulation of the immune system's response is finally accepted by the medical profession. Various researchers who have examined the link between emotions and illness have found a strong association between depression, grief and the overall suppression of immune functioning. But more importantly, dysfunction frequently arises from a lack of self-love. Persistent negative self-images and loss of self-worth do more physiological damage than is currently recognised. This is due to the law of resonance, like attracts like, so what we dwell on day after day attracts more of the same. We can switch our negative thought patterns into positive resonance patterns; this attracts even more positive energy, which is vital to healing.

To recap, the heart chakra is associated with compassion, empathy and love. It rules over our beliefs about love and relationships, one-ness, the physical heart, lungs, breasts, thymus, the immune system, lymph glands and the sensory channel of touch. Malfunctions include lung disease, asthma, heart disease; shallow breathing, high blood pressure, heart attack, tension and cancer; problems with arms, hands and fingers; fears about betrayal, co-dependence and melancholia. Negative heart chakra imbalances or states are demanding attention, overly critical, possessive, moody, melodramatic, manic-depressive, using money to control people, buying love or friendship, the martyr syndrome 'I have sacrificed myself for you', conditional love 'I will love you if', controlling love 'If you loved me you would', or feeling sorry for yourself, the 'poor me' syndrome. Also indecisiveness, paranoia, fear of letting go, fear of getting hurt, feelings of abandonment, fear of rejection, feeling unworthy and feelings of shame - and seeking constant reassurance and validation.

Your heart is the centre of your body - when your heart energy flows, your whole being follows. The heart centre allows you to transcend the limits of your ego and identify with other people, plants, animals, crystals - all life. If you wish to heal yourself and others, a requirement is an open balanced heart chakra. Very often I have found those who could feel 'nothing' from a crystal could feel 'nothing' from other people too. At some time in their development as a human being they had chosen to close off their heart chakra. Very often as therapists most of our work is to get people to allow their hearts to open and then heal. This puts a tremendous responsibility on a vibrational therapist to have integrity, so when a client finally does 'open' up, we behave in a pristine, compassionate manner and in no way abuse or exploit a client to feed our ego-centred cravings.

The fourth chakra, the heart, is experienced as feminine; loving; integrating; yin and eventually the need to surrender the ego. The traditional sound for the heart chakra is the *bija* mantra YAM in the Hindu tradition, and a slightly altered and even more powerful YANG in the Tantric Buddhist tradition of Nepal and Tibet.

The traditional symbol is the 12-petal green lotus flower, the inner centre containing two intersecting triangles called *trikonas* in Sanskrit; they make up a perfect six-pointed star, demonstrating the balance between the downward-pointing spirit descending towards matter and the upward-pointing matter ascending towards spirit. Yet, if we care to look deeper, going into the heart further, we find that it is in the heart chakra that the triangle form is most strongly represented; by being made double it generates six smaller triangles aiming out in all directions, just like the arms of Avalokiteshvara sending the *anahata bija* vibration out to all the other six chakras. The image is *so* very powerful that if one only meditates on the heart chakra, such intense loving energy will eventually bring the whole being into perfect alignment as to facilitate enlightenment. The heart chakra represents *Bakti* Yoga - this closely resembles Christianity, in its devotional aspect. It is the Christian cross that helps us locate our heart chakra with ease: all you have to do is raise your arms out to each side and tune in to the midpoint in your chest where the horizontal meets the vertical - there is your heart.

The ultimate message of the kundalini goddess is that it is an act of surrender through enlightened willpower, not blind faith or subjugation, that brings the heart chakra into perfect alignment. Therefore, only by an of act of focused Herculean-will can we cause the full manifestation of the perfection of our being to be fully revealed in all dimensions and on all levels of our being.

The colors green, pink and gold are always associated with this chakra. The green ray is for soothing, healing, growth, balance, discrimination, ecstasy, unconditional love; merging the physical with the Divine; transmutation with love; marriage of physical and spiritual. Meditation on the green ray of the heart chakra gives the sound of *anahata*, the 'primal sound' or *Sabdabrahman*. It also bestows pure qualities, cosmic love and various psychic powers. This central green heart chakra within the sevenfold system is the heart of our journey on the physical plane. It balances between the worlds of spirit and matter. Through this balance we relate compassionately and unconditionally with all life, with love. Remember, this 'love' is not dependant on others. It is not the tribal love of the root chakra or the sexual love of the sacral chakra, or the materialistic love of the solar plexus chakra, but is a state of being, enduring and constant. It also means self-love and self-acceptance. The color pink is for love and harmony in all our relationships; hope; being receptive, intimate; affection and kindness. It melts and dissolves resentment and any residual resistance we may have to healing. It will bring the activation of *Karuna* (compassion, pity, tenderness; it also implies devoted action to alleviate all suffering in ourselves and others). The gold is the Sun-gold ray of wisdom, knowledge and understanding - the end of the rainbow is the pot of gold that we all seek on our pathway to enlightenment. It aids the assimilation of knowledge, bringing spiritual vitality and spiritual abundance. It rids the body of parasites and parasitic energies on all levels.

Our guides are the inner goddess *Kakini*, who is the color of gold, of lightning, of a candle flame. Once this flame has been ignited, our inner *Linga* (Goddess) will illuminate the three-fold flame in our heart, lighting our path on the journey home. Our other guide is Archangel Raphael, whose name means 'whom God has healed'. Raphael is our guide whenever we choose to heal ourselves or others. Other guides will appear - when we are ready to heal ourselves. The lovely figure of the goddess Venus really represents 'the female holocaust' whereby the female energy (yin) has been made base and subjugated by the male (yang) dominance or ego into believing she is less than human, or certainly less than a male - to be conquered, exploited, abused, denied and murdered. It is not the feminine energy that is base or sinful, only the male interpretation of the mystical feminine that causes dysfunctional dread and fear amongst the male egos on the planet over the millennium (this male/female - yin/yang balance is vital). In reality, we can only find access to the Father through the Mother and, as the Qabala points out so succinctly, we are all female on planet Earth. A final guide is the associated creature, the black antelope. This creature is strong, yet sensitive; it leaps high in the air, but is still earthbound. In the Native American tradition the deer or antelope represents the energy of love; by following this animal spirit, if it comes to you during meditation, you can come closer to your own heart spirit.

Crystal Web of Light - Tranquil Heart
Crystals:
    1 kunzite, natural, tumbled or faceted
    1 hiddenite, natural, tumbled or faceted
    1 morganite, tumbled, faceted or natural
    1 rhodochrosite, tumbled, faceted, slice or natural
    1 rhodonite, tumbled or natural
    2 large rose quartz, natural or tumbled.
    16 clear quartz points

Uses: This crystal web of light works on all parts of the body, mind and spirit. It is used for the newborn to help them integrate their energies into the earth vibration, for birth and re-birth, for new beginnings and for mid-life crisis as a heart opener. It is also used as a heart consciousness wakener. It comforts and heals the heart and old "heartache". Very often, when we do not deal with bereavement, loss, rejection, hurt or pain that deeply affects our heart chakra, we close it down and store these negative experiences within our physical body. Unless we eventually choose to release them to the golden rose-pink light of love, they will cause our spiritual demise.

This crystal web of light has a great balance of compassion, peace and freedom. It is good for the immune system and can clear anaesthetics from the system. It is also good for convalescence and aids recovery from long-standing immune system disorders. Because the web contains hiddenite, which is used at the heart chakra, it brings in the green ray of tender, gentle heart healing. It is not the powerful emerald green ray, rather the fragile new beginning, a bud just starting to open. It is soft and gentle, like a whisper that holds the promise that all will be well. It will gently dispel negative emotions, thoughts and feelings. It also releases feelings of failure and it is good for those who put on a brave face when their heart is full of pain; it helps you to honour these feelings and gently release them.

It works physically on the thymus, heart, shoulders, chest and lungs. It completely stabilizes the emotional body, giving much needed comfort and support. When used in healing, this crystal web of light *is* very potent. It teaches forgiveness and can help you to fulfill your true emotional potential. It will help you develop mature emotional strength and universal love and forgiveness, allowing your heart to become a nurturing place for your soul. This is the life lesson of the heart chakra, forgiveness and compassion for yourself and others. The emotional dysfunctions of the heart chakra are co-dependency, melancholia, fears concerning loneliness, commitment or betrayal. All dis-ease starts with a lack of love.

1 kunzite, placed on the third eye chakra - this brings a head-heart balance - choose a pale-pink to lilac stone, with the 'violet ray' being clearly visible when viewed down the axis of the crystal.

1 hiddenite, placed on the heart chakra - brings in the green ray of tender, gentle heart healing.

1 morganite, placed on the heart chakra - this brings in the rose-gold ray of healing; it also minimises a healing crisis, by holding the emotional body stable.

1 rhodochrosite, placed on the solar plexus chakra - choose a peachy-pink stone.

1 rhodonite, placed between the feet - choose one with a lot of black mixed in the pink.

2 rose quartz, placed one in the palm of each hand - choose ones that really feel good to hold.

16 clear quartz single terminated crystals, placed evenly around the body in a circle to form a light-emitting halo. The terminations should point towards the body.

Process:

1. Cleanse all the crystals and programme the clear quartz for healing.

2. Choose a warm comfortable place where you can lie down undisturbed for at least an hour. Never rush a crystal web of light process. View it as a sacred, silent, healing space, so you need to make sure it is energetically clean. Make sure you are wearing warm, loose, comfortable clothes.

3. Relax by consciously becoming aware of your breathing and heartbeat. You can play soothing music, light candles and burn incense.

4. Lay the stones around and on the body and hold the rose quartz in your hands.

5. Allow 20 minutes to facilitate the integration of the crystal vibration.

6. Feel free to remove the crystals sooner, if you have integrated the crystal energy very quickly.

7. Remove the crystals in reverse order of placement.

8. Make sure you are fully grounded, centred and balanced.

9.   Cleanse your crystals (using your chosen method).

10.   Finish by giving thanks and asking mentally that all the healing work you have just accomplished is closed, sealed and protected with Divine love and wisdom.

11.   Give yourself sufficient time to integrate the crystal therapy session.

12.   As a general guideline it is suggested a period of twice the length of time you were actually lying in the crystal therapy web be allowed for integration.

Clear Quartz - See the Root Chakra for details of properties.

Kunzite

Kunzite, the pale pink to lilac gem variety of the mineral spodumene, is named as a tribute to George Kunz, the legendary gem scholar, gemmologist and gem buyer for Tiffany & Co at the turn of the century. The author of 'The Curious Lore of Precious Stones', Kunz searched the globe for old stories and legends about gems as he searched for new varieties and new deposits. Kunzite was first found in Connecticut, USA, but the first commercially significant deposit was discovered in 1902 in the Pala region of California, where morganite beryl was also first discovered. Spodumene occurs typically in lithium-bearing granite pegmatites, together with minerals such as lepidolite, tourmaline and beryl. Very large crystals have been recorded, some reaching 16 metres in length and weighing up to 90 tons. Kunzite should be protected from heat and continued exposure to strong light which can gradually fade its color.

Kunzite carries the energies of the pale pink to lilac ray, which is the ray of spiritual love. It works on all parts of the body, mind and spirit. It is used for the newborn to help them integrate their energies into the earth vibration, for birth and re-birth, for new beginnings and for mid-life crisis as a heart opener. It is also used as a heart consciousness wakener. It comforts and heals the heart and old "heartache". Kunzite has a great balance of compassion, peace and freedom. Kunzite has a hidden magic: it can reveal and heal a lost childhood where, due to circumstances, you had to grow up too soon. Kunzite is good for the immune system and can clear anaesthetics from the system. It is also good for convalescence and aids recovery from long-standing immune system disorders. It makes an excellent gemstone essence.

Spodumene has a green form, hiddenite, that brings in the green ray of tender, gentle heart healing. It is not the powerful emerald green ray, rather the fragile new beginning, a bud just starting to open. It is soft and gentle, like a whisper that holds the promise that all will be well. It will gently dispel negative emotions and feelings by releasing old heartache pain and self- hatred. Hiddenite releases feelings of failure and it is good for those who put on a brave face when their heart is full of pain; it helps you to honour these feelings and gently release them. Hiddenite works on the thymus, heart, shoulders, chest and lungs. When combined in a gemstone essence with its sister kunzite, it completely stabilizes the emotional body, giving comfort and support.

Affirmation: I now open my heart to receive love.

Morganite

Morganite is the pink variety of beryl. Other gemstone color varieties that belong to beryl include emerald, heliodor and aquamarine. Other colors of beryl are simply referred to by their color, such as red beryl. Morganite is colored by trace amounts of manganese that find their way into the crystal structure. It is named after J. P. Morgan, a famous American industrialist.

Morganite is universal love and compassion; the love of humanity, of honouring each being for their own unique expression of their intrinsic Divinity; of unity within diversity. Morganite contains the energy of high affection - affection without ulterior motive. It melts any resistance you may have to being truly in love or truly giving love freely. In crystal therapy morganite clears the way, by preparing the body to receive 'healing'. It soothes the physical body, making it more open and relaxed. This is the beginning and the end of all healing; if your client is not open to 'receiving', all vibrational therapy is in vain. Very often someone will give 'lip service' to the notion of healing, but they can't or won't change; being the victim does have its rewards. It makes them special. They may even compete with other victims to see who has suffered the most. Morganite helps these souls to remove the miasm that has lodged within the emotional body and is the source of the pre-disposition towards their victim mentality. These 'casualties' need love, not the co-dependant love of looking outside themselves for the love they crave and looking only to draw strength from others, but the mature love of high affection and deep soul healing, of nurturing into wholeness and self-reliance. Easier said than done!

Morganite's signature is very special: it holds the emotional body stable as you let go of pain and painful memories; this is the key to its use. Very often, as people begin to truly heal, they find their emotions are volatile - healing sometimes brings up painful memories; it is easy to get swamped and give up, rather than having the courage to go with the flow. If a crystal therapist uses the vibrational signature of morganite, the emotional backlash is minimised. Physically, morganite works on the digestive system; affection is nourishment. It also heals any part of the body and emotions we have rejected as being un-lovely or un-lovable. It is a good crystal to use after surgical procedures, especially where a body part has been removed or modified. It is good for those undergoing chemotherapy and long-term conventional drug therapy. It works with the patterns of dis-ease and rejection. Morganite helps clients reassess old ideas and issues, allowing them to melt and dissolve away. It is also good for skin eruptions and rashes.

Spiritually, morganite has a very active and beautiful guide who has worked for aeons to free humanity from the bonds of ignorance and suffering. Avalokiteshvara (Quan Yin), the chief Bodhisattva of Amitabha, whose name means infinite light, the Buddha of the West. Avalokiteshvara is the Bodhisattva of Compassion, who has a heartfelt longing to rescue all living beings from the burning house of *samsara*.

Affirmation: Universal Love, healing and compassion are made manifest in every cell and fibre of my being.

Rhodochrosite - See the Solar Plexus Chakra for details of properties.

Rhodonite

Rhodonite is an delightful mineral that is often carved and used in jewellery. It is named after the Greek word for rose, *rhodon*. Its rose-pink color is distinctive and can only be confused with rhodochrosite. Rhodochrosite, however, is streaked with white minerals such as calcite. Rhodonite is usually associated with black manganese minerals and pyrite. Crystals of rhodonite, while not in nearly the same abundance as massive rhodonite, are still found and distributed on the mineral markets. Other characteristics: may tarnish to a brown or black color upon exposure.

Rhodonite is an amazing crystal. Whenever I see someone drawn to it, my first thought is - what have you got bottled up inside you? It always indicates something is lying dormant and buried. If the person works metaphysically, it also means those who don't want to give up anything and lose control. It can show that a person needs to be in control; not just physical and emotional control, but occult control. This crystal also indicates an empty emotional self-destructive life. The black within the pink can also be restriction dominance, depression, withholding empty power used out of selfishness and weakness. But out of the black can come new beginnings. By seeing that which is hidden, women or men who choose this crystal need to review their emotional health. It is the same with the aura: if you ever view black within a person's aura it indicates disease, illness and darkness of the soul.

When used in healing, this crystal *is* very potent. It will quickly bring these seeds of soul destruction to the surface to be healed with the vibrant rose pink ray of universal love. Rhodonite's rose pink has healing beauty within its vibration. It will support you when you feel betrayed, let down or abandoned, or unloved. It teaches forgiveness and can help you to fulfill your true emotional potential. It will help you develop mature emotional strength and universal love and forgiveness, allowing your heart to become a nurturing place for your soul. This is the life lesson of the heart chakra, forgiveness and compassion for yourself and others.

The emotional dysfunctions of the heart chakra are co-dependency, melancholia, fears concerning loneliness, commitment or betrayal. All dis-ease starts with a lack of love. Rhodonite should be used with caution by crystal therapists, as it can surface incredible anger, hatred, resentment and bitterness, which must be dealt with in a constructive, empowering manner. Otherwise it can be like 'a loose cannon' - you never know when it will go off. Rhodonite's rose pink healing energy is very good for healing skin complaints, cuts and wounds.

Affirmation: My heart is open to healing and love.

Rose quartz

Rose quartz is one of the most pleasantly seductive varieties of quartz. The pale-pink to rose-red color is caused by titanium and iron. Rose quartz is usually too cloudy or pale to be used as a cut gemstone, although a few exceptional pieces are found with enough clarity and color to make fine gems. Most gemmy rose quartz is used as cabochons, where the clarity is not as important as the depth of color. Rose quartz is also a very attractive ornamental stone and is carved into popular spheres, pyramids, healing wands and obelisks. Rose quartz is found in Brazil, Madagascar, India and several localities in the USA. Brazil is also the only source of true well-formed crystals of rose quartz. All rose quartz was believed to be only massive, found primarily in the cores of pegmatites. This lack of crystals is somewhat of a mystery, because quartz crystallizes into well-formed crystals in all its other macroscopic varieties. So amazing are the crystals of rose quartz that the first ones discovered were dismissed as 'fakes' by mineralogists from around the world.

Rose quartz transmits a soft love energy, which is soothing and calming to the emotions. The vibration or resonance signature of rose quartz is good if a person has been assaulted in any way. It is wonderful to use in mid-life crisis when dissolution of old patterns and reassessment is imperative. The paler the rose quartz goes colorwise, the wider, higher and deeper the love vibration extends. The very pale natural rose is highly tuned and sensitive; it carries the promise of spiritual fulfilment. Rose quartz is very good for children, the newborn and those yet to be born. It is also ideal for those who are giving birth to their inner child or any new venture; the red within the pink activates the energy, while the white spiritualises the endeavour.

Rose quartz can fully balance the emotional body. It is used to attune to the love vibration. The rose quartz ray works dynamically on the heart chakra, gently cleansing and then transmuting all stored putrefied negative issues of self-worth, self-confidence and self-acceptance. It contains within its beautiful pink mandala the ray of hope. The pink warmth melts and dissolves resistance to allowing the full manifestation of love into every corner of the heart. It will allow the integration of positive energy within all levels of the chakra system, the positive energy being love, compassion, understanding of unity within diversity, bringing tolerance, forgiveness and ultimately the complete expression of universal love and self-love to every corner of the microcosm and macrocosm. Think pink!

The guardian or Angel of rose quartz is very affectionate, deeply understanding and non- judgemental. Many people who tread the Angel path are passionately aware of the potent force of this Divine pink manifestation. It is ideal to carry and wear in stressful situations. It is good to use after operations or dental surgery. Rose quartz is comforting, it mollifies, it is a peace offering. Pour pink on troubled waters. It is great in a crisis and it has been documented many times that the wearer of a rose quartz pendant has had the stone shatter on impact of 'bad news'. This stone really knows how to love you, it will even teach you 'sacrificial love'. It will sacrifice itself for you; rather it breaks, than your heart breaks. It is affordable and so useful; it is a give-away crystal. Many crystal people carry spare pieces of rose quartz just to give to others in times of stress. Rose quartz is also humble; it teaches humility by truly understanding the unconditional love vibration. It is a good ally in times of anxiety, when life is just one long struggle. This wonderful stone has also been used to great effect to treat heart problems on all levels, those who are soul weary, Alzheimer's disease, senile dementia, Parkinson's disease. Great benefit has also been gained from easing the pain and speeding the healing of severe burns and scalds. It makes a wonderful gemstone essence and is said to keep the skin young and supple.

The asterised rose quartz is the most powerful gemstone of the pink ray and as such is sought after by crystal therapists and those who work as 'channels for the Angels and Ascended Masters'. The rutile needles contained within the rose quartz structure stop any unwanted outside interference from both the physical and spiritual worlds. Rutile is used for healing and balancing the aura by repelling negative energy. It works on the physical, etheric and astral bodies.

The well-formed crystals of rose quartz from Brazil are so beautiful and seem especially focused for directing the energy of the pink ray. They have been used in gemstone essences, Earth healing ceremonies and pyramid activation. The energy appears to be incorruptible and, unlike normal rose quartz, the asterised never seems to need the same cleansing procedure, only a light cleansing with the intent. It has been placed in several special sites around the planet to affect planetary peace.

Affirmation: My soul dances to the music of universal peace and love.

Crystal Web of Light - Healing Calm

Crystals: 1 larimar, natural, tumbled or cabochon
                       1 lepidolite, natural, tumbled or cabochon
                       2 moonstone, tumbled or natural
                       1 rose quartz, tumbled, faceted, slice or natural
                       1 sugilite, tumbled or natural
                       12 small clear quartz points

Uses: This crystal web of light will bring the energy of acceptance and wisdom beyond the energy of duality. It has an inner strength and hidden power. The moonstone gives personal resilience and calms the mind. It is nurturing to the soul and heals the subtle energy system by comforting and aiding serene contemplation. Moonstone will lull, soothe, console, comfort, bring personal peace, tranquillity and deep soul connection. The larimar, this beautiful heavenly blue stone, gently transmits pure spiritual substance into the higher chakras above the head. Larimar contains 'Grandmother Earth' energies and will assist you in finding your true path in life. It will also assist you in removing the blocks you have placed on your path to personal power and radiant good health.

The lepidolite can desensitise the nervous system very effectively, thereby numbing pain. It contains an extremely high vibration and works on the brain's pain centres, which helps with drug addiction. It also gives you your own space back, so you can heal, so it is good for convalescence. Lepidolite also clears anaesthetics from the system. It facilitates the energy of no mind, thus relieving stress. It is also used for balancing both sides of the brain. In meditation it feels like a gentle wave of energy flowing through the mind. Lepidolite is especially good for insomnia. The 'Spirit' keeper or Angel of lepidolite facilitates its use as a 'dreamtime' crystal, an astral guide. It changes our way of consciously viewing the world, by accessing other dimensions and realities. It can be used to clear the mind of unwanted debris before meditation, so it aids deep meditation practice. It stops the head ruling the heart, by bringing about a balanced polarity. It teaches us to use an integrated approach. It stops depression, obsessional thinking and confusion. It alleviates symptoms of sensitivity to pollutants, chronic exhaustion, epilepsy and Alzheimer's. Lepidolite also strengthens the immune system and has great healing powers. It gives a rest for the troubled heart and brings inner peace and emotional healing.

1 larimar, placed on the throat chakra.

1 lepidolite, placed on the solar plexus chakra.

2 moonstone, placed one in the palm of each hand.

1 rose quartz, placed on the heart chakra.

1 sugilite, placed on the third eye.

12 clear quartz single terminated crystals, placed evenly around the body. The terminations should point towards the body.

Process:

1.   Cleanse all the crystals and programme the clear quartz for healing.

2.   Choose a warm comfortable place where you can lie down undisturbed for at least an hour. Never rush a crystal web of light process. View it as a sacred healing space, so you need to make sure it is energetically clean. Make sure you are wearing warm, loose, comfortable clothes.

3.   Relax by consciously becoming aware of your breathing and heartbeat. You can play soothing music, light candles and burn incense.

4.   Lay the stones around and on the body and hold the moonstone in your hands.

5.   Allow 20 minutes to facilitate the integration of the crystal vibration.

6.   Feel free to remove the crystals sooner, if you have integrated the crystal energy very quickly.

7.   Remove the crystals in reverse order of placement.

8.   Make sure you are fully grounded, centred and balanced.

9.   Cleanse your crystals (using your chosen method).

10.   Finish by giving thanks and asking mentally that all the healing work you have just accomplished is closed, sealed and protected with Divine love and wisdom.

11.   Give yourself sufficient time to integrate the crystal therapy session.

12.   As a general guideline it is suggested a period of twice the length of time you were actually lying in the crystal therapy web be allowed for integration.

Clear Quartz - See the Root Chakra for details of properties.

Larimar

This variety is actually a rock, being composed of more than one mineral, but is mostly composed of pectolite. It has been given the trade name "Larimar". Only discovered in the Bahamas and Dominican Republic in the last twenty years, it has enjoyed success in the semi-precious stone market. Its translucent sky blue color is attractive and has a loyal following of admirers. It has a turquoise look to it, although the color is distinctly more blue. Larimar has been used in the same manner as turquoise and is even seen in contemporary Native American jewellery. Pectolite is one of the zeolites and is found in cavities in basalt and other volcanic rocks. It often exhibits chatoyancy.

Larimar is etherial in its nature and has an other-worldly feel. This beautiful heavenly blue stone contains an energy of peace and tranquillity. It gently transmits pure spiritual substance into the higher chakras above the head. Larimar contains 'Grandmother Earth' energies and will assist you in finding your true path in life. It will also assist you in removing the blocks you have placed on your path to personal power. For women it will activate your own Goddess energies, bringing understanding of the Divine maiden, mother and crone. It is useful for connecting those who feel disorientated and out of step with the earth. It has been called the Dolphin stone, due to its watery energy, though this is another aspect of 'mystery' about this stone, as its birth is definitely fire in nature. It is best worn as a pendant for long periods of time; this facilitates its magical properties, allowing them to fully manifest in your life. The best way of understanding larimar's fire is through our own fiery emotions, which very often are released through our watery tears. Our tears are our very own ocean, which has been gifted to us to facilitate our personal cleansing process. The Dolphin energy contained within the stone is also playful in nature and it will activate a deep healing of our emotional inner child or, as has been observed, activate our own Angelic inner child.

Our Angelic inner child has never been damaged and its integrity and purity have remained intact; it is beyond the traumas which may have affected our inner child. Your Angelic inner child will show you the ways of joy, gratitude, playfulness, and nurturing into wholeness. Larimar asks the question "when was the last time you took some time to play? - to explore your inner creative childlike nature?"

Larimar helps in crystal reflexology, as it fully opens the meridians of the feet, so bringing greater awareness of the cause of the initial disease, via the painful area of the foot, which is a reflection of the whole body; just as water is reflective, so is larimar. It may be placed on any area of pain, bringing a cooling, peaceful healing energy into the blocked energy centre. It is good for all throat ailments and has been effective in healing heart trauma. Many people have been guided to use larimar as a meditation stone, where it has facilitated deep meditative states, bringing insight and intuition. It definitely has its own Angelic spiritual guidance and has been used to access the Angelic Realm. It has facilitated contact with the Angels who work with the elements of water and healing. It has been used to contact Dolphins and Whales; this has led to joyful encounters with the guardians of the oceans and the keepers of the sacred records.

Affirmation: I no longer deny my etherial nature and allow it to guide me home.

Lepidolite

Lepidolite is a mica and has just in the past decade become available on the mineral market in great quantities. Lepidolite means *scale stone*; it is an ore of lithium and forms in granitic masses that contain a substantial amount of lithium. Lepidolite, like other micas, has a layered structure of lithium aluminum silicate sheets, weakly bonded together by layers of potassium ions. Lepidolite crystals accompany such other lithium-bearing minerals as tourmaline, amblygonite and spodumene and can add greatly to the value of these specimens. Single large plates or 'books' of lepidolite can have appealing violet-lilac color.

Lepidolite can desensitise the nervous system very effectively, thereby numbing pain. It contains an extremely high vibration and works on the brain's pain centres, which helps with drug addiction. It also gives you your own space back, so you can heal, so it is good for convalescence. Lepidolite also clears anaesthetics from the system. It facilitates the energy of no mind, thus relieving stress. It is also used for balancing both sides of the brain. In meditation it feels like a gentle wave of energy flowing through the mind. Lepidolite is especially good for insomnia. The 'Spirit' keeper or Angel of lepidolite facilitates its use as a 'dreamtime' crystal, an astral guide. It changes our way of consciously viewing the world, by accessing other dimensions and realities. Lepidolite is a good space clearer; it can emit an immense force field that will keep anything negative at bay. It has a pushing - pulsing - exploding kind of energy (like popcorn).

It can be used to clear the mind of unwanted debris before meditation, so it aids deep meditation practice. It can fully activate and integrate the crown chakra, bringing alignment to the higher trans-personal chakras above the head. Lepidolite's energy is the positive female aspect of the negative warlike male vibration - Pallas Athena, who sprang fully-armed and protected from the head of her father, Zeus. So lepidolite is beneficial for men who are trying to balance their female polarity and learn to nurture themselves into wholeness. It stops the head ruling the heart, by bringing about a balanced polarity. It teaches us to use an integrated approach.

It stops depression, obsessional thinking and confusion. It alleviates symptoms of sensitivity to pollutants, chronic exhaustion, epilepsy and Alzheimer's. Lepidolite also strengthens the immune system and has great healing powers. It gives a rest for the troubled heart and brings inner peace and emotional healing.

Affirmation: I recognise the need for silence, relaxation and stillness in my life.

Moonstone

Oligoclase is not a well-known gemstone but has been used as a semi-precious stone under the labels of sunstone and moonstone. Sunstone has flashes of reddish color caused by inclusions of hematite. Moonstone shows a glowing shimmer similar to labradorescence, but it is much more subtle. Moonstone is a variety of feldspar and the shimmer, which is called schiller or adularescence, is caused by the intergrowth of two different types of feldspar, with different refractive indexes. Moonstones come in a variety of colors and can range from colorless to grey, brown, yellow, green, blue or pink. The clarity ranges from transparent to translucent. The best moonstone has a blue sheen, perfect clarity and a colorless body color. Sometimes moonstone will have an eye as well as a sheen. Another related feldspar variety is known as rainbow moonstone. In this variety of labradorite feldspar, the sheen is a variety of rainbow hues. Moonstone appears mysterious and magical, with a ghostly shimmering glow floating in a crystalline material. The Romans thought that moonstone was formed out of moonlight. In Europe, moonstone is considered the birthstone for June.

As *the* talisman of the Goddess, moonstone is the female power stone. Due to its close association with lunar energies it facilitates the wearer's deep understanding and celebration of the cycles of life, of the ebb and flow of birth, death and regeneration - the tides of life. Throughout the ages, people have celebrated the role of the goddess in maintaining balance and harmony. In recent history (the last two thousand years) the goddess has been eclipsed by the solar male energy; she has been subjugated, ignored, humbled and vanquished. People forget that the moon and the goddess energy is in reality our true salvation; by honouring the earth and respecting the feminine we will begin to redress the imbalance. We live in a culture that feeds misogyny - the female holocaust. Moonstone is acceptance and wisdom beyond the energy of duality. It has a soft lustre, an inner strength and hidden power. Moonstone gives personal resilience and calms the mind. It is nurturing to the soul and heals the subtle energy system, by comforting and aiding serene contemplation. Moonstone will lull, soothe, console, comfort, bring personal peace, tranquillity and deep soul connection. Moonstone instigates ceremony and ritual by observation and honouring the feminine: the Divine driving force of the universe. Moonstone makes an excellent gemstone essence and meditation stone. It is good for aiding peaceful sleep and when used in body layouts it is very soothing, except for the peach variety, which is creative and inspiring.

Affirmation: The great mystery guides and nurtures me, it activates my inner strength and hidden power.

Rose Quartz - see Web of Light - Tranquil Heart

Sugilite

Sugilite is a very distinctive opaque waxy purple stone. It comes from the Southern states of Africa and Japan. It was discovered in 1944 in Japan by Dr Kenichi Sugi, for whom it was named. It is found in association with manganese and is often streaked with black or bluish lines.

Sugilite is the third eye activator; it works on the pineal gland, the top of the head, the crown and heart chakras, as well as the brain and scalp. Sugilite has a potent mature Universal Consciousness. It is very matriarchal and nurturing; it does seem to 'mother' the 'Star Children', giving them feelings of security and protection against the harsh climate of the negative earth vibration of hostility, rage, anger and fear. It is good for those who feel abandoned and dis-connected from their 'home' and source of emotional nourishment. It has also been used by very gentle sensitive souls who find it difficult to screen out the negativity and hostility of others. It is very protective, as well as gently grounding. It can integrate the spiritual body to the physical body, which is very helpful for those amongst us who 'space out' easily. Many people on the spiritual path have utilised sugilite for grounding their spiritual experiences into their everyday life. Above all, sugilite brings peace, dignity, humanitarianism and mental creativity. It really does develop psychic abilities, allowing for mystical experiences. It can develop faith and inner strength. It teaches you personal mastery, that you have a Divine right to your own point of view and inner truth. Sugilite also contains the spirit of mercy and it is very dignified; it allows you to work with the highest levels of thought and gives a thorough understanding of the thought process. Sugilite is the aristocrat of the purple gemstones; it commands respect as it guides you towards spiritual perfection. It has a richness and quality about it that lead to refined psychic perception. It is good for those who meditate and teach meditation and healing disciplines: its vibration can produce great mystical leaders and enlightened gurus. Sugilite has been used by cancer sufferers; it has brought relief to many souls. It has helped with all kinds of cancer, from brain tumours to breast cancer; this one use alone deserves complete medical research. It also helps problems associated with the immune system. It has been used to help internal inflammation and skin eruptions. Sugilite can subdue palpitations of the heart and jangled nerves. The lighter shades of sugilite can calm emotional turbulence and help with the pain of neuralgia and acute inflammation of the nerves. Lilac sugilite also has great healing powers; it can strengthen the immune system and is good for convalescence. It also flushes from the system the residue of anaesthetics.

Affirmation: I have a Divine right to my own point of view and inner truth.

Crystal Healing Meditation - Heart Chakra

Clearing dis-stress or emotional stress.... from the physical, etheric, emotional, mental, astral and etheric blueprint bodies, via the thymus witness point and heart chakra.

Everyone has at some time in their lives experienced stress or a stressful situation, whether it is a visit to the dentist or a driving test, perhaps a job interview or a person or situation that regularly stresses you out. It could even be some incident in your past that causes you emotional pain or heartfelt sorrow, maybe a bereavement, loss or rejection. Whatever it was......when we become dis-stressed or stressed, our bodies no longer function with a balanced flow of energy.

Very soon we find we can no longer cope with the stressful person, situation or even a memory. The stress builds and builds until we either become ill, or can no longer cope at all. This may take place over many years. The following application will clear dis-stress and current stress from the physical, etheric, emotional, mental, astral and etheric blueprint bodies, etc. - the auric shell or luminous egg.

1. Choose a warm comfortable place where you can sit down undisturbed for at least an hour. Never rush a meditation. View it as your own sacred healing space. You need to make sure it is energetically clean. Make sure you are wearing warm, loose, comfortable clothes......we will use a rose quartz crystal; this is a really effective and totally safe procedure even for a beginner in crystal therapy.

2. Prepare and cleanse your crystal ready for use and place it at your left side as you:

    Sit in a comfortable steady posture, with the spine and neck held erect but not tense. This helps steady the mind and aids concentration. The psychic current must be able to travel freely from the base of the spine to the top of the head. Any comfortable cross-legged posture provides a firm base for the body. It makes a triangular pathway for the energy flow, which must be contained rather than dissipated in all directions, and keeps the lungs free to move naturally with as little effort as possible.

3. Place the hands in the lap, with the right hand resting on the left, and pull the shoulders back ever so slightly and the chin in a little so that there is a small pull on the back of the neck; this will ease the blood-flow to the brain. Close your eyes and, with the mouth ever so slightly open, rest the tip of the tongue on the roof of the mouth just behind the teeth. This placement of the tongue is vital because it naturally maintains the flow of energy to the head whilst keeping the jaw relaxed. There are two major energy channels (acupuncture meridians). The Yin channel (the conception vessel) begins at the perineum and flows up the front centre of the body and

ends at the tip of the tongue. The Yang channel (the governing vessel) begins at the perineum and flows up the back centre of the body, over the top of the head and back down to the roof of the mouth. The tongue connects these two important currents when touched to the highest point in the roof of the mouth.

(An easy way to open this energy channel is to sit in a relaxed posture. Allow your energy to complete the loop by letting your mind flow along with it. Start in the mouth and mentally circulate your attention with the energy. Eventually the current will begin to feel warm in some places as it loops around. Relax, try to bring your mind directly into the part of the loop being focused on. Experience the actual feeling of the flow of chi in that part of your body. Once the circuit is going smoothly, inhale as you go up the spine and over to the third eye, and exhale as you go down from the third eye to the perineum).

4. Now - consciously regulate the breath. Begin with five minutes of deep abdominal breathing to bring oxygen to the brain. Then slow it to an imperceptible rate. Now simply turn your full attention to the movement of your breath. Do not try and control your breathing, simply be aware of the breath. Then begin to follow the breath entering and leaving your body and gradually feel the effect this conscious breathing has on your body.

5. Next, with your right hand, tap the witness point three times (which is on your breastbone between your heart and your throat, just at the thymus point). Then return your right hand into your lap and become aware of the witness point. You may feel a tingling or throbbing sensation as it begins to activate.

6. Then, pick up your rose quartz crystal, hold it in your left hand and gently hold your crystal to the witness point.

7. Begin to think about the problem or stressful situation you have chosen to 'heal'. Really feel all the emotions associated with the stress, remember everything you can, actually bring the full memory back into your conscious awareness, allow the stress to really well up in your body - what happens next is nothing short of miraculous. You will feel all the stress draining away and your emotions will quickly become calm and focused.

8. Keep holding the rose quartz crystal at the witness point, because very often you will feel another surge of energy as the crystal goes even deeper to 'heal' the stress. This process may happen several times as your body takes the healing energy from the crystal. Each time you feel the surge of energy be aware that your body has chosen to use the healing crystal vibration to go to deeper and deeper levels.

This will remove the stressful memory which has become encoded deep within your cellular structure. This facilitates healing to take place on all levels, physical, emotional, mental, etheric etc.

We always use the witness point on the human body, as this is the area where the etheric blueprint joins all the other levels. Whether you are aware of it or not, the etheric blueprint body was formed before the astral, mental, emotional and physical bodies, and by using this point healing will occur on all lower levels.

You may use this technique on yourself and others as many times as needed. Try not to overdo this procedure though; remember to allow your body time to integrate the new flow of energy before attempting to heal another stressful situation.

Please also recognise that everyone heals at their own pace. Some people choose to take the crystal energy and integrate it very quickly, others may take longer. We are all unique and each disease is unique, so allow the healing to be natural to the person you are helping with the crystal healing vibration.

9. Allow yourself or your client to return to everyday awareness and normal breathing.

10.   Finally, drink plenty of pure fresh clean water; this will flush any toxins from your physical body that may have been released during the crystal therapy session.

Sometimes the witness point may feel sore, tight or tingling for several hours; this is quite normal and will pass.

Kundalini Heart Chakra Meditation

The next kundalini awakening meditation underpins all Pranayama. It is the ancient discipline as taught by the great Yoga teacher Patanjali. It is just as fresh and potent a vehicle for spiritual development today as it was when he taught it several thousand years ago. I learned this process myself some 29 years ago.

Alternate-Nostril Breathing - To maintain a balance in the heart chakra you should practise equally on a daily basis both of the techniques I am going to explain.

Technique 1 - Downflow - This is the integration of the lower three chakras with the heart chakra and it will energize the physical body.

1.   Sit comfortably with your spine straight and just focus on your normal breathing pattern for several breaths - just watch your breath coming and going.

2.   Now, raise your right hand to your nose, palm towards your mouth. Place your thumb besides your right nostril and your forefinger besides your left nostril, so that you can close off one air passage or the other, with slight gentle pressure.

3.   Now move your focused attention to your three lower chakras: you are going to energise them with a downflow of loving heart energy from above. Simply close the right nostril with your thumb, while you exhale through the left nostril.

4.   At the bottom of your exhale, simply be empty for a moment, send your focus of attention as far down to the root chakra as possible......then release the thumb from the right nostril and press with your forefinger on the left nostril, so that you inhale through the right nostril.

5.   At the top of this inhale, keep your fingers the same as on the inhale, and exhale through the same right nostril until you are empty of air.....hold on empty......

6.   Now reverse the process ...by releasing your forefinger from your left nostril and pressing your thumb on the right nostril....inhale through the left nostril....hold at the top a moment, keep your fingers the same, then exhale through the same left nostril.

7.   Continue in this pattern, where you inhale and exhale on one side only, then switch nostrils.

8.   Inhale fully, do not switch nostrils....exhale fully from the same nostril.....

Now switch nostrils...inhale.....exhale

Now switch nostrils....inhale...exhale

Now switch nostrils....inhale....exhale

9.   Continue in this pattern for 12 to 20 rounds.

Practise this exercise until you can do it automatically and you are clear about the process.

Technique 2 - Heart Consciousness Rising - This technique will raise your consciousness upwards into your head to give a unified head-heart balance.

To reverse the breath exercise, the secret is to remember that you want to make the switch between nostrils at the top of your inhales......to take the energy upwards, as opposed to making the switch at the bottom of your exhales.... to energise your lower chakras with your heart energy.

With the reversed breathing pattern, you will move pranic energy up into your head with every inhale.

163

Hold on the full breath for several seconds, then switch to the other nostril as you exhale. Inhale on the same side, bringing more energy up to the head. Then switch over to the other nostril for the next exhale-inhale cycle.

So....

Exhale...don't switch nostrils...inhale.

Now switch nostrils.....exhale....inhale.

Switch...exhale....inhale......and continue .....for as long as it takes to master the technique without looking at this book.

Now we will practise the heart chakra meditation...of course it should follow naturally on from the last three kundalini chakra meditations.....so....after you have done the breath of fire, the solar plexus mantra RAM and meditated on the solar plexus mandala....you are now energised and ready to move into the heart chakra.

1.   Practise the heart consciousness rising pranayama you have just learnt.

2.   The heart chakra bandha or energy seal is very simple...you just need to pull your shoulders back, until you feel a gentle pull on them.....this fully opens the heart chakra....allowing the free-flow of energy through this vital centre. Of course you should have all the other energy seals in place that you have learnt in the previous three kundalini meditations.

3.   Breathing easily....you are now ready to focus on and vocalize the fourth chakra mantra... YAM....as before, allow the sound to manifest in your mind....feel it effortlessly rising from your inner being........as the Y (pronounced eeeeeeeyy)....A........M... sound gently moves to awaken your heart chakra.....opening yourself to the sound of the universe, as it joins you in sounding the YAM........continue for as long as you want........and when you are ready, visualise or feel your heart chakra begin to turn upwards.....towards your crown chakra....this brings spiritual energy into your heart chakra and allows for your full attention to be focused upwards towards your enlightenment.......

4.   Now visualise or look directly at the heart chakra mandala....use the one in this book......become aware of the chakra mandala as you focus on the energy movements and shapes it contains.......

5.   Continue to visualise or gaze at the mandala as long as you want.........

6.   When you are ready, allow the gentle loving energy you have created to flow up your spine through all your upper three chakras in sequential order.........and pour out of the top of your head like a fountain of light............this sacred divine loving energy brings your whole energy field to life...........

7.   Allow yourself plenty of time to integrate this new awareness.......you need to practise this meditation on a daily basis; it is the culmination of the first, second, third and fourth chakra kundalini activation you have learned thus far.....don't forget to reverse the root chakra to point downwards and the sacral, solar plexus and heart chakras to point outwards.....as you once more anchor yourself on the earth plane of ego existence......

Part 16

The Throat Chakra

The fifth or throat chakra is also known as the communication or self-expression chakra. In Sanskrit the name is *visuddha*, which translates as pure; it also means purification. It is the first of the spiritual triad of higher centres and resonates most vibrantly with the blue ray. At the psychic level, this chakra is associated with clairaudience, or the ability to hear things at a subtle energetic level. It is located in the throat region, just above the base of the neck - directly situated over the thyroid gland. This is where our basic communication tool, the voice box or larynx, is situated also. This remarkable organ enables us to take the outflow of air through our windpipe and transform the torrent of air into a vibratory message for the outside world to respond to. The way people respond depends on the vocalisation you make. The human voice as a whole is very revealing; in fact it reflects the mental, emotional, spiritual and physical condition of a person.

Your voice, as you will come to recognise, is a direct expression of your soul. Understanding the voice is an excellent discipline of self-awareness and it is central to the art of active listening. The way you use your voice gives vital insight into your complete being; your vocalizations reveal how your energies, feelings, thoughts, emotions and intuition collaborate to produce your unique vocal style. This vocal style reacts to external influences as well as the feelings inside you. It evolves through time as your emotions and past experiences accumulate, develop and mature. Therefore the voice is diagnostic as well as therapeutic. By listening to the voices of others and by objectively tuning in to the nature of your own voice, you can find out many aspects of health and emotional well-being. Try listening to the individual words and their meanings in context, to the subtle layering of implications and associations behind the words and between the lines, to the pauses, gaps and silences; to the non-verbal utterances such as sighs and sobs, and to the voice itself - its pitch and tonal qualities, its rhythm and pace. In addition, look at the posture and the body language, as well as those more mysterious nuances of perception which we call intuition and instinct. Thus the nature of the voice reveals the nature of the soul; it can help us to identify and diagnose problems, which we can utilize to start the healing process.

A healthy voice reflects a healthy soul - the hallmarks of a healthy voice are versatility, sensitivity, compassion, warmth, joy, wisdom and purity of tone; it is clear, bright and open, with no hint of forcing or straining. Above all, a healthy voice possesses vitality - the abundance of vital energy that can triumph over hardship, disaster, disappointment or pain.

Body language concerning the throat chakra is also interesting - the next time you are in a situation, especially a group situation, and you observe someone who appears to have difficulty expressing themselves, see if their chin is held down towards the chest, obscuring the throat area. This shows that the person is very vulnerable or weak in the throat chakra. Such people have frequently to clear the throat because esoterically it is being choked or strangled by the truths they have swallowed. They usually speak in an apathetic monotonous tone. They may attempt to contribute to group discussions, but because of inarticulateness or lack of enthusiasm they are frequently not heard by others. Holding the head down towards the chest is also a sign of depression. If you raise your head and look upwards on a regular basis, it will lift your energy. In fact this very movement of looking up will raise your energy. When we are sad or depressed we usually slump our shoulders and take very shallow breaths. If we sit up straight and breathe deeply, it is much more difficult to stay sad or depressed. In this way anything that makes us look physically upwards subtly makes us more open to feeling happy, optimistic and cheerful in spirit.

165

The throat chakra is concerned with all communication including the written word; as I write the words in this book I am communicating directly with you. I am employing a great deal of energy from the fifth chakra, since this is the chakra of interpersonal communication. Without the throat chakra there would be no interchange of ideas from one person to another and virtually no human civilization at all. We should remember that up until a few hundred years ago, with the invention of the printing press, the vast majority of human communication was through vocal exchange.

The throat chakra also involves learning self-discipline or self-mastery over the incarnating ego's small-will. This controlled expression of the higher will is another important issue of the throat chakra. At a time when self-indulgence has become commonplace, the development of discipline in one's life is an important stepping stone towards any type of personal or spiritual transformation. So by activating the kundalini energy we are made aware of our communication on all levels and in all dimensions. In fact the throat chakra could be called 'kundalini in action' chakra. Many people do not realise this communication is also with their guides, Angels, Masters and teachers including their higher self.

Long ago it was conjectured that there existed a fifth element beyond the four visible elements of earth, water, fire and air; the ancients called it the *akasha* in Sanskrit and 'ether' in the West. This fifth element was the realm where spirits were said to live. It was believed to be at a higher or faster vibration than the other elements, so it was only available to the adepts, those elite souls who could raise their vibratory rate sufficiently high or fast enough to encounter or view its elusive dimension.

The throat chakra also works with the sensory channel of sound. This is the most direct of the chakra correspondences and often the easiest for the Western mind to grasp. Talking about the Western mind - it shows how the throat chakra can become overactive to a detrimental degree. This is because the throat chakra is also intimately associated with the parts of the brain that generate complex thought-flows. My experience as a therapist and teacher has been that most people in our society fixate on the fifth chakra, living in a world of concepts, theories, ideas, dreams and fantasies. With the advent of the Internet, hyperspace has been added to this list, where you can live out your life on the information super-highway in virtual-reality - which is fine, but when it comes to taking action on these ideas, bringing our dreams into reality, we must drop down into the second and third chakras for the necessary creativity and power. Otherwise we spend a great deal of our time living in a fantasy world of what we would like to happen, but never having the drive and enthusiasm to bring our ideas to life, or having the sheer stamina, strength and courage to anchor them on the Earth plane of reality with our first chakra's finest qualities. In other words 'walk our talk', or bring our conceptual 'brain child' to life. The other problem with a lot of people today is that they forget to engage the higher chakras in their conceptual or cognitive domain. They live their lives in the theory stage, or stuck in a fifth chakra world of endless conceptual consciousness with ideas on God, without having first-hand direct personal encounters.

When the communication chakra is dormant or inactive, we are mentally asleep, not thinking things through adequately in order to lead a productive, fulfilling life. These people tend to shut themselves off from society and normal human interaction. Conversely, when the throat chakra is overactive, it drains energy from all the other chakras.......and other people too. We have all encountered this negative draining effect of the person who does not know the meaning of the word moderation; silence can really be 'golden'. These souls who have hyperactive throat chakras can also be caught up in the energy of thinking-thinking-thinking without tuning in to their heart enough (the affective domain) or the solar plexus chakra (the psychomotor domain) to give the necessary power to these ideas. Great thinker - ineffective doer. They can be manipulative too, always seeking the help of others to carry out their grandiose unrealistic plans.

The throat chakra can really become unbalanced through a severe lack of soul connection. The energy of the two higher chakras is needed to truly manifest your divine path with heart; not only must you 'walk your talk', but you should 'walk your way to heaven and anchor it here on earth'. This will stop the abuse of the solar plexus power chakra and the throat chakra's cognitive abuse of the planet and its inhabitants. I do not mean in any way to demean the throat chakra's technological advances though; without the latest technology I would not be able to sit here at my notepad and write this book. When technology is at its finest, it is used for the good of all that lives.

166

I have also found throughout my years of teaching that some people view the chakras as concepts, or ideas - they try and 'get their head around them' to think them through. May I ask you, have you done this? Have you read through this book so far without trying out the meditations? Especially the chakra - kundalini awakening meditation? How real are your chakra energy centres?

So to recap and explore further, the throat chakra is associated with communication, self-expression, sound, voice, speech, writing, typing, singing, chanting and active listening. It also relates to dreaming, imagination and out-of-body experiences and the astral realm. I have had so many clients over the years who were totally fixated with the astral dimension of the throat chakra. This is because not only does the throat chakra give out communication to others, it is where we receive communication from others. This includes the realm of 'spirit'. These non-physical realms contact us via our throat chakras; if our two higher chakras are unbalanced or non-functioning, we can spend our whole lives 'hypnotised' by low level entities. These lower level 'spirits', as anyone who has read a Carlos Castaneda book will know, can be very strange and intimidating - fascinating and sometimes frightening.

So it is very important when working with any chakra healing or vibrational therapy system to give equal attention to all the energy centres, so that they balance and complement each other beautifully. I should state, however, that visions are an integral part of the throat chakra; they relate very much to our own personal fantasies and unconscious activities, very much the way dreams do. If the visions come to you, it is perfectly fine; everyone has this capacity, just as everyone has the capacity to dream. The secret is not to fixate on them, or become overly attached to them. The world of *maya* - illusion, of holding on to images and visions instead of moving beyond them - is a fifth chakra function. Always be ready to let go of your visions in order to move upwards into sixth chakra, non-conceptual, non-duality consciousness. Be open to immense fifth chakra visions that play out your conceptual imagery of spiritual awakening, but be ready to leave them far behind as you move onwards and upwards into the higher chakras.

Physically the throat chakra rules over the thyroid gland, parathyroid, lungs, vocal cords, jaw and breath. Malfunctions include stiff necks, colds, sore throats, thyroid and hearing problems, tinnitus, asthma. It also includes stiff-necked attitudes, dogma, religious dogma, the illusory masks of the self, perfectionism and the inability to express emotions in a constructive non-destructive manner; also blocked creativity is a result of an ineffective throat chakra.

The fifth chakra, the throat, is masculine; manifesting; logical and yang. Its symbol is the 16-petal blue lotus flower. As we progress through the chakras we find the colors becoming cooler and cooler and the vibrations of the colors faster and shorter. The warm earth frequencies (red) are the longest and lowest, as we would expect, and as we move heavenwards the cool blues begin to manifest. Contained within the lotus flower is a downward-pointing triangle representing spirit, within which is a circle representing the full silvery-blue moon. The moon represents the astral energy of the Akashic records. The moon's silver reflection is only an illusion of light. It contains no light of substance of its own. It is when we move into the third eye and crown chakras that the illusion vanishes, as duality and separation end. The sixteen petals of the lotus flower are very significant in this chakra; each petal represents a vowel of the Ancient Sanskrit alphabet. This allows us to relate to the *Sabdabrahman* or original sound and it is through the throat chakra that we disperse the energy of all the other chakra mantras throughout our body and aura. Through the use of these primal *bija* sounds, the throat chakra has a vast potential to carry us towards enlightenment. The traditional sound for the throat chakra is the *bija* mantra HAM in the Hindu tradition, and a slightly altered and even more powerful HANG in the Tantric Buddhist tradition of Nepal and Tibet.

Anahata sounds or the melody are the mystical sounds heard by the meditator at the start of their cycle of meditation. They are called the voice of your inner God/Goddess (Higher Self). This subject is termed *Nada-Anusandhana* or an enquiry into the mystic sounds. This is a sign of purification of the *Nadis*, due to *Pranayama*. These sounds are heard through the right ear with or without closing the ears. The sounds are very distinct when heard through closed ears. The ears can be closed by introducing the two thumbs into the ears through the process of *Yoni Mudra*. Occasionally, you can hear the sounds through the left ear also. Practise to hear the sounds only through the right ear. The reason you should only hear distinctly with the right ear is to make sure your nadis are balanced. The solar (yang) pingala is on the right side of the nose. The *Anahata* sound is also known as *Omkara Dhvani*. The sounds you hear are due to the vibration of *Prana* in the heart.

There are 10 kinds of sounds. The first is *chini* (like the sound of the word chini) which resembles the sweet sound of a nightingale; the second is *chini-chini*; the third is the sound of a bell; the fourth is that of a conch - as the melodious song of an ocean-sprite imprisoned in its shell; the fifth is that of *tantri* (lute); the sixth is *tala* (symbols); the seventh is that of a bamboo flute; the eight is that of *bheri* (drum); the ninth is that of *mridanga* (double drum) and the tenth is thunder.

The color blue associated with the throat chakra gives communication with Divine guidance and right use of will. When this chakra is fully activated with the blue ray of wisdom you have a beautiful voice and your speech is clear and fluent. Your intellect increases, as does your understanding of the Divine scriptures. You have complete knowledge of the past, present and future. You have wisdom, patience, truth, mental attainment, good communication, contentment, artistic inspiration, deep meditation, spiritual and philosophical contemplation, personal integrity and loyalty.

Finally, your guides to this chakra are any Ascended Master, Guru or Angelic being that you feel a strong heartfelt, loving connection to, or a deep devotion to. This is where you need to engage your heart chakra in your daily meditations. It is foolish in the extreme to open to the Akashic records if your heart chakra is not balanced. Be aware, though, that you have the right to 'challenge' any 'being' that appears as your guide (more about this in the chapter on the crown chakra). It is important to establish their goodwill and intent towards you right from the start. It is just the same as any relationship you have with 'beings' on the physical plane of human existence. They should always have your best interest at 'heart' - any being that tries to control, manipulate, dominate, exploit or belittle you in any way is to be firmly banished immediately - this goes for the earth plane too, in my opinion. The associated creatures for the throat chakra are a white lion and *Airavata*, the many-tusked white elephant.

Crystal Web of Light - Sacred Sounds

Crystals: 2 apatite, 1 yellow and 1 blue, tumbled, faceted or natural
                                1 aquamarine, tumbled, faceted or natural
                                3 lapis, tumbled or natural
                                1 iolite, tumbled, faceted or natural
                                6 clear quartz points

Uses: The crystal web of light - sacred sounds includes three pieces of lapis, which is a high intensity etheric blue stone. It contains the energies of royalty, wisdom, patience, truth, mental attainment, good communication, contentment, artistic inspiration, deep meditation, spiritual and philosophical contemplation, personal integrity and loyalty. It is the 'Spirit of Truth'. So this crystal web of light will balance the throat chakra. How you tell if the throat chakra is unbalanced by being too open or spinning too fast is that the person is over-talkative, dogmatic, self-righteous or arrogant. If the throat chakra is too closed, or spinning sluggishly, the person is unreliable, holds inconsistent views and holds back from heartfelt self-expression.

This web of light works on the thyroid, parathyroids, the throat, upper lungs and arms, the base of the skull and body weight. It teaches you the power of the spoken word. Because the blue ray governs the throat, infections in this area are psychologically related to 'talking inwards', not speaking out. Psychologically speaking, coughing is because a person has swallowed their thoughts and cannot bring themselves to speak out. It teaches you to 'give voice to your truth'. It counteracts harshness. If somebody is acting insensitively in a situation, the blue ray will help them become more compassionate. The cool blue ray gives relief from pain, both physical and psychological, and combats cruelty and brutality. This web of light is good to meditate in, as its high intensity etheric nature means you can really bring your energy into line with its refined vibration. It contains a higher order of intelligence and wisdom, 'intellectual integrity'. The crystal web of light also heals the martyr syndrome: 'I am going to punish myself in order to make you suffer'.

It aids discrimination of wisdom; it is very penetrating. It teaches you to reach for the stars. The yellow apatite brings in the energies of the solar plexus chakra, to activate, energize, align and integrate the throat chakra. The blue apatite facilitates true heartfelt communication when used and has instigated new levels of love, compassion and wisdom. Blue apatite is the healer of emotions of the heart; it teaches you to 'talk from the heart' and say what you feel, instead of what is appropriate. It calms the nerves. The lapis in this web of light also teaches you that you have no chance of developing a balanced purified throat chakra until you have successfully worked through and balanced the lower four chakras to obtain the necessary purification to fully activate this centre. Lapis also teaches the mastery of active listening by integrating the full faculties of hearing. We need to fully develop the outer ear, before the subtle inner ear can be available to us for inner guidance. All too often Divine guidance is not heard, because of not truly listening to the 'wisdom' behind the words.

The aquamarine in this crystal web gives freedom from the impressions and influences of others. Calming, soothing to the emotions, cooling and an excellent meditation stone, it helps you go with your own 'flow', finding your perfect karmic path with courage, fortitude and, most of all, compassion for yourself. It will shield the aura from anger, hatred, envy and hostility. It opens the gateways to understanding the archetypal realms, gives mental and emotional stability, promotes greater understanding of the dramas we may be caught up in and facilitates being able to step out of the drama to see the underlying emotion. Finally, the iolite is included as a vision quest guide and guardian to those who go on inner or outer journeys of self-exploration. It awakens innate inner knowledge and wisdom; it assists in reducing confusion by virtue of understanding the life situation that is currently causing the confusion. All confusion arises from the inability to claim one's own 'intuitive power' and act according to the needs of the individual, not the needs of society, or the sentimental tribal mentality which one has been born into.

1 apatite (yellow), placed on the solar plexus chakra.

1 apatite (blue), placed on the heart chakra.

1 aquamarine, placed at the throat chakra.

1 iolite, placed at the third eye chakra.

3 lapis, placed at the crown chakra and in the palms of both hands.

6 clear quartz single terminated crystals, placed in a star of David (Merkaba) web.

Process:

1.   Cleanse all the crystals and programme the clear quartz for healing.

2.   Choose a warm comfortable place where you can lie down undisturbed for at least an hour; never rush a crystal web of light process. View it as a sacred healing space, so you need to make sure it is energetically clean. Make sure you are wearing warm, loose, comfortable clothes.

3.   Relax by consciously becoming aware of your breathing and heartbeat; you can play soothing music, light candles and burn incense.

4.   Lay the stones around and on the body and hold a lapis in each hand.

5.   Allow 20 minutes to facilitate the integration of the crystal vibration.

6.   Feel free to remove the crystals sooner, if you have integrated the crystal energy very quickly.

7.   Remove the crystals in reverse order of placement.

8.   Make sure you are fully grounded, centred and balanced.

9.   Cleanse your crystals (using your chosen method).

10.   Finish by giving thanks and asking mentally that all the healing work you have just accomplished is closed, sealed and protected with Divine love and wisdom.

11.   Give yourself sufficient time to integrate the crystal therapy session.

12.   As a general guideline it is suggested a period of twice the length of time you were actually lying in the crystal therapy web be allowed for integration.

Apatite

A fine gemstone with a vast color range of white, yellow, green, blue and violet, it is a calcium phosphate, with some fluorine or chlorine in the composition. Apatite is a widely distributed mineral. It occurs as small crystals as an accessory mineral in a wide range of igneous rocks. Large crystals occur in pegmatites and in some high-temperature hydrothermal veins. It also occurs in both regional and contact metamorphic rocks, especially in metamorphosed limestone. In sedimentary rocks, apatite is a principal constituent of fossil bones and other organic matter. The name collophane is sometimes used for such phosphatic material. The name comes from the Greek word *apatao*, meaning 'to deceive', because apatite, particularly the gem variety, is easily mistaken for other minerals.

Blue apatite helps with communication on all levels, whether it is communication by speech, writing or self-expression through art and music. It has been worn and carried by world-famous musicians who have used its energy for its truly remarkable inspirational qualities. It also aids communication with other realms of existence and has facilitated many past life karmic visions. Many people who have worn or carried the blue apatite have found beneficial high level spirit guides of a humanitarian nature. Blue apatite facilitates true heartfelt communication when used by groups, whereby the altruistic energy has instigated new levels of group love, compassion and wisdom. Blue apatite is connected to the throat and chest. It is the healer of emotions of the heart; it teaches you to 'talk from the heart' and say what you feel, instead of what is appropriate. It calms the nerves and is a great crystal to wear if you appear before the public (especially when combined with rose quartz). Large opaque crystals of the blue variety are freely available, but many people are drawn to the rare yellow variety for its beneficial solar energies. These wonderful yellow stones can be used to energise the solar plexus chakra, which then eases any problems associated with an underactive solar plexus. Blocked or stagnant energy in the solar plexus is exhibited in myriad ways, the most common being a lack of energy, depression, M.E., feelings of low self-worth, nightmares, poor digestion and food assimilation, lack of concentration, poor learning abilities, low stamina, restlessness and a short attention span. It helps with problems of the bones and teeth.

The yellow variety has successfully been used as an appetite suppressant in the form of a gem essence, as it is good for removing cellulite. Yellow apatite is the great eliminator; it cleans and removes waste from the system. Faulty elimination is the cause of the beginning of most disease. Apatite also works on the pancreas, liver, gall-bladder, spleen and middle stomach. The liver is known as the seat of anger, where our emotional upsets and hurts are stored; yellow apatite can help with the release of this stored anger.

Affirmation: I now communicate my inner truth, I delight in my self-expression and in all my creative pursuits.

Aquamarine

The most popular color for aquamarine is a clear sky-blue, but most are a bluish-green color. This does not affect the healing properties, for both shades are excellent. Under this group may be added the clear green beryls which owe their color to iron and do not have the verdant green of the chromium-colored emerald. Large crystals have been found and sometimes, due to particular growth conditions, striations (lines) are clearly visible on the surface. Aquamarine, the "gem of the sea", derives its name from "sea water". The reference is obvious: aqua sparkles like the sea and its color is pale to medium blue, sometimes with a slight hint of green. Legends say that it is the treasure of mermaids, with the power to keep sailors safe at sea. Aquamarine is said to be a particularly strong charm when immersed in water. The ancients also believed aquamarine gave protection against the wiles of the devil and to dream of aquamarine meant that you would meet new friends. Aquamarine is always a pastel blue, but the darker the color, the more value it has. Therapists also prefer a pure blue, with no green in it. If you prefer a greenish tinge, you will find that these stones are much less expensive. The word brilliance is probably derived from the ancient Greek word for beryl, *berullos*, which means crystal. Heliodor, or golden beryl, is named after the Greek words for sun - *helios* - and gift - *doron*. Red beryl is the rarest member of the beryl family. It is mined in only one place: the Wah Wah Mountains in Utah. Colorless beryl, which is also known as goshenite, is also relatively rare. It is named after a deposit where it was found in Goshen, Massachusetts. The Greeks used colorless beryl as lenses; the first spectacles were probably beryl. Aquamarine is the birthstone for March.

Very rarely the crystal has the appearance of ancient writing or hieroglyphs on the surface. These special crystals are record keepers. Aquamarine gives freedom from the impressions and influences of others. Calming, soothing to the emotions, cooling and an excellent meditation stone, it helps you go with your own 'flow', finding your perfect karmic path with courage, fortitude and, most of all, compassion for yourself. It will shield the aura from anger, hatred, envy and hostility. It opens the gateways to understanding the archetypal realms, gives mental and emotional stability, promotes greater understanding of the dramas we may be caught up in and facilitates being able to step out of the drama to see the underlying emotion. Archetypes are universal themes, or models, of the 'human condition'. They are illustrated through myths, fairy stories and even modern plays and films; they serve to provide us with an understanding of our emotional experiences - both what we are and what we would like to become. Once you understand your 'drama' or 'life role' you can then change it for one that is more in tune with the life you really want.

Aquamarine also identifies the underlying patterns we may have embedded into our neural pathways, which are outwardly projected as particular behaviours; we can choose at any moment to discard those that no longer serve us. Aquamarine teaches us to take up our emotional reins and the emotional challenges that face us every day in order that we can choose a different direction and move into a new stage of development. The throat chakra is also fully activated by aquamarine. Indeed it is very stimulating when placed on the throat chakra in a crystal web of light, but we find we can safely use this stone on any area of the body; it will release stored stress and induce peace and healing resonance. It alleviates all problems of the throat, swollen glands, the teeth, jaw and upper chest. Aquamarine really feeds the central nervous system and calms nervous stress and breakdown. The stillness of aquamarine calms the panic that can follow emotional shock. It stops the person running away from their hurt self and the painful situation. It is a good stone to use when encountering problems in relationships. It encourages you to be able to speak what is in your heart. It is useful in overcoming self-sabotage and in centering oneself.

This stone is said to put you in touch with the dolphins and whales, whose loving energy really makes you look at your resistance to being totally loving and forgiving. Anger prepares the body to correct injustice, but it needs to be released from the body. When it is not released, it hardens into hatred. We need to honour our emotions, but we also need to elevate our consciousness, which is an act of will. When we know there is someone or something we cannot forgive, we need to ask ourselves what we would have preferred. When we forgive, we cancel our expectations and conditions for loving. We forgive for our own sakes, but our forgiveness will affect the people we have not been able to forgive. If we hold on to resentment, anger, hatred and bitterness, it gives them power over us and eventually these negative emotions make us sick. Sometimes we refuse to forgive in order to punish. A simple way of releasing anger towards someone is to first acknowledge what you are truly feeling about their behaviour or injustice, then consciously choose not to punish yourself for carrying this feeling. You can say "I now intend to let go and release all my suffering over the situation". Then visualise the person you need to forgive standing in front of you. Tell them what you would have preferred to happen and choose to release the expectations. You now want to be free. They are totally accountable for their own actions. Unite your consciousness into the light of your cosmic self and imagine and experience the light, compassion and love flowing into you. Experience unconditional love for yourself. As this feeling builds in you, send this love to the true self of the person and say "I send this love out to you just as you are and have been, you are responsible for your own Karma". When you feel honestly at peace with the situation, you are ready to release it. Until then, you are bound in karmic chains of hatred and you will be linked to this person or situation for eternity.

Affirmation: I now release and let go of my past suffering and pain, knowing I release others too.

Clear Quartz - See the Root Chakra for details of properties.

Iolite

The property that makes iolite so transformational is extreme pleochroism. Iolite has different colors in different directions in the crystal. A cube cut from iolite will look a violetish-blue, almost like sapphire, from one side, clear as water from the other, and a yellow from the top. Owing to the sapphire-blue color of gem quality iolite, the material was in earlier days miscalled 'water sapphire'. The name iolite is applied to the stone on account of the blue color of the gem material, the name being derived from the Greek word *ios* for violet.

Star stone: looking at this stone is like looking at the summer night sky. It has a very high vibrational rate. It is ideal for the awakened 'star children' on the earth plane. A vision-prophecy stone for the 'Shaman/Shamanka', it contains powerful 'medicine'. It is safe to carry or wear iolite, but when placed on the third eye chakra it gives full psychic activation and integration, though only if the lower five chakras are fully balanced; otherwise there is a danger of over-stimulation. This is why it is 'wise' to consult a suitably qualified crystal therapist who will use this stone in an integrated or full chakra web of light. Often we choose to be blind to the potential illuminated by our third eye. In its connection with the higher functions of consciousness, the third eye is a psychic tool reminding us that everything we see, hear, smell, touch or taste started as an inner vision or in-sight.

An unbalanced, blocked, distorted or closed third eye is shown by the person being undisciplined or distrustful; they may fear success and may have a tendency towards schizophrenia. An unbalanced third eye that is too open or spins too fast is observable by the person being highly logical, dogmatic, authoritarian or having reforming fervour; the religious fanatic or fundamentalist. A balanced third eye chakra means the person is charismatic, intuitive, not attached to material possessions and will experience visions in meditation.

Iolite is a vision quest guide and guardian to those who go on inner or outer journeys of self-exploration. It awakens innate inner knowledge and wisdom; it assists in reducing confusion by virtue of understanding the life situation that is currently causing the confusion. All confusion arises from the inability to claim one's own 'intuitive power' and act according to the needs of the individual, not the needs of society, or the tribal mentality which one has been born into. (The tribal mentality alludes to your family, friends, work colleagues and any self-limiting group who have a vested interest in your controlled behavioural patterns and the survival of the patterns, which may serve the group, but do not necessarily serve you as an individual).

Iolite teaches us not to get too attached to ritual, but to look for our own path via a balanced third eye chakra; it takes you into the realms of personal inner knowing. Iolite assists in lessening fatty deposits on the body - the fatty deposits are 'stored negative emotions' - and rids the body of toxins - 'old belief systems'. It alleviates all addiction by virtue of allowing us to understand what an addiction is and why we 'need' this person, food or substance etc. in the first place. It brings the passionate expression of your true potential - 'rather than society's expectations and stereotypes'. Iolite helps with stored anger and pain, bringing relief via the release of the stored anger and pain. It is excellent as a gemstone essence.

Iolite holds the key to the indigo ray of devotion, which is a mixture of dark blue and dark violet. Parts of the body iolite helps are: the pituitary gland; the skeleton; lower brain; eyes and sinuses. Its uses are: aids intuition and spiritual knowledge; strongest painkiller of the rainbow spectrum; releases negativity from the skeletal structure; astral antiseptic and astral toxin release (clears negative thought forms); kills bacteria in food, water or air; clears pollution on all levels; heals chronic sinus complaints (unshed tears); cures insomnia; releases migraine headaches and pain; heals overactive thyroid conditions; breaks up tumours and growths; helps ease kidney complaints. Indigo-iolite helps to control diarrhoea; eases bronchitis, asthma, lung conditions; lowers high blood pressure; heals back problems, especially sciatica, lumbago, any spinal complaint, or neurological disturbances; transmutes and purifies negativity; is good for spiritual teachers and writers with its great inspirational guidance. Iolite contains the domain of mystery and psychic understanding. It is the stone of artists and the acting profession; iolite is very theatrical, it teaches you to let go of the 'masked' self to find the inner self.

Affirmation: I now acknowledge my intuitive power and ask it to fully manifest in my life.

Lapis Lazuli

Lazurite is a popular but generally expensive mineral. Well-formed, deep blue crystals are rare and valuable. It is more commonly found massive and combined with other minerals into a rock called lapis lazuli. Lapis lazuli, or lapis for short, is mostly lazurite, but commonly contains pyrite and calcite and traces of some other minerals. The rich blue color is due to the sulphur that is inherent in the structure of lazurite. Small crystals of pyrite are always present in lapis and their brassy yellow color is both attractive and diagnostic in distinguishing lapis from its also blue cousin - sodalite rock, which lacks pyrite. The calcite produces white streaks in the lapis and too much calcite will lower the value of the stone. The name lazurite is often confused with the bright blue phosphate mineral lazulite. The beautiful blues in paintings from the Renaissance are thanks to the blue of lapis lazuli, the blue rock cherished by the ancients, from Mesopotamia to Egypt, to Persia, to Greece and Rome. The ancient city of Ur had a thriving trade in lapis as early as the fourth millennium BC. The name is international, from the Latin, *lapis*, which means stone, and from the Arabic, *azul*, which means blue. When lapis was first introduced to Europe, it was called ultramarinum, which means 'beyond the sea'. The Romans believed that lapis was a powerful aphrodisiac. In the Middle Ages it was thought to keep the limbs strong and free the soul from error, envy and fear.

Lapis is a high intensity etheric blue stone. It contains the energies of royalty, wisdom, patience, truth, mental attainment, good communication, contentment, artistic inspiration, deep meditation, spiritual and philosophical contemplation, personal integrity and loyalty. It is the 'Spirit of Truth'. Lapis lazuli will heal an unbalanced throat chakra. How you tell if the throat chakra is un-balanced by being too open or spinning too fast: the person is over-talkative, dogmatic, self-righteous or arrogant. If the throat chakra is too closed, or spinning sluggishly, the person is unreliable, holds inconsistent views and holds back from heartfelt self-expression. Lapis works on the thyroid, parathyroids, the throat, upper lungs and arms, the base of the skull and body weight.

Lapis teaches you the power of the spoken word. Because the blue ray governs the throat, infections in this area are psychologically related to 'talking inwards', not speaking out. Psychologically speaking, coughing is because a person has swallowed their thoughts and cannot bring themselves to speak out. Lapis teaches you to 'give voice to your inner truth'. It counteracts harshness. If somebody is acting insensitively in a situation, lapis will help them become more compassionate.

Lapis gives relief from pain, both physical and psychological, and combats cruelty and brutality. Lapis is an interesting stone to meditate with, as its high intensity etheric nature means you really have to reach high to bring your energy into line with its refined vibration. It contains a higher order of intelligence and wisdom, 'intellectual integrity'. Lapis also heals the martyr syndrome: 'I am going to punish myself in order to make you suffer'. Lapis aids discrimination of wisdom; it is very penetrating and does not suffer fools gladly, or those who are fooling around with other people's spirituality. Lapis teaches you to reach for the stars and looking at lapis reminds you of a summer night's sky. The small crystals of pyrite which are always present in lapis and the streaks of white calcite produce starry pictures, which will aid your intuition. The white calcite brings in the energies of the crown chakra and the yellow pyrite brings in the energies of the solar plexus chakra to activate, energize, align and integrate the throat chakra. Lapis teaches you that you have no chance of developing a balanced purified throat chakra until you have successfully worked through and balanced the lower four chakras to obtain the necessary purification to fully activate this centre. Lapis also teaches the mastery of active listening by integrating the full faculties of hearing. It is a sad fact that active listening is totally neglected in our society. We need to fully develop the outer ear, before the subtle inner ear can be available to us for inner guidance. All too often Divine guidance is not heard, because of not truly listening to the 'wisdom' behind the words. Lapis makes an excellent gemstone essence which can release a person from emotional bondage and mental suffering.

Affirmation: I allow the spirit of truth to set me free.

Healing Meditation - Throat Chakra

1. Choose a warm comfortable place where you can sit or lie down undisturbed for at least an hour. Never rush a meditation. View it as your own sacred healing space. You need to make sure it is energetically clean. Make sure you are wearing warm, loose, comfortable clothes......

2. Breathe slowly.....encouraging energy to flow up and down your nervous system.....and begin to relax your body......go through your whole body starting at your feet and consciously relax each part, moving up and finishing at your head.....allow yourself to really let go....and deeply relax....feel yourself sinking into the chair, floor or bed........

3. Allow yourself to tune in to your breathing....as you do so I want you to visualise a perfect blue sky.....the blue sky of *shunyata*...the endless blue that is beyond all limitations and restrictions...stretching out in all directions....a vast ocean of blue....begin to breathe in this blue energy, filling your nose....mouth....throat....head....eyes...ears...your mind....as you do so, you feel your throat relaxing even more......

4. Now you are going to use the blue energy to release any restrictions you may have placed around your throat, so feel this blue energy soothing and relaxing your throat, caressing your neck, easing any restrictions, tightness or pain .....allow it to flow through your mind, releasing any rigid mental attitudes that have stopped your personal, healing or spiritual progress.... allow the blue energy to wash away anything you no longer need.......try to cultivate the feeling that your old personality with its faults and self-doubt has disappeared, vanished into the blueness......

5. Now I want you to visualise a perfect pale blue lotus flower right in the centre of your heart. On top of the flower is a white moon mat, a perfect white circle....sitting on the white circle of light is your perfect enlightened compassionate self......

6. As you begin to observe yourself.....you see this image changing into a rainbow of light....it contains all the colors, red, orange, yellow, green, blue, indigo and violet.....it begins to rotate clockwise if you are male and anticlockwise if you are female......

7. As it does so, rainbows pour from it, filling your body and purifying it, until finally you sit in the midst of the vast blue sky, your body filled with rainbows.......

8. Having filled your body, the rainbows overspill from the crown of your head and cascade like a fountain in all directions....this purifies and cleanses the auric shell....the subtle bodies........stay in this rainbow meditation for as long as you like....it will revitalise and renew you......

9. When you are ready and all energy movements have ceased, begin to become aware of your energy field.........your aura.....by now it should be energized and full of healing rainbow

light....you should stay where you are for five more minutes......keep breathing steadily....allowing the energy to fully integrate into every level of your body and aura.....

10.   Come out of meditation very slowly, like a cat having an after-nap stretch.....by using the blue energy.....followed by the rainbow.....it brings the power of all the chakras to aid you in your quest for perfect health, healing and enlightenment....it also stops you fixating on one energy centre....to allow you to open....in balance and grace.....

Kundalini Throat Chakra Meditation - Resonance

The next kundalini awakening meditation is humming....this induces resonance....

1.   Without making any effort to alter your breathing, simply tune in to the actual physical sensations you feel in your nose as air rushes in and out of your nasal passage......with every new breath.......be sure to relax your jaw and tongue........at the same time tune in to the sounds created as the air rushes in and out of your nose.....feel the sensations in your chest as you breathe..........

2.   Allow your awareness to slowly expand to include the tip of your nose....your hands and fingers.....your feet and toes....your whole body, here in the present moment....relax and enjoy the pure experience of effortless breathing and deep meditative calm.....tune in to your heart beating...

3.   Very gently, as softly as possible, begin to allow your vocal cords to vibrate as you exhale, generating a very quiet humming sound with your lips closed.....and your eyes closed as well....

4.   At the bottom of your exhale...fall naturally silent....and inhale silently....feel the vibrations continue throughout your body from your humming a moment before......this is resonance....

5.   Continue with this humming meditation for a number of breaths until you feel you are becoming pure sound yourself......pure resonance.....pure vibration.....

6.   Then allow yourself to be quiet, while you continue breathing....allow the vibrations in your body to remain in your consciousness so that you are listening to every cell and every chakra....

Now we will practise the throat chakra meditation...of course it should follow naturally on from the last four kundalini chakra meditations.....so....after you have done the alternate nostril heart consciousness rising pranayama and the heart chakra mantra YAM and meditated on the heart mandala....you are now ready to move into the throat chakra.

1.   Practise the humming.....resonance.......meditation you have just learnt.

2.   Then just relax....allow the resonance to build in your body....

3.   You are now ready to focus on and vocalize the fifth chakra mantra...HAM....as before, allow the sound to manifest in your mind....feel it effortlessly rising from your inner being........as the H......A........M... sound gently moves to awaken your throat chakra.....opening yourself to the sound of the universe, as it joins you in sounding the HAM........continue for as long as you want........now visualise or look directly at the throat chakra mandala....use the one in this book......become aware of the chakra mandala....as you focus on the energy movements and shapes it contains.......be open to any visions that may come to you.....continue to visualise or gaze at the mandala as long as you want........and when you are ready, visualise or feel your throat chakra begin to turn upwards.....towards your crown chakra....this brings spiritual energy into your throat chakra and allows for your full attention to be focused upwards towards your enlightenment.......

4.   Gently ease the shoulders back ever so slightly and the chin in a little so that there is a slight stretch on the back of the neck, easing the blood-flow to the brain. Keep your mouth slightly open and rest the tip of the tongue on the roof of the mouth just behind the teeth. This placement

of the tongue is very important because it naturally maintains the flow of energy to the head whilst keeping the jaw relaxed. (The tongue placement is the bandha or energy seal for the throat chakra...when you are not actually chanting a mantra, this placement of the tongue is vital, if you wish to move energy into the higher chakras).

5.   When you are ready, allow the energy you have created to flow up your spine through your upper two chakras in sequential order.........and pour out of the top of your head like a fountain of light............this sacred divine loving energy brings your whole energy field to life...........

6.   Allow yourself plenty of time to integrate this new awareness. You need to practise this meditation on a daily basis.......don't forget to reverse the root chakra to point downwards and the sacral, solar plexus, heart and throat chakras to point outwards.....as you once more anchor yourself on the earth plane of normal everyday awareness......

Part 17

The Third Eye Chakra

The third eye chakra in Sanskrit is known as *ajna*, which means to command, or to know. It is also known as the brow chakra. It is located right between and just above the physical eyes; it corresponds to the space between the eyebrows, the *trikuta*. All the chakras, except for the crown and root chakras, can be approached from the back as well as the front. Therefore the sixth chakra is also located in its rear aspect at the base of the skull, at the medulla oblongata. In the 'New Age' movement this position at the back of the head is sometimes called the 'causal' chakra. It is also known as the mouth of God; very often when you are going into deep meditation, you may feel a strong pressure at this point, or even a pushing sensation on the roof of your mouth. These sensations are normal, although some people who have a fear-based mentality are afraid they are being 'taken over' - they are, by their Higher Selves.....the 'little ego' does not give in very easily and it can make you feel fearful; it really does not want to surrender anything, especially its hypnotic control of your senses. This is what the third eye is all about - the surrendering of your dualistic concepts and feelings of separation from your source of Divine wisdom, inspiration and bliss.

It is very difficult to talk about the third eye chakra, because we are using fifth chakra concepts throughout this book, or any book for that matter. In reality, the third eye, our sixth chakra, is beyond the fifth chakra's conceptual realm. Many people stay stuck in the fifth chakra their whole lives, thinking grandiose thoughts about the sixth chakra. Making the move upwards proves immensely difficult for many people, as I have found out both with my clients and students over the years. Ultimately the sixth chakra is beyond concepts.

So, having said that, I shall give you just a few key points which you can reflect upon, before experiencing the realm of sixth chakra awakening. The first primal chakratic concept that has existed for several thousand years is the Hindu and Buddhist understanding of the intricate workings of the kundalini system. There are two major conduits through which kundalini energy rises up the spine. These are the female *Ida* and the male *Pingala*, the yin and yang. Energy enters through the left side, Ida, and exits through the right side, Pingala. These female and male opposites intertwine intimately like lovers as they twist their way up through the first five chakras. Then something extremely awesome happens: they merge in the sixth chakra. Sanskrit tradition says they merge in the pineal gland or, as perhaps some modern neurologists hypothesise, in the pituitary. Here they generate the third eye, which lies within the brain, just behind the centre of the brow. It is here that the earthly duality ends, yin and yang unify to become whole. This marriage of opposites causes the manifest and un-manifest to merge.

I remember as a child reading in the Christian Bible the following statement attributed to Jesus:

> *"The light of the body is the eye: therefore when thine eye is single, thy whole body also is full of light"*, Luke 11:34.

This fascinated me as a child, because of my direct personal experiences, but it was not until my study of the Yogic tradition, which started when I was eighteen, that I found my answers. It clearly explained that when a human being finally lets go of concepts, of dualities, of opposites - which is to say when the Ida and Pingala merge - a great downpouring or flood of light comes into the body, caused by the awakening of the *bija* energy of the sixth chakra centre. This I could do at will; furthermore, I found the yogic descriptions of sixth chakra visions to be identical to my direct personal experiences. Through further study I began to realise the original concepts of duality, of darkness and light; they come from our polar relationship with the Earth and Sun. In a very real sense, it is this energetic relationship between these two forcefields that makes life on earth possible. By going into both the darkness of the centre of the earth and the unlimited brightness of the sun, we are guided into the unity of the third eye chakra.

So before the third eye opens, you see through the two eyes; you experience a duality between your normal self (your conscious mind, intellect, ego) and your Higher Self (your intuitive mind, Spirit). I don't believe you should force yourself to shed your ego. I believe with regular meditation practice on *all* your chakra centres you will eventually merge with the Higher Self and become one with the Divine. When this happens all the masks of the ego-self fall away, you no longer identify with what you thought you were, who you thought you ought to be, who your parents, teachers and the tribal mentality of society said you should be. Suddenly you 'are', your true self shines through, there is no longer any need for pretence, guilt or illusion.

The Yogis say that the pineal gland is the seat of memory, so as the kundalini energy pierces the third eye and your being is flooded with light you have total access to all your past lives. You can let go of the multi-level veil of illusion, *Avidya* - because you are no longer afraid, judgemental or full of guilt. You are flooded with compassion, love, wisdom and understanding for yourself and others. You view your past lives for what they are, and you see yourself in everyone and everything. You no longer have any karmic debts; the kundalini has burned away all the debris of past lives by showing you they were the illusion of the ego or *maya*. The *Panchadasi*, an ancient Indian text, asserts: "Man's present miseries and sufferings, his pains and limited pleasures, births and deaths, are all due to his erroneous identification with the five sheaths and three bodies". The physical, astral and causal body make up the three bodies, while the five sheaths represent the first five levels of the aura and the first five master chakras along the spine; they are, in sequential order, the food sheath, emotional/vitality sheath, the mental sheath, the intellectual sheath and the bliss sheath. Even identifying with the bliss sheath means you have attachments - by wishing to become enlightened. It is only when you move beyond attachments into the sixth chakra that you can be free of *maya*; in other words, you are still trapped in *avidya*.

The sixth chakra, the third eye, is definitely feminine, intuitive, mysterious and yin. It forms the final chakra in the triad of feminine - yin chakras, the other two being the heart and sacral. They are each surrounded by masculine - yang energy centres. As the energy flows upwards and, as you have discovered, downwards, it moves between the alternating male-female chakras. The feminine chakras are the driving force for the male chakras, with the ultimate balance of the whole being centred in the loving power of the heart chakra.

The third eye chakra is associated with intuition, pituitary gland, left eye, the base of the skull. In the sixth chakra the mind is looking directly at itself. The combined interaction of the pineal with the pituitary gland activates this chakra. The element is *Avyakta*, the primordial cloud of undifferentiated energy and matter or light. Malfunctions include headaches, nightmares, eye problems, poor vision, neurological disturbances, glaucoma. Also learning difficulties and hallucinations.

Its symbol is the pure white lotus flower which has two large pure white petals. The words on the petals are *ksham* and *ham*. They are on each side of a pure white circle, within which is a downward-pointing white triangle containing the *bija* seed letter *Om*. The white triangle represents the light of the soul, in its downward path. When activated by the *Om*, it causes duality to vanish as the soul illuminates the body. The basic image also includes the vision of the Ida and Pingala energy upflows merging in the centre of white light. This mandala can also be seen to represent the two sides of the human brain, the opposing forces of cognitive and intuitive. The traditional sound for the third eye chakra is the *bija* mantra OM in the Hindu tradition and in the Tantric Buddhist tradition of Nepal and Tibet. You should devote a great deal of time to this mantra: it is the pathway to the great white light of brilliance. The associated creature of this chakra is the white owl - its natural mantra asks, who are you? This is similar to the Zen Buddhist *koan*, as a question that leads directly to spiritual realisation.

178

The color ray associated with this chakra is indigo (a mix of dark blue and dark violet) which represents devotion to the truth - idealism, obedience, intuition and perception - the ability to look to the future. Indigo transmutes and purifies; it is the transformer. Indigo is the color of the priest or priestess. When you meditate on the third eye chakra and it becomes fully activated, you can successfully destroy the karma of all past lives and become a liberated soul. Intuitional knowledge is obtained through this chakra; it is the seat of primordial power and soul. It is here that yogis consciously place their Prana at the time of death. This is where the un-manifested and manifested meet. This is where yin and yang merge. This is where we move beyond dualism.

There are two more very important chakras above the third eye. The first one is the fourth eye chakra. Its Sanskrit name is *soma*, which means water. The colors violet, white and indigo are associated with this chakra. It is located just above the third eye chakra in the centre of the brain. This chakra controls the body temperature and balances the power chakra in the solar plexus, bringing the male-female balance to the whole body system. The balance is maintained via the breath. Erratic breathing causes imbalances in the body and upsets this polarity.

The next one is the fifth eye chakra; its Sanskrit name is *lalata*, which translates as forehead. The colors violet, white and gold are associated with this chakra. It is located at the top of the forehead. Its full activation brings man to be master of his own destiny. You choose your destiny moment by moment; remember you always have the choice. You can buy into the illusion of pain and suffering or duality, or you can go into the light of the truth - into the light of the soul, where all illusion vanishes and all suffering ends. It's your choice.

Crystal Web of Light - Inner Vision

Crystals:
2 amethyst, tumbled or natural
1 charoite, tumbled or natural
1 iolite, tumbled, faceted or natural
1 lepidolite, tumbled or natural
1 sugilite, tumbled or natural
1 tanzanite, tumbled or natural
3 clear quartz points

Uses: This crystal web of light has a very high vibrational rate. It is ideal for those who regularly meditate or wish to make daily meditation practice part of their life. The iolite, when placed on the third eye chakra, gives full psychic activation and integration when used in this integrated web of light. Often we choose to be blind to the potential illuminated by our third eye. In its connection with the higher functions of consciousness, the third eye is a psychic tool reminding us that everything we see, hear, smell, touch or taste started as an inner vision or in-sight.

It will 'heal' an unbalanced, blocked, distorted or closed third eye, which is shown by the person being undisciplined, distrustful; they may fear success and may have a tendency towards schizophrenia. An unbalanced third eye that is too open or spins too fast is observable by the person being highly logical, dogmatic, authoritarian or having reforming fervour; the religious fanatic or fundamentalist. A balanced third eye chakra means the person is charismatic, highly intuitive, not attached to material possessions and will experience mystical phenomena in meditation. Iolite is a vision quest guide and guardian to those who go on inner or outer journeys of self-exploration. It awakens innate inner knowledge and wisdom; it assists in reducing confusion by virtue of understanding the life situation that is currently causing the confusion. All confusion arises from the inability to claim one's own 'intuitive power' and act according to the needs of the individual. Iolite teaches us not to get too attached to ritual, but to look for our own path via a balanced third eye chakra; it takes you into the realms of personal inner knowing.

Iolite assists in lessening fatty deposits on the body - the fatty deposits are 'stored negative emotions' - and rids the body of toxins - 'old belief systems'. It alleviates all addiction by virtue of allowing us to understand what an addiction is and why we 'need' this person, food or substance etc. in the first place. It brings the passionate expression of your true potential, rather than society's expectations and stereotypes. Iolite holds the key to the indigo ray of devotion, which is a mixture of dark blue and dark violet. It is good for spiritual teachers and writers with its great inspirational guidance. Iolite contains the domain of mystery and psychic understanding. It is the stone of artists and the acting profession; iolite is very theatrical, it teaches you to let go of the 'masked' self to find the inner self. It can unquestionably bring out the spiritual characteristics of those who wear it and work with it. The amethyst used in this crystal web of light is a transformational healer, which will bring spiritual growth and Divine understanding. It purifies all the chakra centres.

Amethyst aids comprehension and enhances the faculty of judgement by stimulating the spiritual body, which ultimately brings detachment from worldly concerns. It helps you to retain a good temper, avoid errors and achieve self-discipline and high standards in life. Amethyst encourages you to become your own leader and master. Amethyst works on the pineal gland, the top of the head, the crown chakra, the brain and the scalp. Amethyst can be beneficial to help calm people who are emotionally erratic. It protects those who are unable to protect themselves - babies, small children, the sick and vulnerable and the animals. It also affords protection to those who are opening spiritually.

The charoite used in this crystal web of light is a stone of vast spiritual transformation and deep personal healing; charoite activates the *Bodhisattva* energy. Charoite activates and balances the crown chakra. This stone will also facilitate past life recall. Since it was discovered in 1976, it has made a huge impact on the vibrational healing scene and has truly 'activated' many 'lightworkers'. Charoite will give protection from nightmares and insomnia. It releases deep hidden fears. The lepidolite is used for balancing both sides of the brain. In meditation it feels like a gentle wave of energy flowing through the mind. Lepidolite is especially good for insomnia. The 'Spirit' keeper or Angel of lepidolite facilitates its use as a 'dreamtime' crystal, an astral guide. It changes our way of consciously viewing the world, by accessing other dimensions and realities. Lepidolite is a good space clearer; it can emit an immense forcefield that will keep anything negative at bay.

The sugilite is the third eye activator; it works on the pineal gland, the top of the head, the crown and heart chakras, as well as the brain and scalp. Sugilite has a potent mature Universal Consciousness. It is very matriarchal and nurturing; it does seem to 'mother' the 'Star Children', giving them feelings of security and protection against the harsh climate of the negative earth vibration of hostility, rage, anger and fear. It is good for those who feel abandoned and dis-connected from their 'home' and source of emotional nourishment. It has also been used by very gentle sensitive souls who find it difficult to screen out the negativity and hostility of others. It is very protective, as well as gently grounding. It can integrate the spiritual body to the physical body, which is very helpful for those amongst us who 'space out' easily. Many people on the spiritual path have utilised sugilite for grounding their spiritual experiences into their everyday life. Above all, sugilite brings peace, dignity, humanitarianism and mental creativity. It really does develop psychic abilities, allowing for mystical experiences. It can develop faith and inner strength. It teaches you personal mastery, that you have a Divine right to your own point of view and inner truth. Sugilite allows you to work with the highest levels of thought and gives a thorough understanding of the thought process. Sugilite is the aristocrat of the purple gemstones; it commands respect as it guides you towards spiritual perfection. It has a richness and quality about it that lead to refined psychic perception. It is good for those who meditate and teach meditation and healing disciplines: its vibration can produce great mystical leaders and enlightened gurus.

Metaphysically, the tanzanite is mesmerising. The pleochroism facilitates altered states of reality. These can cause radical shifts in consciousness, by raising the vibratory signature of the user; this expands their personal mandala or 'original blueprint', allowing for 'downloads' of information which is activated from the Akashic records. Tanzanite is then used for inner/outer journeys. Your raised vibratory rate will cause you to see a thinning of the veil between the various planes of consciousness, allowing for clear communication with Ascended Masters, Angels, Spirit guides and other enlightened beings from dimensions not usually available to your normal conscious awareness. Tanzanite facilitates, with dedicated use, deep meditation, astral journeys and materialisation. It can activate and integrate the energies of the base, sacral, heart, throat, third eye, fourth eye, fifth eye and crown chakras, as well as the chakras eight to fourteen above the head, facilitating a situation in which the mind and psychic abilities are activated and are guided by the wisdom of an enlightened heart. The energized throat chakra allows for clear communication of this integrated understanding.

2 amethyst, placed one in the palm of each hand.

1 charoite, placed on the solar plexus chakra.

1 iolite, placed on the throat chakra.

1 lepidolite, placed on the heart chakra.

1 sugilite, placed on the third eye chakra.

1 tanzanite, placed above the crown chakra.

3 single terminated crystal points, placed to form a triangle of light, one crystal above the head, the other two at the feet. The terminations should point towards the body.

Process:

1.   Cleanse all the crystals and programme the clear quartz for healing.

2.   Choose a warm comfortable place where you can lie down undisturbed for at least an hour; never rush a crystal web of light process. View it as a sacred healing space, so you need to make sure it is energetically clean. Make sure you are wearing warm, loose, comfortable clothes.

3.   Relax by consciously becoming aware of your breathing and heartbeat; you can play soothing music, light candles and burn incense.

4.   Lay the stones around and on the body and hold an amethyst in each hand.

5.   Allow 20 minutes to facilitate the integration of the crystal vibration.

6.   Feel free to remove the crystals sooner, if you have integrated the crystal energy very quickly.

7.   Remove the crystals in reverse order of placement.

8.   Make sure you are fully grounded, centred and balanced.

9.   Cleanse your crystals (using your chosen method).

10.   Finish by giving thanks and asking mentally that all the healing work you have just accomplished is closed, sealed and protected with Divine love and wisdom.

11.   Give yourself sufficient time to integrate the crystal therapy session.

12.   As a general guideline it is suggested a period of twice the length of time you were actually lying in the crystal therapy web be allowed for integration.

Amethyst

The violet and purple varieties of quartz provide the most prized and in many respects the most interesting of the large family of quartz minerals. Amethyst, the name by which this variety of quartz is known, is of ancient derivation. Pliny stated that the gem was so called from the color being near to, but not quite reaching, that of wine. The name is also said to have been derived from the Greek word 'amethustos', which is translated as 'not drunken', and was assigned to the stone from the belief that the wearer would not suffer from excess consumption of alcohol.

The legend of the origin of amethyst comes from Greek myths. Dionysius, the god of intoxication, was enraged one day by an insult from an insignificant mere mortal and vowed to revenge himself on the next mortal that crossed his path, creating fierce tigers to carry out his wish. Along came unsuspecting Amethyst, a beautiful young maiden on her way to pay tribute to the goddess Diana. Diana turned Amethyst into a statue of pure crystalline quartz to protect her from the brutal claws of the tigers. At the sight of the beautiful statue, Dionysius wept tears of wine in remorse for his action. The god's tears stained the quartz purple, creating the gem we know today.

Amethyst was carried into battle to preserve the wearer from harm. As an amulet it was supposed to dispel insomnia and sharpen the intellect and it was also used as an antidote against poison. Leonardo Da Vinci wrote *"Amethyst was able to dissipate evil thoughts and quicken the intelligence"*. In Tibet, amethyst is considered to be sacred to Buddha and mala beads are often fashioned from it. In ecclesiastical communities the spiritual amethyst has always been held in very high esteem. Many of the finest quality specimens of this variety of quartz are set in the finger rings of bishops. Although amethyst is always violet in hue, the range of color play is very wide, from nearly colorless with the faintest of mauve tinges to a fabulous deep purple. The color is due to an iron impurity via radiation-induced effects. If the earth then heats them, they can turn brown, red or green.

Purple is a dignified color which has long been considered a royal color, so it is not surprising that amethyst has been so much in demand during history. Splendid amethysts are highlighted in the British Crown Jewels; they were also a favourite of Catherine the Great and Egyptian royalty. The pale amethyst colors are sometimes called "Rose de France" and can be seen set in Victorian jewellery. The deep colors are the most valuable, particularly a rich purple with rose flashes. Amethyst is mined in Bolivia, Brazil, Uruguay and Argentina, as well as in Namibia, Zambia and other African countries. Amethyst is the birthstone for February.

> *'Man is a spiritual being who, in order to be truly spiritual, needs a body'*
> (St Thomas Aquinas).

Amethyst, with its purple polarity, truly embodies these words. It can unquestionably bring out the spiritual properties of those who wear it and work with it. Amethyst is a transformational healer, which will bring spiritual growth and Divine understanding. It purifies all the chakra centres and can be used anywhere on the body and on all levels of the aura, giving relief from addictions and addictive traits within the personality. It works as an amplifier of healing and spiritual energies. When consciously directed it will break down and transform blocked or stuck energies. Its pain-relieving properties have been demonstrated over and over again, so much so that it never seems to fail in drawing out pain. Amethyst is a very approachable crystal and has been involved in human evolution for eons; as such, it has instigated the activation of many people into the healing properties of gemstones and minerals. The guardian or over-soul of all the amethyst on the planet is probably the most friendly of all the Crystal Angels. Time and time again, if you ask crystal therapists which was the very first crystal they used or wore, you will find the beautiful amethyst at the top of the list. It also helps protect from over-indulgences which have lodged in the emotional body; it calms the mind and thereby aids spiritual and personal growth, giving understanding into the cause of the indulgence.

Amethyst aids comprehension and enhances the faculty of judgement by stimulating the spiritual body, which ultimately brings detachment from worldly concerns. It helps you to retain a good temper, avoid errors and achieve self-discipline and high standards in life. Amethyst encourages you to become your own leader and master. It also gives a stable mind, removes outrage and anxiety and absorbs excessive body heat: as such it is very beneficial to menopausal women who are suffering from hot flushes, due to rapid changes in hormone levels. Amethyst is full of originality and inspiration and is a great teacher. It is power and humility combined and it will instill these qualities in those who wear it and work with it. Amethyst brings spiritual dedication, which makes it a powerful and positive meditation stone. Amethyst works on the pineal gland, the top of the head, the crown chakra, the brain and the scalp. Amethyst can be beneficial to help calm people who are emotionally erratic. It treats any kind of internal inflammation. It also treats heart palpitations and hearing disorders, the skeletal system, nervous system, immune system, digestive tract, stomach, heart, skin and teeth, insomnia, mental disorders, eye problems, headaches, migraine and pain. It is used for regression and it links to the unborn child, hence its use in infertility. It protects those who are unable to protect themselves - babies, small children, the sick and vulnerable and the animals. It also affords protection to those who are opening spiritually.

A group or cluster of amethyst will cleanse the environment of large amounts of stuck or blocked energy, easily raising the overall vibratory level to a much higher frequency of light, which is always beneficial to health.

Affirmation: I am full of spiritual originality and Divine inspiration.

Charoite

Charoite is an unusual mineral and of unique occurrence. It is found in only one location: along the Charo River at Aldan, in Russia, from whence it acquired its name. It forms a swirling pattern of interlocking crystals. The color of charoite is described as stunning. The look of charoite is unlike any other mineral and cannot be mistaken. It simply looks unnaturally beautiful.

A stone of vast spiritual transformation and deep personal healing, charoite activates the *Bodhisattva* energy. Whatever methods one uses to bring it about, the *Bodhichitta* can arise and establish itself firmly within one's innermost spiritual heart. Here it grows and becomes the 'path of service'. There are aspirant Bodhisattvas, who are people trying to 'act' as Bodhisattvas, keeping the Bodhisattvas' precepts, which basically are to *'solely pledge to be the unfailing champion and guardian of all life in its battle to overcome suffering'*. Bodhisattvas normally compose their own vows or can use a formula used by previous Bodhisattvas. However, it is one thing to 'feel' the Bodhichitta arise and a great leap of faith and love to 'live' the Bodhisattva vows.

Charoite activates and balances the crown chakra. You can tell when someone has a balanced crown chakra: they have a magnetic personality, they achieve 'miracles' in life, they are at peace within themselves. Charoite heals a blocked crown chakra. You can tell when someone's crown chakra is blocked or distorted: they seem to be constantly exhausted, they cannot make decisions and have no sense of belonging. Charoite will also re-balance a crown chakra that is too open or one that spins too fast. You can tell if someone's crown is too open: they are psychotic or manic depressive, they may have a confused sexual expression, or be frustrated and feel a sense of unrealized power and direction in life. Charoite has also been known to fully activate and integrate the heart, third eye and throat chakras.

This stone will also facilitate past life recall, not in the spirit of 'look, I was Cleopatra, Queen of the Nile', which only serves to feed the ego, but in the spirit of 'seeing the numerous past lives of all those on the planet'. This view shows us the futility of war, waged over and over again for millennia, with no one ever really winning and the repeated misery and suffering caused by brutality, hatred, prejudice, desire, craving and ignorance. Yes, this is a unique transformational stone! Since it was discovered in 1976, it has made a huge impact on the vibrational healing scene and has truly 'activated' many 'lightworkers', who can no longer buy into the illusion of the twenty-first century of consumerism, greed, power abuse and corruption, nor the pollution of the planet and the wilful squandering of the earth's beauty and resources. Charoite also helps infants to sleep peacefully and will give protection from nightmares and insomnia. It releases deep hidden fears. Soothing to the body, it will reduce heat and fevers.

Charoite transmutes the symptoms of dis-ease. It is used for disorders of the eyes, heart and mind. Charoite will improve degraded conditions of the liver (after alcohol abuse) and pancreas (due to excess refined sugars) and regulate the blood. It makes a wonderful gemstone essence and should be kept as a standby essence for any physical emergency or emotional turmoil, as it will steady the emotional body and ground excess pain and trauma.

Affirmation: I now fully activate and integrate my heart, third eye and throat chakras; this brings spiritual transformation and deep personal healing.

Clear Quartz - See the Root Chakra Section for Properties

Iolite - See the Throat Chakra Section for Properties

Lepidolite - See the Heart Chakra Section for Properties

Sugilite - See the Heart Chakra Section for Properties

Tanzanite

The source of its enchanting color is that tanzanite is trichroic: that is, it shows different colors when viewed in different directions. One direction is blue, another purple, and another bronze, adding subtle tones and depth to the vibrant color. When tanzanite is found in the ground, the bronze color is evident. The unofficial story has it that the effect of heat was first discovered when some brown zoisite crystals lying on the ground with other rocks were caught in a fire set by lightning that swept through the grass-covered Merelani heartland north-east of Arusha. The Masai herdsmen who drive cattle in the area noticed the beautiful blue color and picked the crystals up, becoming the first tanzanite collectors. Tanzanite is relatively new on the metaphysical scene. Its blue-lavender color is unique and a wonderful addition to gemstone therapy. Found in Tanzania (hence the name) in 1967, it has since become a well-known, extensively used and highly respected gemstone for crystal therapy. Pleochroism is very pronounced in tanzanite and is seen as three different color shades in the same stone. In viewing a tanzanite stone, the colors dark blue, green-yellow and red-purple can be seen, all a result of pleochroism. Poorer quality stones may have a brownish color, due to the mixing of blue, purple and green.

Metaphysically, Tanzanite is mesmerising. The pleochroism facilitates altered states of reality. These can cause radical shifts in consciousness, by raising the vibratory signature of the user; this expands their personal mandala or 'original blueprint', allowing for 'downloads' of information which is activated from the Akashic records. Tanzanite is then used for inner/outer journeys. Your raised vibratory rate will cause you to see a thinning of the veil between the various planes of consciousness, allowing for clear communication with Ascended Masters, Angels, Spirit guides and other enlightened beings from dimensions not usually available to your normal conscious awareness. Tanzanite facilitates, with dedicated use, deep meditation, astral journeys and materialisation.

It can activate and integrate the energies of the base, sacral, heart, throat, third eye, fourth eye, fifth eye and crown chakras, as well as the chakras eight to fourteen above the head, facilitating a situation in which the mind and psychic abilities are activated and are guided by the wisdom of an enlightened heart. The energized throat chakra allows for clear communication of this integrated understanding.

Tanzanite works to alleviate problems associated with the upper lungs, throat, ears, thyroid, parathyroid, pineal, head, mouth, upper arms, shoulders, bones and skeletal structure. It holds a lot of healing potential and is carried, worn or used by those who work to alleviate dis-ease in others. As a gemstone essence it has been used for meditation and healing. It combines well with other high vibration gemstones, especially phenacite, danburite, moldavite, azeztulite and quartz. When combined with aquamarine and moldavite in a gemstone essence it causes old patterns of dis-ease to simply fall away, which allows for new patterns to be integrated very quickly.

Those crystals that exhibit the full tanzanite spectrum - violet-blue, purple and bronze, or dark blue, green-yellow and red-purple - are very potent in their healing application, as they contain a vast spectrum of possibilities and applications. They make an exceptional gemstone essence which can be used to alleviate problems that have manifested as dis-ease anywhere in the body or aura.

Affirmation: I am open to enlightened altered states of reality; I now choose to transform my life and become free.

Healing Meditation - Third Eye Chakra

1.   Choose a warm comfortable place where you can sit or lie down undisturbed. View it as your own sacred healing space. You need to make sure it is energetically clean.

2.   Breathe slowly.....encouraging energy to flow up and down your nervous system.....

3.   Now, turn your full attention to your forehead....now I want you to imagine your forehead is made of perfectly clear glass.........and I want you to place the forefinger of your right hand directly onto the third eye area.....

4.   Now, with the unlimited power of your mind, I want you to imagine you can see the finger tip.....actually see the finger....very clearly.....now, don't press your finger hard against the area....just be aware of its presence....when you can imagine you see your finger very clearly, remove it and place your right hand back down to your side or back on your lap.

5.   Now, I want you to see or feel a brilliant white light.....coming into your third eye.....this light floods into your physical eyes....and as it does so it relaxes your eyes....they begin to feel heavy.....and relaxed.....the white light flows into the rest of your head.....through your mind....bringing peace and relaxation as it flows....feel your mind relaxing....

6.   Now the white light begins to flow into your throat... your chest.... and abdomen....bringing relaxation, peace and deep soul healing....feel it flowing right through your body....to the very tips of your fingers and toes.....your whole body is now completely relaxed and at peace.....a calmness pervades your body and mind........breathe deeply of the light.....

7.   Just allow yourself to relax deeper and deeper.....with every breath you feel yourself slipping deeper and deeper into this calm relaxation.......breathe deeply....letting go........more and more.....allowing the healing peace that transcends all understanding to descend on you....feel this peaceful vibration spilling over into your auric shell.....bringing a calmness......allow yourself to relax more and more....really let go......

8.   If you notice any areas of pain, tension or restriction...I want you to allow the white light to just gently wash them away.....allow yourself to heal......on all levels of your being, as the white light gently heals you....physically.....mentally......emotionally......spiritually.......allow yourself to be completely held in the light of your higher self.....feel the love this energy brings....there is no judgement in it......just total acceptance.....of you....just as you are....right now.....you don't have to behave in any particular way.....just being you is enough......it always has been enough.....

9.   Now, just let go of all the things in your life that have harmed or hurt you....that have made you feel small....frightened or vulnerable......let go of all judgement....of yourself or others.....let go of all the times others have judged you.....or made you feel less than perfect....you are perfect...just as you are......this energy of your higher self.....was always with you......you have felt it before....and from now on you will feel it more and more.........as it gently transforms your life....breathe deeply of this energy........

10.   Stay with this energy as long as you like.......you can release a lot of stored negativity and personal pain.....come out of meditation very slowly, like a cat having an after-nap stretch and remember wherever you are this light is always with you......just ask and it will descend.

Kundalini Third Eye Chakra Meditation

We have been learning different pranayama exercises as we have moved through the kundalini meditations. You have already learnt a powerful basic breath meditation for awakening the sixth chakra - the alternate nostril breathing technique. So now we will learn another technique - equally if not more powerful - except this one happens naturally as a by-product of advanced meditation. So how much better to learn the technique early, so if it does happen to you spontaneously you will not feel afraid.

This technique (if it happens spontaneously) is called *Kevala Kumbhaka* or natural retention of breath without *Puraka* (inhalation) and *Rechaka* (exhalation). Obviously at this point I can't teach you how not to breathe, so what I can teach you is the Pranayama Kumbhaka or breath control.

There are different variations on the Kumbhaka breath, but the one I want you to use for the kundalini meditation is the 'Kumbhaka breath - Super-Charge Upwards'. I will teach you this first. It is used for moving energy upwards, or for directly pulling kundalini energy up the spine. This is a good technique to master, because if you are ever feeling 'spacey' or ungrounded and you need to be totally grounded, you just reverse the process. Or if you wish you can balance both extremes by holding the energy on full inhale and on the empty exhale. This balanced Kumbhaka breath marries heaven and earth within your chakra system.

Kumbhaka Breath - Super-Charge Upwards - use in moderation, as it is very powerful.

Inhale for the count of six......

Hold for the count of six......

Exhale for the count of four....

Breathe in immediately for the count of six......

Hold for the count of six......

Exhale for the count of four....

Breathe in immediately for the count of six......and repeat the pattern a number of times.....this breathing formula focuses energy into the top two chakras.

Kumbhaka Breath - Balanced Breath - use often to balance your energy.

Inhale for the count of two..

Hold for the count of four....

Exhale for the count of six......

Hold on empty for the count of four....

Repeat the pattern a number of times.........this breathing formula must be a quick count of two: this moves energy from the base chakra quickly up the spine, while the long six breath out allows energy to flow down the spine slowly, from the crown chakra.

Kumbhaka Breath - Calming and Grounding - use this breathing pattern to bring yourself back down into your lower chakras.

Exhale for the count of six......

Hold for the count of six......

Inhale for the count of four....

Don't hold your breath at all on full...

And repeat the pattern a number of times....until you feel calm and grounded. Make sure on the hold of six you really focus on the lower chakras and breathe energy right down into the base chakra.

So we are now ready to either do a full kundalini meditation, from the first chakra right through to the sixth, or you can just focus on the sixth chakra meditation, third eye meditation programme.

1.   Practise the Kumbhaka breath - Super-charge Upwards.

2.   Breathing easily....you are now ready to focus on and vocalize the sixth chakra mantra...OM....as before, allow the sound to manifest in your mind....feel it effortlessly rising from your inner being.......as the OM sound generates tremendous power in your third eye

region, feel it energising the third eye chakra.....opening yourself to the sound of the universe, as it joins you in sounding the OM........continue for as long as you want........

3.   Now visualise or look directly at the third eye chakra mandala....use the one in this book......become aware of the chakra mandala as you focus on the energy movements and shapes it contains..........when you are ready, visualise or feel your third eye chakra begin to turn upwards.....towards your crown chakra....this brings spiritual energy into your third eye chakra and allows for your full attention to be focused upwards towards your enlightenment.......

4.   Continue to visualise or gaze at the mandala as long as you want.........

5.   When you have finished gazing at the third eye chakra mandala, allow your eyes to close....and with closed eyes..... you will focus your physical eyes and your entire undivided attention on the third eye chakra; this is the bandha or energy seal for the third eye chakra......

6.   Allow yourself plenty of time to integrate this new awareness..........you need to practise this meditation on a daily basis; it is the culmination of the first, second, third, fourth, fifth and sixth chakra kundalini activation you have learned thus far....don't forget to reverse the root chakra to point downwards and the sacral, solar plexus, heart, throat and third eye chakras to point outwards ....as you once more anchor yourself on the earth plane of normal, grounded, waking reality.......

Part 18

The Crown Chakra

Infinite bliss or the crown chakra, as it is called, is so far beyond the mundane physical level and concepts that it defies an explanation. Any words used are merely a shadow play, a tiny reflection of the enormity of the encounter; it genuinely defies description. It should truly be encountered without preconceptions of any kind that will interfere with your direct personal experience. I can give the location and attributes though; these will help you to the direct encounter with your own personal experience of unlimited bliss, enlightenment, Christ consciousness, or samadhi as it is sometimes called. I think you should also be aware that just one momentary brief glimpse will enthral you, so you go further into samadhi, because there are levels of samadhi.

In *Nirvikalpa* samadhi the lower mind is withdrawn from the external objective world. The individual mind becomes one with the cosmic mind or *Hiranyagarbha* or the Oversoul, the Soul of the Universe, the 'One Common Thread Soul'. The function of the intellect, the objective mind and the senses are suspended. The experience of enlightenment places the experiencer on a new plane of existence. All body consciousness falls away. Reading books and abstract reasoning will not give you samadhi. You need to practise meditation daily; this gives you direct personal experience, which is the source for higher intuitional knowledge or divine wisdom. This experience is superconscious or transcendental.

The person who experiences Cosmic Consciousness acquires many *Siddhis* or powers; these are described in the ancient *Raja Yoga Sutras* of *Patanjali Maharishi*. Though many people may originally seek enlightenment to gain these powers, if enlightenment happens these powers are then viewed as worthless, because at that point you have no desire for them. Cosmic Consciousness is the perfect awareness of the oneness of all life. The differentiating mind that splits everything up has gone, vanished. All barriers, all sense of duality, differences, separateness have disappeared. There is no time or space, you realize they are merely an illusion of the mundane mind. There is only eternity and supreme joy and bliss. This state is beyond description. You will have to realise this for yourself. The bliss state is not something we can force into existence in our minds. It comes only after we have prepared ourselves through such techniques as we have been learning in this book. Even then, it comes when we are truly ready, in its own perfect moment. Sometimes we move into crown chakra bliss after doing formal kundalini meditation for half-an-hour to an hour - sometimes it happens spontaneously, when we least expect it. I suspect you have all experienced it many times as a child, just as I did.

As you move upwards through the chakras, if you have been practising the kundalini meditations daily, you will be aware that as you balance all your chakras so you become aware of all the chakras at once. This can happen almost simultaneously after you become practised in mental expansion - especially when you do the full hour-long kundalini meditation I will describe in the Soul Star chapter. Although if you have been practising the techniques I have been teaching you by activating each of your chakras in sequential order, by the time you have reached the seventh, the crown chakra, you have already made intimate direct contact with this chakra many times in meditation. So arriving at the crown chakra is simply a final expansion into infinite bliss. Please remember the final expansion stage relies on resonance, the vibrating in harmony of all your chakras, which is a beautiful experience in itself - your personal symphony.

The Sanskrit name for the crown chakra is *sahasrara*, which means a thousand; it can also mean 'to multiply by a thousandfold'. The crown chakra through which you will experience samadhi is located at the crown of the head, known as the anterior fontanelle in a newborn child. It is called

189

Brahmarandhra, the "hole of Brahma". At the time of death the advanced meditator separates him/herself from the physical body, it bursts open and the *Prana* escapes through it. Please remember, although the crown chakra is situated at the top of the head, its swirling vortex of energy reaches far above the head. The crown chakra is associated with enlightenment, cosmic consciousness, the element of thought, right eye, cerebral cortex, pineal gland, upper skull and the skin. The malfunctions of the crown chakra are confusion, lack of clarity, depression, obsessional thinking, sensitivity to pollutants, chronic exhaustion, epilepsy and Alzheimer's. The seventh chakra, the crown, is masculine, pure bright light and yang. The crown chakra's sensory channel is experience - beyond self.

The seventh chakra's symbol is the thousand-petal lotus flower on which are repeated the fifty letters of the *Sanskrit* alphabet. It is represented as open in full bloom, which means you are fully open to the light of the soul. In the Sanskrit tradition it is the abode of *Shiva*. This is the seat of true wisdom, through deep meditation. When this chakra is fully activated you are filled with joy and develop a beautiful spiritual aura, your light body has anchored onto the physical body, your DNA spiral of life has downloaded your personal keys to ascension and you have transformed into a rainbow warrior of light.

In Buddhism the lotus is a token or symbol for that which transcends the mundane. It is the alchemy energy whereby we transmute our lower nature into our higher nature; thus we turn 'lead into gold'. It is also a symbol of spiritual receptivity. To understand the 'perfection' of wisdom we have to be prepared to stand under it and learn from it. In doing so we may even have to accept that we do not know anything about anything, spiritual or mundane. We need to discipline and develop our rational faculty, not try and dispense with it once we have fully trained our perfect intellect, then we can turn it to the perfect wisdom and let it discover for itself its inadequacy in apprehending reality. The rational mind has to be developed to a point where it can see through itself - and thus acknowledge its own limitations. The lotus is also known as the wisdom goddess, *Prajnaparamita* in Sanskrit, *Sherappkyi Pharoltuchinma* in Tibetan Buddhism.

The crown chakra colors are traditionally violet, gold and white. The violet ray represents those who search for the spiritual truth in all life. It is the ray of spirituality and spiritual service. It contains a balance of blue and red. It is the highest and fastest vibration in the rainbow. The body parts it rules are the pineal gland, top of the head, the crown, brain and scalp. It brings spiritual dedication and aids psychic abilities. It allows for full soul development and the clearing of karmic debris. It also allows psychic protection. The white ray of peace contains all other colors. It can also be the clear ray of brilliance, bringing enlightenment, cosmic awareness, blissful reunion with our source - allowing the 'Holy Spirit' to flow downward into our lives for the ultimate healing and inspirational power of the universe. We transcend our individual minds and enter into perfect conscious harmony with the infinite wholeness of the universe. Infinite love, infinite bliss. Enlightenment is to be filled with light, to comprehend the light, to function in the light, to radiate the light and merge with the light. When *Kundalini Shakti* is united with *Shiva* at the *sahasrara*, the *yogi/yogini* experiences extreme bliss. He/she attains the superconscious state and the highest knowledge. The clear ray of brilliance can be used anywhere on the body and aura. The sun-gold ray is of knowledge and divine understanding - "at the end of the rainbow is the pot of gold". Its uses are that it aids assimilation of knowledge, brings vitality and spiritual abundance. It rids the body of parasites and parasitic energies on all levels (karmic debris and negative thought patterns, your own and those of others). It also brings the attunement to the Sun and Solar Lords of Light.

The traditional sound for the crown chakra is the *Bija* mantra of silence or silent OM. As you gently move from the sixth-chakra chanting of the OM to the seventh chakra, simply allow the Om chant to fall silent. This vibratory sound energy will continue throughout your chakra system. It becomes a silent but all-pervasive mantra; it is the sound of the universe singing your soul back home. It wakes up the bliss sensation in every cell of your body; just when you feel yourself entering this blissful state, stay aware of your breathing, so that it doesn't contract at the awesomeness of the experience; be aware, but don't control it; you will find that you become entrained in harmony with the universe. This is the bliss breath. Allow the universe to 'breathe' you. You will find this a joyful feeling of perfect abandonment. All your thoughts stop, there is only the Soul of the universe.

Your guides to the crown chakra are Archangel Metatron, who is Archangel Sandalphon's twin; also the Solar Lords of Light. As with the throat and third eye chakras, you will also get guidance from any Ascended Master, Angel or tutelary Deity, Sages or Saints that have a deep personal loving connection to you, and who are trying to encourage you onwards on your path to enlightenment, peace and bliss. There are two kinds of forms you will see as you progress through your chakras, especially the higher chakras. The lustrous forms as I have described above, and the mundane forms. Believe me, the lustrous forms are just that - dazzlingly beautiful and full of brilliant light. The mundane forms are just that - ordinary - they are to be avoided. They are the forms you will see during the early part of your meditation. They belong to the lower astral world. They are similar to human beings, but without the physical body; they only possess an astral body. They have desires and human attributes - love, hate, anger, resentment, bitterness, hostility etc. They can move about freely, but only in the lower astral realm. They can hypnotise and trick you if you let them, because some of them do have powers, such as dematerialisation, materialisation, multiplying and clairvoyant vision of a very inferior order. Do not become enmeshed with them or ensnared in their powers. You will know the difference. Your true guides are so bright, vast and beautiful beyond words. It will soon become evident to you; the difference is such a marked contrast as to be beyond mistake.

You may also see visions of beautiful flower gardens, vast shining palaces, mountains, rivers and temples; they are very beautiful. Sometimes during meditation you will see the infinite blue sky of *shunyata*, ethereal space. Sometimes you will appear in the centre, as a black dot. Other times, you will notice highly vibrating, rotating particles of light; stars and galaxies will unfold before you. You will also see human forms, men, women and children; these are objective and subjective, your own mental attributes or finer planes of existence. The Universe consists of many planes and levels. Visions may be purely imaginary, from your own mind, intense crystallized thought patterns; you must learn discrimination, because in the end you must let all these visions go. You must move beyond the attachment to these visions. They are there only to encourage you onwards towards the supreme goal of total union with your true self, your God/Goddess self, which is beyond the duality of the mundane self, to become a part of the One Thread Soul of the universe.

Crystal Web of Light - Pleiadean Star

Crystals: 11 moldavite, natural, tumbled, faceted or pyramid-shaped
             7 clear quartz points

Uses: This crystal web of light activates and balances the crown chakra, through an integration and a synergetic entrainment of resonance, whereby all the master chakras, plus the hands and feet chakras, are brought into the symphony of the self. Old belief patterns and blocked or stagnant energy is released, distorted chakras will come into perfect alignment. The chakra system as a whole is realigned and a massive vibrational shift in consciousness causes an expansion and vibratory raising on all levels and in all dimensions. This crystal web of light has been used by hundreds of people in Europe; it has formed part of the crystal webs of light which can be experienced on the second year of the crystal courses I have personally taught for the last 14 years and the courses the qualified crystal tutors I have trained have taught. It is not compulsory on the course, only available if the students wish to experience it. In fact all the crystal webs of light within this book and the meditations have been used by hundreds, if not thousands, of people, both as an experience in personal development, then later by the students and qualified crystal therapists in their clinical practices.

You can tell when someone has a balanced crown chakra: they have a magnetic personality, they achieve 'miracles' in life, they are at peace within themselves, they transcend the day-to-day worries of ordinary folk, they are not attached to possessions. This crystal web of light heals a blocked crown chakra. You can tell when someone's crown chakra is blocked or distorted: they seem to be constantly exhausted, they cannot make decisions and have no sense of belonging anywhere; they can even be paranoid. This crystal web of light will also rebalance a crown chakra that is too open or one that spins too fast. You can tell if someone's crown is too open: they are psychotic or manic depressive, they may have a confused sexual expression, or be frustrated, feel a sense of unrealized power and experience no joy in life. This crystal web of light has also been used to fully activate and integrate the heart, third eye and throat chakras into the higher realms of cosmic consciousness.

11 moldavite, one on each master chakra, one at each foot, one in each hand.

7 clear quartz points, placed to form a Pleiadean star. The terminations should point towards the body.

Process:

1. Cleanse all the crystals and programme the clear quartz for healing.

2. Choose a warm comfortable place where you can lie down undisturbed for at least an hour; never rush a crystal web of light process. View it as a sacred healing space, so you need to make sure it is energetically clean. Make sure you are wearing warm, loose, comfortable clothes.

3. Relax by consciously becoming aware of your breathing and heartbeat; you can play soothing music, light candles and burn incense.

4. Lay the stones around and on the body and hold a moldavite in each hand.

5. Allow 20 minutes to facilitate the integration of the crystal vibration.

6. Feel free to remove the crystals sooner, if you have integrated the crystal energy very quickly.

7. Remove the crystals in reverse order of placement.

8. Make sure you are fully grounded, centred and balanced.

9. Cleanse your crystals (using your chosen method).

10. Finish by giving thanks and asking mentally that all the healing work you have just accomplished is closed, sealed and protected with Divine love and wisdom.

11. Give yourself sufficient time to integrate the crystal therapy session.

12. As a general guideline it is suggested a period of twice the length of time you were actually lying in the crystal therapy web be allowed for integration.

Clear Quartz - See the Root Chakra Section for Properties

Moldavite

Tektites are still poorly understood. They are irregularly - and at times elaborately - shaped nodules and blobs of a glassy substance. They have no crystal structure and are therefore similar to obsidian, but are not associated with volcanic processes. Their chemistry is unique and unexplained. The leading theory concerning their origin is the "Meteorite Impact Theory". It is postulated that many odd events occur during a meteor's impact, because of the tremendous heat and pressure produced. Tektites may be fused glass that formed during an impact of a meteor with layers of rock on the earth's surface. Tektites occur in broad bands in specific localities in different parts of the world. These bands produce characteristically similar tektites and are sometimes loosely associated with meteorite craters or suspected craters. Could these fields represent splash material from an impact? Many believe so and this idea is gaining acceptance from many scientists. The odd and diverse chemistry of the tektites could be a result of unique meteorites hitting unique rock types with the combinations producing particular effects.

Tektites, which have been found on every continent, are tar black or blackish brown, while moldavites, which have been found only in the Moldau river valley in Czechoslovakia, are a deep green color. The only known fall of moldavites occurred about 15 million years ago. They were prized by humans at least as long as 25,000 years ago, for archaeologists have discovered moldavite shards and pieces in cave dwellings of that era. Moldavites are the rarest of gems, perhaps rarer than diamonds, rubies or emeralds. Since their origin is not of the earth, the discovery of new deposits seems unlikely. Moldavites are sometimes cut as gemstones or put into jewellery as natural uncut pieces to show off their often eerie and exquisite intricate shapes.

Although moldavite has been known of as a gem for thousands of years, it remained in obscurity until recently, the only reference being an article in the Lapidary Journal in 1958 about a strange stone with some kind of mystical properties. In 1986 the wonderful book "Moldavite, Starborn Stone", by Bob Simmons and Kathy Warner, was published. It brought the truly transformational stone moldavite to the attention of millions of 'Lightworkers' around the planet.

The five keys to moldavite's transformational properties are its:

*   Amorphous nature - inner structure
*   Cosmic birth - growth conditions
*   Verdant green hue - color vibration
*   Intense resonance - vibration
*   'Spirit' or Angel guide - inspiration

Amorphous Nature - Inner Structure

Basically, moldavite has no structure; this means it can take you beyond your self-limiting belief system into uncharted realms of infinite possibilities. Moldavite contains the nature of *shunyata*, the vast emptiness (which contains all potentiality), stretching in all directions, absolutely clear, pristine and radiant. By this clear starry night sky stretching into infinity we can gain an understanding, a feeling for the expansiveness and freedom which could be ours if we did not allow our horizons to become narrow, clouded and limited, if we did not permit our minds to become fixated and hypnotised by cravings and worries centred on what really are empty passing phenomena.

Cosmic Birth - Growth Conditions

Moldavite's chemistry is unique and unexplained. The leading theory concerning its origin is the "Meteorite Impact Theory". It was born from a meteor's impact because of the tremendous heat and pressure produced. This makes the energy of moldavite very fast, hot and cosmic. It was sent here for the awakened 'star children', to help their ascension into the higher realms of cosmic consciousness. This massive vibrational shift is happening right now, that is why so many people feel a magnetic attraction to the cosmic transformational tool of moldavite.

Verdant Green Hue - Color Vibration

Green is a balance color; it is the bridge, a gateway into the heart of the body; the lesson of love that needs to be learned in order to grow spiritually. Green will encourage your spiritual growth. It wants you to take your proper place in life. Green gives you harmony and balance. Green does not just follow rules blindly, it creates better ones where the old ones have failed. Green holds the keys to memory - it can remember that which needs to be re-membered, so it unlocks the deep and hidden that is the cause of our psychological and physical dis-ease. It is the diagnostic color: this makes moldavite one of the best diagnostic crystals we have available. An aversion to moldavite or the color green often indicates that we do not feel at ease with our emotions. It shows a deep fear of opening our heart chakra fully to unlimited unconditional love.

Intense Resonance - Vibration

Metaphysically, we have within us the light body and this contains encodements of information like files. When we hold moldavite this data is released. Very often many people are not consciously aware of the information being unlocked, they just feel what has commonly been called 'the moldavite flush', a huge wave of powerful energy which actually flushes through the body; this can cause sweating or a bright 'red' face. Interestingly, red is the green ray's balance color. Others experience the decoding or download as heat surging up their spine. Still others experience the download as an emotional release of tears or laughter. Others find the vibrational download shift and the resulting rise in their vibrational rate as too intense; they may become fearful. Others experience it as dizziness or headaches. There is no doubt, though, the download does cause massive spiritual growth. It can take years to fully integrate the download of information. In fact the more people resist the integration of their Divine blueprint being decoded from the Akashic records, the longer it takes.

'Spirit' or Angel Guide - Inspiration

When we hold, wear, meditate or carry moldavite our energy field changes. The universal law of resonance says that what we focus on becomes our reality. Like attracts like. When we understand that every thought is sent out and attracts like energy which strengthens it, then comes back to us like a boomerang, we begin to grasp how the higher vibration of moldavite increases our sensitivity and increases our clairaudience and clairvoyance abilities. We literally attract a higher form of guidance. Moldavite does have an Oversoul Spirit Guide, which is a vast cosmic Angel. The moldavite Angel can help in all areas, including connecting you to other high vibrational guides and Ascended Masters. These Cosmic Masters have been around for aeons and are able to work with anyone whose vibration has been raised sufficiently. You don't have to use moldavite, though, to attract Cosmic Masters. Many people who have refined their vibration through meditation have accessed this guidance.

The 'Grail Stone' is another name for moldavite: it is its 'Spirit' name. Legend has it that anyone who touches the 'Grail Stone' will have a spiritual transformation. Those who choose to wear, carry, meditate or heal with moldavite carry the energy of moldavite within their Divine blueprint. This makes them the ambassadors for transformation; indeed their energy is raised to such a high vibration of resonance they become the instruments of the enfoldment of the Divine plan for Planet Earth, as she and her children make the vibrational shift into the next dimension.

Affirmation: I release all limiting thought patterns: I am transformed.

Healing Meditation - Crown Chakra

1.   Choose a warm comfortable place where you can sit or lie down undisturbed for at least an hour. Never rush a meditation. View it as your own sacred, silent, healing space. You need to make sure it is energetically clean. Make sure you are wearing warm, loose, comfortable clothes.

2.   Breathe slowly, encouraging energy to flow up and down your nervous system and begin to relax your body......go through your whole body, starting at your feet, and consciously relax each part, moving up and finishing at your head.....allow yourself to really let go and deeply relax... feel yourself sinking into the chair, floor or bed........

3.   Allow yourself to tune in to your breathing.....as you do so, I want you to visualise a perfect white lotus flower.....imagine it at first like a cap of a thousand white petals gently hugging your head.

4.   Now, with the warmth of your focused attention.....feel the petals beginning to turn upwards.... towards the Sun of your own Divine Source......through the centre where the petals meet is an opening through which pours the Light of Your Soul.....it can be brilliant white....violet...or gold....or a mixture of all three.......

5. Allow this pure pristine energy to flow into you.....filling the whole of your body with light...as it does so, you feel a peace....... a love that transcends all understanding.....perfect peace.....a calmness pervades your body and mind.....a deep soul connection is taking place....allow yourself to really absorb this light....until your whole body and aura are pure light................

6. You feel your mind relax....and let go....as you allow yourself to totally merge with the Light of your Soul.....you are at peace with yourself, the world and everyone in it.......breathe deeply of the light................

7. You are the light....you are becoming enlightened.....and the more you practise this meditation the deeper is the soul connection......your life is becoming transformed......you are moving into synchronisation with your Soul.....allowing all the earthly mundane thoughts to fall away as you merge with the Light of your Soul..................

8. This energy has always been there for you....loving you....guiding you....from now on you will listen to the gentle whisperings of your Soul.....by doing so, you allow your Soul to guide you to a new way of being.....a new way of living.....you are going home.......nothing can stop you now.....you and your Soul have merged......into the One......the energy of enlightenment pervades your whole being..........peace............love.......joy..........bliss........enlightenment....

9. Stay with this energy as long as you like.....come out of meditation very slowly....and remember...wherever you are..... this light is always with you......just ask....and it will descend like a cloud of bliss....bringing peace and a deep soul connection......

Kundalini Crown Chakra Meditation

We have been learning different pranayama exercises as we have moved through the kundalini meditations. The next one is the bliss breath; it consists of letting the universe breathe you. The bliss breath follows naturally from the kundalini sixth chakra meditation.

The Bliss Breath

1. You will need to have all six bandhas or energy seals in place......and all your chakras turned upwards.....towards your crown chakra....this brings spiritual energy into all your lower chakras and allows for your full attention to be focused upwards towards your enlightenment.......

2. As you move into the seventh chakra, the crown.....your breathing should become totally uncontrolled, spontaneous and peaceful.....it is as though you just allow the universe to breathe you....I can describe it in no other way..... except to add it feels completely different from any other kind of breathing....it feels different in your chest....it is a feeling of pure joy...of calm...heightened awareness....an altered state of awareness......a unity with all life....as one soul...

3. The crown chakra mantra of OM...will sound in and through you as never before....allow the sound to manifest in your mind....feel it effortlessly rising from your inner being........as the OM sound generates tremendous power.....opening yourself to the sound of the universe, as it joins you in sounding the OM........continue for as long as you want........you are the vibration.....

4. Visualise the crown chakra mandala....use the one in this book......become aware of the chakra mandala....as you focus on the energy movements and shapes it contains.......or just visualise a beautiful pristine white lotus flower on the top of your head....your crowning glory.....

5. Allow yourself plenty of time to integrate this new awareness.........you need to practise this meditation on a daily basis; it is the culmination of the first, second, third, fourth, fifth, sixth and seventh chakra kundalini activation you have learned thus far......don't forget to reverse the root chakra to point downwards and the sacral, solar plexus, heart, throat and third eye chakras to point outwards.....as you once more anchor yourself on the earth plane of normal, everyday, grounded, waking reality.......

Part 19

The Earth Star

As you have been reading this book, you have probably realised that I have been trying to teach you core meditative techniques. The reason kundalini meditation possesses such universal appeal at this point in time is that it offers a clear experienced-based approach for awakening our mundane minds to the presence of our true higher nature. We are really spiritual beings having a human experience.

Through kundalini meditation we can master the quieting of our habitual flows of thought. These thought flows block us from deep spiritual reflection and enlightened realisation. Although it is not always acknowledged, the divine nature of our Higher Selves pushes us onwards through the many obstacles and learning experiences that this life has to offer. Negative or self-depreciating feelings that inhibit the flow of spiritual energies into the physical reality create problems with not only the 'little ego' but also the physical body. These dysfunctional patterns of thinking and feeling inhibit energy movement through the chakras and ultimately disturb the physiological balance of the physical body. As we fall victim to our faulty belief systems, we block the flow of higher consciousness into our daily lives. These faulty perceptions of reality, of ourselves and the world around us, create disharmony and stress at unconscious levels. As we become disconnected from our spiritual roots, we fall prey to the untold forms of dis-ease that civilization has created. Many of these dis-eases are core reflections of the struggle taking place within the human race as we seek to uncover, or rediscover, our true divine nature. It is crucial that we begin to understand the importance of our connectivity to our spiritual roots, because it is the spiritual element which is vital to health and well-being that is left out of the human equation by traditional physicians.

Along with spiritual imbalances, the negative influences of environmentally-produced miasms have created difficulties in the immune system of many people. These miasms have made many people more susceptible to viruses and bacterial infections. In addition, there are other forms of stress which can affect the health and well-being of human beings. One of these stresses is electromagnetic radiation itself. Others are unseen subtle toxicities of harmful environmental substances, chemical pollutants, background radioactivity and electromagnetic radiation, living in an environment of high-voltage transmission lines, microwave ovens, cathode ray tubes and other powerful electronic devices which do produce negative biological effects. On a more ethereal level are the toxic dangers of living or working in an environment of negative thought energies. Our thoughts carry a vibration which can pollute the earth if they are negative, just as areas of the world that have wars or conflicts also add to the overall negative pollution of the planet.

The use of vibrational healing or vibrational medicine to correct disturbances within the human energy system involves a process of not only rebalancing the physical body, but also lifting the consciousness of the individual to new levels of spiritual attunement and awareness. This also includes enlightening the individual client by introducing life-style changes and mind-style changes which impact upon their overall health. If we do not educate people to change their awareness we find that a dis-ease that is a 'core negative issue' will only manifest in another way. This also happens in conventional medicine: a surgeon will cut out a dis-eased part of the body, but because the 'core negative issue' that caused the original dis-ease is not dealt with at all, the 'core negative issue' will quickly manifest as another dis-ease in another organ. This will then be removed surgically too.

We may live in a dis-eased stressed-out society but we can all work in our own way towards not only healing our own dis-ease but helping others to raise their own awareness too. The combined efforts of millions of 'Lightworkers' around the planet will begin to turn the tide of disease and distress within the planetary grid, which in turn will raise the awareness of the whole planet. I am not of the doom and gloom brigade; in fact just as the Dalai Lama recently said, "I am very hopeful for the future". I believe with all the spiritual awakenings on the planet, which includes the Native Peoples on many continents, we will soon move into a new world view. This will be Global awareness and Global responsibility. It will allow us to honour each being for their uniqueness. Unity within diversity will be celebrated.

So with this Planetary World view in mind, let us explore the Earth Star chakra, which is beneath our feet, as it directly entrains our energy field with that of the Earth's energy field. At some point in your spiritual awakening, on your path to enlightenment, you will become aware that the force of gravity is very important. You will also need to make sure you are at peace with not only yourself but all life: this includes the earth and living in harmony with her. Many times in your life you will have felt a powerful sense of oneness in your heart - a sense of total immersion in the natural world around you. Can you recall special moments when your body was charged with life force, when your spirit was burning very bright, when you were really alive. Perhaps it was while gazing at a flower, holding a crystal, watching the sunrise or sunset, the magic of being in a deep green forest, walking on the beach or out in the desert landscape. You may have felt these 'shifts in perception', as the land is suddenly 'alive'. The landscape begins to take on a dream-like quality. The stones and rivers, the cliffs and sea, the trees and grasses, the birds and animals are suddenly 'different'. Then you are part of the wind, the air you breathe is supercharged with vital life force, you hear the earth murmuring and breathing. You breathe with her, she breathes you, you are one. The scene shimmers in front of you in brilliant colors: the awe-inspiring grandeur of oneness makes you humble - the timelessness of eternity. This brief glimpse is gone, you awaken as if from a dream and you are just a mundane creature once again, crawling about in the mud. But the beautiful lotus flower has its roots deep in this same mud too. It learns to grow upwards towards the sun. You can learn to do the same, only you will move upwards through your chakra system towards enlightenment, whereby you will view the world with a heightened sense of awareness. These heightened states will last longer and longer until your world and awareness will shift into new levels of being and relating to all life. The one thing enlightenment brings is the total knowledge that you are everyone and everything - there is nothing that is not you.

So in order to grow to great spiritual heights you need to make sure your roots are firmly established in the earth. This may mean finding your spiritual roots or going out into nature, working with crystals, becoming aware of your environment and any global issues you feel drawn to. It means tuning in to the Earth; she has many stories to tell of the Dreamtime, of the Mirror of the Celts (miracles); every rock, every stream, every blade of grass is alive. It can also mean making sure your feet chakras are fully open, alive, vibrant and functioning. If they are blocked, distorted or not functioning at optimum level, your root chakra at the base of your spine will also be blocked. This will impede the life force for the kundalini energy, which in turn will greatly reduce your chance of finding the necessary balance and resonance in your chakras, especially your heart chakra. For your total healing into an enlightened state of living you need heart, you need love, you need to be in the present moment, right now here on earth.

The Earth Star chakra beneath your feet relates not only to your feet, but your ankles, knees, legs, hips and root chakra; it resonates with black, iridescent black. In truth the earth is full of color, the earth contains crystals of every hue from rich rubies to palest amethyst to the brightest diamond. All crystals have the ability to tune you in to the earth and the highest heavens. They are our rainbow bridge. Your guide is Archangel Sandalphon, Metatron's twin from the crown chakra. Sandalphon is a massive bright Angel of Light; she will teach you the ways of the earth, of the animals and birds, trees and flowers, rocks and streams; the ways of the fairies, elves, gnomes, sylphs and undines, those unique nature spirits that are the guardians of the sacred places. There are sacred places left on the earth; it is not desolate as many people would have you believe. When you take the time to go out into the forests and woods, the beach or the desert, you will find the nature spirits, these sacred guardians, are so grateful that you care enough to take some time to just be.

The Bija seed sounds for the earth star chakra are the sounds of nature. So try a nature listening exercise. Go out into the open air and focus your ears and mind on the natural sounds that surround you. Make a mental list of those you hear: bird song, rustling leaves, humming insects, barking dogs, rustling leaves, people talking, children laughing, babies crying, the gently lapping waves, swishing grass, even the silence. Do you tend to notice sounds by volume, loudest first, or by frequency, high pitched first, or low pitched first. Which sounds are the most obvious, which did you hear first? What sounds make you feel happy or sad? Which sounds may help you reach heightened states of awareness?

Crystal Web of Light - Earth Star Connector for Protection and Purification

Crystals: 1 aragonite, natural
                     1 dioptase, natural
                     2 hematite, tumbled
                     2 labradorite, tumbled, slice or natural
                     2 obsidian, tumbled or natural
                     1 smoky quartz, natural or tumbled.
                     12 clear quartz points

Uses: This crystal web of light contains powerful earth-healing energy. It is totally stable and safe. It makes you think very deeply, which teaches you to think before acting. The aragonite within the crystal web is used for general strengthening, grounding, stabilizing and centering of physical energies. It connects you to the Goddess. It can be used to stabilize the base and sacral chakras, attuning you to the positive force of gravity, allowing for your interconnectedness to the earth, your past and childhood. Aragonite brings immediate warmth to the body when it is chilled from colds or flu, allowing for the full power and passion of the base chakra to be fully activated. Aragonite gives a cloak of security and earthly support during times of stress. It is soothing; it allows us to snuggle up to the bosom of Mother Nature. It is very good for spinal problems and will find the root of the problem by gently rooting you back into the earth, where you will feel supported.

The hematite within the crystal web of light is good for calming the nerves and soothing the emotions. It has a strong grounding quality. The spiritual tranquillity associated with hematite brings about a fluid state of consciousness. It will restore equilibrium and stability, so it is good for headaches, dizziness and the feelings of being spaced out. This stone is also a powerful ally or shield against the negativity of others. When consciously directed it will instantly stop outside intrusive unwanted negative energies affecting your energy field. It is good for stopping nightmares. But be aware it is a very strong stone.

The labradorite within this crystal web is truly an enchanting, fascinatingly beautiful mineral; it is metaphysically known as the 'bringer of light', the illumination on the path. It works by dispelling darkness. Enchanting labradorite is connected to mystery: it points to magic and esoteric knowledge via its labradorescence or luminescence. It contains the mesmerizing dark moon energies of dreaming, of altered states of reality. It facilitates initiation into deep hidden sacred knowledge and past life encounters. It is a gateway to other worlds and dimensions. Labradorite is a shape-shifter; it plays with the light, it moves it and bends it and plays with illusion. It skilfully removes the 'hooks and ensnarements' of other people's mental projections, allowing one to completely clean the auric shell of other people's emotional debris. It removes negativity and depression that have been caused by disappointments in life. It teaches you to look beyond the visible world, to use your sixth sense. Its energy can see beyond the illusion of time and space. It heals the stress and anxiety related to emotional turmoil.

The obsidian within this crystal web of light has no restrictions or limitations. This is due entirely to its amorphous structure; it teaches us to let go of our limitations and self-imposed fear restrictions. It teaches us to flow and expand. It has a soul mirror quality that is all its own. Its 'Spirit' name is the 'Warrior of Truth'. On the path to our own personal wholeness, healing and health we must confront our deepest fears, phobias, pains, hurts and shame. Obsidian will also shield us from all unkind energies which seek to use our energy and manipulate our energy field for their own benefit. It also dissolves all negative energy within our environment. It is an excellent grounding stone for when we feel spaced out or disorientated from reality. It quickly dissolves blocks, trauma, shock, fear and 'reality shock'. It helps us to deal with feelings of betrayal and exploitation. Pain is quickly removed when obsidian is placed on the affected area. It removes toxins from the body after exposure to pollution and toxic areas of the earth. It purges negativity from the meridian system and is being used instead of needles in acupuncture. The smoky quartz teaches you the right use of power and keeps you 'grounded' in fearful situations. It stops destructive power that is used out of selfishness, greed, manipulation, evil or weakness. It is very protective. It stops depression and restriction. It connects you to the deep philosophical thoughts, ideals and wisdom of the land; it can also throw up energetically a smoke-screen of protection that will temporarily hide you - nothing permanent though, just a breathing space while you gather your scattered emotions and ground yourself or 'go to ground'.

Smoky quartz is a great teacher: it can take you deep inside the earth to work with the elementals for healing. Smoky quartz teaches the simple pleasure of a happy, joyful heart, of peace and brotherhood/sisterhood. It shows you friendship and trust are worth their weight in spiritual gold. Smoky quartz is stimulating and purifying to the first chakra, so it is good for meditation practice. It can bring you back to earth to everyday normal waking reality. It eases despair, despondency, gloom, melancholy and suicidal tendencies. It can help you bring your dreams into reality. There is nothing weak about smoky quartz. It enhances the survival instinct; it is a life-saver. Smoky quartz allows for clarity of thought and contemplation. It has been used against the negative effects of radiation, including electrical equipment negativity.

1 aragonite, placed on the sacral chakra.

1 dioptase, placed on the heart chakra.

2 hematite, placed one at the base of each foot.

2 labradorite, one placed six inches below and between the feet, in the Earth Star chakra, and the other one on the third eye chakra.

2 obsidian (black), placed one in each hand.

1 smoky quartz, placed on the throat chakra.

12 clear quartz single terminated crystals, placed evenly around the body. The terminations should point towards the body.

Process:

1. Cleanse all the crystals and programme the clear quartz for healing.

2. Choose a warm comfortable place where you can lie down undisturbed for at least an hour. Never rush a crystal web of light process. View it as a sacred, silent, healing space, so you need to make sure it is energetically clean. Make sure you are wearing warm, loose, comfortable clothes.

3. Relax by consciously becoming aware of your breathing and heartbeat. You can play soothing music, light candles and burn incense.

4. Lay the stones around and on the body and hold the obsidian in your hands.

5. Allow 20 minutes to facilitate the integration of the crystal vibration.

6. Feel free to remove the crystals sooner, if you have integrated the crystal energy very quickly.

7. Remove the crystals in reverse order of placement.

8. Make sure you are fully grounded, centred and balanced.

9. Cleanse your crystals (using your chosen method).

10. Finish by giving thanks and asking mentally that all the healing work you have just accomplished is closed, sealed and protected with Divine love and wisdom.

11. Give yourself sufficient time to integrate the crystal therapy session.

12. As a general guideline it is suggested a period of twice the length of time you were actually lying in the crystal therapy web be allowed for integration.

Aragonite

Aragonite, a dimorphous form of calcium carbonate which crystallises in the orthorhombic system, is very often twinned in its growth. It occurs as a deposit from hot springs and in association with beds of gypsum. The shells of certain molluscs are made of aragonite and many fossil shells now composed of calcite were probably formed originally of aragonite. The name comes from the province in Spain where it was first noted.

This stone has a powerful earth healer energy which is not wildly exciting but is totally stable and safe. It makes you think very deeply, which teaches you to think before acting. Aragonite is used for general strengthening, grounding, stabilizing and centering of physical energies. It connects you to the Goddess and earth-healing energies. It can be used to stabilize the base chakra, attuning you to the positive force of gravity, allowing for your interconnectedness to the earth, your past and childhood. It is good to place on the body to facilitate the grounding process and has been used in this way to access past lives. It can be used for all the solid elements of the body, including the bones and teeth. It helps mend broken bones and helps with calcium absorption. Aragonite brings immediate warmth to the body when it is chilled from colds or flu, allowing for the full power and passion of the base chakra to be fully activated. Aragonite gives a cloak of security and earthly support during times of stress. It is soothing; it allows us to snuggle up to the bosom of Mother Nature. An extremely good way of working with aragonite is to go out into nature, where you will feel growth and renewal channelled through the stone and into your energy system. It is very good for spinal problems and will find the root of the problem by gently rooting you back into the earth, where you will feel supported. One interesting feature of aragonite is its ability to tune you in to the recycling process that is an aspect of conservation. It teaches you moderation in all things, to only 'take' what you need.

Affirmation: I am connected to Mother Earth and know the security of being grounded.

Clear Quartz - See the Root Chakra Section for Properties

Dioptase

This wondrous emerald-green crystal is a copper silicate and has a chemical likeness to chrysocolla. Dioptase is not common, but is found in oxidized parts of copper sulphate deposits. The best deep green dioptase is currently coming out of Russia. Dioptase works primarily on the thymus, heart, chest, shoulders and lower lungs. It has an intense emerald quality and some healers feel it is a 'young' emerald. As therapists we find that an aversion to the green ray often indicates that we are uncomfortable with our emotions. The key is held in childhood, where our 'conditioning' would have been a 'British' stiff upper lip - no emotions, thank you.

Dioptase is best used as a bridge, a gateway to emotional freedom. Dioptase can reveal the health of your emotional heart and your physical heart. It shows your potential in relating to others. Wearing or carrying dioptase will not only help you gain empathy with others, it will make you more approachable. Often those who are deeply damaged emotionally as children, through severely dysfunctional parents, find it very difficult, if not impossible, to open emotionally as adults. They may even find that when they do open emotionally they get hurt again and again, often very badly and from those they least expect 'abuse' from. This is due to the negative 'victim' energy remaining in the auric shell as negative thought forms. On a subconscious level it is 'read' by everyone they meet and, human nature being what it is, unless they are surrounded by saints, it will be acted upon and they will be punished again. The key to this negative release is held in the shoulders; by applying the beautiful dioptase energy to the shoulders the release mechanism is activated.

Dioptase gives direction - so it can be used when you are desperately trying to make up your mind or heart, or both. It is a must for those who don't know what to do next, who feel lost. Dioptase helps biliousness and soothes headaches. It is a good detoxifier and good for controlling blood pressure and liver complaints. It is excellent for the treatment of fatigue and even shock; it is a soporific and can calm hyperactive children. It is also an excellent nerve tonic. Its beautiful green ray is the ray of the great healers and healing. It will draw positive Pranic healing energy towards those who use it and wear it, restoring their vitality and making them feel glad to be alive. It carries the energy of balance, stability and commitment.

Affirmation: The gateway to unconditional love for myself and others is through my heart chakra.

Hematite

Hematite is the most important iron source and is widely distributed. In addition to its use as iron ore, hematite is used as a pigment and a polishing powder. The name is derived from the Greek word for blood and is descriptive of the color of the powdered mineral. Hematite has several varieties, each with their own unique names. Hematite rose is a circular group of bladed crystals giving the appearance of the flower of a rose. Tiger iron is a sedimentary deposit of approximately 2.2 billion years old that consists of alternating layers of silver-grey hematite and red jasper, chert or even tiger eye quartz. Kidney ore is the massive botryoidal form and gives the appearance of lumpy kidney-like masses. Oolitic hematite is a sedimentary formation that has a reddish brown color and an earthy lustre and is composed of small rounded grains. Specularite is a micaceous or flaky stone that is sparkling silver grey and sometimes used as an ornamental stone. Ancient superstition held that large deposits of hematite formed from battles that were fought and the subsequent blood that flowed into the ground, hence its ancient name of 'bloodstone'.

Hematite reflects back mistakes without distortion, apology or bias. A mistake is only a learning experience and some of our greatest learning experiences come from our mis-takes. Like filming, you just do it again until you get it right. It teaches us to work with what we know, rather than from what we see - for our world is only an illusion, a distorted mirror of the true nature of the universe. Very often when people open spiritually, they realise what a huge task it is. You very soon realise that the more you 'know' the more you realise just how 'little' you know. We have all spent thousands of lifetimes trying to 'get it right' and learn as much as possible. Your greatest teacher is your own direct personal experience. I realise you will also meet many teachers on your path; each should be working from direct personal experience too.

Hematite is good for calming the nerves and soothing the emotions. It has a strong grounding quality. The spiritual tranquillity associated with hematite brings about a fluid state of consciousness. It calms the hormones. Hematite is good for the functioning of the kidneys, beneficial in use on fluid flows of the body. It will restore equilibrium and stability, so it is good for headaches, dizziness and the feelings of being spaced out. This stone is also a powerful ally or shield against the negativity of others. When consciously directed it will instantly stop outside intrusive unwanted negative energies affecting your energy field. It is good for stopping nightmares and staunching bleeding. But be aware it is a very strong stone and if you 'over' use it by always carrying or wearing it on the same area on your body it can begin to give a localised distortion in your energy field, as well as being a skin irritant. The iron energy vibration in hematite will purify and strengthen the blood and aid absorption of iron in the small intestine.

Affirmation: I now tune in to the great substance of the Earth to give grounding to my spiritual work.

Labradorite

Labradorite is truly an enchanting, fascinatingly beautiful mineral. It is a mineral whose bewitching charm is not fully noticed and may be overlooked if not viewed from the proper position; generally a drab-looking mineral with no special virtue until the colorful schiller is observed glowing on the surface. Labradorite can produce a colorful play of light across cleavage planes and in sliced sections, called labradorescence. The usually intense colors range from the typical blues and violets through greens, yellows and oranges. The color display is from lamellar intergrowths inside the crystal. These intergrowths result from compatible chemistries at high temperatures becoming incompatible at lower temperatures and thus a separating and layering of these two phases. The resulting color effect is caused by a ray of light entering a layer and being refracted back and forth by deeper layers. This refracted ray is slowed by the extra travel through the layers and mixes with other rays to produce a light ray coming out that has a different wavelength than when it went in. The wavelength could correspond to the wavelength of a particular color, such as blue. The labradorescence is truly a one of a kind mineralogical and metaphysical encounter and must be observed in person in order to truly appreciate its beauty. Notable occurrences include Labrador (from where it derives its name), in Canada, and the Scandinavian Peninsula.

Labradorite is metaphysically known as the 'bringer of light', the illumination on the path. It works by dispelling darkness. Enchanting labradorite is connected to mystery: it points to magic and esoteric knowledge via its labradorescence or luminescence. It contains the mesmerizing dark moon energies of dreaming, of altered states of reality. Labradorite asks you "where do you go when you sleep?" - then it shows you - where you go - when you are not you. It facilitates initiation into deep hidden sacred knowledge and past life encounters. It is a gateway to other worlds and dimensions. Labradorite is a shape-shifter; it plays with the light, it moves it and bends it and plays with illusion.

It skilfully removes the 'hooks and ensnarements' of other people's mental projections, allowing one to completely clean the auric shell of other people's emotional debris. It removes negativity and depression that have been caused by disappointments in life. It teaches you to look beyond the visible world, to use your sixth sense. Its energy can see beyond the illusion of time and space. It can see right through you - it will expose all your flaws, shams, corruptions and shame, then it teaches you to heal them. Labradorite heals relationships; it shows you where there is no substance, just delusion and denial. It heals the stress and anxiety related to emotional turmoil. It calms the hormones and is good for the kidneys and all fluid functions of the body. It soothes the digestion. It has been used as a gem tincture and meditation stone with the Goddess groups. It is a powerful, mesmerizing, bewitching female ally and guide. Labradorite is here to offer you in-sight, clairvoyance, truths to the questions of the universe. It teaches you to exercise your third eye, by letting your intuition guide you daily. Why don't you try using labradorite and keeping an intuitive journal?

Affirmation: I am enchanted as my soul illuminates my path through life.

Obsidian

Obsidian is of very low significance as a material for gemstones, but the so-called glasses provide considerable interest for the many uses to which they have been put by aboriginal man and by the enigma of their genesis. Obsidian is formed by the rapid cooling of volcanic lava which, had it been allowed to cool slowly, would have developed a crystalline structure and assumed the character of granitic rocks. Obsidian is normally black or grey in color and owes any attraction it may have to an iridescent sheen caused by reflections from minute bubbles or inclusions of water or gas. The silver and gold sheen obsidian is highly prized and much sought after. In the United States of America a variety of obsidian having spherulitic inclusions of a white mineral on the black groundmass is cut and polished and goes under the name of 'flowering obsidian' or 'snowflake obsidian'. A variety banded black and red is known as 'mountain mahogany'. A transparent leaf-green is also available, but it is extremely rare and most transparent green obsidians are usually found to be moldavites or merely green glass. Red and blue obsidians have also been found, but these are also very rare.

Marekanite is the name applied to smoky-brown, grey or black decomposing perlitic obsidian found along the banks of the Mareikanka river at Okhotsk, in Siberia. Glassy pebble-like solid cores of unaltered glass, about an inch or more across, from the decomposed obsidian of the American south-west, are known as 'Apache tears'. The fracture of obsidian is extremely conchoidal and it is due to the facility with which the material can be broken into sharp-edged flakes that obsidian was so valued by Stone Age people who lived in areas where it was common, the easily controlled flaking allowing the production of keen-edge spear points, knives and tools. These have been discovered in ancient burial sites.

Obsidian has been quarried since the days of the North American Indians, who used it for arrowhead material. Obsidian was used by the Aztecs and their predecessors for the sharp points of their weapons, for mirrors and masks, and for ear ornaments. They called the material *Iztli* and surnamed it *Teotetl* (Divine stone) because of its manifold uses, one of which was the 'smoking mirror' used by the Mayan priests for scrying to predict the future. Obsidian occurs throughout the world at those places where volcanic activity occurs or has occurred in the past. In Iceland it is known as 'Iceland agate'. It has also been called 'Glass agate', 'Glass lava', 'Montana jet', 'Mountain jet', 'Nevada diamond', 'Nevada topaz', 'Rainbow obsidian', 'Iridescent obsidian' and 'Volcanic glass'. Obsidian derived its name from the Roman Obsius who, according to Pliny, found the stone in present-day Ethiopia.

Obsidian is a master mineral in the art of the hidden, lost or forbidden. It has no restrictions or limitations. This is due entirely to its amorphous structure; it teaches us to let go of our limitations and self-imposed fear restrictions. It teaches us to flow and expand. It has a soul mirror quality that is all its own.

Its 'Spirit' name is the 'Warrior of Truth'. When consciously directed, obsidian reflects our shadow side back to us for deep soul healing. Obsidian then teaches us how to bring more light into our darkness or shadow side. On the path to our own personal wholeness, healing and health, we must confront our deepest fears, phobias, pains, hurts and shame. Very often we desperately try to ignore our shadow side; these are the parts of us that we have judged, rightly or wrongly, to be bad, ugly or shameful. We have been conditioned since our births to conform to other people's ideas of good and bad, right or wrong. This is our personal 'conditioning', our 'robotic programming'. This programming *does* serve a vital function, it makes us easier to control and manipulate. These rules of good or bad constantly change, depending on our personal circumstances and present life situation; they are influenced by our religious beliefs, teachers, parents, relatives, politicians, scientists, the media and our peers. These rules do not represent Eternal Divine Truth, only the current civilisation's accepted truth. As we, as individualised perfect expressions of the sacred life force, claim our Divine birthright and personal power, we will have to confront all our demons of darkness and shine the light of truth into these murky recesses. These demons of darkness will otherwise manifest as illness, pain and feelings of separation from our source of love, inspiration and wisdom.

Obsidian draws the quality of our Divine essence into our physical body; this purges the negativity and activates 'the Divine essence within'. Obsidian will also shield us from all unkind energies which seek to use our energy and manipulate our energy field for their own benefit. It also dissolves all negative energy within our environment. It is an excellent grounding stone for when we feel spaced out or disorientated from reality. It quickly dissolves blocks, trauma, shock, fear and 'reality shock'. It helps us to deal with feelings of betrayal and exploitation.

It has been used for divination and scrying. This is accomplished by the process of soul integration, bringing our spiritual invulnerable self into our consciousness for attunement and integration, until we have a refined clairvoyance that encompasses eternal truth and integrity. Pain is quickly removed when obsidian is placed on the affected area. It has been used in the treatment of arthritis and all joint pain. It easily relieves cramp and the pain from injury or operation scars. It has been used to shrink enlarged prostates and ameliorate the painful side- effects of an enlarged prostate. It removes toxins from the body after exposure to pollution and toxic areas of the earth. It purges negativity from the meridian system and is being used instead of needles in acupuncture. It has helped remove and relieve painful areas in AIDS patients. It is soothing and comforting, but has the ability to deeply penetrate problems and degraded illnesses. Green obsidian is very purifying to the heart and throat chakras.

Because obsidian was used as an implement of death by Stone Age people who lived in areas where obsidian was common - you may have an initial resistance or fear of its energy.

Obsidian spheres have been used to unwind negative energy from dysfunctional chakras and painful areas of the body. They have also been used in meditation and scrying. An obsidian sphere used for meditation has been likened to an 'iron fist in a black velvet glove', so please have a sphere of clear quartz ready to help you fully integrate the energies a black obsidian sphere can unearth as it shatters your mirror of illusion.

I personally have obsidian as one of my spirit guides. The spirit of obsidian chose me, not the other way round. As we begin to work with crystals, we very often find some of them become 'very' special to us. They choose to act as a personal totem energy or ally. A totem energy is wholly reliable in all situations and acts as a guide on all levels, in all situations, very much like a Guardian Angel. In the late summer of 1990 I was teaching a crystal course in Manchester; it was the first week-end of this particular course, so I had not met all the students. The night before I had a dream in which a beautiful Goddess appeared; she was dressed in flowing iridescent sparkling black clothes and she wore a headdress of black feathers intertwined with shimmering jewels. As she stood before me she held out her hand: on it were three very long strange-looking claws like crystal blades; they were curved, dark, translucent and very exotic-looking. She said "choose one". As I gazed at them in wonder I asked "what are they?" She replied "crows' claws". In the Native American shamanic tradition, Crow Medicine is Truth, Wise Counsel, Wisdom and Resourcefulness. I then chose a 'claw'. The next day, during the lunch-time break in teaching the crystal course, one of the students approached me; she looked very shy, hesitant and a little perplexed. She said "yesterday I was in a crystal shop in London, close by where I live, and I was looking at these. I have never seen anything like them before. I was told spiritually to buy three; one is yours". As she stood before me, she held out her hand; on it were three very long exotic-looking claw-like crystal blades; they were curved, dark, translucent and very strange-looking. She said "choose one". Yes, you have guessed it, they were a type of natural obsidian blade I had never seen before. Yes, I was chosen.

Since then I have discovered more about these natural obsidian blades and have purchased them from the lady who 'harvests' them from her obsidian 'mine' in America. Because of the special formation, each blade can take her hours to unearth. They are quite fragile and range in size from a few inches long to huge specimens of 20 inches. I have used them continually in my healing work.

Affirmation: I am a spiritual warrior of truth.

Smoky Quartz

Smoky quartz is a popular variety of quartz. It is also popular as an ornamental stone and is carved into spheres, wands, pyramids, obelisks, eggs and Vogel crystals. The color of smoky quartz is variable from brown to black and sometimes smoky grey-colored specimens are included as smoky quartz. The cause of the color of smoky quartz is in question, but it is almost certainly related to the amount of exposure to radiation that the stone has undergone. Natural smoky quartz often occurs in granitic rocks which have a small but persistent amount of radioactivity. Most smoky quartz that makes its way to crystal shops and to some gem cutters has been artificially irradiated to produce a dark black color.

Smoky quartz is the Celtic Warrior; it was carried into battle as late as the first world war. It teaches you the right use of power and keeps you 'grounded' in fearful situations. It stops destructive power that is used out of selfishness, greed, manipulation, evil or weakness. It is very protective. It stops depression and restriction. It connects you to the deep philosophical thoughts, ideals and wisdom of the land - of ancient battles of good versus evil, of the right to hold your own values and stand your ground. But don't think for one moment that it is masculine. Smoky quartz has a balanced polarity of male and female energies. Remember the womenfolk of the Celts went into battle too. Ancient Celtic Queens like Boadicea fought for her land against the might of Rome.

It has been used for scrying; it intensifies your visionary ability by releasing your fear, fear of failure or fear of the unknown. Smoky quartz contains hidden riches; it can also throw up energetically a smoke-screen of protection that will temporarily hide you - nothing permanent though, just a breathing space while you gather your scattered emotions and ground yourself or 'go to ground'. Smoky quartz is a great teacher: it can take you deep inside the earth to work with the elementals for healing.

It can help you to find your hidden treasure - a strong and healthy body and a calm, peaceful stress-free mind. Smoky quartz can be practical; it likes you to lead a useful life, one in service to others who are less well-off spiritually. Spiritual poverty is rampant today - people with all the money in the world and they are so poor. Smoky quartz teaches the simple pleasure of a happy, joyful heart, of peace and brotherhood/sisterhood. It shows you friendship and trust are worth their weight in spiritual gold.

Smoky quartz is stimulating and purifying to the first chakra, so it is good for meditation practice. It can bring you back to earth to everyday normal waking reality. It eases despair, despondency, gloom, melancholy and suicidal tendencies. It can help you bring your dreams into reality. There is nothing weak about smoky quartz. It enhances the survival instinct; it is a life-saver. Smoky quartz allows for clarity of thought and contemplation. It will balance the male/female polarities; it relieves headaches and congestion of the intestines, helps heal the feet and legs and eases lower back pain. It also relieves cramp - not just physical muscular cramp, but soul cramp too. Its pain-relieving properties are wonderful: it just draws out pain. It has been used against the negative effects of radiation, including electrical equipment negativity.

Affirmation: I now free myself from the daily battle to survive; I trust in the Universe to support me in all I do.

Healing Meditation - Earth Star Chakra

1. Choose a warm comfortable place where you can lie down at leisure for at least an hour. Never rush a meditation. View it as a sacred silent healing space, so you need to make sure it is energetically clean. Wear warm, loose, comfortable clothes.

2. Breathe slowly, encouraging energy to flow up and down your nervous system.....and begin to relax your body. Go through your whole body, starting at your feet, and consciously relax each part, moving up and finishing at your head. Allow yourself to really let go and relax, feel yourself sinking into the floor or bed.

3. Visualize yourself outside in nature.....it is a perfect day, the sky is blue, the sun is shining and the birds are singing....you can hear the gentle hum of insects.....you feel relaxed...... at peace and totally at ease.......

4. See yourself walking on a red pathway.......feel the firm red earth beneath your feet.....you begin to follow the path.........it leads onwards and upwards.....soon you are climbing up a gently sloping green hillside........as you get to the top you notice a deep cave.......stand at the entrance.......you see ancient symbols carved into the rock........this is an ancient megalithic site.........allow your fingers to trace over the symbols........

5.   As you do so...........you feel the energy of the symbols flowing through you........... feel them unlocking doors in your mind.........bringing back ancient memories........of important things you have forgotten...........

6.   Now it's time to move towards the inside of the cave........as you do so, you see the cave is full of crystals..........as you gaze at the crystals, one in particular seems to draw your attention......it has an inner light, glowing brighter than all the rest..............

7.   You go over and gently touch it......... as you do, it comes loose from the cave wall........you get a very strong impression that it has been gifted to you by the guardian of the cave...........allow yourself to hold the crystal to your heart..........stay with this energy as long as you want..........feeling the crystal connecting you back to the earth........back to your past........back to your roots.........to ancient memories and long-forgotten knowledge........allow any thoughts, feelings or impressions to come into your mind.......

8.   When you are ready........begin to come back to everyday waking reality......and allow yourself to become grounded, centred and focused in the present moment.

9.   Write down any thoughts feeling, visions or impressions you got during this meditation.

Kundalini Meditation - Chanting Session

For this meditation you need to have practised all the chakra chants which have been offered in this programme, each of which can be done as a five minutes to an hour meditation in itself, or in any combination. Sometimes it is very enjoyable to go through all the seven chakras in order, with the focus being on a chanting kundalini awakening session. If you feel one of your chakras is low on energy you could just concentrate on that chakra. Just pause for a few minutes......tune in to your breathing experience for several breaths......expand your awareness to include your heartbeat......become aware of your whole body in the present moment.......feel the energy flows in your body.....when you are ready, begin the chanting session...........

1.   Root chakra LAM or LANG

2.   Sacral chakra VAM or VANG

3.   Solar chakra RAM or RANG

4.   Heart chakra YAM or YANG

5.   Throat chakra HAM or HANG

6.   Third eye chakra OM

7.   Silent OM

Part 20

The Soul Star

The soul star chakra is located about six inches above your head. It is sometimes referred to as the eighth chakra and it is the first of the non-physical ones above the head. You have other chakras or energy centres above your head, but this is the one that gives you access to all the other levels, spheres or dimensions. You also need to keep in mind that as the kundalini energy rises up into the seventh chakra it bursts free of your personal energy system, which is intimately tied to the energy system of the earth, and merges with the infinite energy system beyond you. At the same time, unless you are profoundly unbalanced, or you have distorted your chakras, a remarkable light energy will flow down into you. This flow downwards into your body fills each chakra with the sensation of bliss. Meditators experience it as bliss, even though the words bliss, ecstasy, exhilaration, elation are wholly inadequate. Right in the centre of your entering the bliss state, when you are just beginning to explore ....be aware of your breathing, otherwise you may contract or disturb your energy system at the vastness of the unique encounter.

The key to experiencing the crown chakra and the non-physical chakras above your head and leaving your physical body - this is sometimes called astral travel or astral journey - so you materialise there by drawing the necessary materials either from *Asmita (Ahamkara)* or the universal storehouse (ocean of elements), is a thorough understanding and knowledge of your chakra system, plus pranayama, mudras, mantras and meditation. If you take the time regularly to do the kundalini meditations I have described, you can advance deeper and more consciously into kundalini bliss, power, compassion, wisdom and realization. This is a lifetime programme, although it is possible to speed the process up considerably with the crystal webs of light. I have found through my many years as a teacher and therapist most people need to cleanse their bodies considerably before full balanced kundalini movement happens. Therefore it is wise to remove as many toxins from your body and mind as possible. If you are lucky enough to experience your refined astral body, then you must identify yourself with the mind and then you function at first on the mental plane with this refined body, just as you do on the earth plane. Through controlled concentration, you rise above body-consciousness; through meditation, you rise above the mind or mental level; and finally through Samadhi you become one with the One Thread Soul.

Remember always - you are opening yourself to your own inner Master and Higher Self; they will guide you onwards. You can also draw on the energy of all the Spiritual Masters of all time and all dimensions, as well as all the other meditators on the planet. As you advance spiritually, you join the hierarchy of enlightened souls. This will be a joyful experience of compassion; as more and more souls join consciously into the One Thread Soul, we shall experience global bliss. Always remember we are not talking about some vague esoteric practice for the elite: this experience is your divine birthright.

Please note, once you have started the awakening process you may find when you retire for sleep that without any effort on your part you will experience the light in your head; this is with your eyes closed. It will be as if a bright sun is shining. This can also happen in the morning as you are between sleep and waking; it is quite normal. You may find you need a lot less sleep, especially after the crystal webs of light; once again, this is quite normal. Many changes will manifest in your physical body; you may develop an aversion to certain foods, especially meat, fish and dairy products, which are of a very low vibration and, in Yogic understanding, to be avoided. You may experience a lot of new sensations in your body; these are quite normal. Mostly it will be your nervous system getting ready to take a more refined energy. You may experience emotional upset or mood swings; once again, this is part of the process of the body cleansing itself of toxins. It is sometimes referred to as a healing crisis. (I have covered this extensively in my first book, "Crystal Healing"). Through meditation, many secrets withheld from the conscious mind may be discovered.

There is another way to experience the soul star chakra and the other non-physical chakras above the head - this is through 'downloading' or 'channelling' information from the Higher Self. This channelling, as it is commonly called, can be from other beings besides your Higher Self; it can be from an Ascended Master, Angel or tutelary Deity, Sages or Saints, who have a deep personal loving connection to you and who are trying to encourage you onwards on your path to enlightenment, peace and bliss. This 'channelling' or 'downloading' happens all the time, whether you are consciously aware of it or not. You may have noticed the aha! moments in your life, when try as you may to solve a problem, you can't - then, all of a sudden, aha! and you can. You can begin to experience this more and more in your life: the more you observe your divine intuition, the more you are aware of it, the more it happens. I am always surprised when people find 'channelling' strange. Everyone, whether they are aware of it or not, does it all the time. If you go to sleep you do it - regardless of any fear or phobia, religious or otherwise, placed around your beliefs regarding channelling, everyone, even the most hard-headed scientist who has no belief in God, does it all the time every day!

Conscious channelling has to pass through the vehicle of the channel; this can 'color' the information to some degree, as the information will take on the personality characteristics of the channel. This is why some of the 'New Age' information available at this present time is so interesting and endearing. But with practice and a through cleansing of your energy system the information received becomes more and more refined, reliable and less colored by the incarnate ego's personality. It is wise to always check your own hidden agenda before a conscious channelling session; if you are asking a question where you have a great deal of attachment to the answer, it will always be more difficult. This is why some people seek advice from others who have no vested interest in the outcome of the channelling session. The crystal courses I have run over the last 14 years have produced some of the finest conscious channels on the planet. They did not do the crystal course to become a channel, it was a by-product of the course as they developed spiritually, as were all the other talents they unearthed and refined.

Channelling Meditation

True conscious channelling is simple, easy, safe and effective. The following are practical points regarding the basic techniques and stages. They are primarily intended for the beginner, although even the most experienced channel will find a review of them useful.

1. Have a regular time, place and practice.

2. The most effective times are dawn and dusk.

3. Try to have a separate room.

4. Keep it free from other vibrations and influences.

5. Purify it with incense and have a large amethyst crystal which serves to purify the environment (an amethyst cluster will also work).

6. When sitting, face north or east to take advantage of favourable magnetic vibrations.

7. Sit in a comfortable steady posture with the spine and neck held erect but not tense. This means that the base of the spine needs to be higher than the knees, thus tilting the pelvis forwards to a position where the spine naturally remains upright when relaxed. The easiest way of doing this is to put a small, firm cushion beneath the base of the spine. The psychic current must be able to flow unimpeded from the base of the spine to the top of the head.

8. Sit cross-legged; this forms a triangular path for the energy field and stops it dissipating in all directions.

9.   Command the mind to be still for a specific length of time.

10.   Forget about the past, present and future, come alive in the eternal now.

11.   Consciously tune in to your normal breathing pattern.

12.   Allow your awareness of your breathing to expand effortlessly.

13.   In the middle of your breathing experience your heartbeat.

14.   Experience your sense of balance as gravity pulls on your body and your muscles respond with perfect precision to keep upright.

15.   Allow your awareness to expand to encompass the whole of your body and aura.

16.   As you inhale slowly, consciously focus upon the sensation of energy flowing up from the earth into your root chakra and then on upwards in sequential order through each chakra......now as you exhale slowly, open up to receive a spontaneous flow of energy from above......experience a downflow of light, insight and power into your body....moving through each chakra in turn until all seven chakras have been illuminated from above.....and you are empty of air............then again, without effort, let your breath spontaneously come rushing into you......allow energy to flow up from the earth into your chakras.....all the way to the crown........rather than just visualising this, see if you can actually feel this experience happening inside you.....

17.   Again, after the full inhale, reverse the experience.....opening to the downflow of universal energy into your personal energy system........continue with this pattern for a number of breaths....

18.   Once you have cleared the energy in your spine and have a good earth connection and Higher Self connection (the downflow of light) you are now ready to begin to focus on your third eye chakra.

19.   Once you have an active third eye chakra alignment, you are now ready to ask your Higher Self for answers to any problems you may be experiencing....if it's a morning session you may want to ask for guidance about your day........make sure you formulate your question very clearly.....

20.   Be still and wait for an answer....it will come.....even if it happens later in the day as an aha! moment.

21.   When you receive an answer, give thanks immediately. Write down the answers at the end of the session. At the end of the channelling session, ground, centre and focus yourself in your normal everyday waking reality.

Crystal Web of Light - Ascension into Cosmic Consciousness

Crystals: 1 amblygonite, tumbled, faceted or natural
                   2 angelite, tumbled or natural
                   1 danburite, tumbled, faceted or natural
                   1 moldavite, tumbled, faceted or natural
                   1 petalite, tumbled, faceted or natural
                   1 phenacite, tumbled, faceted or natural
                   6 clear quartz points

Uses: This crystal web of light will clear the etheric body and can be used to activate the higher centres above the head. It brings the consciousness of the Higher Self into the spiritual body and sends your intent out into the universal streams of energy. It will also balance your emotional body. Its message is 'follow your heart, for that is where true joy lies'. The brilliance of danburite contained within this crystal web carries a very high vibration of the supreme ray; it works to stimulate the third, fourth, fifth eye and crown chakras, plus the 8th to 14th chakras in the etheric body. Danburite can also activate the 'heart' chakra and integrate it with these higher energies. Danburite can help one to connect to the communication currents of the Angelic Domain. It will also promote lucid dreaming. The brilliance that danburite carries is not a color, it is the original light; not an earthly vibration, but cosmic light representing the Universal Intelligence. It has the purity of the trinity - love, power and wisdom.

Danburite clears away any cloudiness in a person's aura to add lustre and beauty. The moldavite within this crystal web contains the essence of *shunyata*, the vast emptiness (which contains all potentiality), stretching in all directions, absolutely clear, pristine and radiant. By this clear sky stretching into infinity we can gain an understanding, a feeling for the expansiveness and freedom which could be ours if we did not allow our horizons to become narrow, clouded and limited, if we did not permit our minds to become fixated and hypnotized by cravings and worries centred on what really are empty passing phenomena. The petalite will activate higher states of cosmic consciousness.

The phenacite will activate the light body to consciously experience one's existence in higher dimensions. Phenacite encourages you to become a spiritual hero - to soar into the higher regions of bliss. Phenacite is a multi-dimensional energy device: it can teach you astral travel. It knows the gateways to other realms and worlds of infinite bliss. Initiation into the ancient mysteries are stored within its vibrational structure. Phenacite gives the full activation and initiation of the ascension process by downloading the information stored within your Divine blueprint on the Akashic records into your energy body. When used to clear the chakra system it is a healer of the soul, heralding the soul force into the vibration of ascension. Phenacite, most of all, is the Guardian of the gateway guardians. It has frequently initiated contact with Ascended Masters and Angelic guides for those who choose to work in this way. Cosmic Consciousness is an inherent natural faculty of all women and men; this crystal web of light will fully activate the ascension process. It is used for conscious connection to the Angelic realms via attunement to the heavenly vibration. Angelite brings inner peace, tranquillity, calm and focus to the highest realms of heavenly light.

1 amblygonite, placed on the solar plexus chakra.

2 angelite, one held in each hand.

1 danburite, placed on the third eye chakra.

1 moldavite, placed on the heart chakra.

1 petalite, placed on the throat chakra.

1 phenacite, placed on the crown chakra above the head.

6 clear quartz crystal points placed in a star of David configuration. The six-pointed star symbolises the union of heaven and earth.

Process:

1.   Cleanse all the crystals and programme the clear quartz for ascension.

2.   Choose a warm comfortable place where you can lie down undisturbed for at least an hour. Never rush a crystal web of light process. View it as a sacred healing space, so you need to make sure it is energetically clean. Make sure you are wearing warm, loose, comfortable clothes.

3.   Relax by consciously becoming aware of your breathing and heartbeat; you can play soothing music, light candles and burn incense.

4.   Lay the stones around and on the body and hold an angelite crystal in each hand.

5.   Allow 20 minutes to facilitate the integration of the crystal vibration.

6.   Feel free to remove the crystals sooner, if you have integrated the crystal energy very quickly.

7.   Remove the crystals in reverse order of placement.

8.   Make sure you are fully grounded, centred and balanced.

9.   Cleanse your crystals (using your chosen method).

10.   Finish by giving thanks and asking mentally that all the healing work you have just accomplished is closed, sealed and protected with Divine love and wisdom.

11.   Give yourself sufficient time to integrate the crystal therapy session.

12.   As a general guideline it is suggested a period of twice the length of time you were actually lying in the crystal therapy web be allowed for integration.

Amblygonite

A fluophosphate of lithium and aluminum, amblygonite is a very rare mineral which occurs in granite pegmatites together with other lithium minerals. Energetically, these crystals are soothing and inspiring to the mental body, giving a flowing graceful energy of calm and peace. They are very suited to those of an artistic or theatrical nature and give Divine inspiration to those of us who need to, or wish to, express ourselves via writing or poetry. Indeed they are so inspirational that you may find you are almost overwhelmed by the passionate experience, as the ideas and information flow so fast as to cause 'overload'. Using these stones for inspiration is like being tuned in to the creative force of the cosmic universal mind of God/Goddess.

Amblygonite does clear the etheric body and can be used to activate any chakra, especially the higher centres above the head. It brings the consciousness of the higher self into the spiritual body and sends your intent out into the universal streams of energy. This stone will also balance your emotional body and is wonderful to work with when you wish to be heart-to-heart with someone you love. Its message is 'follow your heart, for that is where true joy lies'. For those who wish to acknowledge their creative manifesting gifts for the 'good of all', it will accelerate these altruistic endeavours. Amblygonite combines very well with yellow sapphire and will aid intellectual prowess beyond all former self-imposed limitations.

Regardless of anything else this stone will facilitate, its most potent use will be its stress- reducing properties, which are remarkable. It eases stress and anxiety quickly and has been demonstrated to stop feelings of anger, agitation and hostility within minutes. This is a extraordinary feat; it also releases hostility and self-hatred whereby those who continually self- sabotage themselves due to low self-esteem have been instantly alleviated of this trait completely.

The peaceful flow of this stone is one of being completely de-stressed and inspired. This must be a unique experience for most people and it follows that it is the stone's unique gift or main purpose on the planet at this time. Amblygonite has been used for healing the physical problems of stress, anxiety, stomach disorders, spleen, liver and kidney problems. As well as dispelling fears and phobias caused by wrong mental attitudes, this stone helps you see through the self-limiting illusory world of your own mind. It has been used to view 'masks of the self'. These are often caused by childhood trauma where the 'masked self' was brought up to be seen and not heard, frequently told to 'shut up' and made to feel its opinions were unwanted and useless. The coping mechanism was to hide its 'true self'. This suppressed sad soul remains locked as a child in adult form. It chooses to remain childlike and neglects to take responsibility for its life.

Affirmation: Divine inspiration guides me; I follow my heart, for that is where true lasting joy lies.

Angelite

Anhydrite is a relatively common sedimentary mineral that forms massive rock layers. Anhydrite does not form directly, but is the result of the dewatering of the rock-forming mineral gypsum. This loss of water produces a reduction in volume of the rock layer and can cause the formation of caverns as the rock shrinks. Good mineral specimens of anhydrite were extremely rare, despite its common occurrence. However, fine specimens of anhydrite have been found in Mexico and Peru, showing good

213

crystal habit, a nice blue color and even a play of light internally in the crystal. Lilac-blue anhydrite is sometimes called Angelite for its "Angelic" color.

Anhydrite comes from Mexico, Peru, Germany and New Mexico, but it was adopted by the 'New Agers' as Angelite. This was where it first made its 'appearance' on the New Age crystal scene. This happened when the keepers of 'days' gathered for the Harmonic Convergence of 1986 in Peru. It is used for conscious connection to the Angelic realms via attunement to the heavenly vibration of this pale lilac-blue stone. Angelite brings inner peace, tranquillity, calm and focus to the highest realms of heavenly light. It is one stone that truly holds the energy of the force we know as Karuna: compassion, pity and tenderness. It also implies devoted action to alleviate suffering. It applies itself well to facilitating the practice of *Mantras*, vibrating with high intensity as each chakra is activated with the appropriate sound. With conscious dedicated use it unlocks *Nada* or the inner mystical sounds. When applied to the feet it will also clear the meridians of energy blockages. Angelite's glandular domain is the thyroid and parathyroids. It has also been used for inflammation of the throat and thyroid problems. Its healing vibration is also linked to the upper lungs and arms, the base of the skull and weight. Angelite balances the fluid functions of the body and thereby will release excess body fluid. It has been used as an aura cleanser and activator to bring Angelic attunement.

Blue is the color of the present time, the Aquarian Age. The Aquarian is seen as the truth seeker; however, she or he must go forward in truth, for if they do not go forward, they will go backwards out of fear. Angelite combats this fear. It will help you unlock the secrets of the spoken word, giving voice to your truth. Psychologically, angelite counteracts harshness; if somebody is acting insensitively in a situation, angelite will help them become more compassionate. It also teaches them acceptance of that which cannot be changed. Angelite can be used to relieve pain, both physical and psychological, and combats cruelty and brutality. It has also been used to alleviate the pain of stomach ulcers and sunburn.

Affirmation: The energy of Karuna guides me; I have inner peace and tranquillity.

Clear Quartz - See the Root Chakra Section for Properties

Danburite

Danburite is a calcium borosilicate and the best metaphysical crystals come from Mexico. Danburite is not a well-known mineral, but is growing in popularity. With crystals similar to topaz, its diamond-shaped cross-section and wedge-like termination is a contrast to quartz's hexagonal prisms and pyramidal terminations. Danburite gets its name from its original locality, which is now buried under the city of Danbury, Connecticut. Danburite is found in Danbury, Connecticut, and Russell, New York, USA; Charcas, San Luis Potosi, Mexico; Kyushu Is, Japan; Mogok, Burma; and Uri, Switzerland.

For metaphysical purposes you need the clear form. The brilliance of danburite carries a very high vibration of the supreme ray; it works to stimulate the third, fourth, fifth eye and crown chakras, plus the 8th to 14th chakras in the etheric body. Danburite can also activate the 'heart' chakra and integrate it with these higher energies. Danburite can help one to connect to the communication currents of the Angelic Domain. It will also promote lucid dreaming. The brilliance that danburite carries is not a color, it is the original light; not an earthly vibration, but cosmic light representing the Universal Intelligence. It has the purity of the trinity - love, power and wisdom. Danburite clears away any cloudiness in a person's aura to add lustre and beauty. In everyday use, when worn or carried, danburite will give a joyful connection to the Angelic Realms, giving one access to serenity and inner wisdom in one's daily encounters. Danburite can facilitate one's ability to act with a compassionate heart and an activated mind, guided by the true wisdom of one's connection to spirit.

It is useful to those who wish to consciously access inner guidance. In meditation danburites are powerful aids to the attainment of higher states, because of their natural resonance with the higher frequencies of the human vibrational spectrum. We use this stone when we want to bring about change, major or minor, in our lives. Danburite allows us to wipe the slate clean, to start again. The energy of pure danburite will allow us to move on in a new direction. This can be on any level: physical outer changes, emotional changes, or spiritual changes. It is good for those who are making the transition from life to death.

Danburite has the power to modify any condition and some crystal therapists see it as a 'cure all' - it is - it will bring 'healing' in the 'Angels' wake'. Danburite clears allergies and chronic conditions, it removes toxins from the body, heals liver, kidneys and gall-bladder. Danburite even clears karmic burdens, negative karma patterns and miasms. As a gem essence it is excellent and making and using an aura spray will speed up the healing process. I always use it with my clients at the start of the therapy session and during the therapy session. I have worn a danburite pendant since 1992. Danburite is the main stone in the Angel of Light gem essence I use.

As danburite has such a powerful connection to the Angelic Realm, the Angels of Light and Brilliance, and is overseen by the Ascended Master Serapis Bay, it is useful to keep an Angelic journal when you decide to wear or use it for meditation and dream work. When you choose to use danburite for dream work a natural crystal should be placed in the bedroom. The vibratory signature is so strong that it will transform the entire spiritual climate of the room.

Affirmation: I now choose to release and be cleansed of all negative karma and allow Angelic healing to manifest in my life.

Moldavite - See the Section in the Crown Chakra for Properties

Petalite

Petalite occurs typically in lithium-bearing granite pegmatites along with minerals such as spodumene, tourmaline and lepidolite. Petalite received its name from the Greek word for leaf. Petalite is used to render negative energies impotent. It repels all negative energies, negative entities, evil, black magic, all implants, releases all negative karma and miasms. Petalite releases all binding ties and removes all manipulation. This allows the user to learn discernment in all areas of their life.

Petalite teaches you to avoid fear, anger, hatred, greed, desire, ego manipulation, pride, boastfulness and laziness. Petalite will activate higher states of cosmic consciousness, where you realise that 'powers' such as clairvoyance and clairaudience are not worth striving for because far greater illumination and peace are possible beyond them. If one regularly practises concentration and meditation, psychic powers are bound to come; but they must not be used for selfish gain, otherwise you become a victim of your own ignorance. Physically, each gland in the body has a specific color and vibration of its own. Petalite works on all of them by working on the collective functioning of the endocrine system, so it is ideal to use in a crystal web of light over any area that needs clearing of stagnant or stuck energy.

Petalite also keeps the skin supple and moist, and directly works on the eyes, especially the whites of the eyes. The state of the whites of the eyes is used in diagnosing physical health. Petalite works well with other crystals and as a basic carrier for other energies. It is also good to use when people have 'frozen emotions', withdrawal, their mind is occupied elsewhere; it begins the process of healing. Petalite has a beneficial cooling quality on the whole system and it eases feelings of frustration and isolation by linking you to your 'Divine Essence or Cosmic Consciousness'.

Affirmation: I now activate higher states of Cosmic Consciousness to manifest in my life.

Phenacite

Phenacite is a rare beryllium mineral, but it is found so frequently with precious gemstones that its availability is not in proportion to its rarity. It is found in pegmatitic pockets and is associated with gemstones such as topaz, beryl - especially emerald and chrysoberyl - and smoky quartz. The name phenacite is from a Greek word meaning deceiver, an allusion to its deceptively similar look to quartz. Phenacite is one of the few silicate minerals that has a trigonal symmetry. This symmetry is far more common among carbonates than among silicates. Fine crystals of phenacite can be perfectly clear and, with good hardness, rarity, color and fire, make good choices for gemstone jewellery.

Phenacite is a very rare and beautiful crystal. People who have worked for many years metaphysically with crystals and gemstones classify phenacite as having the highest vibration yet found in any crystal. It is a powerful activator of the upper chakras, especially the crown and the non-physical 8th to 14th chakras above the head. The soul star chakra, which is situated just above the crown chakra, becomes especially energised into full alignment with the Higher Self.

Phenacite allows entrance only to those who know how to access the energies of this mystical stone. You have to 'aim' very high with phenacite. This stone is only for those who can expand their consciousness far beyond the perceived physical plane and who wish to explore their full potential this lifetime. Brazilian phenacite is said to have the highest vibration and is associated with the Angelic feminine energies. The yellow Madagascar phenacite is associated with the extraterrestrial flow and is a powerful tool for manifestation. Colorless Madagascar phenacite is used for grounding the light body into our physical body.

All phenacites help one to activate the light body and to consciously experience one's existence in higher dimensions. Phenacite encourages you to become a spiritual hero in the worldly battlefield, be brave, be undaunted, be a spiritual soldier; to conquer the inner war with the mind and senses, for it is more terrible than the external war; to soar high into the higher regions of bliss.

Clear Madagascar phenacite especially brings this conscious awareness of the Universal Law of resonance, like attracts like. It teaches you to be aware of every thought, word and deed, to purify and refine your vibration, until your whole system on every level is full of pristine light and glory and you become a conscious channel for the light, a force for good. It encourages wisdom, understanding, truth, dispassion, discrimination, serenity, self-restraint, one-pointedness of mind, purity, forbearance, fortitude, patience, forgiveness, the spirit of service, sacrifice and love for all.

Phenacite is a multi-dimensional energy device: it can teach you astral travel. It knows the gateways to other realms and worlds of infinite bliss. Initiation into the ancient mysteries are stored within its vibrational structure. Phenacite gives the full activation and initiation of the ascension process by downloading the information stored within your Divine blueprint on the Akashic records into your energy body.

Phenacite holds the key of the superior human vibration within its structure, for those who choose to use it, to make their ascension in the light. It is a flowing graceful matrix primer of healing, when taken as a gemstone essence. When used to clear the chakra system it is a healer of the soul, heralding the soul force into the vibration of ascension. Clear faceted stones work the best, the clearer the better, but as with all vibrational energy work your intent and dedication will bring good results, regardless of the clarity or size.

Phenacite, most of all, is the Guardian of the gateway guardians. It has frequently initiated contact with Ascended Masters and Angelic guides for those who choose to work in this way. Cosmic Consciousness is an inherent natural faculty of all women and men. Training and discipline are necessary to awaken the consciousness. It is already present in mankind. It is inactive or non-functioning in the vast majority of human beings on account of the force of *Avidya* or ignorance.

Affirmation: I now activate the Divine blueprint of my light body. I am ascending in the light.

Kundalini Seven Chakra Meditation

Without making any effort to alter your breathing, simply tune in to your breathing experience.......
allow your awareness to expand to include your heartbeat and your whole body.....here in the present
moment.....relax and enjoy the pure experience of effortless breathing..........

1.   As you inhale slowly, consciously focus upon the sensation of energy flowing up from the earth

into your root chakra and then on upwards in sequential order through each chakra......now as you exhale slowly, open up to receive a spontaneous flow of energy from above......experience a downflow of light into your body....moving through each chakra in turn until all seven chakras have been illuminated from above.....and you are empty of air...........then again, without effort, let your breath spontaneously come rushing into you....allow energy to flow up from the earth into your chakras all the way to the crown.......actually feel this experience happening inside you.....

2.   Again, after the full inhale, reverse the experience...opening to the downflow of universal energy into your personal energy system........continue with this pattern for a number of breaths....

3.   Then contract the Hui Yin point and just allow your breathing to come and go.... and without any hesitation allow the sound for the root chakra to come as you chant LAM....continue with this chanting as long as you like...now visualise or look directly at the root chakra mandala...focus on the energy movements and shapes it contains......for as long as you want....when you are ready, visualise or feel your root chakra begin to turn upwards.....towards your crown chakra....this brings spiritual energy into your root chakra and allows for your full attention to be focused upwards towards your enlightenment.......

4.   When you are ready, as you inhale imagine you are drawing up energy of a sexual nature and force from the root chakra.....from the very depths of your being...allow it to flow into your genitals....hold your breath for a moment on full.... this allows the charge to be absorbed into your sacral chakra.....then simply let go of the air in your lungs as you breathe out.........just allow yourself to become empty in an effortless fashion........now consciously inhale and draw the energy upwards again......hold your breath for a moment on full....feel the charge of liquid excitement beginning to fill your sacral chakra, then simply let go of the air in your lungs as you breathe out......just allow yourself to become empty in an effortless fashion....continue in this breathing pattern until you feel a charge building up in your sacral chakra.

5.   Without any hesitation allow the sound for the sacral chakra to come as you chant VAM and continue with this chanting as long as you like...now visualise or look directly at the sacral chakra mandala...focus on the energy movements and shapes it contains......for as long as you want....when you are ready.....employ the sacral chakra bandha.......and visualise or feel your sacral chakra begin to turn upwards.....towards your crown chakra....this brings spiritual energy into your sacral chakra and allows for your full attention to be focused upwards towards your enlightenment.......

6.   When you are ready, focus on the breath of fire... rapidly contract your belly muscles, so that you force the air out of your lungs through the mouth almost instantaneously......relax your breathing muscles completely for a short time, so that air flows very quickly into your lungs through your nose, replacing the forced discharge of air...just as soon as the air has rushed into your lungs to replace what you had pushed out, again push the air out with a strong sudden exhale, contracting your diaphragm and abdominal muscles. Let the Huh....sound come out of your throat with each of these exhales, then instantly relax and let air rush in through your nose.......continue in this breathing pattern for as long as is comfortable and you feel deeply centred in your third 'fire' chakra...........then just relax and allow your breathing to slow...........

7.   Without any hesitation allow the sound for the solar plexus chakra to come as you chant RAM and continue with this chanting as long as you like...now visualise or look directly at the solar plexus chakra mandala...focus on the energy movements and shapes it contains......for as long as you want....when you are ready.....employ the solar plexus chakra bandha and visualise or feel your solar plexus chakra begin to turn upwards.....towards your crown chakra....

8.	When you are ready, perform the alternate-nostril breathing....heart consciousness rising...this technique will raise your consciousness upwards into your head..... the secret is to remember that you want to make the switch between nostrils at the top of your inhales......to take the energy upwards.......you will move pranic energy up into your head with every inhale.....hold on the full breath for several seconds, then switch to the other nostril as you exhale.....continue as long as you want..........

9.	Without any hesitation allow the sound for the heart chakra to come as you chant YAM and continue with this chanting as long as you like...now visualise or look directly at the heart chakra mandala...focus on the energy movements and shapes it contains......for as long as you want....then gently ease the shoulders back ever so slightly and the chin in a little so that there is a slight stretch on the back of the neck, easing the blood-flow to the brain......this is the heart chakra bandha........and when you are ready visualise or feel your heart chakra begin to turn upwards.....towards your crown chakra....

10.	Very gently, as softly as possible, begin to allow your vocal cords to vibrate as you exhale, generating a very quiet humming sound with your lips closed.....and your eyes closed as well..... at the bottom of your exhale fall naturally silent....and inhale silently......feel the vibrations continue throughout your body from your humming a moment before.........this is resonance....continue with this humming meditation for a number of breaths until you feel you are becoming pure sound yourself......pure resonance.....pure vibration.....

11.	Without any hesitation allow the sound for the throat chakra to come as you chant HAM and continue with this chanting as long as you like...now visualise or look directly at the throat chakra mandala...focus on the energy movements and shapes it contains......for as long as you want....keep your mouth slightly open and rest the tip of the tongue on the roof of the mouth just behind the teeth. This placement of the tongue is very important because it naturally maintains the flow of energy to the head whilst keeping the jaw relaxed. (The tongue placement is the bandha or energy seal for the throat chakra...when you are not actually chanting a mantra, this placement of the tongue is vital, if you wish to move energy into the higher chakras)......and when you are ready, visualise or feel your throat chakra begin to turn upwards.....towards your crown chakra....

12.	When you are ready, practise the *Kumbhaka* or natural retention of breath super-charge upwards.....inhale for the count of six......hold for the count of six......exhale for the count of four....breathe in immediately for the count of six......hold for the count of six......exhale for the count of four....breathe in immediately for the count of six......and repeat the pattern a number of times.....this breathing formula focuses energy into the top two chakras.

13.	Without any hesitation allow the sound for the third eye chakra to come as you chant OM and continue with this chanting as long as you like...now visualise or look directly at the third eye chakra mandala...focus on the energy movements and shapes it contains......for as long as you want....when you have finished gazing at the third eye chakra mandala, allow your eyes to close....and with closed eyes..... you will focus your physical eyes and your entire undivided attention on the third eye chakra....this is the bandha or energy seal for the third eye chakra.......and when you are ready, visualise or feel your third eye chakra begin to turn upwards.....towards your crown chakra....

14.	When you are ready, allow the crown chakra mantra of OM to sound in and through you as never before....allow the sound to manifest in your mind....feel it effortlessly rising from your inner being........as the OM sound generates tremendous power.....opening yourself to the sound of the universe, as it joins you in sounding the OM........

15.	Continue for as long as you want........you are the vibration.....visualise the crown chakra mandala.... focus on the energy movements and shapes it contains.......or just visualise a beautiful pristine white lotus flower on the top of your head....your crowning glory......imagine it at first like a cap of a thousand white petals gently hugging your head.

16. Now, with the warmth of your focused attention.....feel the petals beginning to turn upwards.... towards the Sun of your own Divine Source......through the centre where the petals meet is an opening through which pours the Light of your Soul.....it can be brilliant white....violet...or gold....or a mixture of all three........

17. Allow this pure pristine energy to flow into you.....filling the whole of your body with light...as it does so, you feel a peace....... a love that transcends all understanding.....perfect peace.....a calmness pervades your body and mind.....a deep soul connection is taking place....allow yourself to really absorb this light....until your whole body and aura are pure light.................

18. You feel your mind relax....and let go....as you allow yourself to totally merge with the Light of your Soul.....you are at peace with yourself, the world and everyone in it.......breathe deeply of the light.................

19. You are the light....you are becoming enlightened.....and the more you practise this meditation the deeper is the soul connection......your life is becoming transformed......you are moving into synchronisation with your Soul.....allowing all the earthly mundane thoughts to fall away as you merge with the Light of your Soul...................

20. This energy has always been there for you....loving you....guiding you....from now on you will listen to the gentle whisperings of your Soul.....by doing so, you allow your Soul to guide you to a new way of being.....a new way of living.....you are going home.......nothing can stop you now.....you and your Soul have merged......into the One......the energy of enlightenment pervades your whole being..........peace............love.......joy..........bliss........enlightenment....... allow the bliss breath to form....as the universe breathes you.....open yourself to the universe........allow yourself to experience.......a beauty and unity beyond normal human comprehension and limitations......you are becoming enlightened....your consciousness soars above the ego confines of the physical body into realms of experience you can only dream of......

21. Allow yourself plenty of time to integrate this new awareness...............don't forget to reverse the root chakra to point downwards and the sacral, solar plexus, heart, throat and third eye chakras to point outwards.....as you once more anchor yourself on the earth plane.

Blessings, abundance, compassion and enlightenment.....to you.........enjoy your journey home.

Glossary

Acupoint: Abbreviation for acupuncture point. An energetic pore in the skin through which subtle energy from the surrounding environment is carried throughout the body via the meridians, supplying nourishing chi energy to the relevant deeper organs, blood and nervous system.

Affirmation: A positive personally inspiring phrase that acts as a powerful therapy tool to counteract previous negative conditioning.

Akashic: Archives of stored information of everything that has ever been or will be within the collective Universal mind of God/Goddess.

Allopathic: Refers to contemporary medical approaches which utilize multiple drugs simultaneously and/or surgery to provide multi-symptom relief and treatment of illness or disease.

Ally: A teacher, guide, totem, spirit, crystal, plant, animal, flower etc. that is wholly reliable and acts as a 'Guardian Angel' on all levels and all dimensions.

Altar: A focal point for contemplation and meditation, usually displaying a collection of meaningful possessions. Sometimes a form of ritual may be involved in the process for enhanced experience.

Angel: *see* Devas.

Angelic Realms: *see* Devic Realms.

Archetype: A universal theme, or model of human emotional development. A level of heightened experience on which everything is imbued with rich symbolic meaning.

Astral: Refers to the energy/matter octave or frequency band just beyond the etheric. Because the astral body is strongly affected by emotionality, astral energy is emotionally linked.

Asuras: Titans, powerful and jealous beings who are prepared to use force and manipulation to gain their own ends. In the Buddhist wheel of life, they are represented as warring with the gods. They may also be seen to represent states of mind, or likened to those who use tribal mentality, big business, politicians, military might, to manipulate us for their own selfish purposes.

Aura: The subtle-energy field surrounding the physical body, invisible to all but gifted individuals and through processes such as aura scans and Kirlian photography.

Bardo: The 'state between' two other states of being.

Bija Mantra: *see* Seed syllable.

Biocrystalline: Refers to the network of cellular elements in the body which have liquid crystal or quartz-like properties. These areas include cell salts, lymphatics, fatty tissue, red and white blood cells and the pineal gland.

Bioelectromagnetic: The energy generated by living cells, including both conventional magnetic fields and subtle magnetic fields.

Bliss (Great): A state of ecstatic happiness achieved through the realisation of the illusory nature of the ego.

Block/Blockage: A dysfunction in the chakra system inhibiting the smooth even flow of subtle- energy.

Bodhichitta: The compassionate desire to gain Enlightenment for the benefit of all living beings.

Bodhisattva: A being pledged to become a Buddha so as to be in the best position to aid all other beings to escape from suffering by gaining Enlightenment.

Brilliance: *see* Clear light.

Buddha: A title meaning one who is awake. A Buddha is someone who has gained Enlightenment - the perfection of wisdom and compassion. In particular the title applied to Siddhartha Gautama, also known as Shakyamuni, the founder of Buddhism.

Cerebral hemispheres: The right and left halves of the cerebral cortex, the highest centres of function within the brain. The left hemisphere controls analytical and linear thought, while the right hemisphere controls symbolic and non-linear thought processes.

Chakra: An integrated system of metaphysical energy centres which affect physical, emotional, mental and spiritual well-being. The chakras process subtle energy and convert it into chemical, hormonal and cellular changes in the body.

Channelling: The phenomenon whereby an individual allows a higher level of consciousness to flow through them, often verbally, as in trance channelling, but also through automatic writing or channelling the higher self or other 'being' consciously.

Chi: Ancient Chinese term for a nutritive subtle-energy which circulates through the acupuncture meridians.

Clairaudience: The psychic ability of hearing at higher vibrational levels. This usually occurs as a by-product of long-term meditation and involves the energy of a refined throat chakra.

Clairvoyance: The psychic ability of seeing higher subtle-energy patterns (from the French, literally meaning 'clear seeing'). An aspect of the third eye or ajna chakra which usually results after prolonged meditation practice as a by-product of spiritual development or scrying.

Clairvoyant reality: A state of seeing and feeling that transcends the normal superficial senses. It is an experience of true reality beyond the confines of time and space boundaries, which allows one to experience the interconnectedness of all things.

Clear light: The experience of the natural state of the mind, of consciousness 'undiluted' by any tendency to move towards sensory experience. Recognition of the nature of this state is synonymous with Enlightenment. Cosmic light. The original light.

Crystal: Solid organic material with ordered internal atomic structure of regular repeating three-dimensional patterns.

Crystal webs of light: Crystals arranged in geometric arrays which have an amplified or synergetic effect greater than the sum of the individual crystals, often used for specific healing or meditative practices.

Devas: Long-lived or eternal beings who experience refined and blissful states of mind. They thus inhabit a heavenly realm. These realms can be interpreted as objective or symbolic. Some individuals can contact these heavenly beings.

Devic Realms: These realms can be interpreted as objective or symbolic for states of mind in which human beings can dwell, or which they can 'contact' for guidance and help. Sometimes known as Angelic Realms.

Dharma: A word with numerous meanings, but in the context of this book it stands for all those teachings and methods which are conducive to gaining Enlightenment, and thereby seeing things as they truly are, particularly the teachings of the Buddha.

Dis-ease: A frequently used term for illness. It implies that sickness is the result of the individual being 'ill at ease' with some aspect of his or her higher self or Divine consciousness. By realigning with the higher self, the soul's purpose can be fulfilled and dis-ease disappears.

Distilled water: Produced by a process of converting the water to steam and condensing the steam back into water, making a very pure product.

Divine Essence Within: The Divine aspect that dwells in each of us, that once acknowledged and integrated is a positive loving guiding force.

DNA: Deoxyribonucleic acid, the helical macromolecule which encodes the genetic information that participates in cellular growth and development at the molecular level. The DNA spiral of life.

Download: Information from the Akashic archives released into the conscious awareness of the individual.

Dowsing: Another term for radiesthesia. An intuitive skill used for finding hidden or lost objects and mineral resources, and in this book for diagnostic use and healing illness and dis-ease.

Ego: The incarnating personality as expressed through this present physical embodiment.

Emptiness: *see* Shunyata.

Endocrine system: One of the body's major physical control systems that transmits hormones produced from a series of ductless glands throughout the body. The system corresponds roughly to the position of the seven master chakras.

Energy blockage: A general term referring to the interruption of the natural flow of subtle- energy throughout the human energetic system, often due to abnormal function in one or more chakras.

Enlightenment: A state of perfect wisdom and limitless compassion. The only permanently satisfying solution to the human predicament. The achievement of a Buddha.

Enzyme: A specialized protein molecule which acts to catalyse or accelerate a particular chemical reaction in the body.

Etheric: The frequency band, octave or vibration just beyond the physical realm. Etheric energy vibrates at speeds beyond light velocity and has a magnetic quality.

Grounding: The importance of maintaining connection to the earth in order to be fully centred.

Guru: A spiritual teacher who, through his/her teachings and/or personal example, aids other people to follow the path to Enlightenment.

Higher dimensions: A term that describes subtle-energy systems which vibrate at speeds faster than light, i.e. non-physical energies.

Higher self: That part of ourselves from which, once tuned in, we can receive Divine guidance.

Holistic: A synergistic approach which deals with combined physical, mental, emotional and spiritual aspects of human health and illness.

Hui Yin: A muscular contraction which is a necessary part of first chakra awakening. The Hui Yin point is between the anus and the genitals. This point must be held for the entire time you are practising a kundalini meditation. Contraction is to prevent Chi from escaping from this point.

Karma: The reincarnational principle, sometimes stated as 'as ye sow, so shall ye reap'. An energetic system of credits and debits, positive actions or negative actions, which allows the soul to experience the full range of perspectives on life, through learning universal laws of resonances. Literal translation 'action'.

Kosas: *see* Aura.

Kundalini: Mythical serpent goddess said to rise upwards through the chakra system in the journey towards Enlightenment.

Light body: Another term for subtle body.

Lingam: Hindu phallus, a symbol of the Hindu God, Lord Shiva.

Mala: Buddhist rosary, used for counting, often with 108 beads.

Mandala: An abstract universal symbol used as an aid to meditation practice in inducing higher states of awareness. Also, in the context of this book, a personal energy signature or pattern.

Mantra: Mantras, being sacred sound vibrations, are composed of sacred syllables representative of, and containing within, great spiritual power or energy. Utilising mantras allows us to concentrate and focus this spiritual energy. The word 'mantra' is composed, in Sanskrit, of two root words: 'man' means 'mind', or 'thinking', and 'tra' to 'release' or 'free' or 'strengthen'. Therefore the meaning is to 'free and strengthen the mind'.

Meridian: A channel through which subtle-energy flows through the body.

Miasm: An energetic state which predisposes an organism to future illness. This can be due to subtle effects of a particular toxic agent or micro-organism. There are four types: acquired, inherited, karmic or planetary in nature.

Moola Bhanda: *see* Hui Yin.

Mudra: In this book it is used in the sense of a hand gesture imbued with symbolic significance.

Multidimensional: Refers to the total spectrum of human energies or levels: physical, mental, emotional, spiritual, astral and higher spiritual levels.

Nadis: The thread-like subtle pathways of energy flow from the chakras to the various regions of the body and aura.

Paranormal: A term used to describe psychic phenomena, i.e. telepathy, clairvoyance, etc., that are outside the normal materialistic tribal scientific everyday reality.

Parasite: *see* Thought-form.

Piezoelectric: A phenomenon observed in crystals whereby physical pressure is converted into electrical fields.

Prana: An ancient Yogic term for a nutritive subtle-energy thought to be taken in during breathing.

Psychoneuroimmunology: Medical term for the evolving discipline which studies the integrated interaction between the body, mind and the immune system in illness or health.

Purified water: Distilled water is purified water, but the definition of purified water includes water that has been filtered and/or de-ionised.

Qi: The Japanese term for chi, sometimes spelled Ki. A term for a nutritive subtle-energy which circulates through the acupuncture meridians.

Reiki: Energy 'medicine' where practitioners have been 'attuned' in special 'ceremonies' given by a Reiki Master to become channels of Universal Life Force or Reiki energy.

Resonance: The phenomenon of sympathetic vibration between two similarly tuned oscillators.

Samadhi: Blissful Divine experience that arises when the ego and the mind are dissolved. It is a state to be attained by one's own effort. It is limitless, divisionless and infinite, an experience of being and of pure consciousness.

Samsara: The cyclic round of birth and death, marked by suffering and frustration, which can only be brought to an end by the attainment of Enlightenment.

Scrying: *see* Clairvoyance.

Seed atom: This is the same permanent atom that dwells in all people from the soul's original creation through all incarnations. This divine spark looks like a star: it expands your philosophical skills to gradually understand concepts of God/Goddess.

Glossary

Seed syllable: Subtle sound-symbols through which Enlightened beings can communicate the Dharma to those on advanced stages of the path to Enlightenment. They are often visualised in chakra meditation.

Shakti: Divine cosmic female power. In reality she has no form. It is the coiled-up, sleeping Divine Shakti that lies dormant in all beings.

Shunyata: Literally 'emptiness' or 'voidness'. The ultimate nature of existence, the absolute aspect of all cognizable things. The doctrine of shunyata holds that all phenomena are empty (shunya) of any permanent unchanging self or self-essence. By extension it can mean the transcendental experience brought about by the direct intuitive insight into the empty nature of things.

Subconscious: That part of the personality that dwells below the surface of waking consciousness and controls automatic human functions. It subliminally records all information taken in by the senses and is conditioned/programmed by rewards, punishments and messages that subtly build up our internal picture and worth.

Subtle body: A term referring to any of the subtle-energy bodies which exist in the higher frequency octaves beyond the physical, i.e. the astral, etheric, mental, spiritual.

Subtle-energy: A general term denoting energy that exists outside the ordinary space/time frame and which moves faster than light.

Superconscious: The part of the higher soul structure which can be 'tuned in' to. It controls the higher wisdom.

Sushumna: Energetic equivalent of the spine; vertical column within which the master chakra system is located.

Tantra: A form of Buddhism making use of yogic practices of visualisation, mantras, mudras and mandalas, as well as symbolic ritual and meditations which work with subtle psychophysical energies.

Thought-form: A manifestation of a strong thought or emotion as an actual energetic structure within an individual's auric field. It can be caused by personal repeated negative or positive thoughts. It may also be placed there by another individual to control or manipulate the person; in this case it would be parasitic and wholly undesirable.

Universal Life Force: Inexplicable natural source of all life, which plays a vital role in health and healing.

Vajra: A ritual sceptre, which symbolically combines the qualities of both diamond and thunderbolt.

Vibrational: Refers to subtle or electromagnetic energy in varying frequencies and amplitudes.

Vibrational medicine: That healing philosophy which aims to treat the whole person, i.e. mind, body and spirit complex, by delivering measured quanta of frequency-specific energy to the human multidimensional system.

Visualisation: A method of meditation involving the use of imagination to create vivid symbolic forms.

Witness: A biological specimen or other energetic signature of a patient used as a focal point for attunement by a crystal or vibrational therapist in dowsing or absent healing. It can also be a crystal which acts as a witness in crystal therapy.

Yin and Yang: According to Ancient Chinese philosophy, the two opposing but complementary forces at work in all nature.

Yoga: A Sanskrit word which means 'to link with God' or 'union with God'. It can refer to methods of meditation or physical postures designed to bring about spiritual development.

225

Explanation of Back Cover

Starting at the top left-hand corner, going clockwise round each color mandala of crystals:

Orange ray
Aragonite (natural crystal formation)
Jasper, red (cut)
Amber (cabochon)
Rhodocrosite (natural crystal formation)
Opal, fire (cabochon)
Sunstone, orange (cabochon)
Garnet, hessonite (tumbled)
Agate, fire (cabochon)
Carnelian (tumbled)
Zincite (natural wand)

Violet ray
Quartz, amethyst (natural crystal formation)
Quartz, ametrine (tumbled)
Opal, blue/violet (cut fancy shape)
Lepidolite (slice)
Iolite (natural crystal formation)
Quartz, violet aura (natural single-terminated crystal)
Quartz, amethyst (Vera Cruz natural crystal)
Sugilite (cut shape)
Tanzanite (natural crystal formation)
Fluorite, purple (natural crystal formation)
Charoite (cut shape)
Quartz, amethyst (faceted)

Pink ray
Smithsonite, pink (natural crystal formation)
Quartz, rose (rough)
Quartz, rose (cut double-terminated wand)
Quartz, rose (natural crystal formation)
Opal, fire/pink (cabochon)
Tourmaline, watermelon (slice)
Tourmaline, pink (natural crystal formation)
Quartz, rose aura (natural single-terminated crystal)
Tourmaline, pink/violet (natural wand formation)
Rhodocrosite (cut shape)
Rhodonite (tumbled)
Morganite (rough)
Kunzite (natural crystal formation)
Calcite, pink (tumbled)

Yellow ray

Calcite, golden stellar beam (natural crystal formation)
Quartz, sunshine aura (natural single-terminated crystal)
Apatite, yellow (natural crystal formation)
Amblygonite (rough)
Quartz, citrine (natural/untreated cut crystal shape)
Jasper, yellow (tumbled)
Calcite, amber (tumbled)
Tiger eye, yellow (tumbled)
Sunstone, yellow (natural crystal formation)
Labradorite, golden (tumbled)
Topaz, yellow (natural crystal wand)
Pyrite (tumbled)
Quartz, citrine (cut double-terminated wand)
Quartz, citrine (faceted)

Blue ray

Quartz, aqua aura (natural single-terminated crystal)
Kyanite (natural blade)
Topaz, blue (tumbled)
Quartz, Siberian blue (cut double-terminated wand)
Agate, blue lace (tumbled)
Turquoise (cabochon)
Tourmaline, blue (natural)
Azurite (natural crystal formation)
Chrysocolla, druzy (cut triangle shape)
Quartz, blue aura (natural single-terminated crystal)
Calcite, blue (rough)
Quartz, rainbow aura (natural single-terminated crystal)
Angelite (cut pyramid shape)
Lapis lazuli (cabochon)
Chrysocolla (cabochon)
Sapphire, blue (river-washed pebble)
Apatite, blue (natural)
Larimar (tumbled)
Aquamarine (natural crystal formation)
Labradorite (cut petal shape)
Chrysocolla (heart shape)

Green ray

Moldavite (natural tektite formation)
Malachite (tumbled)
Emerald (natural)
Hiddenite (natural crystal formation)
Quartz, clear/chlorite phantom (cut crystal shape)
Aventurine, green (tumbled)
Jasper, green (tumbled)
Epidote (tumbled)
Quartz, aqua aura/green aura (natural single-terminated crystal)
Quartz, green (cut double-terminated wand)
Calcite, green (rough)

Agate, green moss (tumbled)
Chrysoprase (cut fancy shape)
Tourmaline, green (natural wand)
Peridot (natural crystal formation)
Peridot (faceted)
Prehnite (tumbled)
Dioptase (natural crystal formation)
Prehnite (natural crystal formation)

Earth crystal ray
Actinolite (natural crystal formation)
Boji stones (natural crystal formation)
Obsidian, snowflake (tumbled)
Hematite (tumbled)
Agate, Botswana (tumbled)
Tourmaline, black (natural wand formation)
Quartz, smoky (natural, double-terminated crystal)
Tourmaline, black (tumbled)
Moqui marbles/shaman stones (natural crystal formation)
Agate, black (tumbled)
Agate, crazy lace (cabochon)

Clear ray
Calcite, white (rough)
Danburite (natural crystal formation)
Moonstone (tumbled)
Quartz, rutile (cabochon)
Quartz, Herkimer diamond (natural double-terminated crystal)
Quartz, opal aura (natural single-terminated crystal)
Quartz, clear (cut double-terminated wand)
Selenite (natural wand)
Quartz, clear (carved into a vajra)
Calcite, clear (natural crystal formation)
Phenacite (natural crystal formation)
Azeztulite (rough)
Quartz, milky/snow (tumbled)
Petalite (rough)
Quartz, clear (faceted)

Red ray
Calcite, red (rough)
Pietersite (tumbled)
Zircon, red (natural crystal formation)
Tiger eye, red (tumbled)
Chiastolite (tumbled)
Quartz, ruby/green aura (natural single-terminated crystal)
Bloodstone (tumbled)
Garnet, red (tumbled)
Garnet, almandine (natural crystal formation)
Quartz, ruby aura (natural single-terminated crystal)
Ruby (cabochon)